RESEARCH IN PERSONNEL AND HUMAN RESOURCES MANAGEMENT

RESEARCH IN PERSONNEL AND HUMAN RESOURCES MANAGEMENT

Series Editors: M. Ronald Buckley, Anthony R. Wheeler, John E. Baur, and Jonathon R. B. Halbesleben

Earlier Volumes:

Volumes 1–10:	Edited by Kendrith M. Rowland and Gerald R. Ferris
Volumes 11–20:	Edited by Gerald R. Ferris
Supplement 1:	International Human Resources Management: Edited by Albert Nedd
Supplement 2:	International Human Resources Management: Edited by James B. Shaw and John E. Beck
Supplement 3:	International Human Resources Management: Edited by James B. Shaw, Paul S. Kirkbridge, and Kendrith M. Rowland
Supplement 4:	International Human Resources Management in the Twenty-first Century: Edited by Patrick M. Wright, Lee D. Dyer, John W. Boudreau, and George T. Milkovich
Volumes 21–22:	Edited by Joseph J. Martocchio and Gerald R. Ferris
Volumes 23–27:	Edited by Joseph J. Martocchio
Volume 28:	Edited by Joseph J. Martocchio and Hui Liao
Volume 29:	Edited by Hui Liao, Joseph J. Martocchio, and Aparna Joshi
Volume 30:	Edited by Aparna Joshi, Hui Liao, and Joseph J. Martocchio
Volume 31:	Edited by Joseph J. Martocchio, Aparna Joshi, and Hui Liao
Volumes 32–36:	Edited by M. Ronald Buckley, Jonathon R. B. Halbesleben, and Anthony R. Wheeler
Volumes 37–40:	Edited by M. Ronald Buckley, Anthony R. Wheeler, John E. Baur, and Jonathon R. B. Halbesleben

RESEARCH IN PERSONNEL AND HUMAN
RESOURCES MANAGEMENT VOLUME 41

RESEARCH IN PERSONNEL AND HUMAN RESOURCES MANAGEMENT

EDITED BY

M. RONALD BUCKLEY
University of Oklahoma, USA

ANTHONY R. WHEELER
Widener University, USA

JOHN E. BAUR
University of Nevada, USA

AND

JONATHON R. B. HALBESLEBEN
University of Texas at San Antonio, USA

United Kingdom – North America – Japan
India – Malaysia – China

Emerald Publishing Limited
Howard House, Wagon Lane, Bingley BD16 1WA, UK

First edition 2023

British Library Cataloguing in Publication Data
A catalogue record for this book is available from the British Library

ISBN: 978-1-83753-389-3 (Print)
ISBN: 978-1-83753-388-6 (Online)
ISBN: 978-1-83753-390-9 (Epub)

ISSN: 0742-7301 (Series)

Printed and bound by CPI Group (UK) Ltd, Croydon, CR0 4YY

CONTENTS

ABOUT THE CONTRIBUTORS

Anthony P. Ammeter (Ph.D. University of Texas) holds a joint appointment as an Associate Professor in Management and Management Information Systems in the School of Business Administration at the University of Mississippi, where he also serves as an Associate Provost. His research intersects organizational behavior issues, including leadership, political skill, trust, and accountability, and the management of technology and technical workers. He has published in leading journals such as *Information Systems Research*, the *Journal of Management*, the *Leadership Quarterly, Information & Management, Group and Organization Management*, the *Academy of Management Learning & Education*, and the *Journal of Business Ethics*.

John E. Baur is an Associate Professor and Director of the MBA and Executive MBA programs at the University of Nevada, Las Vegas. He took his Ph.D. from the University of Oklahoma and has research interests within several areas including leadership, deviance, prosocial deviance, team dynamics, and organizational power. His work has been published in journals including *The Leadership Quarterly, Human Resource Management Review, Journal of Business Research, Journal of Leadership and Organizational Studies, Small Group Research, Group & Organization Management*, and *Organizational Dynamics*.

M. Ronald Buckley is the JC Penney Company Chair of Business Leadership and a Professor of Management and a Professor of Psychology in the Michael F. Price College of Business at the University of Oklahoma.

Chad P. Diaz II is a Ph.D. Candidate in Business Administration with an emphasis in Management Information Systems at the University of Mississippi. His research is focused on the emergence of discursive leadership in online communities. He has conducted research using big data repositories to explore how the lexical features of online posts affect the perception of online community members who become leaders. He works as a Leader in Software Configuration at Corelogic.

Martin Götz, Ph.D., is currently a Senior Research Associate in the Division of Social and Economic Psychology of the University of Zurich's Department of Psychology. His primary research interests are norms and individuals' deviation thereof – be it at the workplace, in economics, or in science in general. His work has been published in outlets such as *Journal of Organizational Behavior, Small Group Research*, and *Psychological Bulletin*. He is a Member of the Editorial Boards of the *Journal of Personnel Psychology* and *Small Group Research*.

Jeffrey H. Greenhaus is Professor Emeritus of Management in Drexel University's LeBow College of Business. His research focuses on work-family relationships and career dynamics. A Fellow of SIOP and the Association for Psychological Science, he is the Author of numerous journal articles, chapters, and books, including most recently *Advanced Introduction to Sustainable Careers* with Gerry Callanan (Edward Elgar, 2022) and *Making Work and Family Work: From Hard Choices to Smart Choices* with Gary Powell (Routledge, 2017).

Jonathon R. B. Halbesleben is Dean, Bodenstedt Chair, and Tom C. Frost Distinguished University Chair for Business Excellence in the Alvarez College of Business at the University of Texas at San Antonio.

Rebecca Hewett is an Associate Professor in Human Resource Management at the Rotterdam School of Management, Erasmus University, in the Netherlands. Her research focuses on understanding the human experience of HR practices, particularly motivation and well-being, and the role of managers in implementing HR practices. Her research has been published in journals including *Journal of Management, Journal of Management Studies, Human Resource Management Review, Human Relations, Journal of Organizational Behavior*, and *Journal of Vocational Behavior.* In recent years she has published a number of papers and chapters on the role of attributions in HR processes. She is currently an Associate Editor for *Human Resource Management Review*.

Paul D. Johnson, Ph.D., is an Associate Professor, the Thomas W. Colbert Lecturer in Venture Capital and Entrepreneurial Finance, and Associate Dean in the School of Business Administration at the University of Mississippi. He is the Author of numerous publications on innovation, creativity, and motivational processes in entrepreneurial teams. His work appears in the *Journal of Management*, the *Journal of Applied Psychology*, and the *Journal of Organizational Behavior*, among others. After attending the University of Oklahoma for a BS in Zoology and an MBA, he received his Ph.D. from Oklahoma State University in 2010.

Anthony C. Klotz is an Associate Professor of Organizational Behavior in the UCL School of Management at University College London. He received his Ph.D. from the University of Oklahoma's Price College of Business. His research focuses on understanding employees' relationship with work through the lenses of resignations, citizenship behavior, and biophilic design. His research has been published in top management journals, but he is best known for having coined the phrase "The Great Resignation" in an interview with Bloomberg Businessweek in May 2021.

Joel Koopman is an Associate Professor and TJ Barlow Professor of Business Administration in the Mays Business School at Texas A&M University. He earned his Ph.D. from Michigan State University. He serves on a number of Editorial Boards and is currently an Associate Editor at *Organizational Behavior* *and Human Decision Processes*. His research interests include organizational justice, daily employee self-regulation and well-being, and research methodology.

Ellen Ernst Kossek is the Basil S. Turner Distinguished Professor of Management at Purdue University's Mitchell E. Daniels School of Business. A Fellow of the Academy of Management, SIOP and APA, she received her Ph.D. from Yale University and is the first elected President of the Work Family Researchers' Network. Her research focuses on relationships between leader and organizational work-life interventions and gender and work-life equality. She has won a work-life legacy award for building the work-life movement and serves on a National Academies of Sciences Expert Committee to provide evidence-based guidance on how to support family caregivers working in STEMM.

Brenda A. Lautsch is the Beedie Professor and Associate Dean at Simon Fraser University's Beedie School of Business. She received her Ph.D. in Industrial Relations and Human Resource Management from the M.I.T. Sloan School of Management and an MIR from Queen's University. Her current research examines work-life relationships, how flexibility can be implemented to enhance work-life equality and inclusion, and how work and leisure can be more meaningful. Her articles appear in leading journals such as the *Journal of Management* and the *Academy of Management Annals*.

Yizhen Lu is a Ph.D. Candidate in Management and Organization at the National University of Singapore. Her research interests are in workplace political correctness, prosocial behavior, humor, and employee well-being. Her topics tend to explore phenomenon-driven issues, how to draw on cross-disciplinary research to help managers address these organizational issues and close the scientist-practitioner gap. Her research has been published in journals like *Academy of Management Journal* and *Frontiers in Psychology*.

Caleb Lugar, Ph.D., is the Director of Oasis International School – Kosovo. He is the Author of book chapters and journal articles in collections including *Journal of Management History, Leadership, Economics Ecology Socium*, and *Nova Science Publishers*. His research interests include leadership, education, and self-initiated expatriates. In addition to research activities, he is a Practitioner who has held leadership roles in international organizations in the USA, South America, Africa, Southeast Asia, and Europe.

Tarani J. Merriweather is a Research Scholar in Organizational Behavior and Human Resources in the Department of Management at Purdue University's Daniels School of Business, where she Co-chaired the Dismantling Bias Conference and is co-PI on a grant funded by the NIH. She earned her Ph.D. in Social-Organizational Psychology from Columbia University's Teachers College after attending Spelman College and gaining extensive experience living and working abroad in Paris, France. Her research is focused on applying an intersectional lens to the work-life literature, including interrogating how systems are embedded in contexts within and across cultures.

Jeremy D. Meuser (Ph.D. University of Illinois at Chicago, 2016) was selected as a 2021 Western Academy of Management Ascendant Scholar, a prestigious award given to the very best early career scholars in Management recognizing excellence in research, service, and teaching. He brings an eclectic background to the study of leadership, holding degrees in several different disciplines. He is an Associate Editor for leadership articles at *Group and Organization Management* and the *Journal of Managerial Psychology*. He also serves on the Editorial Review Board for *The Leadership Quarterly*. He currently serves as Co-president of the Network of Leadership Scholars.

Milorad M. Novicevic (Ph.D. University of Oklahoma) is an Associate Professor at the University of Mississippi and Former Chair of the Academy of Management – Management History Division. His research is focused primarily on the global and historical aspects of leadership and human resource management. He has published more than 170 articles in journals such as *Organizational Behavior and Human Decision Processes, Leadership Quarterly, Academy of Management Learning and Education, Human Relations, Journal of World Business, Strategic Management Journal, Human Resource Management, International Journal of Human Resource Management, Human Resource Management Review, Journal of Vocational Behavior,* and *Career Development International.*

Ernest H. O'Boyle is a Professor of Organizational Behavior and Human Resources and holds the Dale M. Coleman Chair of Management in the Kelley School of Business at Indiana University. His work on such topics as the Dark Triad of personality, workplace deviance, superstar effects, and research integrity has been published in leading outlets such as *Journal of Applied Psychology, Journal of Management, Personnel Psychology,* and *Psychological Bulletin.* His work has also been featured in such popular press outlets as *NPR's Morning Edition*, *Wall Street Journal*, and *Bloomberg Businessweek*.

Matthew B. Perrigino is an Assistant Professor of Management at Baruch College's Zicklin School of Business. He completed this work as an Assistant Professor of Management at Iona University's LaPenta School of Business. He previously served as an Assistant Professor of Management at Elon University's Love School of Business and earned his Ph.D. from Purdue University's Krannert School of Management. His research focuses on the work–nonwork interface including how supervisors engage in leadership styles that support employees' well-being and the implementation of work-life balance policies in organizations.

Karin Sanders is a Professor of Human Resource Management and Organizational Psychology at the School of Management and Governance, University of New South Wales (UNSW) Business School, UNSW Sydney, Australia. Her research focuses on the human resource (HR) process approach, in particular, the impact of employees' understanding and attributions of HR practices on their attitudes and behaviors. She published on these and other topics in journals such as *Human Resource Management (Wiley), Human Resource Management Journal, HRM Review, Journal of Vocational Behavior, Academy of Management Learning and Education, Organization Studies*, and *Organization Science.* She is an Associate Editor for *Human Resource Management* (Wiley) and *Human Resource Management Review*. Finally, she is on the Editorial Boards of several (HR) management and organizational psychology journals.

Pok Man Tang is an Assistant Professor of Management in the Terry College of Business at University of Georgia. He received his Ph.D. from Texas A&M University. His research interests include human–nonhuman interactions at work (i.e., interaction with artificial intelligence, robots, algorithms, animals, and nature), behavioral ethics & stereotypes, and emotions & well-being. His research has appeared in internationally renowned journals, for instance, *Academy of Management Journal, Journal of Applied Psychology, Personnel Psychology, and Organizational Behavior and Human Decision Processes.*

Elijah X. M. Wee is an Assistant Professor of Management in the Foster School of Business at University of Washington. He received his Ph.D. from University of Maryland. He examines the conditions that disrupt hierarchies in organizations and its downstream consequences. He studies social hierarchies, employee creativity, and inclusion in organizations. He has published in top-tier management journals and received recognition for his research, including the Williams A. Owens Scholarly Achievement Award, and the S. Rains Wallace Dissertation Award.

Anthony R. Wheeler is Dean of the School of Business Administration and Professor of Management at Widener University. He completed his Ph.D. in Industrial-Organizational Psychology at the University of Oklahoma and is known for his research in employee turnover and retention. He has published peer-reviewed research in outlets such as Journal of Applied Psychology, Journal of Management, and Journal of Organizational Behavior. He recently published a book that examines the future of HRM in an age of automation, artificial intelligence, and machine learning.

Huadong Yang is a Reader at the Management School, University of Liverpool in the UK. His current research interests are on HRM process, in particular, on HRM strength, HRM implementation by line managers, and employee HRM sensemaking. His work has appeared in journals such as *Human Resource Management* (Wiley), *the International Journal of HRM*, and *Journal of Organizational Behavior*. He is one of the Associate Editors of the *International Journal of HRM* and sits on the Editorial Boards of *Human Resource Management* and *Human Resource Management Journal.*

CHAPTER 1

FORTY VOLUMES OF *RESEARCH IN PERSONNEL AND HUMAN RESOURCES MANAGEMENT*: REFLECTING ON IMPACTFUL CONTRIBUTIONS AND CONTINUING OUR MISSION INTO THE FUTURE

Anthony R. Wheeler, John E. Baur,
Jonathon R. B. Halbesleben and M. Ronald Buckley

This volume celebrates a milestone for *Research in Personnel and Human Resources Management* (*RPHRM*) as the oldest and most prestigious annual series in human resources management (HRM). For 40 years, leading scholars within various domains of HRM have published their work which has helped to shape the body of knowledge used by researchers around the globe. This current volume, the 41st in the series, continues that legacy. As the current editors of this series, we take this opportunity to reflect on the history of the series from the original inception and founding editor. We then particularly celebrate five articles that we believe typify the quality, and trendsetting nature, of articles that *RPHRM* publishes each year. Selecting five manuscripts that represent more than 40 years of collective research presents challenges, as we cannot judge a manuscript as being qualitatively or quantitatively better than another. Rather,

Research in Personnel and Human Resources Management, Volume 41, 1–6

Published under exclusive licence by Emerald Publishing Limited
ISSN: 0742-7301/doi:10.1108/S0742-730120230000041003

we chose to highlight these five manuscripts as representing the types of research that have made *RHRM* the premier HRM annual series.

William Glueck, a distinguished professor at The University of Georgia, was contracted by JAI Press to be the first editor of this series. He passed away in May 1980 before producing a volume. The ubiquitous unfilled need for this research series was then passed on to two world-class scholars who became the editors of the initial volume – the late Kendrith M. Rowland (Professor of Management at the University of Illinois) and Gerald R. Ferris (then a doctoral student in Management at the University of Illinois – who developed into one of the most important contributors to research and a celebrated thought leader in HRM). Their vision was to create an annual series dedicated to publishing long-form, conceptual research for HRM scholars, analogous to the annual series *Research in Organizational Behavior*. Although organizational behavior and HRM complement each other, each field has distinct bodies of knowledge that are independent of the other.

The focus of the new research series was that every published *RPHRM* manuscript must prominently address HRM issues.

Since its inception, the editors of RPHRM have maintained two key requirements for authors who seek to publish a manuscript. One, *RPRHM* only publishes conceptual HRM research. Readers of the series will not see empirical research in any of the published volumes. Two, authors must commit to publishing more-than-typical-journal-length manuscripts, which typically amount to 20,000- to 40,000-word monograph-length manuscripts and published importantly in 1983. *RPHRM* seeks to publish conceptual research that does not just summarize past research on a given topic but pushes theory and research forward in new, important, fecund, and provocative ways. Thus, readers should notice that most *RPHRM* articles contain novel research questions or frameworks that establish and suggest future directions for research.

Folger and Greenberg (1985) perfectly demonstrated how scholars have used the series to not only summarize previous research but also to extend research in new directions. They selected a nominally organizational behavior topic – organizational justice – but extend research into an HRM domain. Both Folger and Greenberg established robust research streams on social comparisons and perceptions of equity that arise from those comparisons. Until their *RPHRM* publication, HRM scholars focused more attention on equity perceptions, often distributive equity perspectives, in compensation settings. After all, it is in the compensation setting that employees most often experience justice considerations early in their employment in terms of monetary exchange. Folger and Greenberg widened the lens on justice and HRM to explicate how procedural justice perceptions infiltrate entire HRM systems. They also expanded the consideration of procedural justice throughout total HRM systems. That focus on process and systems also laid the foundations for strategic HRM research that abounded in the early 1990s through the early 2000s.

Employers and managers who standardize discrete HRM processes develop more trust between employers and employees. Folger and Greenberg (1985) later published multiple empirically based articles that provided evidence to support their conceptualizations in their *RPHRM* manuscript; simply put, if companies strengthen their processes around selection, performance management, and even decisions whereby employees receive training opportunities, employees will experience a greater sense of fair treatment. That in turn tends to increase positive employee and company outcomes such as stronger organizational commitment, improved job satisfaction, and reduced turnover. From a 2023 vantage point, these findings seem mundane; but at the time, Folger and Greenberg's conceptualization created a framework that they and others used to create a common body of knowledge around the interplay between fairness perceptions and HRM systems.

RPHRM has published several manuscripts that advanced the body of knowledge for strategic HRM, but the manuscript by Delery and Shaw (2001) stands out for several reasons. *RPHRM* published this manuscript as the early empirical research on strategic HRM was peaking. Several strategic HRM theories, such as the resource-based view of HRM (e.g., Boxall, 1996), agency theory (e.g., Tosi & Gomez-Mejia, 1994), and transaction cost theory (e.g., Wright & McMahan, 1992), had gained empirical support. Delery and Shaw systematically summarized the empirical findings supporting the various theories, while also clearly identifying opportunities for scholars to address voids in the literatures of those theories.

The Delery and Shaw (2001) manuscript has been cited more than 1,000 times since its publication, and it has served as the foundation of meta-analyses (e.g., Jiang et al., 2012), multilevel models of strategic HRM (e.g., Ployhart & Moliterno, 2011), and explorations of international HRM (e.g., Takeuchi et al., 2007). A more underappreciated aspect of the Delery and Shaw manuscript is the identification of commonalities among the various strategic HRM theories. It is this type of conceptual research that advances fields of study by breaking down silos and pushing for more comprehensive, perhaps even meta-theories that again kickstart new empirical research.

Whereas *RPHRM* has published several highly cited strategic HRM manuscripts, the series also has published functional HRM manuscripts that have pushed respective bodies of knowledge forward. Bauer et al. (1998) advanced newcomer socialization research into new directions. Notable in Bauer et al.'s summary of previous research on newcomer socialization was the work they did to fully summarize the costs associated with unsuccessful orientation programs. Increasingly, in the 1990s, and perhaps spurred by the connections that strategic HRM research made to the value and costs of HRM systems, HRM researchers even in the functional area made specific attempts to connect those functions to what were viewed as important organizational performance metrics, namely productivity and turnover. Bauer et al. provided a comprehensive review of the linkages between organizational socialization and employee productivity and turnover cost estimates.

Bauer et al. (1998) then systematically identified voids in the research around organizational socialization. From methodological issues to often ignored temporal aspects to process issues to newcomer learning issues, Bauer et al. highlighted voids and noted opportunities for scholars to advance the body of knowledge for organizational socialization. From the view of the field in the early 2020s, Bauer et al. also specifically address a topic that is at the forefront of researchers' minds now, but one that was not often addressed two decades ago: the role of diversity. They highlighted research not only on cultural diversity (e.g., how newcomer socialization occurs in the USA vs. Japan) but also on how individual diversity characteristics can affect newcomer socialization. Bauer et al. laid out a series of propositions around cultural and individual diversity that would go on to be tested over the decades to come.

RPHRM also has published manuscripts on emerging bodies of knowledge in HRM. Glomb et al. (2011) published a manuscript on the confluence of mindfulness and HRM. Whereas research on mindfulness has become mainstream, even to the point of popular media attention on the topic, mindfulness research in organization in the early 2000s was not considered mainstream. The application of an emerging body of knowledge such as mindfulness to HRM represented boundary expansion to an even greater level at the time.

Glomb et al. (2011) begin their chapter discussing the emergence of mindfulness, particularly noting that the topic had gone mainstream in such a rapid period of time that a backlash had already emerged, which was fueled in part by beliefs that mindfulness had explicit religious connotations. Perhaps the rapid ascent of interest in mindfulness as a popular media panacea for workplace stress and employee burnout coincided with the full maturation of the internet era, that is, mindfulness went viral, especially in the realm of mental health and individual well-being.

Glomb et al. (2011) sought to formulate this increased popular and research attention into a coherent theoretical framework that explained how and why mindfulness impacted employee performance and well-being. They connected research previously siloed outside of the organizational context with research emerging inside of the organizational context. It is this type of theorizing in which *RPHRM* manuscripts shine. Authors can utilize the monograph-length parameters of *RPHRM* to make theoretical connections, propose connective processes and mechanisms, and proffer testable propositions for empirical scholars and approaches to evaluate. In the decade since Glomb et al. connected disparate literatures to organizational literatures, their manuscript has been cited nearly 500 times.

We have focused attention on four manuscripts that have become the foundations for now established research. However, the final *RPHRM* manuscript we highlight here focuses on a topic that dominates the consciousness of individuals, organizations, and societies across the world. The topic is social media. Kluemper et al. (2016) provided one of the first extensive explorations into the role that social media plays in how organizations and HRM can operate. Although ubiquitous now, back in 2016, very little research existed on the topic of social media in organizations, and almost none existed on the topic of social media and HRM. This pushed Kluemper et al. to delve into myriad emerging literatures to theorize about a future where social media would in fact make significant impacts on how organizations run and HRM systems connect with social media applications.

How do you forecast the impact of social media on organizational operations when limited research exists on that topic? That was the challenge for Kluemper et al. (2016). At the time when *RPHRM* published their work, *Facebook* had yet to turn 10 years old. *Twitter* existed but did not have the same cache as it does now. *LinkedIn* functioned more like an online recruiting platform instead of the true social network, backed by artificial intelligence, we see today. Kluemper et al. (2016) summarized disparate literatures around organizational branding, employee recruitment and selection, communication channels, and counterproductive work behaviors to then project forward the power of social media in the organizational context. We take this for granted now due to pervasiveness of social media in every aspect of daily life, but Kluemper et al.'s work in the mid-2010s required the ability to see trends and play them forward.

What is next for *RPHRM*? In the near term, we as editors have consciously committed to seeking out researchers who can provide manuscripts on nascent or emerging topics that will become mainstream research topics over the next decade. To do so, we actively work to identify thought leaders, nascent scholars, and area experts within HRM. We endeavor to help the field get ahead of the next wave. We have lived through a once-a-century global pandemic that reoriented how modern organizations function. Although telework has existed in some form for multiple decades, work-from-home policies have expanded to the point where some companies have started to develop work-from-office policies. What does the future hold for HRM scholars who study how HRM functions and HRM strategy works in an in-person, remote, or hybrid workplace?

The pandemic also accelerated the adoption of technologies associated with the "Fourth Industrial Revolution" – automation, artificial intelligence, machine learning, and the internet of things. We should expect the adoption of those technologies to accelerate over the next decade as those technologies mature. Inevitably, this will lead to disruption across jobs, organizations, industries, and societies. How will HRM adapt to this disruption, and how will HRM scholars develop an understanding of the causes, effects, mechanisms, and processes around this disruption? The pandemic and "Fourth Industrial Revolution" coincide with a larger macro trend, that of climate change. This exogenous, multidimensional threat will reorient every aspect of society. Expect more manuscripts in *RPHRM* that will seek to explicate the relationships between climate change and how organizations strategize and operationalize their HRM systems.

Taking a step back and looking at the broad scope of *RPHRM* over the past 40 years, this important research series has provided HRM scholars with the opportunity to describe what, when, how, and why the future of work will exist. In this current volume of *RPHRM* – number 41 of the series – we present five manuscripts that again push the study of HRM forward in thought-provoking ways. As the current editors of this series, we take great pride in continuing the tradition of moving HRM research forward; a trend that Professor Kendrith M. Rowland and Professor Gerald R. Ferris established over 40 years ago!

REFERENCES

Bauer, T. N., Morrison, E. W., & Callister, R. R. (1998). Socialization research: A review and directions for future research. *Research in Personnel and Human Resources Management* (Vol. 16, pp. 149–212). JAI Press.

Boxall, P. (1996). The strategic HRM debate and the resource-based view of the firm. *Human Resource Management Journal*, *6*(3), 59–75.

Delery, J. E., & Shaw, J. D. (2001). The strategic management of people in work organizations: Review, synthesis, and extension. *Research in personnel and human resources management* (Vol. 20, pp. 165–197), Emerald Group Publishing Limited.

Folger, R., & Greenberg, J. (1985). Procedural justice: An interpretive analysis of personal systems. In K. M.Rowland & G. R. Ferris (Eds.), *Research in personnel and human resources management* (Vol. 3, pp. 141–183). JAI Press.

Glomb, T. M., Duffy, M. K., Bono, J. E., & Yang, T. (2011). Mindfulness at work. In A. Joshi, H. Liao, & J. J. Martocchio (Eds.), *Research in personnel and human resources management (research in personnel and human resources management)* (Vol. 30, pp. 115–157). Emerald Group Publishing Limited.

Jiang, K., Lepak, D. P., Hu, J., & Baer, J. C. (2012). How does human resource management influence organizational outcomes? A meta-analytic investigation of mediating mechanisms. *Academy of Management Journal*, *55*(6), 1264–1294.

Kluemper, D. H., Mitra, A., & Wang, S. (2016). Social media use in HRM. In *Research in personnel and human resources management* (Vol. 34, pp. 153–207). Emerald Group Publishing Limited.

Ployhart, R. E., & Moliterno, T. P. (2011). Emergence of the human capital resource: A multilevel model. *Academy of Management Review*, *36*(1), 127–150.

Takeuchi, R., Lepak, D. P., Wang, H., & Takeuchi, K. (2007). An empirical examination of the mechanisms mediating between high-performance work systems and the performance of Japanese organizations. *Journal of Applied Psychology*, *92*(4), 1069.

Tosi, H. L., Jr., & Gomez-Mejia, L. R. (1994). CEO compensation monitoring and firm performance. *Academy of Management Journal*, *37*(4), 1002–1016.

Wright, P. M., & McMahan, G. C. (1992). Theoretical perspectives for strategic human resource management. *Journal of Management*, *18*(2), 295–320.

CHAPTER 2

COBBLERS, LET'S STICK TO OUR LASTS! A SONG OF SORROW (AND OF HOPE) ABOUT THE STATE OF PERSONNEL AND HUMAN RESOURCE MANAGEMENT SCIENCE

Martin Götz and Ernest H. O'Boyle

ABSTRACT

The overall goal of science is to build a valid and reliable body of knowledge about the functioning of the world and how applying that knowledge can change it. As personnel and human resources management researchers, we aim to contribute to the respective bodies of knowledge to provide both employers and employees with a workable foundation to help with those problems they are confronted with. However, what research on research has consistently demonstrated is that the scientific endeavor possesses existential issues including a substantial lack of (a) solid theory, (b) replicability, (c) reproducibility, (d) proper and generalizable samples, (e) sufficient quality control (i.e., peer review), (f) robust and trustworthy statistical results, (g) availability of research, and (h) sufficient practical implications. In this chapter, we first sing a song of sorrow regarding the current state of the social sciences in general and personnel and human resources management specifically. Then, we investigate potential grievances that might have led to it (i.e., questionable research practices, misplaced

Research in Personnel and Human Resources Management, Volume 41, 7–92

Published under exclusive licence by Emerald Publishing Limited
ISSN: 0742-7301/doi:10.1108/S0742-730120230000041004

incentives), only to end with a verse of hope by outlining an avenue for betterment (i.e., open science and policy changes at multiple levels).

Keywords: Academic-practice divide; credibility of science; open science; philosophy of science; replicability crisis; reproducibility crisis; science-practice gap

Cordwainer. (Old-fashioned) A person who makes new shoes from leather.

Cobbler. (Old-fashioned) A person who repairs shoes.

The health of an applied science, such as personnel and human resources management (PHRM), and, more generally, industrial and organizational psychology (I/OP), can be broadly captured as a multiplicative function of its (a) relevance to practitioners, (b) rigor of its methodology, (c) accuracy of its findings and claims, and (d) ability to build cumulative knowledge. We stress multiplicative because if any one of these four hallmarks is absent or lacking, then the health of the entire scientific field will be poor, regardless of the strength of the other hallmarks. We put forth that all of these hallmarks are present in the PHRM field. Further, in many respects, each hallmark has increased the overall health of PHRM research over time. For example, advances in statistical analysis, increased grant funding for PHRM research, open access (OA) publishing, and growing membership in both PHRM academic and practitioner societies all suggest the current scientific paradigm is robust and relevant. However, improvements in the questions we ask, the advances in methodologies and statistics we employ, and greater access to the cumulative knowledge of the field for both researchers and practitioners are not the only changes seen in PHRM. For each of these improvements to the PHRM health, there are detriments and unintended consequences.

These detriments and unintended consequences manifest as (a) academic navel gazing in the form of research with little chance (or interest) in practitioner implications or implementation, (b) insufficient forethought in study design and measurement, which leads to (c) an overreliance on statistics to analyze what should have been designed around, and (d) a rose-tinted literature containing a non-trivial amount of findings that appear rigorous and relevant but are in fact tainted by non-ideal research and reporting practices.

In this chapter, we review and, at times, critique the current state of PHRM rigor and relevance. We begin with a review of the PHRM science along with the four hallmarks of a healthy science introduced above. We then propose a set of impeding factors that detriment PHRM research by adversely affecting one or more of the four hallmarks. We then offer a set of recommendations that reflect both strategies successfully employed in other social sciences as well as the unique features of the PHRM and I/OP domains.

In framing this paper, we use the distinction in the English language between a cordwainer and a cobbler: While the former makes new leather shoes, the latter fixes them. As can be seen, the two professions have a symbiotic relationship with both professions needing one another. These professions make for an apt analogy of the research process. Cordwainers develop, propose, and, at times, preliminarily test new theory while cobblers validate, replicate, and if found to be robust, apply the new theory in other contexts. With this symbiotic relationship in mind, we argue that we, as a field, have far more (perhaps too many) cordwainers and far fewer (certainly too few) cobblers. Although old-fashioned, the parallel between these professions and ours carries to the present day. Consider how the rise of fast fashion and throwaway culture have led to many more shoes being produced with few ever intended to be repaired, has grave unintended consequences in the form of plastic waste, toxic emissions, sweatshops, etc. Likewise, when coupled with other concerning issues in PHRM and I/OP research (e.g., unreliability in the review process and norms regarding openness and transparency) the vast proliferation of new theory with few ever to be tested through replication has generated its own form of "theory pollution" with its own grave unintended consequences in the above-mentioned forms of navel gazing, reduced care in study design, overreliance on statistics, and questionable research practices.

From the perspective of PHRM and I/OP researchers, and broadly keeping a threefold structure of theory, methods, and statistics in mind, we contribute to the literature in three ways: (1) We outline current issues in social scientific research; (2) we present an overview of possible promising solutions of these current limitations; and (3) we sketch bridges of how we, as a field, could move toward a better future. In doing so, we present scholars with a thorough assessment of the current PHRM and I/OP research and publication life cycle and provide potential cobblers with a realistic job preview that combines, at times, a stark assessment of the profession with just enough hope to take the job anyway.

We also wish to highlight that this chapter is intended for both academics and practitioners. Although there are some technical aspects that may require an understanding of, for example, the general linear model, we tried to write in a manner free of academic jargon. As we will discuss, one of the many reasons PHRM research struggles to find relevance among HR practitioners is that even with access to the research (a far from certain thing without either extensive funds or academic library access), the writing is often needlessly complex. A relatively simple step to increase our relevance as an academic and applied field is describing the research in a way that is actually relevant and understandable to the very individuals tasked with putting the research into practice.

SONG OF SORROW: THE CURRENT HEALTH OF PHRM SCIENCE

Before the ode to the cobbler, let us first sing their song of sorrow about the current state of social scientific research and the ecosystem it has produced – and vice versa – with a focus on PRHM. To be clear, bemoaning the current state of the science that one belongs to is an age-old practice (e.g., Dienes, 2008; Ferguson, 2015; R. A. Fisher, 1956; Koch, 1992; Kuhn, 1996; Lakatos, 1970; Meehl, 1967,

1978, 1990; Merton, 1957; Pearson, 1911; Popper, 1956/1983), and we draw from a number of these past critiques in assessing the PHRM field. However, the song of sorrow for PHRM is a novel harmony and arrangement, and these unique aspects must be considered. As such, we embed our understanding of the PHRM field within the larger social science framework. However, where applicable, we highlight the intricacies of our field, and how these intricacies might be leveraged or mitigated to ensure that the research we do is trustworthy, accurate, and relevant to those studying, and practicing PHRM.

The Norms of Science

As the name implies, the song of sorrow is a dirge. It bemoans where we are, and how we got there. To understand the lyrics, we first must understand where we want or ought to be. Science operates within a social system (i.e., community), and every social system is eventually governed by norms. Norms are the shared set of acceptable behaviors within a community that are learned and reinforced by its members – Cristina Bicchieri (2005) poignantly considered norms *the grammar of society*. Broadly speaking, there are two types of norms: injunctive and descriptive. Injunctive norms refer to the behaviors that are the espoused or spoken beliefs of what is acceptable or not. For example, most laws are a reflection of previously developed and reinforced injunctive norms. Descriptive norms, on the other hand, are what most people actually do. In short, injunctive norms are what a community thinks one *should* do and descriptive norms are what community members *typically* do (see also Cialdini & Trost, 1998; J. Gross & Vostroknutov, 2022; Lapinski & Rimal, 2005).

In many cases, the injunctive norms and descriptive norms of a community align. For example, there is an injunctive norm against driving on the wrong side of the road as well as the descriptive norm that most people do not drive on the wrong side of the road. However, there are times when these two categories of norms do not align and are in fact in opposition to one another. For example, although there is an injunctive norm against exceeding the speed limit on an interstate highway, the descriptive norm, in the United States at least, is that you stay with the flow of traffic which typically runs several miles above the speed limit. There is ample research on which types of norms are most salient in a given context, but more often than not, it is the descriptive norms that most impact our behavior (e.g., Borsari & Carey, 2003; Jacobson et al., 2020; Yip & Schweitzer, 2022). For example, consider your first job. How much of your behavior was influenced by the employee manual (injunctive norms), and how much was influenced by observing how the other employees behaved (descriptive norms)?

Robert K. Merton described the "extension of certified knowledge" as "the institutional goal of science" (1942, p. 117). In turn, he prominently described the norms that should govern a scientific system in that these render principles of desirable behavior (e.g., 1942; *cf.* Mulkay, 1976, 1980). Specifically, he outlined the following four injunctive norms: (1) communality, (2) universalism, (3) disinterestedness, and (4) organized skepticism. First, *communality* refers to the ideal of shared ownership of scientific methods and findings. As such, scientists should openly share their findings, and how their respective procedure how they arrived at them; at the very least, with their fellow scholars. Second, *universalism* refers to the ideal that scientific findings should solely be judged on the basis of their merit, without taking irrelevant characteristics, such as the researcher's status, or affiliation, into account. In other words, scientists should always have "Does this get us closer to the respective truth?" as a guiding principle in mind. Third, and closely related, *disinterestedness* refers to the understanding that scientific work should be exclusively motivated by the desire for knowledge and discovery, and not by self-interest, or the pursuit of status and wealth. Fourth, *organized skepticism* refers to the ideal that scientific findings are made available for collective scrutiny in accordance with accepted scientific standards. In other words, researchers should consider all new evidence, hypotheses, theories, and innovations, even those challenging or contradicting their own work.

These Mertonian norms were later extended by Anderson et al. (2010), also who formulated (5) governance, and (6) quality as injunctive norms of science. Specifically, and fifth, *governance* refers to the system in which researchers "debate, negotiate, and come to decisions about issues that drive scientific inquiry, methods to be used, distribution of resources, and attention to scientific initiatives" (M. S. Anderson et al., 2010, p. 378). In other words, researchers should be responsible for the direction and control of science through governance, self-regulation, and peer review. Finally, sixth, *quality* refers to the ideal that researchers should judge each other's contributions to science primarily on the basis of quality. Against the background of the distinction of norms regarding injunctive and descriptive norms, we consider Merton's norms of science as the injunctive ones in that we *should* follow them (Anderson et al., 2007a, 2007b, 2010; see also M. S. Anderson et al., 2010).

Yet, as Merton and Barber (1963/2017) noted, there are also counter-norms that create ambivalence regarding acceptable behavior aligned with injunctive norms and create contrasting social pressures. In light of the introduced distinction between injunctive and descriptive norms, we consider the counter-norms of science to be the current *descriptive* ones and stick with this nomenclature in what follows (see also Anderson et al., 2007a, 2007b). Specifically, Merton and Barber (1963/2017) stated that their "analysis of sociological ambivalence proceeds from the premise that the structure of social roles consists of arrangements of [injunctive] norms and [descriptive] norms which have evolved to provide the flexibility of normatively acceptable behavior required to deal with changing states of a social relation" (p. 104). For example, as a general rule, one should not tell lies (injunctive norm) but the descriptive norm in certain circumstances provides the flexibility to if not outright lie, at least stretch the truth, such as when a new parent asks, "Isn't my baby beautiful?," or a police officer asks, "Do you know how fast you were going?" Where community threatening problems emerge is when the descriptive norms in conflict with the injunctive norms become so pervasive and powerful that the injunctive norm is essentially abandoned.

Building on Merton's work, Mitroff (1974) identified the descriptive (i.e., counter) norms of science as; (1) secrecy, (2) particularism, (3) self-interestedness, and (4) organized dogmatism. First, *secrecy* refers to researchers protecting their newest findings to ensure priority in publishing, patenting, grant applications, etc. Second, *particularism* refers to researchers assessing new knowledge, and its applications based on the reputation, and past productivity of the individual or research group. Third, *self-interestedness* refers to researchers competing with others in the same field for journal space, grant funding, and recognition of their achievements through tenure, status, income, awards, etc. Fourth, *organized dogmatism* refers to researchers investing their careers in promoting their own most important findings, theories, or innovations.

In extending the Mertonian norms of science, Anderson et al. (2010) also extended Mitroff's (1974) counter-norms accordingly, by also acknowledging (5) administration and (6) quantity. In particular, fifth, *administration* refers to practice of researchers relying on "administrators to direct the scientific enterprise through management decisions scientist" (Anderson et al., 2010, p. 379). And, finally, *quantity* scientist assesses each other's work primarily on the basis of numbers of publications and/or amount of grant funding. As can be seen quickly, these counter-norms are the direct opposites of the injunctive norms of science, as formulated by Merton (1942) and extended by Anderson et al. (2010).[1]

The key question is which set of norms dominates current PHRM and I/OP practices. To be clear, adherence to one of these descriptive norms of science is not inherently bad or inherently contradictory to the injunctive norms. Secrecy, for example, has a place in science, such as when the research has national security implications, or includes trade secrets (e.g., Hannah, 2005). Likewise, self-interest and the pursuit of glory and riches have incentivized and driven a tremendous amount scientific progress and is at the heart of many economic models (e.g., Camerer, 1999; Hargreaves Heap, 2013; von Neumann & Morgenstern, 2007). For example, the Breakthrough Prize (https://breakthroughprize.org/) is an annual award worth several million dollars that is given to researchers achieving a scientific breakthrough in the areas of physics, life sciences, and mathematics. To the extent that the prize (or any other incentive) motivated the award winners beyond their intrinsic motivation and disinterestedness can be viewed as strengthening the hallmarks of good science and by extension improving the overall health of those particular fields (see also Gallus & Frey, 2016).

When descriptive and injunctive norms are not aligned, understanding the degree and prevalence of misalignment is critical to understanding the health of the community (for a far from complete contrasting juxtaposition, see Table 1). Just as an occasional "white lie" may provide a degree of social niceties when interacting with a new parent and their less than beautiful child, if lying were to become the injunctive norm (i.e., you should always tell lies), the community would suffer. Likewise, to *consistently* default to research secrecy, to let the baubles and accolades of academia color *all aspects* of the research process, to *routinely* ignore if and how one's research is applied, or to allow any of other descriptive norms to become the exclusive or dominant driver of scientific inquiry hampers advancement, accuracy, implementation, and practical relevance. In other words, when Mitroff's (1974) descriptive norms supersede Merton's (1942, 1973; Merton & Barber, 1958/2004) injunctive ones, then the exception becomes the rule and the community of scholars and those they are alleged to serve will most assuredly suffer.

Table 1. Injunctive Norms and Descriptive Norms of Science.

Injunctive Norms With Examples From PHRM	Descriptive Norms With Examples From PHRM
Communality a. Prominent journals (e.g., *Journal of Applied Psychology* and *Personnel Psychology*) including OA publishing options b. Adoption of American Psychological Associations' Journal Article Reporting Standards	Secrecy a. Although many journals encourage OA practices, few require or enforce them b. The sharing of data for reproduction and secondary analysis (e.g., meta-analysis) is still uncommon
Universalism a. Internationalization of Academy of Management and Society for Industrial and Organizational Psychology b. Increasing use and development of OA software (e.g., R) commonly used in PHRM research c. Academy of Management's Diversity, Equity, and Inclusion division continues to expand its membership and influence d. Society for Industrial and Organizational Psychology's Anti-Racism Grants	Particularism a. Most samples derive from Western, Educated, Industrialized, Rich Democracies b. PHRM research is dominated by a select few colleges and departments primarily in the United States c. Research outside of the hypothetico-deductive model of research (e.g., qualitative, machine learning, and abductive and inductive approaches) can struggle to publish their work in leading outlets
Disinterestedness a. Efforts and editorials have been made to encourage replication b. Increased data transparency requirements at many journals have increased the ability to reproduce results c. The advent of journals, such as *Journal of Management Scientific Reports*, exclusively publishes replications and tests of previously published theoretical models	Self-interestedness a. Despite widespread recognition that replication and reproducibility studies are necessary hallmarks of good science, the cobbler's work is almost entirely left undone b. Compliance with journal policies around transparency is not consistently enforced
Organized skepticism a. Journals, such as *Academy of Management Discoveries*, encourage abductive research outside the hypothetico-deductive model b. Non-significant results are not entirely absent from the literature New theories and ideas are routinely introduced in the literature	Organized dogmatism a. Substantial evidence of publication bias for findings that fail to support hypotheses or oppose the current zeitgeist b. Bias toward quantitative research that conforms to the hypothetico-deductive model c. Preference given to building new theory or increasing its complexity rather than testing and winnowing extant theory
Governance a. Journals, such as *Human Resource Management Journal*, have instituted Practitioner Notes (short bullet pointed takeaways of the research; e.g., Farndale et al., 2020) b. *Society for Human Resource Management*'s Science-to-Practice Series c. Nearly all PHRM journals are members of Committee on Publication Ethics d. Division 14 (I/OP) regained its American Psychological Association Council Seat	Administration a. Implications for practice are given little attention in most PHRM research b. Most publications in prominent journals exist behind paywalls c. PHRM researchers have essentially outsourced dissemination of their research to consultants, HR practitioners, popular press outlets, and instructors with little concern over if and how their research is applied

(Continued)

Table 1. *(Continued)*

Injunctive Norms With Examples From PHRM	Descriptive Norms With Examples From PHRM
Quality	Quantity
a. To reduce *salami slicing* (i.e., submitting a set of similar papers using the same data to multiple journals), many PHRM journals have instituted requirements to disclose if data have been used in other publications	a. Increasing use and reliance on journal lists in business schools in particular have turned many tenure and promotion reviews into a counting exercise of how many "A" hits (i.e., highly esteemed journals) one has
b. Transparency checklists help reviewers and readers better gauge the rigor and quality of a study	b. In departments and schools strongly reliant on grant funding, the number and amount of grants can be prized more so that the science being conducted with those funds
c. To eliminate reviewers' tendency to judge the methodology based upon the results, some PHRM journals have instituted results-blind manuscripts	c. (a) and (b) coupled with beliefs that only "good" results are publishable have led to influx of questionable research practices

Note. The injunctive norms of science are adapted from Merton (1942) and Anderson et al. (2010), whereas the counter (descriptive) norms of science are adapted from Mitroff (1974) and Anderson et al. (2010). For an in-depth discussion and an empirical assessment of these norms in the scientific context, please see Anderson et al. (2007a, 2007b, 2010).

Hypothetico-deductive Model of Research

To inform our assessment of whether Mitroff's (1974) descriptive norms or Merton's injunctive norms (e.g., 1942, 1973; Merton & Barber, 1958/2004) currently govern PHRM and I/OP research, let us inspect the typically reported research life cycle[2]; the hypothetico-deductive model (Fig. 1; see also Chambers, 2017; Munafò et al., 2017; Popper, 1959/2002). We, as PHRM and I/OP scientists, identify a business problem in need of a solution. Based upon theoretical knowledge drawn from either the I/OP domain, or from a sister field, such as sociology, and economics, apply sound logic and considerable thought in order to develop testable hypotheses as to why this problem exists in the first place, and/or, in turn, what could be done to solve it. Thus, we generate hypotheses about the problem that we then typically test empirically. Doing so requires that we formulate and design an empirical study suitable to allow for collecting data, analyzing it, and finding evidence for or against our original hypotheses. The results derived from the empirical data or findings are then incorporated into a scientific report that is published by a scientific journal and thereby informs fellow researchers, practitioners, and anyone interested in the problem or its potential solutions. Importantly, if our study and/or data did not bring about enough evidence to address the research question fully, the hypothetico-deductive model of science starts over again and we or others in the research community will begin anew deducing what caused the problem and what might fix it.

The overarching goal of this model of research (and others including inductive, and abductive approaches) is the accumulation and advancement of knowledge (Bosco, 2022). This advancement primarily occurs through self-correction where unsupported, overly complex, and ultimately incorrect ideas give way to those correct ideas that are supported with evidence and provide a more parsimonious description and solution to a problem. Philosophers of science claim that

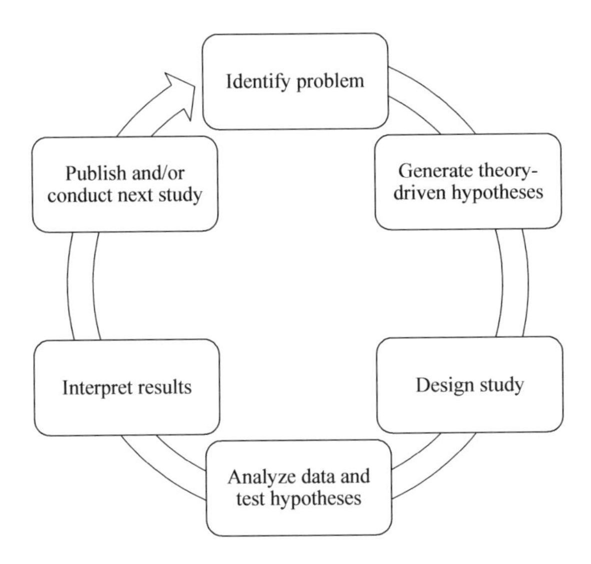

Fig. 1. Hypothetico-deductive Model of Science. *Note.* This (simplified) hypothetico-deductive model of science renders an idealized version regarding confirmatory empirical quantitative research (Chambers, 2017; Johnson et al., 2018; Munafò et al., 2017).

this scientific method is self-corrective by default (e.g., Laudan, 1981; Merton, 1942; Popper, 1959/2002). Specifically, this self-corrective thesis (SCT) proposes that the "(1) scientific method is such that, in the long run, its use will refute a false theory; (2) science possess a method for finding an alternative theory which is closer to the truth than a refuted theory" (Laudan, 1981, p.227; see also Romero & Sprenger, 2021). Importantly, the SCT assumes the six injunctive norms of conducting good science are dominant. If, on the other hand, the descriptive norms of science are pervasive, then there is no guarantee that self-correction will occur in a timely manner or even at all. So the fundamental question is how aligned are the descriptive norms of what scientists actually do with Merton's (1942, 1973; Merton & Barber, 1958/2004) idealized injunctive norms of what they should do?

George E. P. Box famously stated that, "all models are wrong, but some are useful" (Box & Draper, 1987, p.74), meaning also that all theories are oversimplifications of reality and thus require caveats or exceptions to what is proposed in the theory. A theory will ultimately give way to a new theory when it collapses under its own weight of caveats and exceptions (Kuhn, 1970). For example, the theory of geocentrism (i.e., Earth is at the center of solar system) required a massive number of caveats (e.g., Ptolemy's epicycles) to explain the seemingly erratic and unique orbits of the other planets. The compendium of caveats in geocentrism collapsed the theory when presented alongside the far more parsimonious and ultimately correct heliocentric model of the solar system with the Sun at the center. In the case of what orbits what, science did indeed correct itself. Whether SCT is more akin to a geocentric or heliocentric theory requires a review of its own noteworthy caveats (e.g., Ioannidis, 2012; Jussim et al., 2016; Romero & Sprenger, 2021).

The first SCT caveat is that better or stronger theory must be employed to challenge existing theory. If new theory is as equally complex and convoluted as existing theory, then we replace one weak model with another (or worse) one. The second SCT caveat is that science can only self-correct when it is shown repeatedly that the existing model is incorrect. Just as *one swallow does not make a summer*, a single study – even a well-conducted one – still requires replication. That the cordwainer claims their shoes are of the highest quality should be viewed with skepticism until the cobblers have had a chance to report how often the shoes need repair, how much they cost to fix, and whether they fit most people or only a small subset of the cordwainer's choosing. Likewise, SCT requires replication, and reproducibility to be as frequent, if not more frequent, than the proposing and initial test of new theories. The third caveat is that there must be some reliable set of standards by which to judge the support or lack thereof for the theory or finding. Typically in PHRM and I/OP, this reliability initially comes in the form of the peer-review system. If research challenging the collective zeitgeist is suppressed solely because it refutes existing wisdom, then self-correction will not occur. To the extent that the peer-review system is unreliable due to individual and group biases or a misalignment of incentives to encourage thoughtful and thorough assessments of theory and study quality is the extent that the SCT will be slowed or fully stopped.

The fourth and last noteworthy SCT caveat is that science cannot self-correct when it does not know that it is incorrect. Beyond a lack of reproducibility and replication, if unsupported hypotheses are routinely omitted in the initial proposal and test of a theory for the exclusive reason that they were unsupported, then future researchers will assume that the hypothesis remains untested and we end up with researchers devoting time and resources to reinventing the square wheel. In addition, mispresenting the research process by, for example, presenting a post hoc finding as an a priori hypotheses or running a series of models but only reporting the one model with positive findings, also hampers any self-correction. If the cobbler does not know or was misled in how the cordwainer made the shoe, then their ability to repair it is compromised as are any improvements in terms of fit, durability, aesthetics, etc.

DEVIATING FROM THE IDEAL (INJUNCTIVE NORMS)

A multitude of observations has given rise to the perspective that our implementation of the scientific model is flawed, or, at the very least, not correctly carried out on a consistent basis. Taking the research life cycle as a structuring guide, we will discuss the current issues namely (1) the lack of solid theory, (2) the lack of replicability, (3) the lack of reproducibility, (4) the lack of quality control (i.e., the peer-review process), (5) the lack of non-significant findings, (6) the lack of availability, and finally, (7) the lack of proper practical implications.

Lack of Solid Theory

Our understanding and knowledge of the world is typically organized in theories, namely "statement[s] of relations among concepts within a set of boundary assumptions and constraints" (Bacharach, 1989, p. 496; Sutton & Staw, 1995; Weick, 1995). As such, theory is typically generated from observations about the world and then used to make predictions by postulating hypotheses, and testing them (e.g., Popper, 1963, 1956/1983, 1959/2002). Yet, no theory can ever be proven to be truthful but only put to the test of falsification. In other words, "establishing truth is not what science does. No matter how strongly we or others believe a theory, the theory is and always remains just a guess, even if it is our best guess" (Dienes, 2008, p. 5). Because scientists want to accumulate and advance the knowledge of the world, it follows that we should put our theories to the test and refine them with respect to the results of our respective research.

But what makes for a strong theory (e.g., Fiedler, 2017; Sutton & Staw, 1995; Weick, 1995)? In its simplest form, theory assumes an order between constructs of interest in terms of causes and effects. Thus, the constructs of interest as well as their sequence should be defined clearly and distinctly. To make this simple theory stronger, the temporal sequence should be specified – in other words, the time it takes from cause to effect should be specified (e.g., Dormann, 2022; Dormann & Griffin, 2015; Dormann & van de Ven, 2014). In addition, the causal relationships should be quantified and explicated: (1) The relationship is how strong exactly?, (2) Which function (e.g., linear, quadratic, and cubic) does the relationship follow over which window of time?, and (3) What are potential boundary conditions, such as a context for the effect of interest to not occur or occur in a different manner (see also Ferris et al., 2012; Mitchell & James, 2001; Muthukrishna & Henrich, 2019)? We could go on, but the overarching question is which theoretical framework in PHRM and I/OP research effectively and thoroughly address these questions (e.g., Cropanzano et al., 2017; Locke & Latham, 2006; Rosen et al., 2020).

In our assessment, the unfortunate answer to this question in PHRM and I/OP research is "few to none." Micklethwait and Wooldridge (1997) considered management theory to be "bedeviled by obfuscation, jargon, and faddishness" (Hubbard, 2016, p. 1). In other words, the cordwainers have put fashion over function. Even our most foundational theories developed in I/OP lack the necessary specificity. Some of the lack of strong theory is that as PHRM and I/OP researchers we rarely give our theories a workout. For example, despite approaching its 50th anniversary, the Job Characteristics Model (Hackman & Oldham, 1975) has had very few complete tests of the theory with all five job characteristics, all three psychological states, and all four of the originally proposed outcomes of motivation, performance, satisfaction, and absenteeism/turnover. When one considers the moderator of growth needs strength, the number of complete tests of this model falls to zero. As such, it is no surprise that the theoretical precision remains relatively vague such that hypotheses derived from it are accordingly simplistic with little nuance or specificity beyond basic predictions of the direction of effect (Edwards & Berry, 2010).

This is not an indictment of Job Characteristics Model by any means. Even strong theory will atrophy when it is employed in a haphazard or lackadaisical manner. The phrases, "drawing from theory, we hypothesize," and "theoretically derived hypotheses" litter our journals, but far more often than not it is unclear on what exact components of the theory are informing the hypotheses. The reader is given a largely blank map with just a departure (theory) and destination (hypothesis), but little information connecting the two. As quipped by Paul Spector in a December 2022 blog post on why this is the case, he stated that theory has become, "merely a meme – a catchphrase that gives the reader a feeling of familiarity, and perhaps an illusion of clarity" (Spector, 2022). Put differently, authors are aware that theory must be employed for their manuscript to be published so they are paying homage to whatever theory has a passing resemblance to their predictions, measures, study design, and intended analysis.

Hartley (1749/2013) insisted, "only in mathematics can one develop theories which can be rigorously demonstrated. In science, however, we must be content with something less than certainty" (Laudan, 1981, p. 230). This ambiguity in science complicates researchers' ability to leverage theory in meaningful ways, yet it eases researchers' ability to leverage it in simplistic ways. If a PHRM – or I/OP – theory is vague and largely untested, then it can be applied to just about any work context. As an example from organizational behavior, consider the growth of leadership theories and constructs, such as transformational leadership, ethical leadership, authentic leadership, humble leadership, servant leadership, etc. For any given hypothesis involving these different theories of leadership, is there a single instance where substituting one theory for another would invalidate the hypothesis? Put differently, is there a single instance where, for example, servant leadership and humble leadership would make different predictions about follower reactions to a leadership behavior that could be tested via *strong inference* (Platt, 1964) where two competing theories enter the arena and only one theory (or none) leaves?[3]

Our contention is that there are extremely few examples of strong inference tests in PHRM and I/OP because our theories are not strong enough to make differential predictions. And, that this isn't a bug, it's a feature. Strong and thoroughly tested theories make research harder! Whether deliberate or accidental, anemic theory benefits researchers working under the descriptive norms of science. By leaving PHRM and I/OP theories vague and untested, they are endlessly flexible to fit just about any research effort. This allows PHRM and I/OP researchers to sidestep careful deliberation of which theory or theories to employ, how a set of hypotheses might support or refute a theory, or what nuances or contradictions may exist between two or more theories (relatedly, see Borsboom et al., 2021; Oberauer & Lewandowsky, 2019; Proulx & Morey, 2021).

In short, good science is hard. Developing theory-driven predictions is a cumbersome and time-consuming endeavor often taking multiple iterations, but it is what the injunctive norms of science demand. Alternatively, if the descriptive norms of self-interestedness and quantity are dominant in PHRM and I/OP, then researchers can achieve their aims of placement, promotion, and individual prestige and rewards without having to do good science. That is, if a quick, gilded use of theory that only pays it lip service is rewarded the same as a time-consuming and meticulous solid gold use of theory, then there is little incentive or desire for strong theory or strong tests of it (e.g., Cucina & McDaniel,

2016; Pfeffer, 1982; Weick, 1995). Further, incentives in the current system do not encourage the cobbler's finetuning and repairs (e.g., verification of results and replication of findings) as that would only make the cordwainer's job more difficult. When descriptive norms dominate, theory does not need to be precise to be employed by PHRM and I/OP researchers and since it is unlikely to ever be replicated or verified, nor does it really need to be accurate. As such, the "theory fetish" (Hambrick, 2007) in PHRM and I/OP is not around accuracy or utility, it is instead around complexity (e.g., Bettis, 2012; Cucina & McDaniel, 2016; Ferris et al., 2012).

This added complexity only exacerbates the lack the strong theory because more complex theoretical models are harder to test. Saylors and Trafimow (2021) reviewed all articles in *Academy of Management Journal*, *Organizational Behavior and Human Decision Processes*, and *Administrative Science Quarterly* between 2016 and 2018 and found that theoretical models typically contained six constructs or variables proposed to be causally related to one another. Yet, Saylors and Trafimow (2021) simply and strikingly pointed out that "even with a *generous* 80% independent probability of each relation being properly theorized, the joint probability of a six-variable model is about 3.5%" (emphasis added; Saylors & Trafimow, 2021, p.616). Further underscoring this point, Halbesleben et al. (2004) investigated if, and how well, articles from one of PHRM's premier theoretical outlets, the *Academy of Management Review*, were put to the empirical test in the *Academy of Management Journal*. The overwhelming majority of theoretical contributions in the *Academy of Management Review* – despite being oftentimes highly cited works – did not spark empirical follow-ups and thereby were not to put to the much needed empirical test that would allow for judging the predictive value of a proposed theoretical framework or model in the first place (*cf.* Popper, 1963, 1956/1983, 1959/2002). A scientific field that values complexity with little regard for specificity or accuracy creates the ideal conditions for academic navel gazing.

Lack of Replicability

Science should be replicable in that a focal characteristic of a scientific finding should be that it can be found again. More formally, "replicability means that the finding can be obtained with other random samples drawn from a multidimensional space that captures the most important facets of the research design" (Asendorpf et al., 2013, p. 109). One typical distinction is being made between *direct* and *conceptual* replications (e.g., Crandall & Sherman, 2016; Derksen & Morawski, 2022; Schauer, 2022): While the former generally refers to replicating a study sticking as closely to the original protocol as possible (i.e., different sample, *but* same methods), the latter generally refers to replicating a study but varying at least one relevant aspect of it (i.e., different sample, *yet* different methods). A fair amount of meta-scientific literature has discussed the precise meaning of replicability: Regarding one particular effect, one could, for example, judge a replication by the direction, the size, and/or the statistical significance of the effect (e.g., Alister et al., 2021; McShane et al., 2019a; Stanley et al., 2018).

Yet, the general idea in simple terms is that scientific findings should be robust to changes to methods (e.g., sample and materials) and analysis – if this was not the case, then a systematic investigation should, at least, uncover the limits of a scientific finding's robustness. Note that a lack of replicability can be the product of virtually every aspect of the scientific method: Theoretical imprecision, improper methods, misapplied/outdated statistics, and/or biased conclusions.

In general, we see a suboptimal landscape in the (social) sciences when it comes to replicability (e.g., Camerer et al., 2018; Klein et al., 2014; Nosek et al., 2022). Famously, the Open Science Collaboration (2015) conducted replications of 100 experimental and correlational studies from three leading psychology journals and found only 36% of "replications had significant results; 47% of original effect sizes were in the 95% confidence interval of the replication effect size; 39% of effects were subjectively rated to have replicated the original result; and if no bias in original results is assumed, combining original and replication results left 68% with statistically significant effects" (p. 943; *cf.* Gilbert et al., 2016). Similar results were found in preclinical research on cancer biology (Errington et al., 2021), economics (Camerer et al., 2018), and medicine (Morgan et al., 2007). The takeaway from large-scale replication projects is twofold: First, such projects are seldomly undertaken, and, second, the successful (however defined) replications rates are far from optimal, thereby stressing the importance of the first takeaway even more (see also Nosek et al., 2022).

Turning to PHRM and I/OP, replication attempts are essentially absent despite early literature giving room to this important building block of science. Consider what is arguably the premier outlet of I/OP, *Journal of Applied Psychology*. This journal has existed for over a century and as of 2022 published over 26,000 articles. Of these 26,000, a ProQuest search conducted in December 2022 identified 64 instances of "replication" being mentioned in either the title or abstract. Thirteen were published since 2000, and two of these publications (Chen, 2018; Cortina et al., 2017) were lamentations on the lack of replication in PHRM and I/OP.[4] Similarly, Hubbard et al. (1998) found very low levels of replication studies in management and strategic management journals and concluded little solace to respective scholars aiming for a self-correcting and self-assuring discipline. Alas, so few cobblers.

Lack of Reproducibility

Third, there is a striking lack of reproducibility of scientific findings. Defined somewhat formally, "data reproducibility means that Researcher B (e.g., the reviewer of a paper) obtains exactly the same results (e.g., statistics and parameter estimates) that were originally reported by Researcher A (e.g., the author of that paper) from A's data when following the same methodology (Asendorpf et al., 2013, p. 109)."[5] In other words, obtaining the data and analysis script of another researcher's work should suffice to reproduce the statistical finding reported in said work.

Yet, reproducibility seems to be far from the norm (e.g., Artner et al., 2021; Stodden, 2015; Wolins, 1962). Artner et al. (2021) set out to reproduce the focal statistical claims drawn from 46 articles published in 2012 in three American

Psychological Association (APA) journals (i.e., *Experimental and Clinical Psychopharmacology*, *Journal of Abnormal Psychology*, and *Psychology and Aging*). Of the 232 focal claims, Artner et al. (2021) managed to successfully reproduce 70% (i.e., 163), following the respective authors' descriptions in their works. Yet, Artner et al. (2021) stated that the "time-consuming, painstaking nature of validating published statistical results without a code of analysis also means that we will never be able to validate large numbers of articles published in the past – even in the case that the relevant raw data is made available by the authors" (p. 544). Furthermore, the success rate of 70% overall appears to represent the *upper* limit, given that an overwhelming majority (i.e., 62%) of the authors asked to share their original data for the reproducibility project never complied with the request (Artner et al., 2021; Vanpaemel et al., 2015).

Lack of Materials, Data, and Code

Closely intertwined with the observed lack of reproducibility is the lack of data from scientific studies. Data are the cornerstone of research in that it contains the most relevant raw information necessary to make any claims regarding a scientific findings (e.g., Borgman, 2015; Götz & Field, 2022; Martone et al., 2018). As a basis for a self-correcting science, data must be available openly, or, at least, upon request. Only if data are available can it be used to check the validity and reliability of a study's conclusions or build complex meta-analytic models on top of it. On the other hand, if data are not available, there is essentially no way to reproduce a study's results.

Despite data being fundamental drivers of essentially every original research effort, the data are often not available (e.g., Hardwicke et al., 2018; Obels et al., 2020; Vanpaemel et al., 2015). For example, Vanpaemel et al. (2015) inquired the corresponding authors of 394 papers that were published in four leading APA journals in 2012 for their data: Only 38% of the inquiries were properly addressed. Herein we see a clear conflict between the injunctive norm of communality and the descriptive norm of secrecy. This aspect of communality is so integral to the hallmarks of a healthy science that it is even codified in the APA's *Ethical Principles of Psychologists and Code of Conduct* (American Psychological Association, 2017), which prohibits "authors from withholding data from qualified requesters for verification through reanalysis in most circumstances" (American Psychological Association, 2020, p. 14). In close resemblance, Serghiou et al. (2021) compared scientific disciplines regarding, among others, data availability, and estimated only 8% of 27,000 articles from the social sciences published in the PubMed Central data base to provide access to the corresponding data. Juxtapose these results from PHRM and I/OP with physical sciences, such as biology, where roughly 29% of articles provide access to the data (see also Stodden, 2015; Stodden et al., 2018).

While data make up the cornerstone of research, the necessary chisel to make the data usable lies in the respective analysis code (i.e., computational reproducibility; Epskamp, 2019; Stodden et al., 2018). Here, we note an even starker lack of availability across essentially all scientific disciplines (Serghiou et al., 2021).

Artner et al. (2021) began the discussion of their reproducibility project by noting that "the vast majority of successful reproductions in this study are the results of a *painful and frustrating process of trial and error*, because of the existence of multiple, plausible data analytical pathways to calculate the numerical triplet of the primary claim that are compatible with the provided raw data combined with the vague description of the statistical methods in the article" (emphasis added, p. 540). In other words, even when researchers shared their data, the verbal descriptions in the article did not readily allow for a straightforward reproduction of results. To put it differently, providing fellow scholars with one's data is only half the battle, as one has to make sure that future users can also run the code in a reproducible manner (e.g., Cadwallader & Hrynaszkiewicz, 2022; Epskamp, 2019; Hardwicke et al., 2018). We assert that sharing data – let alone, sharing properly prepared data with properly crafted accompanying information to make this data properly usable – is far from a norm in our community as of now.

Lack of Proper Samples

PHRM and I/OP researchers draw samples from reality to eventually make inferences about it and ultimately provide HR practitioners with practical implications. Thus, if our samples are not a proper reflection of reality (i.e., the population to which we seek to generalize), we draw improper inferences and give potentially misleading recommendations. The generalizability of PHRM and I/OP samples is questionable at best (e.g., Bergman & Jean, 2016; Dipboye & Flanagan, 1979; Landers & Behrend, 2015). For one, typical samples from psychology in general and PHRM and I/OP specifically often suffer from being WEIRD (i.e., sampled participants stemming from Western, educated, industrialized, rich, and democratic societies; Arnett, 2008; Henrich et al., 2010; Thalmayer et al., 2021). Regarding PHRM and I/OP specifically, Berman and Jean (2016) investigated the samples used in all articles published in *Journal of Applied Psychology*, *Personnel Psychology*, *Academy of Management Journal*, *Journal of Management*, and *Journal of Organizational Behavior* that were published between 2012 and 2014. Only 9% of the samples drawn focused explicitly on workers, namely wage instead of salary earners in non-executive, non-professional, or non-managerial roles of low to medium skill. Comparing these characteristics to the actual United States and international labor markets, Bergman and Jean (2016) stated the research to be "overrepresenting core, salaried, managerial, professional, and executive employees while underrepresenting wage earners, low- and medium-skill first-line personnel, and contract workers" (p. 84). Further, almost half the studies inspected by Bergman and Jean (2016) drew their samples from crowdsourcing platforms, such as Amazon Mechanical Turk (MTurk), or Prolific (for similar estimates, see C. A. Anderson et al., 2019; Zhou & Fishbach, 2016). These have also become frequently employed in PHRM and I/OP research as they allow for quick, relatively cheap, and easy sampling of a large number of subjects (e.g., Buhrmester et al., 2018; Cheung et al., 2017; Woo et al., 2015). Given the flexibility of crowdsourcing platforms (e.g., used to run surveys, experiments, and even experience sampling studies), as well as the rise of computer-aided methods for data collection, using these platforms promises a very convenient, and efficient way to collect data – particularly in survey-driven disciplines, such as PHRM, and I/OP (e.g., Aguinis et al., 2021; Cheung et al., 2017; Woo et al., 2015).

Given that compensation for participation is relatively small, these online platforms in some respects help researchers connect with workers rather than just managers and organizational leaders. However, they are by no means a panacea. Despite, for example, MTurk promising large numbers of workers available on the platform, recent estimates for active and currently employed workers vary between 2,000 and 7,300 (Difallah et al., 2018; Stewart et al., 2015). Given the popularity of MTurk, these few thousand workers might be the best and most frequently studied population of workers ever assessed in PHRM and I/OP research, but do these workers generalize across the full or even a large swath of employees? There are reasons for concern that the answer is no. Webb and Tangney (2022) report that – after thorough data quality checks and data cleaning – only 2.6% of the sample drawn from MTurk turned out to consist of valid human responses. In a similar vein, Chmielewski and Kucker (2020) report a substantial decrease in data quality in a longitudinal study in the form of "increases in participants failing response validity indicators, decreases in reliability and validity of a widely used personality measure, and failures to replicate well-established findings" (p. 464). Finally, Brodeur et al. (2022) investigated works that sampled from MTurk and that were published in leading journals between 2010 and 2020 to find "evidence of widespread *p*-hacking, publication bias and over-reliance on results from plausibly under-powered studies [...] across the business, economics, management and marketing research fields (with marketing especially afflicted)" (p. 3). Of increasing concern is that recently developed AI tools, such as Queuebicle (TurkerView, 2023), now allow for MTurk participants to "automatically accept HITs [i.e., study invitations] and complete them." Thus, we may be approaching the PHRM and I/OP singularity where our theories and hypotheses are predominantly tested via artificial intelligence. In sum, a lot of PHRM and I/OP research has sampled from a very small, well-trained, but surely not representative population, and that it is not implausible that a non-trivial and growing number of those sampled are not even human.

A final insight regarding the generalizability of scientific findings even using archival data, as is typically done in strategic management research, come from Delios et al. (2022). These authors systematically investigated whether 29 findings from strategic management built on top of archival data were reproducible and generalizable to new contexts and time frames. Only "45% of the reproductions returned results matching the original reports together with 55% of tests in different spans of years and 40% of tests in novel geographies" (Delios et al., 2022, p. 1). These numbers improved starkly, when the original findings were reproducible in the first place.

Lack of Quality Control: The Peer-review Process

Fourth, science should be self-correcting, and one prominent pathway to achieve this is peer review as a means of quality control (for historical perspective, see

Csiszar, 2016; Tennant et al., 2017; Vazire, 2022). By design, a submission to a peer-reviewed journal should get thoroughly checked by, at least, two subject matter experts for sensibility, and correctness to assure a certain robustness, and quality of a finding (e.g., De La Garza & Vashi, 2022; Gottfredson, 1978; Kuhn, 1996). In turn, the reviewers' recommendations provide editors with the basis to, ideally, make an informed decision about the fate of the submission. As time, and therefore work, spent by reviewers indicate, the peer-review system is of utmost importance to the scientific endeavor. For example, Aczel et al. (2021) found that "the total time reviewers globally worked on peer reviews was over 100 million hours in 2020, equivalent to over 15 thousand years. The estimated monetary value of the time US-based reviewers spent on reviews was over 1.5 billion USD in 2020" (p. 1). As such, we should hope that this system pays in full in that it assures a valid and reliable assessment of scientific rigor and resulting body of literature.

In the software industry, *eating your own dog food* refers to the practice that one uses the program or service one has produced him/herself to demonstrate confidence in it. With regard to the scientific peer-review system, the fundamental question is on what grounds this method was conceived and essentially integrated as our quality control mechanism in the first place. It knocks us for a loop that we, as scientists trained in the scientific method, use an instrument for quality control that has essentially never been empirically and thoroughly tested using the scientific method before it was implemented. In other words, the peer-review system as a quality control of scientific findings is surprisingly understudied (see also Elson et al., 2020; B. London, 2021), and there are reasons to suspect that our widespread reliance on it is questionable.

The evidence for peer review being a scientifically sound mechanism to self-correct and better scientific submissions stands in stark contrast to its hallmark position within the system (e.g., Ceci & Peters, 1982; Cicchetti, 1991; R. Smith, 2006). Research on the effectiveness of reviewers as quality controllers demonstrates that reviewers caught only around 30% of the major and minor errors researchers willingly included into their manuscripts (e.g., Baxt et al., 1998; Godlee et al., 1998; Schroter et al., 2008).[6] Furthermore, meta-analytic evidence on the reliability of reviews paints a rather grim picture with upper limits of the reliability coefficients of roughly 0.40, and mean values varying between 0.34 and 0.17 – depending on the reliability coefficient inspected (Bornmann et al., 2010). Of course, it stands to reason that peer review might not only serve a quality control function but also an enrichment function in that it allows for the emergence of controversial findings; despite, or because of disagreement among the reviewers (Horrobin, 1990). As such, high reliability among reviewers as a sole determinant might corrupt the emergence of controversial findings (e.g., Armstrong & Hubbard, 1991) and should not be the only criterion to judge the peer-review system on.

Further, while the peer-review system is typically double-blind, where neither the author nor reviewers are identifiable, the ultimate decider of the manuscript's fate, the editor, is typically not blind in the process and is aware of reviewer and author identities. Merton (1968) famously coined the term *Matthew effect* to describe how submissions by high-status researchers typically gain more traction, are perceived to be of higher quality in the review process, and eventually end up in our body of knowledge more easily. Yet, because the quality of research is not necessarily a consequence of an author's status, Merton (1968) considered the presence of the Matthew effect "a problem in the just allocation of credit for scientific accomplishment" (p. 59). The Matthew effect is alive and well: Huber et al. (2022) provide experimental evidence that a prominent researcher's name (i.e., Nobel laureate Vernon L. Smith) dramatically affected researchers willingness to review a manuscript as well as their overall assessment of it. Compared with the display of a rather unknown researcher's name, the display of the prominent researcher's name lead to higher willingness to review a manuscript in the first place and also more favorable recommendations regarding acceptance/rejection (see also Blank, 1991; Ucci et al., 2022).

Above and beyond issues of reliability and validity of the peer-review process, it being a social process itself with all potential issues of power (ab)usage that come along with that can also an issue (e.g., Bedeian, 2004; Karhulahti & Backe, 2021; Roth, 2002). Specifically, as scholars typically have to get their works published to *make them count*, reviewers and editors can exert certain powers, such as demanding potentially unnecessary changes of the manuscript under review by suggesting their own work for inclusion or reference. Illustrating this point by sharing his personal experience with the peer-review system, Roth (2002) stated that "when one of my articles is finally published, I always have a sense that I am only partially the author, something is lost; this something may well be a part of myself. There are so many other actors [...] who have [...] succeeded in making changes [...] or getting me to make it "in a satisfactory way" that it no longer feels mine in a traditional sense" (p. 15). In turn, "the published version of a manuscript is almost inevitably a compromise between what its authors intended to say and the mandates of an editor and a set of referees" (Bedeian, 2004, p. 199). While the recommendations of reviewers and editors would ideally be mere suggestions to improve scholarly work, they are unfortunately oftentimes considered as demands by the authors (e.g., Bedeian, 2004; Karhulahti & Backe, 2021; Roth, 2002).

The current weaknesses of the peer-review system coupled with the already outlined lack of materials, data, and code also is a reason for concern. If reviewers can seldomly look at the actual materials, data, and code of a scientific study and have to take the authors' writing at face value, then the self-correcting function of the peer-review system is impaired to such an extent that one is left wondering if we even need it. Those skeptical of the value of peer review are in good company. In dramatic words, Nobel laureate Sydney Brenner, stated "I don't believe in peer review because I think it's very distorted and as I've said, it's simply a regression to the mean. I think peer review is hindering science. In fact, I think it has become a completely corrupt system" (Dzeng, 2014).

The low reliability, potential favoritism, and concerns over quality (e.g., correctly identifying clear confounds) may give the impression that reviewers and editors are rushing through manuscripts in order to get back to perhaps more intrinsically, and certainly more extrinsically rewarding work (O'Boyle & Götz, 2022). After all, if the contractor's code of "good, fast, and cheap – pick two" applies, then the fact that most reviewers are unpaid and quality is questionable, then the review process should at least be fast. It isn't though.

The peer-review process in PRHM research can be painfully slow and it appears to be getting slower. The time it takes for a submitted manuscript to receive pagination has steadily increased. The aforementioned Hackman and Oldham (1975) Job Characteristics Model was submitted nine months prior to its pagination. A decade later, Staw and Ross' (1985) seminal work on the dispositional approach to job attitudes was published 14 months after it was submitted. Saks (1995) influential work on onboarding and newcomer adjustment took 22 months to be published. Salanova et al. (2005) took 25 months to publication and a decade later Joseph et al. (2015) were submitted in April 2012 – exactly three years after its original submission. To be clear, these are not cherry-picked examples. They are all well-regarded and highly cited works that appeared on the first page of *Journal of Applied Psychology* results in Google Scholar. Despite being a far from systematic search, it does align with more rigorous reviews of the peer review and publication process (*cf.* Gaudino et al., 2021; Huisman & Smits, 2017; Lyman, 2013).

A lengthy review process is not inherently bad. For example, most seasoned researchers can recall times when the back and forth through the revision process forged a stronger contribution. Similarly, there are times that only after reviewers' careful and meticulous inspection of the manuscript that some fatal flaw is revealed, and what might have initially been seen as a highway to new insights and theory is rightfully recognized as a dead end (relatedly, see Lakens, 2023). However, there are tradeoffs in the slow dissemination of research that can adversely affect PHRM and I/OP researchers and practitioners.

For the researcher, the lengthy review process will be most concerning to doctoral students and junior faculty. Consider four conditions facing new entrants into the field. One, most assistant professors will go up for tenure in their seventh year. Two, the widespread adoption of journal lists means that the space available for publications that *count* for tenure is very limited. Three, more PHRM and I/OP researchers are entering the field than ever before. Four, most manuscripts cycle through multiple outlets and lengthy review processes before finding a home. With only seven years to publish before tenure, how early in a nascent researcher's career is their fate sealed due to the lengthy review process? What sort of pressure does such a delayed peer-review process put on future scholars of PHRM and I/OP research, and how much does that pressure motivate high quality research and how much does that pressure motivate non-ideal scientific practices? Fittingly, van Dijk and van Zelst (2020) reported that the "satisfaction with the publication system does not seem to change when publishing time increases for researchers with tenure, whereas among untenured researchers there is a sharp decrease in perceived justifiability the longer the publishing time lasts" (p. 12). One additional consequence of this ever-increasing lag-time to publication is that doctoral students may delay their graduation and job market entry. In doing so, psychology departments and business schools must continue to fund their education and training further restricting resources (mostly taxpayer funded) that could be invested elsewhere.

For practitioners, there is a positive relation between timeliness and relevance. Practitioners require guidance on what they should do and not what they could have done. Some research is relatively "evergreen" in that the research speaks to underlying, hardwired human and group behaviors. For example, humans tend to gravitate toward information that support preexisting beliefs, so although Paul C. Wason and others' work on confirmation bias predates social media and cable news, it is still highly relevant (e.g., Wason, 1960; Wason & Johnson-Laird, 1972; see also Nickerson, 1998). Conversely, much of the telecommuting work from the 1990s may have certain persisting relevance (e.g., potential feelings of disconnection), but remote work has so radically changed in the past 30 or so years that many of those findings would need to be revisited and replicated with updated technology. Lengthy lags in the review process hamper the ability to update dated results and inform practitioners on recent developments and changes.

Reviewers must carefully assess rigor and relevance, so the "good" of the contractor's code must be present to maintain the four hallmarks and abide by the injunctive norm of quality. And, given the proposed relation between timeliness and relevance, the "fast" of the contractor's code is difficult to exclude. As such, if PHRM and I/OP research wants a review process that is good and fast, then it won't be cheap. We will return to this point in the recommendations and discuss, for example, what role publishers might play in this 19 billion USD a year industry whose major players report profit margins of up to 40% (higher than Coca-Cola, Apple, or BMW; e.g., Beverungen et al., 2012; Hagve, 2020; Larivière et al., 2015).

Lack of Non-significant Findings

Fifth, support for predictions in PHRM and I/OP research largely relies on null hypothesis significance testing (NHST). For the uninitiated, this is an up-or-down, binary decision typically used to claim whether an effect is present or absent. The key statistic that informs this decision is a probability value or *p*-value. Typically, *p*-values less than 0.05 are deemed as supportive (i.e., rejects the null hypothesis and concludes effect is present) and values in excess of 0.05 are deemed unsupportive (i.e., retains the null hypothesis and fails to support the presence of the effect). In general, researchers want to reject the null hypothesis and thereby claim statistical support for their model, or theory.

When a hypothesis is well-grounded in theory, sample size is adequate, measures are reliable and valid, and statistical analyses competently executed and interpreted, there should be a reasonable chance of rejecting the null hypothesis, and supporting one's prediction. But reasonable is not the same as certain. Even with such care in the scientific process, a researcher must not just be right, they need a certain amount of luck, too. One might argue that such luck is an interdisciplinary treat, given the manifold statistically significant estimates in the literature despite the fact that studies are typically underpowered in psychology (Stanley et al., 2018), economics (Ioannidis et al., 2017), and neuroscience (Button et al., 2013). There is always a chance that the theory has an unexpected boundary condition, the sample size ended up being too small, the measures turned out to have some flaw, or the assumptions of the statistical test were inadvertently violated. As such, scientists spend a lot of time being wrong and although frustrating, this is a sign of a healthy science.

In PHRM and I/OP research, this sign of a healthy science is largely absent. PHRM and I/OP scientists seem almost incapable of failing to support their predictions, and, as a result, non-significant findings, and unsupported hypotheses are disappearing from the literature. This has given many the belief that the published literature is rose-tinted through the exclusion of non-significant results and "enhancing" of certain results until they become significant. In situations where one result is favored over another, there is the possibility of what has become known as questionable research practices and outcome reporting bias. Simply put, this occurs when researchers report what data initially works, torture reluctant data until they work too, and any data that does not fold under interrogation is promptly buried and forgotten. We will discuss the specific questionable practices and effect they have on the trustworthiness of PHRM and I/OP research in a later section, but, for now, we wish only to highlight the dearth of non-significant findings.

Van Zwet and Cator (2021), for example, presented more than one million z-values taken from the full text of papers published in Medline (*PubMed*) from 1976 to 2019 (see also Barnett & Wren, 2019; Fig. 2). In order to be statistically significant (e.g., attain a p-value less than .05), researchers need a z-value of around $|2.0|$ or higher. The reader will notice the steep drop in frequencies for z-values between -2.0 and $+2.0$. There are very few plausible explanations for this dearth of findings in this zone of non-significance to naturally occur. Inspecting p-values instead of z-values results in equally concerning findings in economics (Brodeur et al., 2016), psychology (Kühberger et al., 2014), and sociology (Gerber & Malhotra, 2008a), among others (e.g., Gerber & Malhotra, 2008b; Hartgerink et al., 2016; Hubbard et al., 1997). These distributional *black holes* can only be the product of selection bias in the form of publications bias and/or questionable research practices (see also Fanelli, 2012b; Friese & Frankenbach, 2020; Scheel et al., 2021). An alternative explanation of these *black holes*, of course, would be the sheer power of precognition of the combined force of researchers having put out these values – an explanation, we certainly question (but see for yourself: Bem, 2011; Bem et al., 2011; *cf.* Wagenmakers et al., 2011).

Focusing more specifically on p-values in PHRM and I/OP models of moderation, O'Boyle et al. (2019) again found worrisome results. Spanning a time frame of 20 years and covering six leading PHRM and I/OP journals (i.e., *Academy of Management Journal*, *Journal of Applied Psychology*, *Journal of Management*, *Journal of Organizational Behavior*, *Organizational Behavior and Human Decision Processes*, and *Personnel Psychology*), O'Boyle et al. (2019) found two interesting results. The first was that despite moderators typically being severely underpowered (i.e., not enough study participants to have a reasonable chance of detecting an effect) in PHRM and I/OP research (Murphy & Russell, 2017), the majority of published interactions were statistically significant, and the percentage of significant interactions rapidly increased over the 20-year period time from 41% to 69%; all while sample sizes remained unchanged ($r = -.002$). The second finding was that in a model including 15 substantive and methodological features that

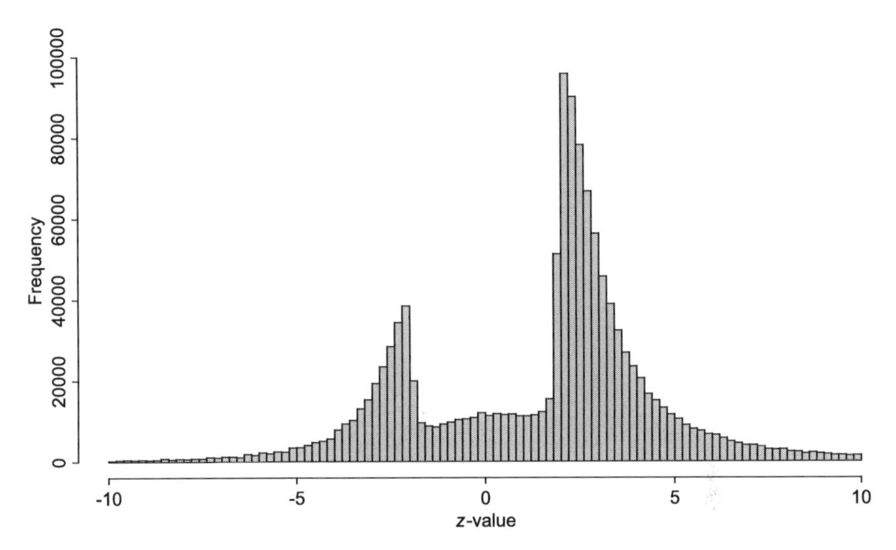

Fig. 2. One Million z-values From 1979 to 2019. *Note*. Reproduced based on the data openly provided by Barnett and Wren (2019) and van Zwet and Captor (2021).

might influence the magnitude of an interaction term (e.g., level of analysis, study design, and intercorrelations of the linear terms), the single best predictor was its sample size ($b^* = -0.571$). As sample size goes down, effect size goes up. This statistical anomaly is difficult to reconcile. All things equal, the relation between effect size and sample size is zero, so for sample size to dominate the model suggest other factors in play and that the lack of non-significant tests of moderation may be due to reasons other than statistical precision and keen theoretical argumentation and insight.

In a similar vein, inspecting the distributions of confidence intervals estimated to test indirect effects (e.g., mediation) for statistical significance, Götz et al. (2021) found troubling aggregate results once again. Sampling all relevant primary works from five leading APA journal (i.e., *Journal of Applied Psychology*, *Journal of Educational Psychology*, *Journal of Personality and Social Psychology*, *Journal of Counseling Psychology*, and *Journal of Consulting and Clinical Psychology*) from 2018 and 2019, hypothesized tests of indirect effects resulted in aggregate distributions that, again, have an inordinate number of results that just barely achieve statistical support (i.e., the confidence interval just excludes zero) and a paucity of results that just barely include zero. Of prime relevance to our work here, I/OP and social psychology have perhaps the most eye-catching – in other words, very skewed – aggregate distributions (Fig. 3). Given the importance of complex statistical procedures, such as interactions, and indirect effects, for generating more and more complex theories about the world, these results hint at our empirical basis of support for many of these tests of mediation have feet of clay (for a replication in marketing journals, see Charlton et al., 2021).

This lack of "negative" findings greatly hinders scientific advancement given how much we can learn from an endeavor that did not go as planned – as a matter

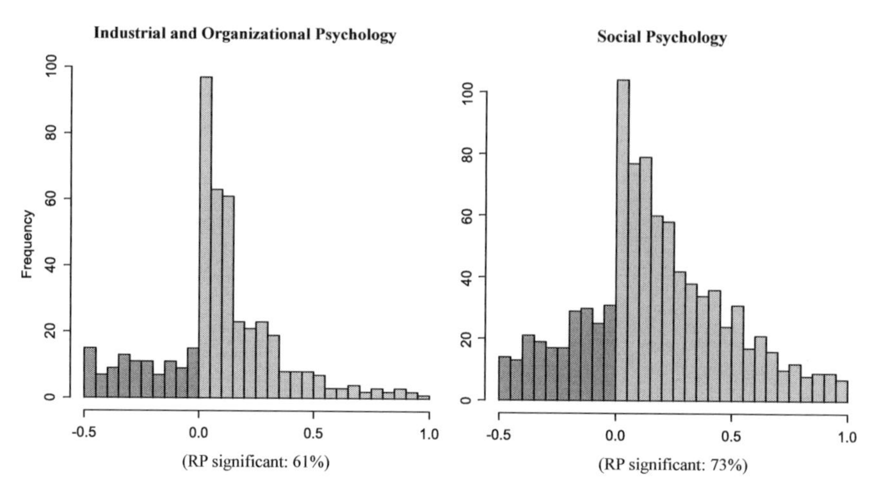

Fig. 3. Relative Proximities of Hypothesized Tests of Mediation in Industrial-Organizational, and Social Psychology. *Note*. Reproduced based on the data openly provided by Götz et al. (2021). Relative proximities (RP) – that is, the distance to zero of an indirect effect's confidence interval as a function of its range – for 488 indirect effects from the *Journal of Applied Psychology* (i.e., as proxy for I/OP) and 991 indirect effects from the *Journal of Social and Personality Psychology* (i.e., as proxy for social psychology) in 2018 and 2019 (Götz et al., 2021). RP below zero indicates a statistically non-significant indirect effect – thus, bars in dark gray represent frequencies of non-significant point estimates, whereas bars in light gray frequencies of significant ones.

of fact, we would argue that one can learn almost more from "failure" than from "success." Consider the beginnings of the coronavirus pandemic that arrived in 2020 – researchers across the globe were rushing to propose adequate countermeasures and developed promising vaccines that eventually helped to contain the pandemic (e.g., Collins, 2021; A. J. London & Kimmelman, 2020; Oliu-Barton et al., 2021). Of course, not all developments of vaccine candidates were successful (Dolgin, 2021) – yet, knowing which vaccines and therapies worked, which did not, and which worked for some but not all was critically relevant information that allowed for much faster and more effective countermeasures (Stefan, 2022). We argue that "null findings" and unsupportive results are just as valuable in PHRM and I/OP research (see also Cortina & Folger, 1998; J. R. Edwards & Berry, 2010; Kepes et al., 2014).

Importantly, such problematic aggregate findings, among others, permeate throughout the body of knowledge in the form of research syntheses (i.e., systematic literature reviews, and meta-analyses; Ioannidis, 2016; Meehl, 1990; Stanley et al., 2018). Generally, research syntheses where the available evidence is collated and aggregated provide a more complete picture of a respective body of knowledge, given their potential to reconcile the drawbacks of any given individual study. "Available" is the operative word here. If available research is not an accurate reflection of the total research, then a systematic review will be systematically biased. After all, what good is a meta-analysis of so and so many hundred cross-sectional studies that more or less all provide statistically significant estimates going to do? The same question can be asked regarding internal meta-analyses where authors attempt to asses/strengthen the evidential value of multiple primary studies reported in one article (Vosgerau et al., 2019). The *garbage in, garbage out*-principle specifically applies to research syntheses built on top of a tainted body of knowledge and ultimately only can provide us with a false sense of certainty (see also Egger et al., 2001; Ioannidis, 2016; Sotola, 2022).

That "negative" findings seem to be drastically underrepresented in the published literature leads to the conclusion that many PHRM and I/OP researchers view findings that do not support their hypotheses with utter dismissiveness. If researchers, reviewers, and editors hold the belief that unsupported hypotheses cannot meaningfully inform future research, then the lack of interest in publishing null findings is quite understandable, but it is nevertheless an incorrect belief that nevertheless hampers our advancement as a field. Although a few editorials of I/OP/management journals have hinted at the willingness of publishing null findings from carefully designed and executed studies (e.g., Bettis et al., 2016; Landis et al., 2014; Miller & Bamberger, 2016; Roloff & Zyphur, 2019), the studies contained within those very same journals have so few non-significant results that calls for change are often drowned out by the cacophony of the status quo.

Lack of Availability

Sixth, the product of our work typically sees the light of day in the form of publications in academic journals. The number of journals as well as the number of articles have substantially increased virtually every year since inception of this form of scholarly communication (Johnson et al., 2018; STM, 2021). Even those researchers that fully embrace the Mertonian norms of communality and disinterestedness – motivated to work only that which advances science and make that work available to all – must nevertheless operate within the for-profit model that is academic publication. Long gone are the days of the cottage industry of tiny publishing houses scattered across the globe. Academic publishing is a consolidated and massive industry with the average revenue per article being roughly 5,000 USD (e.g., Beverungen et al., 2012; Hagve, 2020; Van Noorden, 2013). At the same time, the average production costs of a representative article are estimated to be around 400 USD (Grossmann & Brembs, 2021; Logan, 2017). On the one hand, these revenues keep the publishing houses open for business which in some small ways do trickle down to the various academic institutions in societies relevant to PHRM and I/OP researchers in the form of conference sponsorship, monetary awards, and endowments, and occasionally an editorial stipend. On the other hand, how these funds are generated can conflict with the Mertonian norms of communality and disinterestedness.

Typically, the products of our work (i.e., journal articles) are subject to paywalls that only allow access against sometimes hefty charges (e.g., 35.00 USD per PDF) that have to be put forth by either the individual researchers or their respective institutions. Accordingly, calls for openly accessing scientific works have continued to grow louder – for example, prestigious research funding agencies, such as the US National Institutes of Health, the US National Science Foundation, the European Commission, the UK's Wellcome Trust, as well as the Swiss National Science Fund, among others, have made OA[7] publications mandatory for grantees (e.g., European Commission: Directorate-General for Research & Innovation, 2017; National Science Foundation, 2015; Swiss National Science Foundation (SNSF), 2022; U.S. Department of Health & Human Services, 2022; Wellcome Trust, 2012).

There is a multitude of OA publishing formats – probably the most well-known are the following: (1) Gold OA means that an article is published in an OA journal that is indexed by the Directory of Open Access Journals (DOAJ) – an PHRM-related example is *Personnel Assessment and Decisions*; (2) Green OA means that there is a toll-access on the publisher page, but a free copy in an OA repository is generally allowed; (3) Hybrid OA means that an article is free under an open license in a toll-access journal –PHRM-related examples are *Personnel Psychology* or *Human Resource Management*; (4) Bronze OA means that an article is generally free to read on the publisher page, but a clearly identifiable license is lacking; finally, (5) closed format refers to all publication formats that are under lock and key by the respective publisher, and posting preprints, or OA version of the article is forbidden (e.g., Björk et al., 2010; Johnson et al., 2018; Piwowar et al., 2018). The OA publishing model generally works in such a way that the more open a researcher wants their work to be, the more they have to pay up-front – in other words, publishers are not charities and they will embrace OA up to the point that it costs them money (for an in-depth review, see STM, 2021). If OA stymies sales to the consumer, then that lost revenue is passed on to the researcher that created the research.

OA is on the rise (e.g., Laakso & Björk, 2022; STM, 2021; Wallace & Ollivere, 2022) and even considered inevitable (D. W. Lewis, 2012) – yet, the majority of publications are currently behind publishers' paywalls (e.g., Björk et al., 2010; Johnson et al., 2018; Piwowar et al., 2018). For example, as Piwowar et al. (2018) illustrated comparing OA formats and rates across a multitude of scientific disciplines, only in biomedical research were more than 50% of the samples published in some OA format, whereas in the social sciences, it was only about a quarter. Yet, even the emerging pay-for-open-access-business models provide enough cause for concern, given that the primary goal of for-profit publishers will always be to make a profit, instead of disseminating knowledge by making it accessible (see also Björk, 2012; Husted & de Jesus Salazar, 2006; Pinfield et al., 2016).

Before moving on to the next stanza of the song of sorrow, we wish to note that if you tell someone they are the problem, then don't ask them to be part of your solution. Publishers seeking profit is not inherently problematic or antithetical to Mertonian norms of science. And, publishers play a very important and historic role in science as the meeting places where researchers introduce discoveries and where debate takes place. However, the PHRM and I/OP publication process has changed very little over the past century despite tremendous technological and societal advances. Research is typically created with taxpayer funding in the form of state universities and public colleges or grant funding that is then submitted to a journal. Quality control in the form of reviewing is largely pro bono. Published research is then sold back to the state universities and public colleges at a premium. Our belief is that profits and scientific ideals can be aligned in ways that publishers can still earn large profits while also contributing more directly to the OA movement.

Lack of Practical Implications

Seventh and last, a predominant goal of an applied science is to provide practitioners with insightful, reliable, and pragmatical implications that allow them to address the issues in their businesses and workplaces that motivated the research in the first place. To illustrate this point, in an editorial in *Personnel Psychology*, Michael A. Campion (1993) presented an *article review checklist*, in which the provision of practical implications was considered the second highest criterion for evaluating both the importance and contribution of a submitted work. Relatedly, the APA's most recent iteration of the journal article reporting standards holds practical importance and contributions of the works in essentially equally high regards as theoretical ones (Appelbaum et al., 2018). Further, Thomas G. Cummings (2007) in his 2006 presidential address to the Academy of Management proposed that "the future vitality and success of our profession depends on making sure our research-based knowledge is relevant and useful" (p. 355; see also Hambrick, 1994; Tihanyi, 2020; Van De Ven & Johnson, 2006). Yet, it is our impression that such calls have largely gone unanswered because practical implications seldomly relate explicitly and explicatively to the research at hand (e.g., work on transformational leadership recommends leadership training)[8], and these recommendations for how the research might be incorporated often have feet of clay with little interest or concern with implementation, training fidelity, costs, etc.

Unfortunately, implications for practitioners have been largely redelegated to a blurb at the end of the article, or, alarmingly, completely excised. Bartunek (2007) reviewed the discussion sections of all *Academy of Management Journal* articles published in 2006. They found that over a third of the published articles did not even include a section for practical implications. Of those that did, the overwhelming recommendations for practitioners was to be "more aware" of the topic and/or consider some sort of training. Using a larger sample of journals, Bartunek and Rynes (2010) replicated the results with increased awareness being the most commonly reported recommendation to practitioners. It is difficult to plausibly imagine scenarios where these implication sections influence practitioners directly. The scenario would require (a) knowledge of the journal, (b) access to it, (c) intention to read the article, (d) ability to understand it, (e) believe it as high quality and relevant to themselves and their organizations, and (f) implement it.

For (a), besides perhaps *Harvard Business Review*, awareness of where one might find journals that publish PHRM research is decidedly low. For (b), as stated above, almost all leading journals are behind paywalls. For (c), a typical leader, HR director, or decision-maker's work life is quite busy, and time is at a premium. That practitioners sit down and slog through 30 or more pages of a typical academic article in the hopes that it might be relevant to them is unlikely. For (d), even if the practitioner got their hands on the article and intended to read it, most implications to practice sections are written in such a way to obfuscate any real understanding without what amounts to a PhD. For example, Bartunek and Rynes (2010) reported that despite ostensibly being a section intended for practitioners, implications for practice sections were written in a manner that on average required no less than 17 years of formal education. We stress that this just applies to the implications for practice sections – not the full article which understandably requires a high degree of education and training. In terms of (e), whether the practitioner would trust the findings and see them as relevant to their work, again we see problems. There are large discrepancies between research findings on PHRM and practitioners' beliefs about effective HRM practices (Rynes et al., 2002; Sanders et al., 2008). For example, Rynes et al.'s (2002) survey of almost 1,000 HR professionals found that despite ample evidence that personality-type indicator tests, such as Myers-Briggs, simply do not work in a selection context or really any work context (e.g., Pittenger, 1993, 2005; Stein & Swan, 2019), they were endorsed as valid tools by more than half of the respondents. Notably, this same study has been replicated several times. Sanders et al. (2008) used a Dutch instead of an US sample of HR professionals and found similar results with wide divergence between well-established academic findings and HR professionals practices (e.g., 57% respondents believed that the most important trait of an effective leader is an outgoing, energetic personality). Most recently, Fisher et al. (2021) conducted a conceptual replication with 453 HR practitioners in the USA and Canada and found that the inability to identify HR myths from HR facts has actually gotten worse. However, the worst is saved for last. For (f), the actual successful implementation, this is the least likely step to be completed. How exactly are practitioners supposed to do this when the vast majority of implications are vague, tentative afterthoughts? When the most common recommendations are for practitioners to be "more aware" of the research findings and develop "some sort of training," we as academics are tipping our hand, and signaling how much we actually care (or don't care) about practical impact.

This has not always been the case though. PHRM and I/OP has a storied history of conducting research with specific and actionable practical implications (see also Kieser et al., 2015). For example, consider the following *Journal of Applied Psychology* publications noting their date of publication;

Boudreau, J. W., & Rynes, S. L. (1985). Role of recruitment in staffing utility analysis. *Journal of Applied Psychology*, *70*(2), 354–366. https://doi.org/10.1037/0021-9010.70.2.354

Grigg, A. E. (1948). A farm knowledge test. *Journal of Applied Psychology*, *32*(5), 452–455. https://doi.org/10.1037/h0054644

Hall, G. S. (1917). Practical relations between psychology and the war. *Journal of Applied Psychology*, *1*(1), 9–16. https://doi.org/10.1037/h0070238

Paterson, D. G., & Tinker, M. A. (1931). Studies of typographical factors influencing speed of reading. *Journal of Applied Psychology*, *15*(3), 241–247. https://doi.org/10.1037/h0074261

Rothe, H. F., & Nye, C. T. (1958). Output rates among coil winders. *Journal of Applied Psychology*, *42*(3), 182–186. https://doi.org/10.1037/h0041121

What unites these works – beyond their age and common outlet – is that they all considered the context of the sampled participants, studied these in said context, and provided actionable implications for said context. As we know, context matters tremendously and has to be taken into account particularly when it comes to recommending informed practical implications (e.g., Johns, 2006, 2018; Ostroff, 2019). Take for example the meat processing industry: The increase of belt speed in factories over the years has led to more injuries (Oxfam America, 2015). Furthermore, workers in this industry display very high incidence of musculoskeletal disorders, a leading cause of occupational injury (Tappin et al., 2008). In addition, meat packing workers have been rather prone to contracting COVID-19, infecting their respective communities, and dying from it (Saitone et al., 2021). Just sampling "employees" cannot do the job to achieve insightful and helpful practical implications.

The above-listed works lead with their practical contribution and intended audience. These studies that are heavy on practical implication and less focused on theory building have all but disappeared from the literature. If the research itself is too esoteric to derive actionable and justified practical implications, then the brevity and vagaries of the practical implication section is quite understandable. An apt exception that proves the rule is Gonzalez-Mulé and Cockburn's (2021) study of how job demands and work stress play a role in worker mortality titled, "Worked to death: The relationships of job demands and job control with mortality." The manuscript was rejected from a number of outlets due to *a lack of theoretical contribution*. The DV was death! We struggle to think of a more practically meaningful work outcome and it is no surprise that when this study was eventually published in the top-tier outlet, *Personnel Psychology*, it generated tremendous popular press attention. However, in order to have this study published and accessible to the public, these authors had to go back, and retrofit enough theory to make this crucial and highly practical finding palatable to an academic audience. We put forth that this should not be the norm in PHRM and I/OP research, and that contribution means more than contribution to theory.

All these points combined might explain why practitioners considered academic publishing a "vast wasteland" (Bennis & O'Toole, 2005, p. 99). In turn, they also explain the often-bemoaned science-practice gap (e.g., Banks et al., 2016; Kulikowski, 2022; Rogelberg et al., 2022). Specifically, Bansal et al. (2012) stated that "most of what management researchers do utterly fails to resonate with management practice" (p. 73), and Banks et al. (2016) noted the "widening gap between science and practice [that questions] the relevance of research conducted in the management domain" (p. 2205). Drastically, this led Kulikowski (2022) to state that "for the public dealing with real-life problems, a good evidence-based decision might be to ignore I/OP scholars' communication, which is often based on futile and misdirected research" (p. 273). To our best knowledge, the science-practice gap has more likely widened than closed over the last years or even decades.

POTENTIAL EXPLANATIONS

The second verse of the song of sorrow is how we arrived at our current state of affairs, and we now turn to outlining potential reasons as to why things appear so dire. We start with the often-cited explanation of misaligned incentives. Specifically, what is being rewarded in the PHRM and I/OP research community is failing to motivate the right behaviors and, in many cases, is incentivizing behaviors that detriment the hallmarks of a healthy science. After reviewing this somewhat bleak, but ever-growing literature, we then turn to four specific grievances that played and continue to play dominant roles in detrimenting the four hallmarks of a healthy science. In doing so, we review questionable research/reporting practices only to then more specifically look at issues regarding measurement, methodology, and statistics within the PHRM space and related fields.

We wish to note one potential detriment that we will not discuss – bad faith actors. There are notorious fraudsters, such as Diederik A. Stapel in social psychology, and, closer to home, David S. DeGeest in PHRM and I/OP (especially close to home for the second author of this chapter; see retraction of DeGeest et al., 2017). The destruction they cause in terms of wasted research built of falsified results and loss of credibility for the field can be immense, but we, perhaps being overly optimistic, see this as a rare phenomenon (see also Candal-Pedreira et al., 2022; C. Gross, 2016; Marshall, 2000). We contend that the death of an entire science will not be due to the actions of one or two fraudsters dealing a fatal blow, but rather it will be the death of 1,000 cuts, where each cut is an ever so gradual move away from the injunctive norms of science.

Beyond side-stepping the issue of outright fraud and academic misconduct, we wish to highlight that the current state of social science is undoubtedly a system-problem. We believe that no one – not even those engaged in the most extreme counterproductive behaviors in scientific research – entered the field for the express purpose of misleading practitioners and fellow researchers. Framing these detriments as moral failings, or as a "bad apples" problem will do little to change future practices. System-wide problems require system-wide solutions, and keeping with Merton's norm of communality, this will require collective action from cordwainers and cobblers alike.

Don't Blame the Individual – It's (Mainly) The Ecosystem!

The numbers of journals and publications per year (Johnson et al., 2018) seem to be ever growing, and more and more policy measures are put in place to keep the wheel spinning in terms of increasing the quantity of research output (Chu & Evans, 2021). Yet, the progress in science has been slowing in several major fields, and "papers and patents are increasingly less likely to break with the past in ways that push science and technology in new directions" (Park et al., 2023, p. 135; Fig. 4; see also Chu & Evans, 2021; Purgar et al., 2022). This finding stands in stark contrast to the choir of editors and reviewers who regularly demand some new (theoretical) insight for a manuscript to be accepted for publication. Commenting on these developments, Münch (2014) succinctly stated that "science increasingly proceeds as a struggle for the best statistics required for obtaining a good position in an academic field determined by quality assurance, benchmarking, and ranking" (p. 245). Thus, we might have ended up in a place where we have to accept the fact that we have not gotten as far as the numbers would want us to believe. Given our summary of the current status of the scientific system, we may not be standing in the ruins as of yet, but repairs are desperately needed.

What we aim to produce, knowledge, is a collective good – in Merton's words, scientific findings "constitute a common heritage in which the equity of the individual producer is severely limited" (1942, p. 121). Yet, within the current scientific system, as we have already outlined, knowledge is generally treated as a private good that can be used to advance individual careers, prestige of universities, and profit margins of publishers. This is entirely consistent with the descriptive norms of secrecy, self-interestedness, and quantity. In particular, the norm of quantity plays a key role based on changes in the incentives for PHRM and I/OP researchers. It appears that the move in many fields is toward rigid quantification of impact and research quality. Increasingly, researchers discuss their citations counts, h-indices, number of "A" hits, etc. In business schools in particular where a sizable amount of PHRM and I/OP research derives, the use of journal

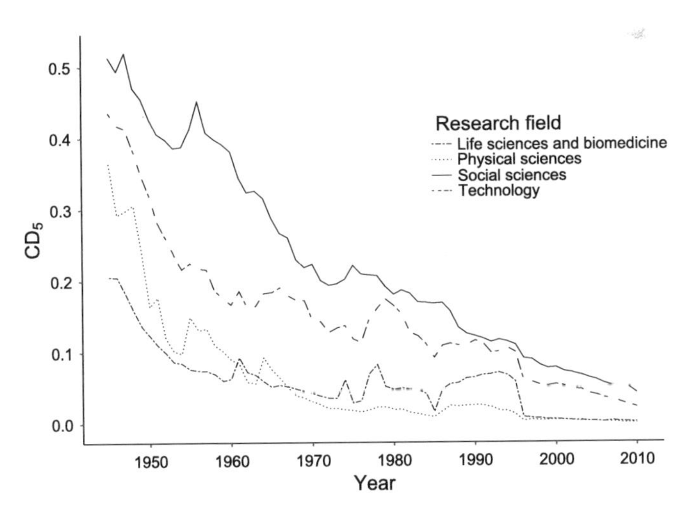

Fig. 4. Decline in Disruptiveness of Research Output Over the Last Decades. *Note*. Reproduced based on the data openly provided by Park et al. (2023). Results from an analysis of 25 million papers in the Web of Science (1945–2010) hint at an overall decrease in research disruptiveness. CD_5 = consolidating/disruptive (CD) index as measured five years after the year of a respective work's publication; range: –1 for the least disruptive to 1 for the most disruptive work.

lists and the weighing of the CV (i.e., how much in grants, how many top-tier publications, how many total publications, and how many citations) have turned promotion and tenure decisions into a counting exercise rather than a qualitative review. This has greatly simplified the tenure process as committee members don't really need to read the papers; they just need to sort the candidate's record into publications that count and sum the various grant funding. However, this simplification comes at great costs. Darley's law (2001) states that the more a quantitative measure is used to gauge rewards, the more it will be corrupted and the more it will distort the behavior of whom the metric is being applied. Put differently, there are unintended consequences to any reward and compensation system and if PHRM and I/OP researchers fixate only on the ends, then the means are sure to be corrupted.

We stress that it is the misaligned nature of the rewards that is the problem and not that PHRM and I/OP researchers have self-interests or desire for rewards and recognition. From a purely economic perspective, human behavior is about incentives and individual preferences (Voslinsky & Azar, 2021). In addition, economists typically adopt a *revealed preference approach* when studying human behavior (e.g., Hands, 2013; Richter, 1966) – as such, economists generally classify peoples' verbal statements as *cheap talk*, and instead only focus on peoples' behavior as indicator of their preferences. From this perspective, economists care little about the espoused injunctive norms of science – they are only concerned with the descriptive norms of scientists' behavior. As Ralph Waldo Emerson succinctly stated, "What you do speaks so loudly that I cannot hear what you say." Against this background, researchers either have preferences for their current behavior or the incentives drive them toward this behavior.

The global dissemination in the 1960s of new public management, a program somewhat ironically built on top of findings from strategic management, and institutional economics, was meant as a measure to modernize, measure, and make better academia (e.g., Kieser, 2010; Münch, 2014, 2015). In this attempt to eventually quantify the generation of knowledge in the form of scientific articles, the sheer number of publications has been made (more or less) the sole grounds for decisions about individual researchers regarding their hiring, salary, promotion, tenure, and grant approval (e.g., Gingras, 2020; Nosek et al., 2012; Wouters, 2020). At the same time, research institutions (e.g., departments and universities) are evaluated and ranked mainly based upon the number of publications achieved per year (e.g., Adler & Harzing, 2009; Kehm, 2020; Schmoch, 2015). As a result, pursuing, generating, and publishing knowledge is no longer the focal incentive for a researcher, but rather getting published – essentially at all costs – is (e.g., Bakker et al., 2012; Giner-Sorolla, 2012; Grimes et al., 2018). It is no wonder that this sheer focus on the quantification of knowledge generation has led to a hypercompetitive social system, which ultimately can lead to the emergence of unethical, careless, and/or irresponsible behavior as we have seen in the physical sciences (e.g., Edwards & Roy, 2017; Molinié & Bodenhausen, 2013; Ronning, et al., 2007) as well as in social scientific research (e.g., Charness et al., 2014; Crick & Crick, 2021; Kacperczyk et al., 2015).

Grievance 1: Questionable Research/Reporting Practices

A particularly prominent account as to why research findings are neither necessarily replicable nor reproducible lies in so-called questionable research/reporting practices (e.g., Gopalakrishna et al., 2022; O'Boyle & Götz, 2022; Wigboldus & Dotsch, 2016). Such practices lie in the *grey area* between proper scientific conduct and fraud in that they can be characterized as making a scientific result more beautiful/publishable than it actually is (e.g., Fanelli, 2012a; Lynøe et al., 1999; Steneck, 2006). In other words, what makes QRPs questionable is that they are a tool to not report the entire (potentially relevant) truth of a research project, knowingly or unknowingly (O'Boyle & Götz, 2022). Specific behaviors that are typically subsumed under the term QRP are, for example, *p*-hacking (i.e., continuously manipulating data until desired results are achieved), hypothesizing after results are known (HARKing; Kerr, 1998), and dropping conditions from experiments that did not bring about the hypothesized results (e.g., Baum & Bromiley, 2019; Bosco et al., 2016; John et al., 2012). Returning to the hypothetico-deductive model of research, QRP might best be described as measures to hot-wire the research life cycle to get from A to B more quickly, or at all (Fig. 5; Munafò et al., 2017).

Results from the *Netherlands Survey of Research Integrity* by Gopalakrishna et al. (2022) indicate that roughly half of the surveyed researchers from the social and behavioral sciences reported to have engaged in at least one of the considered behaviors. Most commonly, researchers did not submit valid negative studies for publication, insufficiently discussed flaws and limitations of their own studies, and did not adequately take note of their research process to assure transparent

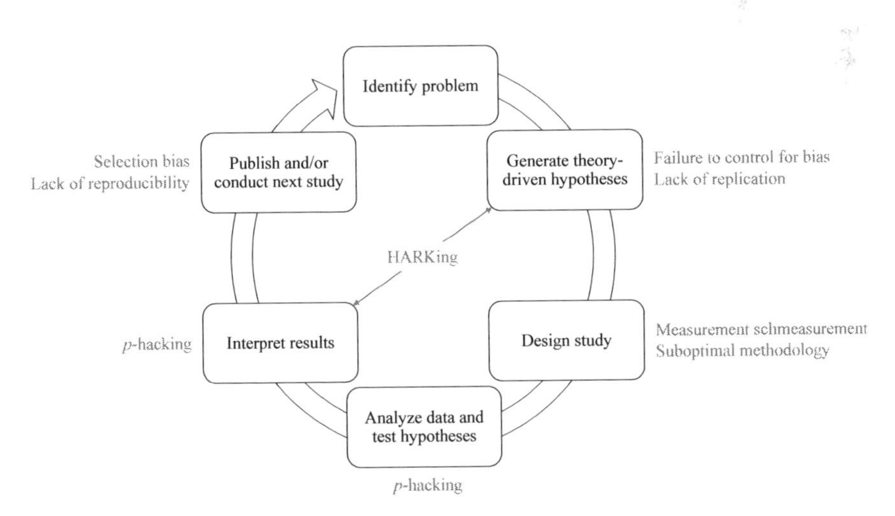

Fig. 5. A Hot-wired Hypothetico-deductive Model of Research. *Note*. The hypothetico-deductive model of research including potential shortcuts in the form of QRPs, such as HARKing, or *p*-hacking (printed in gray; see also Munafò et al., 2017).

and complete reporting. Similar results are reported by John et al. (2012), who found a majority of the surveyed scientists to have failed to report all of a study's dependent variables in a publication, used arbitrary stopping rules regarding data collection (i.e., as soon as the desired results are in), and selectively reported only these (aspects of) studies that "worked" (see also Fiedler & Schwarz, 2016; Fox et al., 2022; Xie et al., 2021). Of course, measuring the occurrence or prevalence of QRPs is cumbersome, given the very private nature of this set of behaviors. Yet, as we know from research on self-report data on sensitive behaviors (e.g., counterproductive work behavior), these estimates should be considered under-estimates rather than overestimates due to self-serving bias, non-response bias, and/or social desirability (e.g., Greco et al., 2015; Yan, 2021; *cf.* Fiedler & Schwarz, 2016; Fanelli, 2022).

Additional evidence comes from O'Boyle et al. (2017) who compared dissertations to the subsequent journal publications. Naturally, there is a winnowing process as dissertations are reduced in length for journal submission, but the changes that did occur during this winnowing process had a tendency to improve the level of hypothesis support far more often than it detrimented them (see also Kepes et al., 2022). The authors referred to this phenomenon as the *Chrysalis effect*. Just as a caterpillar becomes a chrysalis[9] only to eventually turn into a beautiful butterfly, "the ratio of supported to unsupported hypotheses more than doubled (0.82 to 1.00 versus 1.94 to 1.00) [and this] rise in predictive accuracy resulted from the dropping of statistically non-significant hypotheses, the addition of statistically significant hypotheses, the reversing of predicted direction of hypotheses, and alterations to data" (O'Boyle et al., 2017, p. 376). In a similar vein, Judge and Schechter (2009) investigated nine commonly used data sets and found the ones stemming from developing countries to be of poorer quality (i.e., more fabricated observation) compared to the data from the United States (see also Francis & Thunell, 2022; Marchi & Hamilton, 2006; Nye & Moul, 2007).

A final, yet very prominent example from PHRM and I/OP comes from Cortina et al. (2017) who reviewed the reporting practices of latent variable modeling (or structural equation modeling [SEM]; Bollen, 1989; T. A. Brown, 2015; Kline, 2016) in 784 models from 75 papers that were published in *Academy of Management Journal* and *Journal of Applied Psychology*. Here, a little knowledge about SEM allows one to check whether a model reported in an article aligns with the degrees of freedom (i.e., *df*). Problematically, Cortina et al. (2017) found that only about 75% of the models reported enough information that even allowed for the calculation of the respective *df*, and only roughly 62% of the reported number of *df* matched with the respective calculated one. As such, either the research or the reporting practices of latent variables modeling in PHRM and I/OP seem to be in need of betterment to allow researchers to be accurately informed of what model was tested and what specific degree of model fit was attained (see also Credé & Harms, 2019).

As can be seen, the perniciousness of QRPs to the hallmarks of a healthy science is attributable to their frequency, and their frequency is attributable to the descriptive norms of science. The norm of secrecy that discourages sharing of data and study materials allows those engaged in QRPs the opportunity to go undetected. The norm of self-interestedness prioritizes individual glory over scientific advancement. And, the norm of quantity places immense pressure on PHRM and I/OP researchers to publish by any means necessary.

Grievance 2: Measurement Schmeasurement

Given that humans are the primary focus of PHRM and I/OP research, and given the incredible complexities and intricacies of humans, measuring a latent (read, *invisible*) construct is without question a challenging endeavor (e.g., Hand, 2016; Nunnally, 1975; Price, 2017). Nonetheless, whatever construct, phenomenon, or mechanism PHRM and I/OP researchers investigate empirically, it must be measured in a way that assures both validity and reliability. In the words of the physicist Walter H. G. Lewin (2011), "accuracy is the *only* [original emphasis] thing that matters, and a measurement that doesn't also indicate its degree of accuracy is meaningless" (p. 8). To put it differently, no matter how versatile one's methodological, and statistical tools are, or if statistically significant results are achieved between already measured constructs; if the construct of interest is not measured accurately, none of the above matters.

Yet, measurement in the social sciences is often flawed in important ways – Flake and Fried (2020) fittingly coined the term *measurement schmeasurement* for this circumstance (see also Chester & Lasko, 2021). Taking the first indicator of good measurement, reliability, there is an age-old discussion as to which statistical estimate should be used to express reliability. Given that we typically use scales comprising several items in PHRM and I/OP, alpha (or, internal consistency, e.g., W. Brown, 1910; Cronbach, 1951; Spearman, 1910) is most commonly used to indicate a scale's reliability – yet, a vast array of methodological work has criticized exactly this use of the estimate as being flawed (e.g., Cho & Kim, 2015; Cortina et al., 2020; McNeish, 2018). First, only under very strong assumptions can alpha be considered to indicate a scale's reliability; assumptions that essentially never hold in social science nor are they typically tested (Cho & Kim, 2015; *cf.* Peterson & Kim, 2013). Second, although Nunally's (1978) book *Psychometric theory* is generally referred to justify sufficient reliability if alpha exceeds 0.70, Nunnally (1978) very carefully discussed alpha and never made such general recommendations regarding cut-offs. Writing a few years prior to his seminal work, Nunnally (1975) stated, "[r]eliability theory is not highly important for basic research on individual differences, unless the reliability is miserably low, e.g., below .70 [...] In such cases where important decisions must be made about humans on the basis of test scores, even a reliability of .90 is not high enough" (p. 10).[10] Although it is better to have reliabilities that are miserably low than reliabilities that fail to be even miserably low, an alpha of 0.70 is a little cause to celebrate in PHRM and I/OP research. If our purpose is informing practitioners' decisions on what selection instruments they should use, what types of trainings and interventions they should employ and how they should evaluate the individual and team performance of their workforce, then PHRM and I/OP researchers are clearly operating in a space "where important decisions must be made about humans on the basis of test scores." Reliabilities of these HR tools should be increased to match their high stakes implications. Third, as any undergraduate in a HR class can attest, there are very few questions in PHRM and I/OP research that are not answered with "it depends." In other words, most phenomena and theories include moderators (also called interactions). However, when one estimates interaction or moderation effects of two scales in that the reliability of said interaction term is the product of the individual scales' reliability. If, for example, both scales barely made Nunally's (1978) supposed cut-off, the interaction terms reliability would be a "miserably low" 0.49 (Greco et al., 2018). Finally, the famous mantra *correlation does not imply causation* also applies to the hunt for reliability – just because items of a scale display a strong intercorrelation, and a resulting high alpha, does not mean they are actually measuring the same construct.

One prominent statistical technique allowing to acknowledge a measure's unreliability – in other words, allowing to correct for measurement error – is latent variables modeling (or SEM; Bollen, 1989; T. A. Brown, 2015; Kline, 2016). Yet, rather often, the tools provided by SEM to disentangle true score variance and measurement error (i.e., confirmatory factor analysis (CFA)) are not properly put to use, thereby running at the risk of inflating Type I and Type II errors (e.g., Credé et al., 2012; Credé & Harms, 2019; Jackson et al., 2009). Furthermore, even when researchers conduct a proper CFA to illustrate their measurement models' proper fit to the data, they subsequently rather often shy away from modeling also the structural parts of their models, thereby potentially introducing severe bias (e.g., D. A. Cole & Preacher, 2014; Rhemtulla, 2016; *cf.* Rhemtulla et al., 2020). Particularly when interactions are integral part of the structural models, researchers seem to shy away from modeling these in a latent fashion despite the unreliability being particularly problematic in this instance (Cortina et al., 2021).

Unfortunately – a word that will preamble much of our assessment – in lieu of increasing the reliability and validity of our measures and study designs, much attention and effort has been paid to correcting them to be what they might if our measures had higher reliabilities and validities. We will speak to the role of statistics in the current state of affairs shortly, but take the interrater reliability of supervisor ratings of job performance as an example. The interrater reliability in this context refers to how two or more supervisors evaluating the same worker arrive at similar or dissimilar job performance ratings. The degree of interrater reliability ranges from zero (no agreement) to one (perfect agreement). For supervisor ratings, which are highly influential in employment contexts resulting in promotions, raises, and disciplinary actions up to and including termination, it is 0.52 (Viswesvaran et al., 1996). That means that about half of what goes into a supervisor rating is just noise and error. That we have a substantial distance to go before we reach the aforementioned Nunnally criterion of "miserably low" (i.e., 0.70) levels of reliability for what is the most common means of performance evaluation is a non-ideal state of affairs to say the least.

Given the centrality of supervisor ratings and job performance to PHRM and I/OP, it is no surprise that this Viswesvaran et al. (1996) article has generated well over 1,000 citations. However, the majority of these citations are not efforts to improve the reliability or measurement of supervisor ratings. In fact, hardly any of these citations are measurement refinement pieces (notable exceptions include LeBreton & Senter, 2007, and Salgado and Moscoso, 2019). Rather, the bulk of citations to this influential work are meta-analyses using the 0.52 reliability to "correct" observed correlations to what they would be if supervisor ratings weren't so horribly unreliable. Unfortunately, there is no such thing as a free lunch. By greatly increasing the magnitude of the observed correlations through statistical correction rather than through measure refinement, we introduce uncertainty and often untestable assumptions.

As an analogy to this statistical uncertainty, place yourself in the role of buying a racehorse. On the first day of your shopping spree, you arrive in perfect racing conditions and the horse runs the track in exactly two minutes. The next day you arrive to see a different horse, but it is raining, the track is muddy, and it is cold outside. It takes this horse three minutes to run the track. However, the trainer explains three minutes in bad race conditions is equal to two minutes when conditions are perfect. Which horse are you most confident in being able to complete the race in two minutes? The first one of course because it was observed. There were no calculations or conversions for weather or track conditions. You don't need to assume that the trainer is truthful or that the calculations apply perfectly to the second horse. PHRM and I/OP researchers are spending a lot of time on the calculations and conversions, and we contend not nearly enough time on training a faster horse. Applying statistical corrections is important and we, as PHRM and I/OP researchers and psychometricians, should continue this work, but we need to treat this work for what it is – a stopgap measure until we develop more reliable and valid tests (LeBreton et al., 2014).

As with all these detriments, there are normative factors in play. Specifically, the descriptive norm of administration trumping the injunctive norm of governance that turns academics insular and distances them (us) from those we are tasked with serving. Would practitioners benefit more from more accurately calculating what the predictive capabilities of a test or rating would be if it wasn't contaminated by error and noise or would they benefit more from a test or rating that wasn't so contaminated?

Apart from issues with the reliability of our measures, the validity of our measures also provides reasons for concern. Much of our research relies on participant responses to surveys composed of various scales (Credé & Harms, 2019). The specific scales used should be validated through a formal scale validation process (e.g., DeVellis, 2016; Hinkin, 1998; Lambert & Newman, 2022). Yet, it is our observation that in the typical scale validation study construct validity (e.g., convergent and discriminant validity) is seldomly tested in a thorough manner to actually assure that a measure is truly capturing what it is designed to. Or, as Blue and Brierley (2016) state, "doing measurement is not necessarily doing science" (p. 191). Most often, cross-sectional data on some (un-)related and supposedly validated scales are also collected, and then correlations are inspected. The manifold intricacies of validating a measure are, however, generally neglected despite a mountain of methodological research existing (e.g., Heggestad et al., 2019; Vazire et al., 2022; Wetzel & Roberts, 2020).

Furthermore, self-report is our most typical rating source which brings with it all the potential drawbacks of social desirability, active, and passive non-response as well as a diverse set of cognitive biases (e.g., Arnold & Feldman, 1981; Yan, 2021; Ward & Meade, 2023). In that regard, the idea that a measure is more valid if it stems from other sources than the self often comes up – yet, we still have little in the way of conclusive evidence that coworker-, supervisor-, or generally other-reports really help improve validity of a measurement (e.g., Berry et al., 2012; Carpenter et al., 2014; Gartstein et al., 2012).

Furthermore, measuring actual behavior is seldomly engaged in PHRM and I/OP despite many of our focal constructs directly refer to behavior, such as leadership. For example, Banks et al. (2021) systematically reviewed research recently published in top-tier journals, such as *Leadership Quarterly*, and *Journal of Organizational Behavior*, and found only 3% of 2,338 variables studied were behavioral in nature and only 19% of studies included at least one behavioral measure. Furthermore, take recent research syntheses on actual behaviors at the workplace, such as green workplace behaviors (Francoeur et al., 2021), workplace deviant behavior (Mackey et al., 2021), or workplace ostracism (Howard et al., 2020). The overwhelming majority of studies included in each of these did not measure actual behavior.

Finally, there is ample evidence for construct proliferation, namely "the accumulation of ostensibly different but potentially identical constructs representing organizational phenomena" (Shaffer et al., 2016, p. 80) in PHRM and I/OP. Already in the early 1900s, Thorndike (1904) and Kelley (1927) collectively coined the term *jingle-jangle fallacy* to hint at misguided assumptions that either two different constructs are the same because they share the same or similar names (*jingle fallacy*), or that two (almost) identical constructs are different because they are labeled differently (*jangle fallacy*). Taking again the example of leadership, Shaffer et al. (2016) demonstrated that (too) many measures of leadership constructs, such as transformational leadership, charismatic leadership, or leader-member exchange, essentially show intercorrelations of around .95 when corrected for measurement error. Given the ample theoretical backgrounds, and respective bodies of literature, such strong intercorrelations are worrisome (see also Bormann & Rowold, 2018; M. S. Cole et al., 2012; Shaffer et al., 2016). Specifically, these findings directly violate Occam's razor regarding an efficient, and economic science in that *plurality must never be posited without necessity*. In other words, "not everything that can be counted counts [–] not everything that counts can be counted" (Cameron, 1963, p. 13). Or, as more assertively stated by Yankelovich's (1972) discussion of *McNamera's fallacy* (also known as the *quantitative fallacy*):

> The first step is to measure whatever can be easily measured. This is OK as far as it goes. The second step is to disregard that which can't be easily measured or to give it an arbitrary quantitative value. This is artificial and misleading. The third step is to presume that what can't be measured easily really isn't important. This is blindness. The fourth step is to say that what can't be easily measured really doesn't exist. This is suicide.

Grievance 3: Methodology

Causality is a peculiar thing, and eventually our overall goal in generating robust knowledge is to establish causality regarding the relationships between constructs we study (e.g., Imbens & Rubin, 2015; Kenny, 1979; Mill, 1843/1974). There are three conditions such a relationship between X and Y has to fulfill to be considered causal that Kenny (1979) outlined: (1) The cause X has to precede the effect Y (i.e., temporal precedence), (2) there has to be a functional, observable relationship between X and Y, and (3) there must not be any alternative explanation for the relationship between X and Y (i.e., non-spuriousness). From these three conditions it follows that the methodology of a study is key to allowing for causal inferences, whereas statistics are a necessary but insufficient tool. As Wasserstein and Lazar (2016) put it, when discussing the value of *p*-values from a causality standpoint:

> Good statistical practice, as an essential component of good scientific practice, emphasizes principles of good study design and conduct, a variety of numerical and graphical summaries of data, understanding of the phenomenon under study, interpretation of results in context, complete reporting and proper logical and quantitative understanding of what data summaries mean. No single index should substitute for scientific reasoning. (p. 132)

One can calibrate the typical research designs in PHRM and I/OP with Kenny's (1979) three conditions for causality: (1) The typical cross-sectional and time-lagged design can allow for fulfillment of the second condition, namely the test of a relationship; (2) a truly longitudinal design that takes repeated measurements can fulfill two conditions: temporal precedence and observable relationship; and (3) only the randomized controlled experiment (RCT) allows to fulfill all three conditions including non-spuriousness. Of course, each of these designs has intricacies and nuances, some of which we already discussed – for example, you might run a RCT on MTurk measuring your constructs of interest using some supposedly validated scale. Given the inferential issues of MTurk, and the measurement schmeasurement of most of the self-report measures, the level of causality to be expected from the RCT may nevertheless be low despite using the *gold standard* of research designs.

We acknowledge that, particularly in PHRM and I/OP, testing hypotheses in an experimental fashion is often very difficult. Given that we then often start with the disadvantage of not having the option to run a RCT, our research designs should be tailored in a robust way as possible to allow meaningful inferences (for a historical perspective on methodological developments in PHRM and I/OP, see Aguinis et al., 2017).[11] Yes, cross-sectional studies were rightfully put in their generally inferior place over the last several years (e.g., Hamaker, 2023; Maxwell & Cole, 2007; Spector, 2019), and a methodological pluralism emerged (e.g., policy capturing, extreme-group designs, or multilevel research). Yet, for example, upspring of so-called time-lagged studies (e.g., measuring the variables proposed to render a mediation over three occasions, but one at a time) is a marginal improvement. Essentially, such a research design is just a cross-sectional research design stretched over time in that it still holds the same drawbacks. In addition, issues of measurement invariance – questions, such as "Does this measurement instrument work equally well over time?", or "Does this scale work in different cultural spaces as intended in the original validation study?" (e.g., Davidov et al., 2018; Kim et al., 2022; Schmitt & Ali, 2015). Finally, rarely, if ever, are the time-lags between the measurement occasions explicitly specified and justified (e.g., Dormann, 2022; Dormann & Griffin, 2015; Dormann & van de Ven, 2014).

In all fairness, we consider these, and other, methodological shortcomings to be direct consequences of the song of sorrow that we have sung so far: Our theoretical models are complex but underspecified, our measures are underdeveloped or improperly used, our incentives are misaligned in that *statistically significant* is typically confused with *practically or meaningfully significant*, and our inferential tools are often misused or just dull (relatedly, see Aguinis & Vandenberg, 2014; Cortina, 2016; Tourish, 2020).

Grievance 4: Statistics

The final grievance we consider is our usage of statistics, given our earlier bemoaning of the many statistical aggregate anomalies in front of us (e.g., Götz et al., 2021; O'Boyle & Götz, 2022; van Zwet & Cator, 2021). We share Andrew Gelman's (2016) sentiment when he describes the apparent predominant understanding and usage of statistics as of today:

> It seems to me that statistics is often sold as a sort of alchemy that transmutes randomness into certainty, an "uncertainty laundering" that begins with data and concludes with success as measured by statistical significance. (p. 1)

It indeed appears to be the case that statistics are rather often used to render a supposed finding more credible or truthful, whereas it should be used as a mere tool to actually test one's hypothesis, summarize data, or even inspect interesting patterns in the data exploratorily. To allow for a prudent usage of statistics, it is imperative that all stakeholders (i.e., readers, authors, reviewers, and editors) understand the workings and limits of it. The predominant statistical framework in PHRM is, without question, NHST (e.g., Cortina, Aguinis, et al., 2017; Gigerenzer & Marewski, 2015; Hubbard et al., 1997). NHST itself is a homespun hybrid of Fisher's (1956) and Neyman and Pearson's (1933) seminal works that, as we state, is generally misunderstood in its capabilities, its appliance, and its allowance for inferences (e.g., Etz et al., 2022; Gigerenzer, 2004; Gigerenzer et al., 2004). Notably, Gigerenzer (2018) stated that misguided external incentives should not be the sole reason to attribute the lack of credibility of science to. Rather, widespread faith in statistical rituals and *associated delusions* should be considered as well.

Inspecting the inner workings of NHST is beyond the scope of our work here, but given its dominant role, it seems worthwhile to briefly review common misunderstandings of it, and contrast it with the often-evoked alternative, namely Bayesian statistics (e.g., Gigerenzer & Marewski, 2015; Lindley, 2014; McElreath, 2020). First, the definition, meaning, and inferential power of the almighty *p*-value along with the often interchangeably used term *statistical significance* seem to be generally poorly understood (e.g., Gigerenzer, 2004; Greenland et al., 2016; Wasserstein & Lazar, 2016). A *p*-value is clearly defined as "the probability of the observed data (or of more extreme data points), given that the null hypothesis H_0 is true" (Gigerenzer, 2004, p. 595). Yet, Cassidy et al. (2019) examined 30 introductory psychology textbooks only to find that a staggering 89% explained both the definition and the interpretation of statistical significance incorrectly. The manifold misconceptions about *p*-values and statistical significance thus cannot come as a surprise (see also Harlow et al., 2016; Kline, 2013; Ziliak & McCloskey, 2008).

As is well-known, NHST does not allow one to accept the null hypothesis (Kluger & Tikochinsky, 2001). In turn, NHST does not allow one to accept the alternative hypothesis because the alternative hypothesis is not what is being tested (e.g., Gigerenzer, 2004; Greenland et al., 2016; Wasserstein & Lazar, 2016). Some pointed to this and other issues, such as the 0.05 threshold artificially dichotomize the continuous nature of probability which can encourage certain questionable practices, like *p*-hacking. The collective problems with NHST have led some to see it as the cause of the rose-tinting of the literature and go so far as recommending the deinstitutionalization of NHST (e.g., Hubbard et al., 1997; McShane et al., 2019b; Orlitzky, 2012). Although we fully agree with these authors and researchers that NHST is problematic, one should be wary of simple solutions to complex problems.

Abandoning NHST is unlikely to address the problem because whenever one result is favored over another there will be the motivation to "rose-tint" findings. This sentiment is shared by Jacob Cohen (1994) when he wrote "don't look for a magic alternative to NHST, some other objective mechanical ritual to replace it. It doesn't exist" (p. 1001). Fife (2020) interpreted Cohen's words by stating that "there is no *one* alternative to NHST; rather, statistical analysis requires a rather large toolbox in which each tool is adapted to the circumstances under which it is most appropriate. The tool might be, for example Bayes factors, confidence intervals, effect sizes, single-subject designs, preregistration, and/or graphical data analysis" (p. 1055; see also Gigerenzer, 2004). In the words of Abraham H. Maslow (1966) "it is tempting, if the only tool you have is a hammer, to treat everything as if it were a nail" (p. 15) – yet, we should be very wary to not fall prey to the "idol of a universal method of scientific inference" (Gigerenzer & Marewski, 2015, p. 437).

Coming Out of the Dark: Where Should We Go?

We began this chapter by highlighting the four hallmarks of a healthy science as (a) relevance to practitioners, (b) methodological rigor, (c) accuracy of findings and claims, and (d) ability to build cumulative knowledge. We then reviewed the barriers to these hallmarks due to an increasing abidance to the descriptive norms of science rather than striving for the ideals of Merton's injunctive norms. As concerning as the current state of affairs regarding the conduct, meaningfulness, and credibility of PHRM science may be at the moment, we now gladly turn to what we consider a silver lining. In the hopes that you, our dear reader, are still with us, let us intone the final verse of the song of sorrow that actually is one of hope. It is a call to action.

As Thomas S. Kuhn (1996) noted that "to reject one paradigm without simultaneously substituting another is to reject science itself" (p. 79) – and, by no means, do we want to reject science itself. We first stress that doing good science is difficult and while the quantity of scientific output has clearly increased, the increase in per paper quality is less certain. Specifically, we put a light on the tremendous amount of variability in the entire scientific life cycle, and how it can guide cobblers to actually embrace and study it. Then, we will discuss how open science practices can be implemented in a way that does not require extensive training or sacrifice on the part of the cobbler (or cordwainer, for that matter). With a more reliable and robust science, we next turn to doing robust and reliable science that actually matters to practitioners. We then conclude with a discussion of how we can build a bigger tent and expand our understanding to PHRM/I/OP issues encountered in non-WEIRD cultures and with neglected populations.

For each recommendation, we will also discuss the means of incentivizing the behaviors necessary to improve the health of all four hallmarks these recommendations are intended to yield. Although we strongly believe that the intrinsic motivation to do the types of science aligned with Merton's injunctive norms plays a necessary role, exclusively relying on others' altruism and self-sacrifice to achieve a healthier science is a bit naïve. There are a lot of incentives to maintain the status quo, and we have trained multiple generations of PHRM and I/OP researchers in the ways of the descriptive norms – many of whom have somewhat excelled in the current system including the authors of this chapter. The solution to misaligned incentives is alignment not abandonment, and although some of the changes may cause some short-term discomfort, those that help in this realignment will be the beneficiaries of these changes. Their research will be more rigorous and impactful to both practitioners and fellow researchers in ways that will surpass research created under the current model.

Need to Set the Norms Straight

Surely, Merton (1942) has not provided an exhaustive analysis of the entire normative system of science – he described *merely four* norms that he considered to ideally be followed by most researchers. Yet, as we have illustrated, we currently seem to be considerably more aligned with the descriptive counter-norms of science. Indeed, where communality, universalism, disinterestedness, and organized skepticism should reign supreme, secrecy, particularism, self-interestedness, and organized dogmatism actually do. As such, we, as PHRM/I/OP researchers have to ask ourselves: *Whom are we, as a discipline, serving? Theory, practice, or ourselves? Are we developing theory to ultimately provide practitioners with recommendations for real-world problems? Are we collecting data to develop and refine our theories until they are so sharp that we can actually use them to understand and predict the real world? Or, are we trying to find as robust as possible answers to practitioners' real-world questions, regardless if we can properly explain the findings up-front? Or, are we trying to get these two additional lines on our CVs, that (ideally) help us achieve tenure, status, and job security?* Of course, there is no definitive answers in terms of "right" or "wrong" to these questions – yet, we, as a discipline, should carefully think about them and decide who we actually want to be to set the standards for ourselves and our research.

Merton (1942) made the "extension of certified knowledge" (p. 117) out to be a goal of the scientific endeavor, and it is our contention that this should still hold true today. Just consult the preamble of the APA's *Ethical Principles of*

Psychologists and Code of Conduct (American Psychological Association, 2017): "Psychologists are committed to increasing scientific and professional knowledge of behavior and people's understanding of themselves and others and to the use of such knowledge to improve the condition of individuals, organizations, and society." In turn, we have to make sure that we dedicate ourselves to operating under the Mertonian injunctive norms of science and start moving away from Mitroff's (1974) counter-norms. Our assessment of the current state of science so far makes it imperative that changes are implemented: Changes to the way we *do* science, to the ways we *view* science, and to the way we are *incentivize* those who partake in this system. Before we dive in, let us note that we consider the accumulation of knowledge the product of a pluralistic approach – we do not mean to outline a streamlined corset that all scientific endeavors from now on have to fit in. In all, we argue for a normative change, yet we know from research on norms, such change is hard to implement (e.g., Bicchieri & Mercier, 2014; Reynolds et al., 2015; Yip & Schweitzer, 2022). Yet, it is very much needed.

Need to Set Proper Incentives

Before we start diving into potential betterments in terms of moving us as a field closer to the Mertonian norms, let us quickly address needed change to the system in which we actually *do* science. Of course, we are not alone in our assessment that a somewhat perverse hypercompetitive incentive system has been established in academia (and, outside of it, too; e.g., Edwards & Roy, 2017; Molinié & Bodenhausen, 2013; Ronning, et al., 2007). When thinking about the incentives in academia, more than once the TV show *The Wire* crossed our mind (Simon et al., 2002–2008). This show focused on the manifold problems of the city of Baltimore, and some of its major institution, such as the police, and the educational system, among others. A recurrent theme that always comes back as a root of problems is the salience of metrics: The police were obsessed with hitting the numbers (e.g., making enough arrests and solving enough murders), the schools are obsessed with getting enough students to the next level of the school system by *teaching the test*. Yet, the overall drama of the series is that real issues are not properly addressed in an attempt to better them – everyone tries their best in their little yard, but the overall system just keeps on producing more and more issues.

We argue that the same is true for academia, although we can only speak on behalf of our own experiences in our respective systems of higher education (i.e., USA and Switzerland). Our careers, or rather their length and success, are directly determined by the number or papers we publish, the outlets of said papers, and the amount of grants we attain. Typically, we have to fulfill certain thresholds of these metrics to advance to the next stage (e.g., from doctoral student to assistant professor), and the primary means of job security is obtaining a tenured position. If, for whatever reason, one does not make it to the next level of the hierarchy on time, one typically drops out of the system. This is particularly problematic in light of the typical length of a career in academia before the guillotine falls. Most of our former PHRM colleagues dropped out of the university by the age of 35 and many were even younger than that. Although wunderkind such as Albert

Einstein made his most notable contributions well before that age (e.g., theory of relativity by the age of 26), many other scientists were late bloomers. The current PHRM system does not tolerate this and it is unclear to what degree that we are losing highly valuable intellectual capital due to a short window to demonstrate contribution.

Need to Embrace Variability, and Not Shun It

Gelman and Loken (2014) rightfully stated "criticism is easy, research is hard" (p. 464), and, without question, new and powerful ideas about the functioning of the world are *very* hard to come by (e.g., Bloom et al., 2020; Chu & Evans, 2021; Park et al., 2023). Despite the current body of literature might give us the impression that there are somewhat simple binary answers with regard to rather complex questions, there is actually tremendous amount of variability to be found at every single step of the process. In what Simmons et al. (2011) called *researcher degrees of freedom*, they alluded to the fact that researchers are faced with a myriad of questions in the scientific endeavor to which the answers create (dramatically) many degrees of freedom. In close resemblance, Gelman and Loken (2014) used the metaphor of the *garden of the forking paths*. For example, think of the following questions when conceptualizing a study, collecting the data, and analyzing it: *Which materials/scales do we use to manipulate/assess constructs of interest? How many experimental conditions do we need? How much (more) data should be collected? Should we exclude some observations because of this, or that reason? Which experimental conditions might be collapsed, and which might be compared to what? Which control variables should be considered, and how? Should specific measurement instruments be combined or transformed, if necessary?* As should be clear, the list of decision points can easily be prolonged almost indefinitely.

An ample array of research projects has been carried out to illustrate the variability introduced into the findings from research based upon the multitude of researchers' decisions. First, there are the so-called Many Labs projects that regularly demonstrated substantial variation in direct replications (e.g., Ebersole et al., 2020; Klein et al., 2014, 2018). Second, the Many Materials project demonstrated substantial variation in conclusions of psychological experiments, given idiosyncratic operationalizations/materials despite the same hypotheses (Landy et al., 2020). Finally, Many Analysts projects regularly demonstrated substantial variation in conclusions from statistical analyses of the same data set and the same research question (e.g., Botvinik-Nezer et al., 2020; Menkveld et al., 2021; Silberzahn et al., 2018). Given that we consider it is important to see the variability in research first-hand, we now turn to inspecting these projects in more detail.

Many Labs

In 2012, a large-scale meta-science project, the so-called Many Labs project, was kicked off to essentially provide researchers with the first set of direct replications of social psychological findings. Over the course of five iterations, a diverse set of scientific findings was tested for their direct replicability by several teams of researchers from and in many labs (i.e., Ebersole et al., 2016, 2020; Klein et al.,

2014, 2018, 2022). For example, in the first installation, Klein et al. (2014) demonstrated that 10 out of 13 classic effects could be directly replicated across 36 independent samples totaling 6,344 participants. The researchers used the original study materials whenever possible and varied whether the replication study was conducted online, in a lab, using an US sample, or an international one. Interestingly, "most of the variation in effects was due to the effect under investigation and almost none to the particular sample used" (Klein et al., 2014, p. 151). Among the successful replicated effects were Oppenheimer et al.'s (2009) sunk costs, Tversky and Kahneman's gain vs. loss framing (1981), and Jacowitz and Kahneman's (1995) anchoring. More or less randomly selecting further studies for direct replications, the following four iterations of the Many Labs project consistently illustrated high amounts of variability regarding effect sizes across different research teams and effects under investigation (Ebersole et al., 2016, 2020; Klein et al., 2018, 2022). Yet, there is also criticism of the Many Labs projects in that the knowledge to be gained from direct replications is somewhat limited, and our focus as cobblers should be rather on our theories (Stroebe, 2019; see also Ebersole, 2019).

Above and beyond inspecting the variability of scientific findings, what we consider most noteworthy about the Many Labs projects is that they were all coordinated by the *Center for Open Science* (https://www.cos.io/). As such, these projects not only aimed for investigating the replicability of selected scientific findings but also for testing the viability of the *Open Science Framework* (OSF) as a means to openly share materials, data, and code and foster collaboration among fellow researchers – a platform, we will shortly return to.

Many Materials

Direct replications are, as their name suggests, the most direct test of the validity of a scientific finding. Yet, in crafting knowledge, we aim for generalizability in that our conclusions ideally transcend a particular research design, set of materials, or sample in that scientific findings should be found again in reality, even if one uses a different pair of glasses, or looks in a different place for it. Against this background, conceptual replications are also an important ingredient to assure a robust body of knowledge (e.g., Crandall & Sherman, 2016; Derksen & Morawski, 2022; Schauer, 2022). One particular aspect of a study, namely the choice of materials in the form of scales, vignettes, or manipulations, offers great room for creativity, and, of course, variability.

Landy et al. (2020) conducted a meta-scientific research project to inspect whether and how variability due to idiosyncratic choices by researchers crafting study materials might affect the conclusions of a research project. Specifically, they provided fifteen research teams with five hypotheses and asked them to independently design studies to test them. For four out of the five hypotheses, the research teams found drastically differing, but statistically significant effects in opposite directions. In the authors' words, "the subjective choices that researchers make in stimulus design have a substantial impact on observed effect sizes" (Landy et al., 2020, p. 461). This variability in effect sizes was not attributable to the skill of the research team in designing materials, but instead to the hypothesis being tested. Notably, there were no systematic differences between research teams in creating materials that consistently created large effect sizes for all hypotheses.

Many Analysts

Variability is also introduced into the research process by the manifold choices that researchers have to make during the actual analysis of data. Let alone the adoption of the statistical framework one is adopting (e.g., NHST, and Bayes), a myriad of decisions can be made regarding the actual modeling approach, the inclusion/exclusion and transformation of variables, the inclusion/exclusion of data points, the handling of missing data, and so on. Meta-science projects involving many analysts to uncover this typically hidden variability have recently emerged and brought about thought-provoking findings (e.g., Botvinik-Nezer et al., 2020; Breznau et al., 2022; Silberzahn et al., 2018).

For example, Silberzahn et al. (2018) posed the same research claim (i.e., "soccer referees are more likely to give red cards to dark-skin-toned players than to light-skin-toned players" [p. 38]) to 29 research team comprising a total of 61 researchers and provided them all with the same dataset. What resulted were 29 different analytical approaches, 21 unique combinations of considered covariates, and an equally variable answer to the research question: 69% of the teams of a statistically significant positive effect, and 31% did not find one, at all. Furthermore, the estimated effect sizes drastically differed across research teams (*cf.* Auspurg & Brüderl, 2021; Edelsbrunner et al., 2022), rendering referees either as horrifically biased against players with darker skin tones or as paragons of impartiality with no bias whatsoever. Intriguingly, neither analysts' prior beliefs about the effect of interest, nor their level of expertise, nor the peer ratings of the quality of the analyses accounted for this level of variability in the outcomes. Similar projects have resulted in equally large (or larger) amounts of variability due to data analytic decisions in the context of COVID-19 estimates in the UK (Scientific Pandemic Influenza Group on Modelling, Operational subgroup (SPI-M-O), 2020), political science (Breznau et al., 2022), neuroscience (Botvinik-Nezer et al., 2020), economics (Menkveld et al., 2021), and also PHRM (Schweinsberg et al., 2021).

Each analytical path chosen by an analyst can be described as a *universe* and combining all possible analytical paths creates a *multiverse* (e.g., Dafflon et al., 2022; Del Giudice & Gangestad, 2021; Steegen et al., 2016). If we could gather each of the viable decisions at each stage of the research process, then we would have the multiverse. Such a *multiverse analysis* was first conceived of by Steegen et al. (2016) who re-analyzed a published work for illustrative purposes. In doing so, they illustrated that for each decision of the original authors, alternative and justifiable specifications existed that affected the authors' conclusions. Multiverse projects have exemplarily illustrated that decisions regarding (1) data collection/sources permeate into variability regarding the actual data analysis, and the resulting inferences (Harder, 2020), and (2) data preparation can drastically affect the reliability of measures (Parsons, 2022), and data analysis per se can, of course, starkly affect the robustness of inferences to be drawn from a research project (e.g., Gruda et al., 2022; Modecki et al., 2020; Stern et al., 2019).

We reviewed these various projects and multiverse approach to highlight their usefulness to nascent and experienced cobblers alike. What these tools and projects allow is for better understanding of the boundaries of a finding; and all findings have boundaries. In terms of incentivizing cobblers to use these tools we offer three benefits or suggestions for how and why they should embrace the variability. First, cobbling can be a lonely profession so we encourage collaboration. Replication efforts when done with several independent studies create a significantly larger contribution than a single replication. Although we contend that every replication attempt can be valuable, reviewers and editors generally need something more than, "I looked for the same effect as so-and-so and I could (or couldn't) find it." However, across multiple attempts and trials we begin to understand the boundaries and robustness of a finding. We discover the contexts and populations where the effect is strongest or weakest, present or absent, linear or curvilinear, etc., and we can begin to hypothesize and study what might be causing the effect variability. This makes for a much stronger contribution and there is ample evidence that these types of replication efforts are routinely published in the form of meta-analyses.

Meta-analyses are routinely published in top PHRM and I/OP journals. They are some of the most highly cited works in those journals, and some even discuss meta-analyses as (or, combined with) replication efforts (e.g., Carter & McCullough, 2018; O'Donnell et al., 2021; Schmidt, 1992). However, large-scale replication efforts, such as those conducted by Many Labs, have additional benefits beyond meta-analysis. For example, they can be applied to multivariate findings while meta-analysis is almost exclusively geared toward bivariate results.[12] In addition, meta-analysts are beholden to the preferences of the primary data researchers that conducted the studies while large-scale replications allow researchers to a priori design studies that test the various boundary conditions and moderators of a finding. Lastly, large-scale replications are proactive and do not need to wait for a literature to mature enough to meta-analyze. To be clear, meta-analysis is a highly valuable tool – especially within fields where the norm of secrecy is strong and access to raw data is limited. We simply wish to note that showing the robustness of an effect and its boundary conditions is not unheard of PHRM and I/OP research, and it is clear that PHRM/I/OP reviewers and editors value (and publish) these types of contributions, as do fellow PHRM/I/OP researchers that value (and cite) such contributions.

Our second suggestion to best embrace the variability is for cordwainers to begin employing multiverse analysis in their theoretical model tests. We have described the advantages to science that multiverse brings, so let us turn to the advantages for the scientists themselves. Reviewers will have more faith in the robustness of a finding when authors can show that it is not an artifact of the specific forking path they chose. In our experience, many manuscripts are rejected or put through many rounds of revision based on reviewer perception about the robustness of results. If that can be largely addressed at the outset of the review process, reviewers can focus more on those currently neglected areas, such as practical implications.

Our final suggestion is that cobblers need to work closely with cordwainers. Even if reporting standards were greatly improved and more open science practices were adopted, there will likely still be ambiguities in what was reported in the article to replicated and what actually occurred during the research process. For example, the original study may indicate that they removed outliers but not report whether it was based on some rule of thumb (e.g., ±3 standard deviations), or some multivariate statistic (e.g., Mahalanobis distances). Further, replication efforts that show the robustness and boundaries of an effect increase the citations to the original work. Ideally, the replication efforts allow for a more nuanced understanding of the effect and that the replication results largely align with the original findings. So what if the replication effort shows generally weaker results than the original effort? Our answer is it is a foregone conclusion that a series of replications will find different effects from each other and the original work and some of these replication efforts are bound to yield weaker effects than the original study. This is to be expected so it should not be feared. It does not invalidate the original finding. It simply shows that for some conditions, contexts, populations, measures, analytic approaches, etc., the effect is weaker. As such, there's no reason for cordwainers to avoid or stymy a replication effort by a group of cobblers. Rather, they should actively solicit and collaborate with cobblers. Regardless of what the replication effort yields, it highlights the original work and the collaboration.

An added benefit to embrace the variability through the use of large-scale replications and multiverse analysis is that we can have more confidence and understanding of the phenomenon when we communicate it to others. The one place that most PHRM and I/OP researchers routinely disseminate research to practitioners is the classroom. Those of us employed by colleges and universities as well as those consultants and practitioners that routinely teach executives and other practitioners tend to teach similar topics to what we research. Us understanding a phenomenon better will not only increase our confidence in its robustness, it will also make us better at communicating it and presenting it in a way that a student or HR practitioner can have more faith.

Need for Openness

If one wants to implement Merton's norm of communality, one is automatically a proponent of open science in today's world. Presenting an integrated definition of open science, Vicente-Saez and Martinez-Fuentes (2018) focused on four *differentias* to define open science as "transparent and accessible knowledge that is shared and developed through collaborative network" (p. 434). Fuentes et al. (2022, p. 3) suggested understanding open science as a process instead of a product by defining it as "the process of increasing transparency, openness, and data sharing as well as ensuring replicability and reproducibility within the context of the production and dissemination of scientific knowledge" (Crüwell et al., 2019). Beginning in 2023, US National Aeronautics and Space Administration (NASA) invests $20 million per year to advance open science in what it called the Transform to Open Science (TOPS) mission to transform agencies, organizations, and communities to an inclusive culture of open science (Gentemann, 2023). At the same time, research funding agencies have started to demand open science measures to be included in funded research (e.g., data management plans, preregistrations, open data; e.g., Council of the EU and the European Council, 2021; National Science Foundation (NSF), 2016; Swiss Academies of Arts and Sciences, 2021). Also, several psychology journals have started to adopt open science practices and actively reward them with so-called open science badges (Fuentes et al., 2022; Kidwell et al., 2016).

Certain ingredients have become somewhat synonyms of open science so that we will now turn to discussing the most dominant ones, as of today: (1) preregistration, (2) registered report, (3) open materials, data, and code, (4) OA, and (5) platforms to engage in open science. In light of our criticism of the peer-review system as a quality control mechanism that itself essentially never had to stand the test of the scientific method, we first have to state that more empirical work researching the efficacy of open science practices is needed. While there are empirical investigations into the effects, and efficacy of preregistration, registered report, and open data (e.g., Scheel et al., 2021; Soderberg et al., 2021; Toth et al., 2021), it is clear that more science on the way we actually do science, and how to do science better, is surely needed. Yet, we contend that all these measures surely do not make science worse than it is now – that surely is a low bar to pass, but an important one, nonetheless, given the current state of science.

Preregistration

Perhaps the most widely known open science practice is preregistration (e.g., Hardwicke & Wagenmakers, 2023; Simmons et al., 2021a, 2021b). Specifically, preregistration "typically involves specifying, in a time-stamped document, (1) the research question or hypothesis under study, (2) the relevant independent variables, (3) the relevant-dependent variables (and how they will be combined and scored), (4) any relevant control variables (and how they will be combined and scored), (5) how sample size will be determined, (6) the rules for deciding which observations will be excluded from the analyses, and (7) the precise specification of the key analysis typically involves pre-specifying" (Simmons et al., 2021b, p. 154). The most relevant aspect here is that researchers specify these steps of their research project *before* they actually start working on it (e.g., collecting data). As such, preregistration is considered to be an instrument to think more carefully, and thoroughly about one's research project beforehand, and thereby limit one's researcher degrees of freedom as well as potential accusations of engaging in QRP, such as *p*-hacking.

Oftentimes, preregistration is met with criticism in that it allegedly (1) prevents researchers from data exploration, (2) is too onerous, (3) is bad for scientific culture, and (4) does not help with the actual betterment of science (e.g., Pham & Oh, 2021a, 2021b; Simmons et al., 2021b). First, although often stated otherwise, preregistration does not prevent researchers from engaging in exploratory research – it merely sets boundaries in that researchers now should make explicitly clear, which results stem from a confirmatory approach, and which stem from an exploratory one. Second, a preregistration certainly adds to the researchers' to-do list in that they have to, ideally, address, and specify as many steps of the respective research project's life cycle in advance as possible. Yet, we argue that one would ideally have a good grasp of a research project before one begins it (e.g., overview of *all* relevant data to be collected), in the first place – otherwise, one seems to be made up for (unwanted) surprises along the way (e.g., "snap, I forgot that you cannot analyze the data in this way – what now?"). Third, some have also argued that making preregistrations the new default of planning, and managing a research project might create a culture of distrust in science. Yet, we would argue that quite the contrary holds true – if we actually see for ourselves that the results of a research project are indeed the product of an ideas conceived before the project began, we would consider this evidence to be more trustworthy than from other, non-preregistered works. Finally, some argue that preregistration will not help with the deeply engrained issues of science in that it only is a *pseudo-improvement* as a study's flaws would be typically caught during the peer-review process – for the manifold reasons we outlined earlier in this regard, we starkly disagree.

"But are there actual effects of preregistration, and not just seemingly-convincing, out-of-the-blue arguments?," you might ask. Focusing on effect sizes, Schäfer and Schwarz (2019) compared effects from published preregistered studies with non-preregistered ones. They found a rather drastic difference in that effects from the former were essentially half the size (median $r = .16$) than the ones from the latter (median $r = .36$). Furthermore, Toth et al. (2021) compared published preregistered samples with non-preregistered ones and found that the former were characterized by more transparent reporting, and also more rigorous reporting of study methods and analyses. Against this, and the background of interviews with researchers who had not previously preregistered their research, Toth et al. (2021) provided stakeholders in PHRM and I/OP research (e.g., researchers, graduate trainers, reviewers, practitioners, and editors) with actionable steps to implement preregistration.

Despite the obvious advantages of preregistration, it has not necessarily been adopted all too widely – rather, there are stark differences across disciplines. For example, Simmons et al. (2021b) compared adoption rates of preregistration across the journals *Psychological Science*, *Journal of Experimental Psychology: General*, *Journal of Consumer Research*, and *Journal of Consumer Psychology*. Whereas almost half the articles published in *Psychological Science* contained a preregistered study that was only the case for roughly 7% of the articles in *Journal of Consumer Psychology*. From our personal experience as readers of PHRM research, we contend that the prevalence of preregistered studies leaves room for improvement.

Registered Report

While preregistration certainly allows for an overall improvement of the research process, we would argue that a drawback lies in the additional demands placed on the reviewers. For example, think of a typical manuscript that you have to wrap you head around – if it is preregistered, you also need to check the preregistration, and compare whether there were any unreported deviations. Here, an arguably superior solution comes in the form of the registered report. This specific submission/publishing format involves two stages of peer review: At stage one, authors submit essentially the first half of a classical paper (i.e., introduction, theoretical background, hypotheses, as well as planned methods) to a journal for review. Upon in-principle approval, the research project can be undertaken in that it can be carried out according to the plan presented at stage one. Once all the data are collected, and the full manuscript is ready, it can be submitted as stage two report for peer review (e.g., Grand et al., 2018; Nosek & Lakens, 2014; Nosek et al., 2015). In other words, "registered reports require peer review of the research, and acceptance by the journal, before data are collected and analyzed – and thus before results are reported – thereby shifting the focus of review away from conclusions and onto the proposed methods and underlying theory" (Higgs & Gelman, 2021, p. 978). Just as preregistrations, also registered reports were met with criticism, in that it (1) limits the opportunity for discovery, (2) unnecessarily promotes null findings, (3) puts more demands on authors and reviewers, (4) is not suitable for all types of research, and (5) cannot actually better scientific communication (Grand et al., 2018). First, more or less for the same reasons that we mentioned with regard to preregistrations, we disagree with the contention that registered reports hamper creativity, and novelty. Much to the contrary, providing a sound rationale as to why, and how a research project should be conducted before the actual results are in, could be considered a license for creativity, given that the weight lies on the process of research and not merely the results. Second, as we have already outlined, we consider null findings that one arrived at based on a prudent research design very informative (e.g., Dienes, 2014; Ioannidis, 2006; Landis et al., 2014). Third, as authors, and reviewers who have spent a greater amount of resources with bad manuscripts than with good ones, we do not consider registered reports to put more demands on authors and reviewers. As a matter of fact, dissecting a classical paper into sub-components makes the evaluation of each easier and allows for more rigor. Fourth, while registered reports were initially indeed conceived for empirical confirmatory analyses (Wagenmakers et al., 2012), we contend that this publishing format can be readily adapted to a myriad of scientific methodologies. Finally, while we agree that registered reports alone do not render the panacea for all issues identified in the current scientific system, we do not consider this *all-or-nothing* argument helpful. To put this argument in a different context, one might ask whether a single study presenting some incremental insight into to some mechanism should then be allowed to get published, if it did not present a new theoretical model, unequivocal empirical proof for it, and so on.

Investigating the effects of registered reports regarding the credibility of scientific findings, Scheel et al. (2021) compared a random set of classical hypothesis-testing publications with a random set of hypothesis-testing registered reports. Intriguingly, while 96% of the first hypotheses in the classic articles were *confirmed* against statistically significant results, this was only true in half the cases for the registered reports. Yet another recent meta-scientific research project investigated the viability of registered reports (Soderberg et al., 2021; *cf.* Higgs & Gelman,

2021). Specifically, 353 researchers peer-reviewed a pair of papers from a set of either classic publications or registered reports and provided their judgments on a list of fourteen criteria. Intriguingly, the registered reports outperformed the classic publications on a wide set of criteria, such as novelty, creativity, sizeable improvements in rigor of methodology, analysis, and overall paper quality.

Registered reports have become more and more common over the last years – for example, the journals *Human Resource Management Journal*, *International Journal of Selection and Assessment*, and *Leadership Quarterly* already actively invite such formats of submission (see also Timming et al., 2021). Again, we have barely seen a rise of registered reports in PHRM and I/OP research, but we encourage scholars to pick up the pace.

Open Materials, Data, and Code

As we have illustrated investigating the lack of open materials, data, and code, opening up this vital black box of every research project is essential for a more reproducible, and robust science (e.g., Crüwell et al., 2019; Gewin, 2016; Laitin et al., 2021). Only if the study materials (e.g., instructions, stimuli, blank questionnaires, treatment manuals, interview protocols, and/or details of procedures) and collected data as well as respective analysis code are made openly available, can future research build on top of it properly.

Perhaps most prominently, the practice of sharing data openly has been met with criticism, such as (1) not being suitable for all forms of data (e.g., qualitative), (2) concerns about sensitive data, and (3) concerns about intellectual property rights (e.g., Houtkoop et al., 2018; Martone et al., 2018; Prosser et al., 2022). First, while we consider it certainly true that there should be no one-size-fits-all approach to demanding open data by journals, there should, at the very least, be an ongoing inquiry as to what, for example, qualitative data is, and how to make it open. Second, we agree that protecting participants' confidentiality – if not agreed upon otherwise – must be sacrosanct to any researcher collecting data in the social sciences. Yet, there are promising data analytic tools to anonymize, synthesize, and artifice data sets containing potential sensitive information that should be made use of in the process of sharing data (e.g., Grund et al., 2022; Slavković & Seeman, 2023; Wicherts et al., 2022). Finally, there may also be good reasons as to why certain data is subject to intellectual property rights (e.g., copyright and patent) – yet, from our experience, we would consider this criticism to not be particularly relevant in PHRM.

Regarding the effects of open data, we have already discussed the reproducibility endeavors Artner et al. (2021) undertook (see also Hardwicke et al., 2018; Obels et al., 2020). In short, if data were not shared, such investigations into a scientific findings' reproducibility would simply not be possible. In turn, we would, once again, not know how robust a finding is.[13] In addition, Piwowar et al. (2007) traced the citation history of medical publications only to find that the ones that shared their data received a staggering 85% of the aggregate citations. In a similar vein, Christensen et al. (2019) provided results from a natural experiment comparing articles from journals that actively demand open data with the ones that do not. They concluded that "authors who share data may be rewarded eventually with additional scholarly citations" (p. 1). Here, it is important to stress again that one should make sure that one's analysis code is amended with a version control feature to allow future analysts run the code *as-if* it were the original run date (for a solution for package reproducibility in R, see Daniel et al., 2022).

Already in 1983, Ceci and Waker called for a mandate to share all research data openly, and more and more journals, such as *American Economic Review*, *Social Psychological Bulletin*, and *Science*, now actually require open data, or a justification as to why sharing it is not possible. Yet, as of now, we contend that sharing ones' materials, data, and code is far from being the norm in science in general, and in PHRM specifically – specifically, we do not know of any PHRM journal that requires its authors to share their data. Importantly, more and more powerful political have started to stress the importance of open data and demanded change. For example, the G7 nations committed to "promote the efficient processing and sharing of research data as openly as possible and as securely as necessary across the G7 and beyond, by improving the availability, sustainability, usability and interoperability of research data, technologies, infrastructure and services" (Council of the EU and the European Council, 2021, p. 1).

Open Access

Given that most of our research is generally funded by public money (e.g., tax payer money funding the university funding the researcher, and tax payer money funding the national science funding agency funding the researcher), the public should have access to the results of our work. As such, we consider the current status quo of private publishers – essentially as providers of the manuscript handling software, organizers of copy-editing and typesetting, and providers of a PDF – being the final gatekeepers of scholarly work not even anywhere close to ideal. As such, OA to public knowledge must be achieved, and there are multiple OA publishing formats available now (e.g., Laakso & Björk, 2022; STM, 2021; Wallace & Ollivere, 2022). Yet, it stands to reason whether letting the producers of knowledge pay up-front for a publisher's work is much better than letting the consumers of knowledge pay upon-consumption, as typically is the case now. In light of the Mertonian norms, we still would have publishers as administrators of scientific communication, while governing ourselves essentially should be the goal. So, we should consider redirecting the vast amounts of money from the publishers – even under an OA agreement – to a more modern, accessible, and public form of scholarly communication (Brembs et al., 2021).

Platforms to Achieve Openness

We briefly review three particular open science platforms that have grown in popularity over the last years, and that each bring certain advantages to the table for people interested in opening up their science. First, there is AsPredicted (https://www.aspredicted.org/; Simonsohn et al., 2022), a non-profit online platform funded by the

Wharton School of the University of Pennsylvania. The sole focus of AsPredicted is to allow researchers to comfortably and efficiently preregister their studies, and allow others to access those preregistrations. A preregistration can be compiled by answering nine questions about one's research design and analyses (e.g., "What's the main question being asked or hypothesis being tested in this study?"). Upon completion of the preregistration, a time-stamped PDF document is created that can be either kept privately or made publicly, if others should be able to access it. That AsPredicted offers a very straightforward solution for preregistering one's studies can also be seen in its user numbers – in 2020, roughly 1,500 preregistrations were submitted every month (Simmons et al., 2021b).

Second, there is the OSF (Center for Open Science, 2023a), another non-profit online platform that is funded by a variety of philanthropic foundations, and trusts, such Arnold Ventures, or John Templeton Foundation. Essentially, the OSF can be considered the *jack of all trades* device for researchers that want to engage in open science – it allows storing preregistrations, materials, data, code, and even preprints in a time-stamped fashion. Furthermore, the OSF provides users with digital object identifiers (DOIs) that, exemplarily, allow for (1) crediting researchers as authors of a preregistrations, data, and the like, (2) licenses to be posted that clarify how data shared on the OSF can be reused, and (3) metadata descriptions (e.g., data dictionaries; Buchanan et al., 2021; Soderberg, 2018).

Finally, there is ResearchEquals (https://www.researchequals.com/; Liberate Science GmbH, 2023), yet another non-profit online platform that is funded by the Shuttleworth Foundation, and the Mozilla Foundation. Whereas the platforms we already discussed focus on the betterment of science within the current scholarly communication system, ResearchEquals wants to go beyond that by allowing for an entirely modular way of doing, and communicating science (Hartgerink, 2019; Hartgerink & van Zelst, 2018). Modular means that the typical scientific life cycle is broken down into respective research modules (e.g., theory, data, and analysis), each of which can be published individually on ResearchEquals, equipped with a respective DOI. The resulting modules can then be accessed and linked by anyone on the platform which ideally allows for a quick dissemination and usage of scientific findings. ResearchEquals also aims for providing researchers with more wholesome metrics (*cf.* impact factor, and number of citations) in that it allows for the usage of social network analytics – for example, relevant metrics of a researcher in such a system could be the number of modules created, the number of modules linked, the number of offspring modules, and so on.

(Individual) Benefits to Engaging in Open Science Practices

Many of these open science practices will be known to the reader or have otherwise been discussed elsewhere in the literature, so simply repeating their value in moving us closer to Mertonian norms of science is wasted ink. As such, let us focus on what is in it for the typical PHRM and I/OP researcher. First, if publication is the coin of the realm, then certain open science practices will facilitate more coins in one's pocket (i.e., CV). Take results-blind review as an example. The typical process is to derive a theoretical model, design a study, conduct the study, analyze and interpret the data, and discuss theoretical implications and certainly practical ones as well. The hope is that one's labor in this research effort is rewarded with publication. That is a very risky hope! What if there was some confound that was missed by the researcher but caught by the reviewers? What if, as Larry Williams once said, "the data don't share your enthusiasm," and the researcher is left with a stack of unsupported hypotheses? What if one or multiple reviewers is biased against the work for reasons other than rigor and relevance? The end result is an awful lot of unpaid labor. Alternatively, a result-blind submission only contains the theoretical framework and study design before being submitted to a journal. The overlooked confound is identified and corrected before the study is carried out. The degree of statistical support is not considered as it is not even available. In addition, the author will take more care in their theorizing and study planning as there are no results to point that can paint over weak argumentation and methodology. And, even if one or both reviewers' biases lead to a rejection and no coin is paid out, it was at least less unpaid labor.

Consider also study preregistration. Some have viewed it as a straitjacket that locks a researcher into a set of decisions that cannot be altered despite changing circumstances during the conducting of the study. However, this simply is not the case (see Hardwicke & Wagenmakers, 2023; Nosek et al., 2018; Simmons et al., 2021b). Preregistrations routinely submit changes and amendments throughout the research process as circumstances change. The only difference between a preregistered study and the status quo is that the changes are documented and justified. This can be particularly helpful during the review process as reviewers and editors can see the full process, which provides greater faith that the findings reported are accurate and not a function of *p*-hacking, or any other questionable research practices.

Beyond highlighting the benefits to the researcher and by extension the editors and reviewers that can better gatekeep their respective journals, let us also consider how open science practices benefit the publisher. The explosion of content coupled with huge profit margins means that publishers are truly living their best lives right now, and likely wish to keep the status quo. However, that is short-sighted. Using the language of the Boston Consulting Group, academic publishing is a *cash cow*. The top publishers hold a huge market share and the product generates far more cash than it consumes. Yet, there is no guarantee that this model that subsists largely on per article sales for practitioners and library subscriptions for researchers can continue to thrive. Take, for example, the music and movie industry. Throughout the 2000s, top record companies and studios fought a losing battle against filesharing and piracy. Ultimately, what helped turn these industries around was a change in strategy that included fairer pricing structures built around usage and features (e.g., Spotify, and MoviePass), and in the case of cinema, there was a shift in content to media that are purported to be far superior on the silver screen than on a computer monitor (e.g., superhero movies). In the case of the music industry, they too changed the business from using a tour to promote an album to using an album to promote a tour. Although PHRM researchers may not be going on tour and our research may not pack the theaters, if we continue to make our research overly restrictive and expensive, people will find alternative means to acquire it or worse yet, ignore it. Either case will lead to a cash cow becoming a dog (i.e., a product that at best breaks even and ties up lots of resources in the meantime).

Need for Relevance

We documented a disconnect between research and practice. How we reconnect with practice is threefold. First, nobody will pay attention to advice from someone they do not trust. There is a healthy skepticism and lack of trust from practitioners, and it is not entirely undeserved. Questionable research practices, publication bias, outcome reporting bias, and various other efforts to rose-tint the literature have challenged the veracity and degree of certitude we have in our own work. What that might seem from the outside looking in is that we do not conduct trustworthy research. PHRM practitioners cannot tell (nor can PHRM researchers in most cases) what is built upon the bedrock of good science, and what is built upon the sand of data manipulation and post hoc explanations presented as a priori predictions. As such, they are well within their right to dismiss the entirety of PHRM research as hopelessly tainted; and frankly it is difficult to blame them for this perspective. Forgive the vulgar expression, but if you mix 10 grams of manure into 990 grams of candy, you now have a kilogram of manure. We must end the rampant questionable research practices and other biasing factors from our literature to have any hope of regaining trust from practitioners.

Second and one we will discuss in more detail in the subsequent section is the need to work with practitioners to do more research that directly informs their work. There are PHRM-relevant ideas and practices occurring in businesses around the world that PHRM researchers could and should incorporate into their research and the types of research questions they ask. For example, PHRM has a rich history of those graduating with PhDs from I/OP psychology programs and entering practice. These are well-trained PHRM researchers that understand practitioner needs and interact with them daily. Why not co-create knowledge with these individuals? We do not mean simply ask them for access to their organizations for data collection. Rather, it should be a genuine collaboration. Not only will this add legitimacy to the research from practitioners that see, for example, a people analytics publication co-authored by a data scientist at a major tech company, the practitioner can help ground the research into real-world application.

Third, we need to do more experiments and randomized control trials. Practitioners care little for correlation – they want causality. We have a jungle of related constructs in PHRM research and everything relates to everything else (relatedly, see Meehl, 1990a, 1990b; Orben & Lakens, 2020). For some years, we have watched the shift away from designs that allow causal claims in PHRM research under the auspices of external validity. However, if this was the only reason why we moved away from the laboratory, then why aren't we fully embracing the econometric movement toward causality through other means? Why don't we see more instruments and two-stage least squares analysis or difference-in-differences in PHRM journals? Why is almost every limitations section a series of caveats about not the inability to make causal claims due to the study design and lack of foresight? Our recommendation is that if conducting research under the hypothetico-deductive model, then any non-experimental research should begin its methodology section by describing why the PHRM researcher did not or were not able to conduct a true experiment. Even if only a brief statement about the infeasibility or ethical barrier, it would at least focus readers and future PHRM researchers to always start with the gold standard of a RCT before moving onto correlational designs.

Fourth, having a trustworthy product that is co-created with practitioners is all well and good, but it is not enough to drive PHRM research to relevance in a meaningful way. Having a good product does not guarantee sales. We must get better at controlling the dissemination process instead of idly hoping that it finds its way into a practitioner's hands. As PHRM scientists we need to decide what responsibility we have in ensuring that our work is properly interpreted. If we see this as outside of our responsibilities, then we de facto leave dissemination in the hands of those that can monetize it and we must live with the consequences. We lose the right to object to the latest TED talk iconoclast that offers ungrounded and grossly simplistic advice supported with cherry-picked examples and pseudoscience. We cannot bemoan that type indicator personality test whose popularity belies its validity. Likewise, the various blogs, listicles, and unscrupulous consultancies that offer magic (i.e., imaginary) bullets to all practitioner problems must be if not embraced, at least accepted as the cost of keeping our hands clean from the mud and muck of actual application. Most importantly, we cannot blame the practitioner for not incorporating our findings into their organizations. If we make zero effort to sell them, then we cannot object to them not buying it.

The recommendation is obvious – control the narrative. The aforementioned quote by Thomas S. Kuhn (1996) is apt here as well. If we are going to discount or dismiss the current paradigm of knowledge dissemination, then we need to replace it with something else. We know our research better than anyone else in the world. For every bombastic and opportunistic author promising, "Five simple tricks to achieve [insert hot PHRM topic of the day]," we should be right there to clarify, contextualize, and if necessary, publicly refute the misapplication and overextension of our work. That is the reactive component of this recommendation. The proactive component is that nature abhors a vacuum almost as much as a news cycle does. If we truly believe we have made a significant contribution to practice, then it is on us to make that known to practitioners. LinkedIn classrooms, personal blogs, media contacts, community outreach, etc. should be a part of what we do, and it is not a selfish act to promote our research. For example, four of the five most popular TED talks are PHRM topics (i.e., body language during interviews (Cuddy), leadership (Sinek), vulnerability (Brown), and procrastination (Urban)). Of these, one is an academic (Cuddy). Whether you discount power posing or not, that TED talk has been watched more than 67 million times as of January 2023. Whether one believes "starting with why" is a genius insight or trite pablum, one cannot discount 61 million views as having no practical impact. The bottom line is that people want our research; so let's give it to them free of distortion and oversimplification.

Need for Inclusiveness

PHRM research is a vast field operating at multiple levels of analysis and across a wide variety of constructs, methods, and statistical approaches. However, there are two areas where PHRM research is (overly) homogenous. The first is homogeneity of researchers, and the second is homogeneity of participants. For the former, we highlighted in the above section the need for greater input from practitioners, but this can be extended to greater collaboration on the research itself. Part of regaining our relevance to practitioners is to acknowledge that they can be more than study participants. A more diverse group of researchers that includes those outside of academia as collaborators and co-authors allows for more actionable and practical research and it helps to signal to practitioners that knowledge creation is not a one-way street. When a reader sees "one of their own" as a co-author, they may perceive that the study is more likely to be aligned with their specific PHRM needs.

It is not just practitioners that are currently underutilized in the research process. PHRM has concentrated to a point that much of the published research derives from Ivy League and Big Ten schools (e.g., the chapter you are reading). Although there are a number of research powerhouses outside of these two conferences that we will not list for fear of leaving out the reader's alma mater or current employer, the Ivy League and Big Ten do make up a disproportionate amount of PHRM research. For example, given the history of PHRM research among universities in the Big Ten Conference, it is not surprising that several PHRM researchers from these schools appeared in the Winter 2022 issue of *Personnel Psychology*[14] or that Big Ten faculty serve as editors at this journal. However, of the 15 articles published in that issue, 9 are authored by one or more Big Ten researchers. Of the six publications not authored by Big Ten researchers, one was published by faculty at an Ivy and three were published by faculty at private institutions in the US state of Texas (Texas Christian University, Rice University), leaving only two papers not published with at least one author from the Midwestern USA. Similarly, four of the five associate editors were either Big Ten or Ivy League faculty or graduates. Collectively, research production has been dominated by a small group of universities, and gatekeepers (i.e., reviewers, and editors) tend to come from these same universities.

This is not an indictment of those researchers, reviewers, and editors from the Big Ten and Ivy League. Those at these schools with such storied traditions have generated some of the most robust and relevant PHRM research to date. The issue is that through no intentionality we are seeing an attraction–selection–attrition process where diversity of thought and ideas is narrowing as those researchers at colleges and departments that have traditionally succeeded in elite PHRM journals move onto these journals' editorial boards and editorships, and naturally favor research topics and methods they are familiar with and that they employ in their own research. We wish to note that the diminished diversity of thought is at the field level and not the individual level. There is no reason to suspect that any given research effort originating in either the Big Ten or Ivy League is less innovative, creative, or relevant than a research effort generated outside of these conferences.

Yet, this overrepresentation still creates a problem. Consistent with norms theory, we tend to behave in ways shaped by the descriptive norms of what we see, hear, and read. Even if not trained or employed at an Ivy League or Big Ten institution, a researcher still wants to publish in the same journals that those two conferences dominate. The topics they choose to study and how they go about conducting the research will be modeled after past research in the elite journals. If that research tends to share a common perspective and use a common set of tools to conduct research, then even research conducted outside of the two conferences will still be similar to research conducted within them.

Turning to the homogeneity of participants, we need more research outside of WEIRD nations. This is not just about taking concepts and theories developed in WEIRD cultures by researchers primarily living in WEIRD nations. That work is certainly important and PHRM and I/OP researchers should continue to strive to, for example, increase the measurement invariance of their instruments. However, PHRM and I/OP researchers should also seek out those issues that might be unique to those cultures. The Rich in WEIRD means that most of our research is based on people living in affluent societies. As such, we have relatively little insight into how individuals and organizations conduct business in an unreliable infrastructure, and lead a workforce living well below the global poverty line, all while navigating potentially high levels of corruption. For example, WEIRD countries do go to war just like non-WEIRD countries, but the war tends to be fought at arm's length distance. As such, we really don't know what work looks like for a non-combatant in a war zone? At the time of this writing, there is an ongoing war caused by Russia's invasion of Ukraine. People in Kyiv are still going to work. How does one navigate hiring of applicants or leading a change initiative with a full-scale war raging in the background? Or, when the smog is so bad in Delhi that workers can barely breathe, how do you still motivate them? These are extreme contexts for sure, but they are not as uncommon as those residing in WEIRD countries may believe.

Our recommendations for becoming a more inclusive science are rather simple. First, for the individual researcher, we hope that the benefits of a broader and more diverse PHRM and I/OP literature take little convincing. The research will become more interesting and will appeal to a wider cross-section of those we serve. Also, from a purely selfish standpoint, if everyone is doing similar types of research on similar types of topics, it can be very difficult to standout. The concept of "contribution" that is routinely levied against rejected manuscripts is more difficult because one of the most common ways to demonstrate a contribution to the literature is changing what we know or what we thought we knew. If we continue to rehash the same questions, using the same methods, applied to the same data sources, then we will get the same answers. It is a scientific equivalent of the drunk man looking for his keys under the streetlight.[15]

If it can be taken at face value that the field would benefit from more diversity of thought in terms of the research and researchers, then it is not the desire for homogeneity that has created the current state. Rather, it is just a natural diversity entropy that occurs when we select co-authors of similar backgrounds and approaches. Our second suggestion for the researcher is the use of goal setting. If a researcher generally works on five projects a year, can one of those projects benefit from having a practitioner involved in more than a study participant capacity? Especially until academic-practitioner collaborations become more common, there is value in speaking with the authors on these teams about strategies of how research teams that consist of more than just academics work to bring out the best of both.

For editors, we ask that they evaluate where the research published in their respective journals derives and consider ways to diversify research without sacrificing quality. Only by knowing the current state can we gauge the distance to the desired state. Key questions might include what percentage of submissions are from scholars working in non-WEIRD contexts, and what percentage of these scholar's manuscripts are published. If the success rate is markedly lower than their WEIRD counterparts, then is the differential rate attributable to non-WEIRD submissions being lower in rigor and relevance or is it that they just don't look the same as WEIRD submissions? Are there steps that can be employed that might expand the representation and diversity in the journal with grammar and style coaching, assistance with alternative statistical approaches, reviewer training, and/or small grant funding for the conducting of additional studies requested by reviewers. Poorly described or framed research is not necessarily bad research, and and for those that do not have the luxury of being trained and surrounded by leading scholars, some degree of additional effort to better present and frame a rigorous and relevant contribution should be considered.

Another suggestion for editors is the use of special issues and calls for papers. These are effective means to draw attention and incentivize the types of research and researchers that may be underrepresented. Likewise, editorial boards at top PHRM and I/OP journals have greatly expanded in recent years in order to keep pace with the greatly expanded number of PHRM and I/OP submissions. As these boards continue to grow, more deliberate efforts can be made to attract reviewers from diverse, non-WEIRD (or at least, non-Ivy, and non-Big Ten) backgrounds. The incentive for editors to take this tact is that it makes for a more interesting journal which will broaden the readership. Further, PHRM and I/OP researchers tend to read where they publish. Having a more diverse set of authors could draw in a more diverse readership especially in untapped and underserved markets.

Importantly, journals in their role as gatekeepers need to adopt and incentivize these open science practices for them to uncover their full beneficial potential (please avail yourself to the Center for Open Science, 2023b as it holds complete lists of journals that encourage preregistration, registered reports, and so on; see also Torka et al., 2023). The Center for Open Science also formulated the TOP guidelines that are becoming the most widely used tool for implementing open science practices in academic journals (Nosek et al., 2015). The TOP guidelines subsume eight modular standards, each with three levels of respective – as such, journals can adopt different levels of these standards to allow for a greater transparency in scientific communication (see Table 2). Importantly, already more than 5,000 signatories, including the APA, have adopted the guidelines.

Table 2. Transparency and Openness Promotion Guidelines.

Standard	Not Implemented	Level I	Level II	Level III
Citation Standards	No mention of data citation	Journal describes citation of data in guidelines to authors with clear rules and examples	Article provides appropriate citation for data and materials used consistent with journal's author guidelines	Article is not published until providing appropriate citation for data and materials following journal's author guidelines
Data Transparency	Journal encourages data sharing or says nothing	Article states whether data is available, and, if so, where to access them	Data must be posted to a trusted repository. Exceptions must be identified at article submission	Data must be posted to a trusted repository, and reported analyses will be reproduced independently prior to publication
Analytic Methods (Code) Transparency	Journal encourages code sharing or says nothing	Article states whether code is available, and, if so, where to access it	Code must be posted to a trusted repository. Exceptions must be identified at article submission	Code must be posted to a trusted repository, and reported analyses will be reproduced independently prior to publication
Research Materials Transparency	Journal encourages materials sharing, or says nothing	Article states whether materials are available, and, if so, where to access them	Materials must be posted to a trusted repository. Exceptions must be identified at article submission	Materials must be posted to a trusted repository, and reported analyses will be reproduced independently prior to publication
Design and Analysis Transparency	Journal encourages design and analysis transparency or says nothing	Journal articulates design transparency standards	Journal requires adherence to design transparency standards for review and publication	Journal requires and enforces adherence to design transparency standards for review and publication
Study Preregistration	Journal says nothing	Article states whether preregistration of study exists, and, if so, where to access it	Article states whether preregistration of study exists, and, if so, allows journal access during peer review for verification	Journal requires preregistration of studies and provides link and badge in article to meeting requirements
Analysis Plan Preregistration	Journal says nothing	Article states whether preregistration of study exists, and, if so, where to access it	Article states whether preregistration with analysis plan exists, and, if so, allows journal access during peer review for verification	Journal requires preregistration of studies with analysis plans and provides link and badge in article to meeting requirements

Note. For each standard, level 0 illustrates the respective standard as not fulfilled, whereas levels 1 to 3 represent increasingly stringent requirements. (Reprinted from *TOP guidelines*, by Center for Open Science, 2023, https://osf.io/2cz65. Reprinted under the CC0 1.0 Universal license.)

CONCLUSION

The only people who achieve much are those who want knowledge so badly that they seek it while the conditions are still unfavorable. Favorable conditions never come. (C. S. Lewis, 1949/2001, p. 60)

We began this chapter in part using the distinction in old English between a cordwainer and a cobbler: While the former made new shoes, the latter repaired them. Adapted to producing science instead of shoes, the cordwainers seem to be dominant whereas the cobblers seem to have disappeared. This *fast fashion* approach to science of constantly proposed models and alleged breakthroughs with little to no verification and reproduction have left a form of theoretical pollution in the form of unintended consequences, such as academic navel gazing, questionable research practices, weak methodology, and overreliance on statistical showmanship. The result is that the hallmarks of a healthy science are diminished. PHRM research may be under the weather, but a cure is available. Through a recalibration of how we approach our research, who we actually intend it for, how we verify its robustness it, and how we disseminate it, there is an optimistic prognosis. Just as alternatives to fast fashion will create their own challenges and unintended consequences, we, as a discipline, will ultimately need to become more like cobblers and stick to our lasts!

NOTES

1. For the sake of simplicity, we will refer to injunctive norms put forward by Merton (1942), and extended by Anderson et al. (2010) collectively as the six Mertonian norms, and also consider the descriptive norms of science put forward by Mitroff (1974), and extended by Anderson et al. (2010) collectively as Mitroff's six counter-norms.
2. We stress the word *reported*. As will be discussed, the description of the research life cycle in PHRM is not always an accurate reflection of the actual research life cycle.
3. An example of a strong inference test is Newton's theory of universal gravitation and Einstein's theory of general relativity making contradictory predictions about how gravity affects light. The strong inference test in 1919 tested this prediction during a solar eclipse. When the light of background stars "bent," it supported general relativity, and rejected universal gravitation.
4. Other elite journals that routinely publish I/OP research (e.g., *Personnel Psychology*, *Academy of Management Journal*, and *Journal of Management*) fared equally poorly.
5. Note that the term reproducibility is frequently used to refer to replicability in other scientific disciplines (e.g., biology). However, we see important merits in distinguishing these two constructs: While reproducibility is more or less like cooking another person's recipe explicitly based on his or her cookbook with the same ingredients, and cook ware at hand, replicability is a bit like cooking another person's recipe after having seen him/her cook, having tasted the food, or just having heard him or her talk about his/her cooking.
6. To give you an impression of the major errors willfully included into the manuscripts by Baxt et al. (1998): (1) Presenting a randomized controlled experiment in which the randomization device was *flipping a coin at midnight*, (2) measuring a construct of interest with a scale made up on the spot despite several validate measure being available, (3) figures of the statistical analysis clearly indicate no meaningful effect – yet, in text, this very effect supposedly is strongly statistically significant, and so on.

7. The renowned German Max-Planck-Gesellschaft (2003) defined OA as follows: "By 'open access' to the literature, we mean its free availability on the public internet, permitting any users to read, download, copy, distribute, print, search, or link to the full texts of these articles, crawl them for indexing, pass them as data to software, or use them for any other lawful purpose, without financial, legal, or technical barriers other than those inseparable from gaining access to the internet itself."

8. Guitly as charged, we plead for ourselves.

9. A synonym for chrysalis is pupa, but *Pupa effect* just wouldn't sound so nice, would it?

10. An example of basic research would be a psychologist administering a personality test to a group of students and seeing how well certain traits relate to something like social media usage. Alternatively, an example of "important decisions being made about humans" would be to use those personality test scores test to select candidates for internship or employment opportunities. For the former, there is less chance of the test's unreliability doing harm to others than there is in the latter.

11. As a quick self-check, we might ask ourselves if we had taken the COVID-19 vaccine had its safety and efficacy been researched using the typical methodologies in PHRM and I/OP (relatedly, see G. C. S. Smith & Pell, 2003).

12. Multivariate meta-analytic tests, such as subgroup analysis, meta-regression, and meta-SEM have a number of problematic issues, and almost certainly unmet and untestable assumptions (e.g., multivariate normality) caused by the inability to access the raw data.

13. Note that by *robust* we refer to the very basic requirement of a scientific finding that the same data, and the same analysis script should lead to the same results and conclusions that were presented in the original work.

14. As with the examples above from specific journals, the findings from *Personnel Psychology* are consistent with other PHRM and I/OP journals.

15. For those unfamiliar with the expression, the streetlight effect or drunkard's search is an anecdote/joke of a police officer approaching a drunk man crawling around under a streetlight. The officer asks him what he is doing and the man replies, "looking for my keys." The officer then asks if he dropped them under the streetlight and the drunk man replies, "No, I dropped them in the park but this is where the light is."

REFERENCES

Aczel, B., Szaszi, B., & Holcombe, A. O. (2021). A billion-dollar donation: Estimating the cost of researchers' time spent on peer review. *Research Integrity and Peer Review*, *6*(1), 14. https://doi.org/10.1186/s41073-021-00118-2

Adler, N. J., & Harzing, A.-W. (2009). When knowledge wins: Transcending the sense and nonsense of academic rankings. *Academy of Management Learning & Education*, *8*(1), 72–95. https://doi.org/10.5465/AMLE.2009.37012181

Aguinis, H., & Vandenberg, R. J. (2014). An ounce of prevention is worth a pound of cure: Improving research quality before data collection. *Annual Review of Organizational Psychology and Organizational Behavior*, *1*(1), 569–595. https://doi.org/10.1146/annurev-orgpsych-031413-091231

Aguinis, H., Villamor, I., & Ramani, R. S. (2021). MTurk research: Review and recommendations. *Journal of Management*, *47*(4), 823–837. https://doi.org/10.1177/0149206320969787

Alister, M., Vickers-Jones, R., Sewell, D. K., & Ballard, T. (2021). How do we choose our giants? Perceptions of replicability in psychological science. *Advances in Methods and Practices in Psychological Science*, *4*(2), 1–21. https://doi.org/10.1177/25152459211018199

American Psychological Association. (2017). *Ethical principles of psychologists and code of conduct*. https://www.apa.org; https://www.apa.org/ethics/code

American Psychological Association. (2020). *Publication manual of the American Psychological Association: The official guide to APA style*. American Psychological Association.

Anderson, C. A., Allen, J. J., Plante, C., Quigley-McBride, A., Lovett, A., & Rokkum, J. N. (2019). The MTurkification of social and personality psychology. *Personality and Social Psychology Bulletin*, *45*(6), 842–850. https://doi.org/10.1177/0146167218798821

Anderson, M. S., Martinson, B. C., & De Vries, R. (2007a). Normative dissonance in science: Results from a national survey of U.S. scientists. *Journal of Empirical Research on Human Research Ethics*, *2*(4), 3–14. https://doi.org/10.1525/jer.2007.2.4.3

Anderson, M. S., Ronning, E. A., De Vries, R., & Martinson, B. C. (2007b). The perverse effects of competition on scientists' work and relationships. *Science and Engineering Ethics*, *13*(4), 437–461. https://doi.org/10.1007/s11948-007-9042-5

Anderson, M. S., Ronning, E. A., De Vries, R., & Martinson, B. C. (2010). Extending the Mertonian norms: Scientists' subscription to norms of research. *The Journal of Higher Education*, *81*(3), 366–393. https://doi.org/10.1353/jhe.0.0095

Appelbaum, M., Cooper, H. M., Kline, R. B., Mayo-Wilson, E., Nezu, A. M., & Rao, S. M. (2018). Journal article reporting standards for quantitative research in psychology: The APA Publications and Communications Board task force report. *American Psychologist*, *73*(1), 3–25. https://doi.org/10.1037/amp0000191

Armstrong, J. S., & Hubbard, R. (1991). Does the need for agreement among reviewers inhibit the publication controversial findings? *Behavioral and Brain Sciences*, *14*(1), 136–137. https://doi.org/10.1017/S0140525X00065699

Arnett, J. J. (2008). The neglected 95%: Why American psychology needs to become less American. *American Psychologist*, *63*(7), 602–614. https://doi.org/10.1037/0003-066X.63.7.602

Arnold, H. J., & Feldman, D. C. (1981). Social desirability response bias in self-report choice situations. *Academy of Management Journal*, *24*(2), 377–385. https://doi.org/10.2307/255848

Artner, R., Verliefde, T., Steegen, S., Gomes, S., Traets, F., Tuerlinckx, F., & Vanpaemel, W. (2021). The reproducibility of statistical results in psychological research: An investigation using unpublished raw data. *Psychological Methods*, *26*(5), 527–546. https://doi.org/10.1037/met0000365

Asendorpf, J. B., Conner, M., De Fruyt, F., De Houwer, J., Denissen, J. J. A., Fiedler, K., Fiedler, S., Funder, D. C., Kliegl, R., Nosek, B. A., Perugini, M., Roberts, B. W., Schmitt, M., van Aken, M. A. G., Weber, H., & Wicherts, J. M. (2013). Recommendations for increasing replicability in psychology. *European Journal of Personality*, *27*(2), 108–119. https://doi.org/10.1002/per.1919

Auspurg, K., & Brüderl, J. (2021). Has the credibility of the social sciences been credibly destroyed? Reanalyzing the "many analysts, one data set" project. *Socius: Sociological Research for a Dynamic World*, *7*, 1–14. https://doi.org/10.1177/23780231211024421

Bacharach, S. B. (1989). Organizational theories: Some criteria for evaluation. *The Academy of Management Review*, *14*(4), 496. https://doi.org/10.2307/258555

Bakker, M., van Dijk, A., & Wicherts, J. M. (2012). The rules of the game called psychological science. *Perspectives on Psychological Science*, *7*(6), 543–554. https://doi.org/10.1177/1745691612459060

Banks, G. C., Pollack, J. M., Bochantin, J. E., Kirkman, B. L., Whelpley, C. E., & O'Boyle, E. H. (2016). Management's science-practice gap: A grand challenge for all stakeholders. *Academy of Management Journal*, *59*(6), 2205–2231. https://doi.org/10.5465/amj.2015.0728

Banks, G. C., Woznyj, H. M., & Mansfield, C. A. (2021). Where is "behavior" in organizational behavior? A call for a revolution in leadership research and beyond. *The Leadership Quarterly*, 101581. https://doi.org/10.1016/j.leaqua.2021.101581

Bansal, P., Bertels, S., Ewart, T., MacConnachie, P., & O'Brien, J. (2012). Bridging the research–practice gap. *Academy of Management Perspectives*, *26*(1), 73–92. https://doi.org/10.5465/amp.2011.0140

Barnett, A. G., & Wren, J. D. (2019). Examination of CIs in health and medical journals from 1976 to 2019: An observational study. *BMJ Open*, *9*(11), e032506. https://doi.org/10.1136/bmjopen-2019-032506

Bartunek, J. M. (2007). Academic-practitioner collaboration need not require joint or relevant research: Toward a relational scholarship of integration. *Academy of Management Journal*, *50*(6), 1323–1333. https://doi.org/10.5465/amj.2007.28165912

Bartunek, J. M., & Rynes, S. L. (2010). The construction and contributions of "implications for practice": What's in them and what might they offer? *Academy of Management Learning & Education*, *9*(1), 100–117. https://doi.org/10.5465/amle.9.1.zqr100

Baum, J., & Bromiley, P. (2019). P-hacking in top-tier management journals. *Academy of Management Proceedings*, *2019*(1), 10810. https://doi.org/10.5465/AMBPP.2019.10810abstract

Baxt, W. G., Waeckerle, J. F., Berlin, J. A., & Callaham, M. L. (1998). Who reviews the reviewers? Feasibility of using a fictitious manuscript to evaluate peer reviewer performance. *Annals of Emergency Medicine*, *32*(3), 310–317. https://doi.org/10.1016/S0196-0644(98)70006-X

Bedeian, A. G. (2004). Peer review and the social construction of knowledge in the management discipline. *Academy of Management Learning & Education*, *3*(2), 198–216. https://doi.org/10.5465/amle.2004.13500489

Bem, D. J. (2011). Feeling the future: Experimental evidence for anomalous retroactive influences on cognition and affect. *Journal of Personality and Social Psychology*, *100*(3), 407–425. https://doi.org/10.1037/a0021524

Bem, D. J., Utts, J., & Johnson, W. O. (2011). Must psychologists change the way they analyze their data? *Journal of Personality and Social Psychology*, *101*(4), 716–719. https://doi.org/10.1037/a0024777

Bennis, W. G., & O'Toole, J. (2005). How business schools lost their way. *Harvard Business Review*, *83*(5), 96–104.

Bergman, M. E., & Jean, V. A. (2016). Where have all the "workers" gone? A critical analysis of the unrepresentativeness of our samples relative to the labor market in the industrial–organizational psychology literature. *Industrial and Organizational Psychology*, *9*(1), 84–113. https://doi.org/10.1017/iop.2015.70

Berry, C. M., Carpenter, N. C., & Barratt, C. L. (2012). Do other-reports of counterproductive work behavior provide an incremental contribution over self-reports? A meta-analytic comparison. *Journal of Applied Psychology*, *97*(3), 613–636. https://doi.org/10.1037/a0026739

Bettis, R. A. (2012). The search for asterisks: Compromised statistical tests and flawed theories. *Strategic Management Journal*, *33*(1), 108–113. https://doi.org/10.1002/smj.975

Bettis, R. A., Ethiraj, S., Gambardella, A., Helfat, C., & Mitchell, W. (2016). Creating repeatable cumulative knowledge in strategic management: A call for a broad and deep conversation among authors, referees, and editors. *Strategic Management Journal*, *37*(2), 257–261. https://doi.org/10.1002/smj.2477

Beverungen, A., Böhm, S., & Land, C. (2012). The poverty of journal publishing. *Organization*, *19*(6), 929–938. https://doi.org/10.1177/1350508412448858

Bicchieri, C. (2005). *The grammar of society: The nature and dynamics of social norms* (1st ed.). Cambridge University Press. https://doi.org/10.1017/CBO9780511616037

Bicchieri, C., & Mercier, H. (2014). Norms and beliefs: How change occurs. In M. Xenitidou & B. Edmonds (Eds.), *The complexity of social norms* (pp. 37–54). Springer. https://doi.org/10.1007/978-3-319-05308-0_3

Björk, B.-C. (2012). The hybrid model for open access publication of scholarly articles: A failed experiment? *Journal of the American Society for Information Science and Technology*, *63*(8), 1496–1504. https://doi.org/10.1002/asi.22709

Björk, B.-C., Welling, P., Laakso, M., Majlender, P., Hedlund, T., & Guðnason, G. (2010). Open access to the scientific journal literature: Situation 2009. *PLoS ONE*, *5*(6), e11273. https://doi.org/10.1371/journal.pone.0011273

Blank, R. M. (1991). The effects of double-blind versus single-blind reviewing: Experimental evidence from the american economic review. *American Economic Review*, *81*(5), 1041–1067.

Bloom, N., Jones, C. I., Van Reenen, J., & Webb, M. (2020). Are ideas getting harder to find? *American Economic Review*, *110*(4), 1104–1144. https://doi.org/10.1257/aer.20180338

Blue, B., & Brierley, G. (2016). 'But what do you measure?' Prospects for a constructive critical physical geography. *Area*, *48*(2), 190–197. https://doi.org/10.1111/area.12249

Bollen, K. A. (1989). *Structural equations with latent variables*. John Wiley & Sons.

Borgman, C. L. (2015). *Big data, little data, no data: Scholarship in the networked world*. The MIT Press.

Bormann, K. C., & Rowold, J. (2018). Construct proliferation in leadership style research: Reviewing pro and contra arguments. *Organizational Psychology Review*, *8*(2–3), 149–173. https://doi.org/10.1177/2041386618794821

Bornmann, L., Mutz, R., & Daniel, H.-D. (2010). A reliability-generalization study of journal peer reviews: A multilevel meta-analysis of inter-rater reliability and its determinants. *PLoS ONE*, *5*(12), e14331. https://doi.org/10.1371/journal.pone.0014331

Borsari, B., & Carey, K. B. (2003). Descriptive and injunctive norms in college drinking: A meta-analytic integration. *Journal of Studies on Alcohol*, *64*(3), 331–341. https://doi.org/10.15288/jsa.2003.64.331

Borsboom, D., van der Maas, H. L. J., Dalege, J., Kievit, R. A., & Haig, B. D. (2021). Theory construction methodology: A practical framework for building theories in psychology. *Perspectives on Psychological Science*, *16*(4), 756–766. https://doi.org/10.1177/1745691620969647

Bosco, F. A. (2022). Accumulating knowledge in the organizational sciences. *Annual Review of Organizational Psychology and Organizational Behavior*, *9*(1), 1–24. https://doi.org/10.1146/annurev-orgpsych-012420-090657

Bosco, F. A., Aguinis, H., Field, J. G., Pierce, C. A., & Dalton, D. R. (2016). HARKing's threat to organizational research: Evidence from primary and meta-analytic sources. *Personnel Psychology*, *63*(3), 709–750. https://doi.org/10.1111/peps.12111

Botvinik-Nezer, R., Holzmeister, F., Camerer, C. F., Dreber, A., Huber, J., Johannesson, M., Kirchler, M., Iwanir, R., Mumford, J. A., Adcock, R. A., Avesani, P., Baczkowski, B. M., Bajracharya, A., Bakst, L., Ball, S., Barilari, M., Bault, N., Beaton, D., Beitner, J., Benoit, R. G., … Schonberg, T. (2020). Variability in the analysis of a single neuroimaging dataset by many teams. *Nature*, *582*(7810), 84–88. https://doi.org/10.1038/s41586-020-2314-9

Boudreau, J. W., & Rynes, S. L. (1985). Role of recruitment in staffing utility analysis. *Journal of Applied Psychology*, *70*(2), 354–366. https://doi.org/10.1037/0021-9010.70.2.354

Box, G. E. P., & Draper, N. R. (1987). *Empirical model-building and response surfaces*. Wiley.

Brembs, B., Huneman, P., Schönbrodt, F., Nilsonne, G., Susi, T., Siems, R., Perakakis, P., Trachana, V., Ma, L., & Rodriguez-Cuadrado, S. (2021). *Replacing academic journals*. https://doi.org/10.5281/ZENODO.5793611

Breznau, N., Rinke, E. M., Wuttke, A., Nguyen, H. H. V., Adem, M., Adriaans, J., Alvarez-Benjumea, A., Andersen, H. K., Auer, D., Azevedo, F., Bahnsen, O., Balzer, D., Bauer, G., Bauer, P. C., Baumann, M., Baute, S., Benoit, V., Bernauer, J., Berning, C., Berthold, A., … ⊠ółtak, T. (2022). Observing many researchers using the same data and hypothesis reveals a hidden universe of uncertainty. *Proceedings of the National Academy of Sciences*, *119*(44), e2203150119. https://doi.org/10.1073/pnas.2203150119

Brodeur, A., Cook, N., & Heyes, A. (2022). *We need to talk about Mechanical Turk: What 22,989 hypothesis tests tell us about p-hacking and publication bias in online experiments*. Social Science Research Network. https://doi.org/10.2139/ssrn.4188289

Brodeur, A., Lé, M., Sangnier, M., & Zylberberg, Y. (2016). Star wars: The empirics strike back. *American Economic Journal: Applied Economics*, *8*(1), 1–32. https://doi.org/10.1257/app.20150044

Brown, T. A. (2015). *Confirmatory factor analysis for applied research*. Guilford Press.

Brown, W. (1910). Some experimental results in the correlation of mental abilities. *British Journal of Psychology*, *3*(3), 296–322. https://doi.org/10.1111/j.2044-8295.1910.tb00207.x

Buchanan, E. M., Crain, S. E., Cunningham, A. L., Johnson, H. R., Stash, H., Papadatou-Pastou, M., Isager, P. M., Carlsson, R., & Aczel, B. (2021). Getting started creating data dictionaries: How to create a shareable data set. *Advances in Methods and Practices in Psychological Science*, *4*(1), 1–10. https://doi.org/10.1177/2515245920928007

Buhrmester, M. D., Talaifar, S., & Gosling, S. D. (2018). An evaluation of Amazon's Mechanical Turk, its rapid rise, and its effective use. *Perspectives on Psychological Science*, *13*(2), 149–154. https://doi.org/10.1177/1745691617706516

Button, K. S., Ioannidis, J. P. A., Mokrysz, C., Nosek, B. A., Flint, J., Robinson, E. S. J., & Munafò, M. R. (2013). Power failure: Why small sample size undermines the reliability of neuroscience. *Nature Reviews Neuroscience*, *14*(5), 365–376. https://doi.org/10.1038/nrn3475

Cadwallader, L., & Hrynaszkiewicz, I. (2022). *A survey of researchers' code sharing and code reuse practices, and assessment of interactive notebook prototypes* [Preprint]. Open Science Framework. https://doi.org/10.31219/osf.io/tys8p

Camerer, C. F. (1999). Behavioral economics: Reunifying psychology and economics. *Proceedings of the National Academy of Sciences*, *96*(19), 10575–10577. https://doi.org/10.1073/pnas.96.19.10575

Camerer, C. F., Dreber, A., Holzmeister, F., Ho, T.-H., Huber, J., Johannesson, M., Kirchler, M., Nave, G., Nosek, B. A., Pfeiffer, T., Altmejd, A., Buttrick, N., Chan, T., Chen, Y., Forsell, E., Gampa, A., Heikensten, E., Hummer, L., Imai, T., Isaksson, S., … Wu, H. (2018). Evaluating the replicability of social science experiments in Nature and Science between 2010 and 2015. *Nature Human Behaviour*, *2*(9), 637–644. https://doi.org/10.1038/s41562-018-0399-z

Cameron, W. B. (1963). *Informal sociology: A casual introduction to sociological thinking*. Random House.

Campion, M. A. (1993). Article review checklist: A criterion checklist for reviewing research articles in applied psychology. *Personnel Psychology*, *46*(3), 705–718. https://doi.org/10.1111/j.1744-6570.1993.tb00896.x

Candal-Pedreira, C., Pérez-Ríos, M., & Ruano-Ravina, A. (2022). Retraction of scientific papers: Types of retraction, consequences, and impacts. In J. Faintuch & S. Faintuch (Eds.), *Integrity of scientific research: Fraud, misconduct and fake news in the academic, medical and social environment* (pp. 397–407). Springer. https://doi.org/10.1007/978-3-030-99680-2_40

Carpenter, N. C., Berry, C. M., & Houston, L. (2014). A meta-analytic comparison of self-reported and other-reported organizational citizenship behavior. *Journal of Organizational Behavior*, *35*(4), 547–574. https://doi.org/10.1002/job.1909

Carter, E. C., & McCullough, M. E. (2018). A simple, principled approach to combining evidence from meta-analysis and high-quality replications. *Advances in Methods and Practices in Psychological Science*, *1*(2), 174–185. https://doi.org/10.1177/2515245918756858

Cassidy, S. A., Dimova, R., Giguère, B., Spence, J. R., & Stanley, D. J. (2019). Failing grade: 89% of introduction-to-psychology textbooks that define or explain statistical significance do so incorrectly. *Advances in Methods and Practices in Psychological Science*, *2*(3), 233–239. https://doi.org/10.1177/2515245919858072

Ceci, S. J., & Peters, D. P. (1982). Peer review: A study of reliability. *Change: The Magazine of Higher Learning*, *14*(6), 44–48. https://doi.org/10.1080/00091383.1982.10569910

Ceci, S. J., & Walker, E. (1983). Private archives and public needs. *American Psychologist*, *38*(4), 414–423. https://doi.org/10.1037/0003-066X.38.4.414

Center for Open Science. (2023a). *Open science framework*. https://osf.io/

Center for Open Science. (2023b). *TOP guidelines*. https://www.cos.io/initiatives/top-guidelines

Chambers, C. D. (2017). *The seven deadly sins of psychology: A manifesto for reforming the culture of scientific practice*. Princeton University Press. https://doi.org/10.1515/9781400884940

Charlton, A., Montoya, A. K., Price, J., & Hilgard, J. (2021). *Noise in the process: An assessment of the evidential value of mediation effects in marketing journals* [Preprint]. PsyArXiv. https://doi.org/10.31234/osf.io/ck2r5

Charness, G., Masclet, D., & Villeval, M. C. (2014). The dark side of competition for status. *Management Science*, *60*(1), 38–55. https://doi.org/10.1287/mnsc.2013.1747

Chen, G. (2018). Supporting and enhancing scientific rigor. *Journal of Applied Psychology*, *103*(4), 359–361. https://doi.org/10.1037/apl0000313

Chester, D. S., & Lasko, E. N. (2021). Construct validation of experimental manipulations in social psychology: Current practices and recommendations for the future. *Perspectives on Psychological Science*, *16*(2), 377–395. https://doi.org/10.1177/1745691620950684

Cheung, J. H., Burns, D. K., Sinclair, R. R., & Sliter, M. T. (2017). Amazon Mechanical Turk in organizational psychology: An evaluation and practical recommendations. *Journal of Business and Psychology*, *32*(4), 347–361. https://doi.org/10.1007/s10869-016-9458-5

Chmielewski, M., & Kucker, S. C. (2020). An MTurk crisis? Shifts in data quality and the impact on study results. *Social Psychological and Personality Science*, *11*(4), 464–473. https://doi.org/10.1177/1948550619875149

Cho, E., & Kim, S. (2015). Cronbach's coefficient alpha: Well known but poorly understood. *Organizational Research Methods*, *18*(2), 207–230. https://doi.org/10.1177/1094428114555994

Christensen, G., Dafoe, A., Miguel, E., Moore, D. A., & Rose, A. K. (2019). A study of the impact of data sharing on article citations using journal policies as a natural experiment. *PLOS ONE*, *14*(12), e0225883. https://doi.org/10.1371/journal.pone.0225883

Chu, J. S. G., & Evans, J. A. (2021). Slowed canonical progress in large fields of science. *Proceedings of the National Academy of Sciences*, *118*(41), e2021636118. https://doi.org/10.1073/pnas.2021636118

Cialdini, R. B., & Trost, M. R. (1998). Social influence: Social norms, conformity, and compliance. In D. T. Gilbert, S. T. Fiske, & G. Lindzey (Eds.), *The handbook of social psychology* (Issue 1906, pp. 151–192). McGraw-Hill.

Cicchetti, D. V. (1991). The reliability of peer review for manuscript and grant submissions: A cross-disciplinary investigation. *Behavioral and Brain Sciences*, *14*(1), 119–135. https://doi.org/10.1017/S0140525X00065675

Cohen, J. (1994). The earth is round (p < .05). *American Psychologist*, *49*(12), 997–1003. https://doi.org/10.1037/0003-066X.49.12.997

Cole, D. A., & Preacher, K. J. (2014). Manifest variable path analysis: Potentially serious and misleading consequences due to uncorrected measurement error. *Psychological Methods*, *19*(2), 300–315. https://doi.org/10.1037/a0033805

Cole, M. S., Walter, F., Bedeian, A. G., & O'Boyle, E. H. (2012). Job burnout and employee engagement: A meta-analytic examination of construct proliferation. *Journal of Management*, *38*(5), 1550–1581. https://doi.org/10.1177/0149206311415252

Collins, F. S. (2021). COVID-19 lessons for research. *Science*, *371*(6534), 1081–1081. https://doi.org/10.1126/science.abh3996

Cortina, J. M. (2016). Defining and operationalizing theory. *Journal of Organizational Behavior*, *37*(8), 1142–1149. https://doi.org/10.1002/job.2121

Cortina, J. M., Aguinis, H., & DeShon, R. P. (2017). Twilight of dawn or of evening? A century of research methods in the *Journal of Applied Psychology*. *Journal of Applied Psychology*, *102*(3), 274–290. https://doi.org/10.1037/apl0000163

Cortina, J. M., & Folger, R. G. (1998). When is it acceptable to accept a null hypothesis: No way, jose? *Organizational Research Methods*, *1*(3), 334–350. https://doi.org/10.1177/109442819813004

Cortina, J. M., Green, J. P., Keeler, K. R., & Vandenberg, R. J. (2017). Degrees of freedom in SEM: Are we testing the models that we claim to test? *Organizational Research Methods*, *20*(3), 350–378. https://doi.org/10.1177/1094428116676345

Cortina, J. M., Markell-Goldstein, H. M., Green, J. P., & Chang, Y. (2021). How are we testing interactions in latent variable models? Surging forward or fighting shy? *Organizational Research Methods*, *24*(1), 26–54. https://doi.org/10.1177/1094428119872531

Cortina, J. M., Sheng, Z., Keener, S. K., Keeler, K. R., Grubb, L. K., Schmitt, N., Tonidandel, S., Summerville, K. M., Heggestad, E. D., & Banks, G. C. (2020). From alpha to omega and beyond! A look at the past, present, and (possible) future of psychometric soundness in the Journal of Applied Psychology. *Journal of Applied Psychology*, *105*(12), 1351–1381. https://doi.org/10.1037/apl0000815

Council of the EU and the European Council. (2021). *G7 research compact*. Council of the EU and the European Council.

Crandall, C. S., & Sherman, J. W. (2016). On the scientific superiority of conceptual replications for scientific progress. *Journal of Experimental Social Psychology*, *66*, 93–99. https://doi.org/10.1016/j.jesp.2015.10.002

Credé, M., & Harms, P. (2019). Questionable research practices when using confirmatory factor analysis. *Journal of Managerial Psychology*, *34*(1), 18–30. https://doi.org/10.1108/JMP-06-2018-0272

Credé, M., Harms, P., Niehorster, S., & Gaye-Valentine, A. (2012). An evaluation of the consequences of using short measures of the Big Five personality traits. *Journal of Personality and Social Psychology*, *102*(4), 874–888. https://doi.org/10.1037/a0027403

Crick, J. M., & Crick, D. (2021). The dark-side of coopetition: Influences on the paradoxical forces of cooperativeness and competitiveness across product-market strategies. *Journal of Business Research*, *122*, 226–240. https://doi.org/10.1016/j.jbusres.2020.08.065

Cronbach, L. J. (1951). Coefficient alpha and the internal structure of tests. *Psychometrika*, *16*(3), 297–334. https://doi.org/10.1007/BF02310555

Cropanzano, R. S., Anthony, E. L., Daniels, S. R., & Hall, A. V. (2017). Social exchange theory: A critical review with theoretical remedies. *Academy of Management Annals*, *11*(1), 479–516. https://doi.org/10.5465/annals.2015.0099

Crüwell, S., van Doorn, J., Etz, A., Makel, M. C., Moshontz, H., Niebaum, J. C., Orben, A., Parsons, S., & Schulte-Mecklenbeck, M. (2019). Seven easy steps to open science: An annotated reading list. *Zeitschrift Für Psychologie*, *227*(4), 237–248. https://doi.org/10.1027/2151-2604/a000387

Csiszar, A. (2016). Peer review: Troubled from the start. *Nature*, *532*(7599), 306–308. https://doi.org/10.1038/532306a

Cucina, J. M., & McDaniel, M. A. (2016). Pseudotheory proliferation is damaging the organizational sciences. *Journal of Organizational Behavior*, *37*(8), 1116–1125. https://doi.org/10.1002/job.2117

Cummings, T. G. (2007). 2006 presidential address: Quest for an engaged academy. *Academy of Management Review*, *32*(2), 355–360. https://doi.org/10.5465/amr.2007.24349184

Dafflon, J., F. Da Costa, P., Váša, F., Monti, R. P., Bzdok, D., Hellyer, P. J., Turkheimer, F., Smallwood, J., Jones, E., & Leech, R. (2022). A guided multiverse study of neuroimaging analyses. *Nature Communications*, *13*(1), 3758. https://doi.org/10.1038/s41467-022-31347-8

Daniel, F., Hong, O., de Vries, A., Csárdi, G., & Microsoft. (2022). *Package 'checkpoint'* (1.0.2) [R]. https://github.com/RevolutionAnalytics/checkpoint

Darley, J. M. (2001). The dynamics of authority influence in organizations and the unintended action consequences. In J. M. Darley, D. M. Messick, & T. R. Tyler (Eds.), *Social influences on ethical behavior in organizations* (pp. 37–52). Lawrence Erlbaum Associates.

Davidov, E., Muthén, B. O., & Schmidt, P. (2018). Measurement invariance in cross-national studies: Challenging traditional approaches and evaluating new ones. *Sociological Methods & Research*, *47*(4), 631–636. https://doi.org/10.1177/0049124118789708

De La Garza, H., & Vashi, N. A. (2022). The role of peer review in the scientific process. In J. Faintuch & S. Faintuch (Eds.), *Integrity of scientific research: Fraud, misconduct and fake news in the academic, medical and social environment* (pp. 409–416). Springer. https://doi.org/10.1007/978-3-030-99680-2_41

DeGeest, D. S., Follmer, E. H., Walter, S. L., & O'Boyle, E. H. (2017). RETRACTED: The benefits of benefits: A dynamic approach to motivation-enhancing human resource practices and entrepreneurial survival. *Journal of Management*, *43*(7), 2303–2332. https://doi.org/10.1177/0149206315569313

Del Giudice, M., & Gangestad, S. W. (2021). A traveler's guide to the multiverse: Promises, pitfalls, and a framework for the evaluation of analytic decisions. *Advances in Methods and Practices in Psychological Science*, *4*(1), 251524592095492. https://doi.org/10.1177/2515245920954925

Delios, A., Clemente, E. G., Wu, T., Tan, H., Wang, Y., Gordon, M., Viganola, D., Chen, Z., Dreber, A., Johannesson, M., Pfeiffer, T., Generalizability Tests Forecasting Collaboration, & Uhlmann, E. L. (2022). Examining the generalizability of research findings from archival data. *Proceedings of the National Academy of Sciences*, *119*(30), e2120377119. https://doi.org/10.1073/pnas.2120377119

Derksen, M., & Morawski, J. (2022). Kinds of replication: Examining the meanings of "conceptual replication" and "direct replication." *Perspectives on Psychological Science*, *17*(5), 1490–1505. https://doi.org/10.1177/17456916211041116

DeVellis, R. F. (2016). *Scale development: Theory and applications*. SAGE Publications.

Dienes, Z. (2008). *Understanding psychology as a science: An introduction to scientific and statistical inference*. Palgrave Macmillan.

Dienes, Z. (2014). Using Bayes to get the most out of non-significant results. *Frontiers in Psychology*, *5*(July), 1–17. https://doi.org/10.3389/fpsyg.2014.00781

Difallah, D., Filatova, E., & Ipeirotis, P. (2018). Demographics and dynamics of mechanical Turk workers. *Proceedings of the eleventh ACM international conference on web search and data mining* (pp. 135–143). https://doi.org/10.1145/3159652.3159661

Dipboye, R. L., & Flanagan, M. F. (1979). Research settings in industrial and organizational psychology: Are findings in the field more generalizable than in the laboratory? *American Psychologist*, *34*(2), 141–150. https://doi.org/10.1037/0003-066X.34.2.141

Dolgin, E. (2021). CureVac COVID vaccine let-down spotlights mRNA design challenges. *Nature*, *594*(7864), 483–483. https://doi.org/10.1038/d41586-021-01661-0

Dormann, C. (2022). Start even smaller, and then more random. Comment on "Start small, not random: Why does justifying your time-lag matter?" by Yannick Griep, Ivana Vranjes, Johannes M. Kraak, Leonie Dudda, & Yingjie Li. *The Spanish Journal of Psychology*, *25*, e20. https://doi.org/10.1017/SJP.2022.16

Dormann, C., & Griffin, M. A. (2015). Optimal time lags in panel studies. *Psychological Methods*, *20*(4), 489–505. https://doi.org/10.1037/met0000041

Dormann, C., & van de Ven, B. (2014). Timing in methods for studying psychosocial factors at work. In M. F. Dollard, A. Shimazu, R. Bin Nordin, P. Brough, & M. R. Tuckey (Eds.), *Psychosocial factors at work in the asia pacific* (pp. 89–116). Springer. https://doi.org/10.1007/978-94-017-8975-2_4

Dzeng, E. (2014, February 24). *How academia and publishing are destroying scientific innovation: A conversation with Sydney Brenner*. https://www.kingsreview.co.uk/interviews/how-academia-and-publishing-are-destroying-scientific-innovation-a-conversation-with-sydney-brenner

Ebersole, C. R. (2019, May 28). *A critique of the many labs projects*. https://www.cos.io/blog/critique-many-labs-projects

Ebersole, C. R., Atherton, O. E., Belanger, A. L., Skulborstad, H. M., Allen, J. M., Banks, J. B., Baranski, E. N., Bernstein, M. J., Bonfiglio, D. B. V., Boucher, L., Brown, E. R., Budiman, N. I., Cairo, A. H., Capaldi, C. A., Chartier, C. R., Chung, J. M., Cicero, D. C., Coleman, J. A., Conway, J. G., Davis, W. E et al. (2016). Many Labs 3: Evaluating participant pool quality across the academic semester via replication. *Journal of Experimental Social Psychology*, *67*, 68–82. https://doi.org/10.1016/j.jesp.2015.10.012

Ebersole, C. R., Mathur, M. B., Baranski, E. N., Bart-Plange, D.-J., Buttrick, N. R., Chartier, C. R., Corker, K. S., Corley, M., Hartshorne, J. K., IJzerman, H., Lazarevi⊠, L. B., Rabagliati, H., Ropovik, I., Aczel, B., Aeschbach, L. F., Andrighetto, L., Arnal, J. D., Arrow, H., Babincak, P., Bakos, B. E., … Nosek, B. A. (2020). Many Labs 5: Testing pre-data-collection peer review as an intervention to increase replicability. *Advances in Methods and Practices in Psychological Science*, *3*(3), 309–331. https://doi.org/10.1177/2515245920958687

Edelsbrunner, P. A., Sebben, S., Frisch, L. K., Schüttengruber, V., Protzko, J., & Thurn, C. M. (2022). How to understand a research question—A challenging first step in setting up a statistical model. *Religion, Brain & Behavior*, 1–3. Advance online publication. https://doi.org/10.1080/2153599X.2022.2070258

Edwards, J. R., & Berry, J. W. (2010). The presence of something or the absence of nothing: Increasing theoretical precision in management research. *Organizational Research Methods*, *13*(4), 668–689. https://doi.org/10.1177/1094428110380467

Edwards, M. A., & Roy, S. (2017). Academic research in the 21st century: Maintaining scientific integrity in a climate of perverse incentives and hypercompetition. *Environmental Engineering Science*, *34*(1), 51–61. https://doi.org/10.1089/ees.2016.0223

Egger, M., Smith, G. D., & Sterne, J. A. C. (2001). Uses and abuses of meta-analysis. *Clinical Medicine*, *1*(6), 478–484. https://doi.org/10.7861/clinmedicine.1-6-478

Elson, M., Huff, M., & Utz, S. (2020). Metascience on peer review: Testing the effects of a study's originality and statistical significance in a field experiment. *Advances in Methods and Practices in Psychological Science*, *3*(1), 53–65. https://doi.org/10.1177/2515245919895419

Epskamp, S. (2019). Reproducibility and replicability in a fast-paced methodological world. *Advances in Methods and Practices in Psychological Science*, *2*(2), 145–155. https://doi.org/10.1177/2515245919847421

Errington, T. M., Mathur, M., Soderberg, C. K., Denis, A., Perfito, N., Iorns, E., & Nosek, B. A. (2021). Investigating the replicability of preclinical cancer biology. *ELife*, *10*, e71601. https://doi.org/10.7554/eLife.71601

Etz, A., Goodman, S. N., & Vandekerckhove, J. (2022). Statistical inference in behavioral research: Traditional and Bayesian approaches. In L. J. Jussim, J. A. Krosnick, & S. T. Stevens (Eds.), *Research integrity: Best practices for the social and behavioral sciences* (pp. 175–202). Oxford University Press. https://doi.org/10.1093/oso/9780190938550.003.0007

European Commission: Directorate-General for Research & Innovation. (2017). *H2020 programme: Guidelines to the rules on open access to scientific publications and open access to research data in Horizon 2020*. https://ec.europa.eu/research/participants/data/ref/h2020/grants_manual/hi/oa_pilot/h2020-hi-oa-pilot-guide_en.pdf

Fanelli, D. (2012a). The black, the white and the grey areas: Towards an international and interdisciplinary definition of scientific misconduct. In T. Mayer & N. H. Steneck (Eds.), *Promoting research integrity in a global environment* (pp. 79–90). World Scientific Publishing.

Fanelli, D. (2012b). Negative results are disappearing from most disciplines and countries. *Scientometrics*, *90*(3), 891–904. https://doi.org/10.1007/s11192-011-0494-7

Fanelli, D. (2022). Is science in crisis? In L. J. Jussim, J. A. Krosnick, & S. T. Stevens (Eds.), *Research integrity: Best practices for the social and behavioral sciences* (pp. 93–121). Oxford University Press. https://doi.org/10.1093/oso/9780190938550.003.0004

Farndale, E., McDonnell, A., Scholarios, D., & Wilkinson, A. (2020). *Human Resource Management Journal*: A look to the past, present, and future of the journal and HRM scholarship. *Human Resource Management Journal*, *30*(1), 1–12. https://doi.org/10.1111/1748-8583.12275

Ferguson, C. J. (2015). "Everybody knows psychology is not a real science": Public perceptions of psychology and how we can improve our relationship with policymakers, the scientific community, and the general public. *American Psychologist*, *70*(6), 527–542. https://doi.org/10.1037/a0039405

Ferris, G. R., Hochwarter, W. A., & Buckley, M. R. (2012). Theory in the organizational sciences: How will we know it when we see it? *Organizational Psychology Review*, *2*(1), 94–106. https://doi.org/10.1177/2041386611423696

Fiedler, K. (2017). What constitutes strong psychological science? The (neglected) role of diagnosticity and a priori theorizing. *Perspectives on Psychological Science*, *12*(1), 46–61. https://doi.org/10.1177/1745691616654458

Fiedler, K., & Schwarz, N. (2016). Questionable research practices revisited. *Social Psychological and Personality Science*, *7*(1), 45–52. https://doi.org/10.1177/1948550615612150

Fife, D. (2020). The eight steps of data analysis: A graphical framework to promote sound statistical analysis. *Perspectives on Psychological Science*, *15*(4), 1054–1075. https://doi.org/10.1177/1745691620917333

Fisher, P. A., Risavy, S. D., Robie, C., König, C. J., Christiansen, N. D., Tett, R. P., & Simonet, D. V. (2021). Selection myths: A conceptual replication of HR professionals' beliefs about effective human resource practices in the US and Canada. *Journal of Personnel Psychology*, *20*(2), 51–60. https://doi.org/10.1027/1866-5888/a000263

Fisher, R. A. (1956). *Statistical methods and scientific inference*. Oliver and Boyd.

Flake, J. K., & Fried, E. I. (2020). Measurement Schmeasurement: Questionable measurement practices and how to avoid them. *Advances in Methods and Practices in Psychological Science*, *3*(4), 456–465. https://doi.org/10.1177/2515245920952393

Fox, N., Honeycutt, N., & Jussim, L. J. (2022). Better understanding the population size and stigmatization of psychologists using questionable research practices. *Meta-Psychology*, *6*, 1–19. https://doi.org/10.15626/MP.2020.2601

Francis, G., & Thunell, E. (2022). Data detective methods for revealing questionable research practices. In W. O'Donohue, A. Masuda, & S. Lilienfeld (Eds.), *Avoiding questionable research practices in applied psychology* (pp. 123–145). Springer. https://doi.org/10.1007/978-3-031-04968-2_6

Francoeur, V., Paillé, P., Yuriev, A., & Boiral, O. (2021). The measurement of green workplace behaviors: A systematic review. *Organization & Environment*, *34*(1), 18–42. https://doi.org/10.1177/1086026619837125

Friese, M., & Frankenbach, J. (2020). P-Hacking and publication bias interact to distort meta-analytic effect size estimates. *Psychological Methods*, *25*(4), 456–471. https://doi.org/10.1037/met0000246

Fuentes, M. A., Zelaya, D. G., Delgado-Romero, E. A., & Butt, M. (2022). Open science: Friend, foe, or both to an antiracist psychology? *Psychological Review*. Advance online publication. https://doi.org/10.1037/rev0000386

Gallus, J., & Frey, B. S. (2016). Awards: A strategic management perspective. *Strategic Management Journal*, *37*(8), 1699–1714. https://doi.org/10.1002/smj.2415

Gartstein, M. A., Bridgett, D. J., & Low, C. M. (2012). Asking questions about temperament: Self- and other-report measures across the lifespan. In M. Zentner & R. L. Shiner (Eds.), *Handbook of temperament* (pp. 183–208). Guilford Press.

Gaudino, M., Robinson, N. B., Di Franco, A., Hameed, I., Naik, A., Demetres, M., Girardi, L. N., Frati, G., Fremes, S. E., & Biondi-Zoccai, G. (2021). Effects of experimental interventions to improve the biomedical peer-review process: A systematic review and meta-analysis. *Journal of the American Heart Association*, *10*(15), e019903. https://doi.org/10.1161/JAHA.120.019903

Gelman, A. (2016). The problems with p-values are not just with p-values. *The American Statistician, Online Discussion*. http://www.stat.columbia.edu/~gelman/research/published/asa_pvalues.pdf

Gelman, A., & Loken, E. (2014). The statistical crisis in science. *American Scientist*, *102*(6), 460. https://doi.org/10.1511/2014.111.460

Gentemann, C. (2023). Why NASA and federal agencies are declaring this the Year of Open Science. *Nature*, *613*(7943), 217–217. https://doi.org/10.1038/d41586-023-00019-y

Gerber, A. S., & Malhotra, N. (2008a). Publication bias in empirical sociological research: Do arbitrary significance levels distort published results? *Sociological Methods & Research*, *37*(1), 3–30. https://doi.org/10.1177/0049124108318973

Gerber, A. S., & Malhotra, N. (2008b). Do statistical reporting standards affect what is published? Publication bias in two leading political science journals. *Quarterly Journal of Political Science*, *3*(3), 313–326. https://doi.org/10.1561/100.00008024

Gewin, V. (2016). Data sharing: An open mind on open data. *Nature*, *529*(7584), 117–119. https://doi.org/10.1038/nj7584-117a

Gigerenzer, G. (2004). Mindless statistics. *The Journal of Socio-Economics*, *33*(5), 587–606. https://doi.org/10.1016/j.socec.2004.09.033

Gigerenzer, G. (2018). Statistical rituals: The replication delusion and how we got there. *Advances in Methods and Practices in Psychological Science*, *1*(2), 198–218. https://doi.org/10.1177/2515245918771329

Gigerenzer, G., Krauss, S., & Vitouch, O. (2004). The null ritual: What you always wanted to know about significance testing but were afraid to ask. In D. M. Kaplan (Ed.), *The SAGE handbook of quantitative methodology for the social sciences* (pp. 391–408). SAGE Publications. https://doi.org/10.4135/9781412986311.n21

Gigerenzer, G., & Marewski, J. N. (2015). Surrogate science: The idol of a universal method for scientific inference. *Journal of Management*, *41*(2), 421–440. https://doi.org/10.1177/0149206314547522

Gilbert, D. T., King, G., Pettigrew, S., & Wilson, T. D. (2016). Comment on "Estimating the reproducibility of psychological science." *Science*, *351*(6277), 1037–1037. https://doi.org/10.1126/science.aad7243

Giner-Sorolla, R. (2012). Science or art? How aesthetic standards grease the way through the publication bottleneck but undermine science. *Perspectives on Psychological Science*, *7*(6), 562–571. https://doi.org/10.1177/1745691612457576

Gingras, Y. (2020). The transformation of the scientific paper: From knowledge to accounting unit. In M. Biagioli & A. Lippman (Eds.), *Gaming the metrics: Misconduct and manipulation in academic research* (pp. 43–55). The MIT Press.

Godlee, F., Gale, C. R., & Martyn, C. N. (1998). Effect on the quality of peer review of blinding reviewers and asking them to sign their reports: A randomized controlled trial. *JAMA*, *280*(3), 237. https://doi.org/10.1001/jama.280.3.237

Gonzalez-Mulé, E., & Cockburn, B. S. (2021). This job is (literally) killing me: A moderated-mediated model linking work characteristics to mortality. *Journal of Applied Psychology*, *106*(1), 140–151. https://doi.org/10.1037/apl0000501

Gopalakrishna, G., ter Riet, G., Vink, G., Stoop, I., Wicherts, J. M., & Bouter, L. M. (2022). Prevalence of questionable research practices, research misconduct and their potential explanatory factors: A survey among academic researchers in The Netherlands. *PLOS ONE*, *17*(2), e0263023. https://doi.org/10.1371/journal.pone.0263023

Gottfredson, S. D. (1978). Evaluating psychological research reports: Dimensions, reliability, and correlates of quality judgments. *American Psychologist*, *33*(10), 920–934. https://doi.org/10.1037/0003-066X.33.10.920

Götz, M., & Field, J. G. (2022). Data sharing and data integrity. In K. R. Murphy (Ed.), *Data, methods and theory in the organizational sciences: A new synthesis* (pp. 49–72). Routledge. https://doi.org/10.4324/9781003015000-4

Götz, M., O'Boyle, E. H., Gonzalez-Mulé, E., Banks, G. C., & Bollmann, S. S. (2021). The "Goldilocks Zone": (Too) many confidence intervals in tests of mediation just exclude zero. *Psychological Bulletin*, *147*(1), 95–114. https://doi.org/10.1037/bul0000315

Grand, J. A., Rogelberg, S. G., Banks, G. C., Landis, R. S., & Tonidandel, S. (2018). From outcome to process focus: Fostering a more robust psychological science through registered reports and results-blind reviewing. *Perspectives on Psychological Science*, *13*(4), 448–456. https://doi.org/10.1177/1745691618767883

Greco, L. M., O'Boyle, E. H., Cockburn, B. S., & Yuan, Z. (2018). Meta-analysis of coefficient alpha: A reliability generalization study. *Journal of Management Studies*, *55*(4), 583–618. https://doi.org/10.1111/joms.12328

Greco, L. M., O'Boyle, E. H., & Walter, S. L. (2015). Absence of malice: A meta-analysis of nonresponse bias in counterproductive work behavior research. *Journal of Applied Psychology*, *100*(1), 75–97. https://doi.org/10.1037/a0037495

Greenland, S., Senn, S. J., Rothman, K. J., Carlin, J. B., Poole, C., Goodman, S. N., & Altman, D. G. (2016). Statistical tests, P values, confidence intervals, and power: A guide to misinterpretations. *European Journal of Epidemiology*, *31*(4), 337–350. https://doi.org/10.1007/s10654-016-0149-3

Grigg, A. E. (1948). A farm knowledge test. *Journal of Applied Psychology*, *32*(5), 452–455. https://doi.org/10.1037/h0054644

Grimes, D. R., Bauch, C. T., & Ioannidis, J. P. A. (2018). Modelling science trustworthiness under publish or perish pressure. *Royal Society Open Science*, *5*(1), 171511. https://doi.org/10.1098/rsos.171511

Gross, C. (2016). Scientific misconduct. *Annual Review of Psychology*, *67*(1), 693–711. https://doi.org/10.1146/annurev-psych-122414-033437

Gross, J., & Vostroknutov, A. (2022). Why do people follow social norms? *Current Opinion in Psychology*, *44*, 1–6. https://doi.org/10.1016/j.copsyc.2021.08.016

Grossmann, A., & Brembs, B. (2021). Current market rates for scholarly publishing services. *F1000Research*, *10*, 20. https://doi.org/10.12688/f1000research.27468.2

Gruda, D., Karanatsiou, D., Hanges, P., Golbeck, J., & Vakali, A. (2022). Don't go chasing narcissists: A relational-based and multiverse perspective on leader narcissism and follower engagement using a machine learning approach. *Personality and Social Psychology Bulletin*. Advance online publication. https://doi.org/10.1177/01461672221094976

Grund, S., Lüdtke, O., & Robitzsch, A. (2022). Using synthetic data to improve the reproducibility of statistical results in psychological research. *Psychological Methods*. https://doi.org/10.1037/met0000526

Hackman, J. R., & Oldham, G. R. (1975). Development of the job diagnostic survey. *Journal of Applied Psychology*, *60*(2), 159–170. https://doi.org/10.1037/h0076546

Hagve, M. (2020). The money behind academic publishing. *Tidsskrift for Den Norske Legeforening*. https://doi.org/10.4045/tidsskr.20.0118

Halbesleben, J. R. B., Wheeler, A. R., & Buckley, M. R. (2004). The influence of great theoretical works on subsequent empirical work: An investigation of top management journals. *Management Decision*, *42*(10), 1210–1225. https://doi.org/10.1108/00251740410568926

Hall, G. S. (1917). Practical relations between psychology and the war. *Journal of Applied Psychology*, *1*(1), 9–16. https://doi.org/10.1037/h0070238

Hamaker, E. L. (2023). The curious case of the cross-sectional correlation. *Multivariate Behavioral Research*, 1–12. Advance online publication. https://doi.org/10.1080/00273171.2022.2155930

Hambrick, D. C. (1994). 1993 presidential address: What if the academy actually mattered? *Academy of Management Review*, *19*(1), 11. https://doi.org/10.2307/258833

Hambrick, D. C. (2007). The field of management's devotion to theory: Too much of a good thing? *Academy of Management Journal*, *50*(6), 1346–1352. https://doi.org/10.5465/amj.2007.28166119

Hand, D. J. (2016). *Measurement: A very short introduction*. Oxford University Press. https://doi.org/10.1093/actrade/9780198779568.001.0001

Hands, D. W. (2013). Foundations of contemporary revealed preference theory. *Erkenntnis*, *78*(5), 1081–1108. https://doi.org/10.1007/s10670-012-9395-2

Hannah, D. R. (2005). Should i keep a secret? The effects of trade secret protection procedures on employees' obligations to protect trade secrets. *Organization Science*, *16*(1), 71–84. https://doi.org/10.1287/orsc.1040.0113

Harder, J. A. (2020). The multiverse of methods: Extending the multiverse analysis to address data-collection decisions. *Perspectives on Psychological Science*, *15*(5), 1158–1177. https://doi.org/10.1177/1745691620917678

Hardwicke, T. E., Mathur, M. B., MacDonald, K., Nilsonne, G., Banks, G. C., Kidwell, M. C., Hofelich Mohr, A., Clayton, E., Yoon, E. J., Henry Tessler, M., Lenne, R. L., Altman, S., Long, B., & Frank, M. C. (2018). Data availability, reusability, and analytic reproducibility: Evaluating the impact of a mandatory open data policy at the journal Cognition. *Royal Society Open Science*, *5*(8), 180448. https://doi.org/10.1098/rsos.180448

Hardwicke, T. E., & Wagenmakers, E.-J. (2023). Reducing bias, increasing transparency and calibrating confidence with preregistration. *Nature Human Behaviour*, *7*(1), 15–26. https://doi.org/10.1038/s41562-022-01497-2

Hargreaves Heap, S. P. (2013). What is the meaning of behavioural economics? *Cambridge Journal of Economics*, *37*(5), 985–1000. https://doi.org/10.1093/cje/bes090

Harlow, L. L., Mulaik, S. A., & Steiger, J. H. (Eds.). (2016). *What if there were no significance tests?* Routledge. http://books.google.com/books?id=lZ2ybZzrnroC

Hartgerink, C. H. J. (2019). Verified, shared, modular, and provenance based research communication with the Dat protocol. *Publications*, *7*(2), 40. https://doi.org/10.3390/publications7020040

Hartgerink, C. H. J., van Aert, R. C. M., Nuijten, M. B., Wicherts, J. M., & van Assen, M. A. L. M. (2016). Distributions of p-values smaller than .05 in psychology: What is going on? *PeerJ*, *4*, e1935. https://doi.org/10.7717/peerj.1935

Hartgerink, C. H. J., & van Zelst, M. (2018). "As-you-go" instead of "after-the-fact": A network approach to scholarly communication and evaluation. *Publications*, *6*(2), 21. https://doi.org/10.3390/publications6020021

Hartley, D. (2013). *Observations on man: His frame, his duty, and his expectations*. Cambridge University Press. (Original work published 1749)

Heggestad, E. D., Scheaf, D. J., Banks, G. C., Monroe Hausfeld, M., Tonidandel, S., & Williams, E. B. (2019). Scale adaptation in organizational science research: A review and best-practice recommendations. *Journal of Management*, *45*(6), 2596–2627. https://doi.org/10.1177/0149206319850280

Henrich, J., Heine, S. J., & Norenzayan, A. (2010). The weirdest people in the world? *Behavioral and Brain Sciences*, *33*(2–3), 61–83. https://doi.org/10.1017/S0140525X0999152X

Higgs, M. D., & Gelman, A. (2021). Research on registered report research. *Nature Human Behaviour*, *5*(8), 978–979. https://doi.org/10.1038/s41562-021-01148-y

Hinkin, T. R. (1998). A brief tutorial on the development of measures for use in survey questionnaires. *Organizational Research Methods*, *1*(1), 104–121. https://doi.org/10.1177/109442819800100106

Horrobin, D. F. (1990). The philosophical basis of peer review and the suppression of innovation. *JAMA: The Journal of the American Medical Association*, *263*(10), 1438. https://doi.org/10.1001/jama.1990.03440100162024

Houtkoop, B. L., Chambers, C., Macleod, M., Bishop, D. V. M., Nichols, T. E., & Wagenmakers, E.-J. (2018). Data sharing in psychology: A survey on barriers and preconditions. *Advances in Methods and Practices in Psychological Science*, *1*(1), 70–85. https://doi.org/10.1177/2515245917751886

Howard, M. C., Cogswell, J. E., & Smith, M. B. (2020). The antecedents and outcomes of workplace ostracism: A meta-analysis. *Journal of Applied Psychology*, *105*(6), 577–596. https://doi.org/10.1037/apl0000453

Hubbard, R. (2016). *Corrupt research: The case for reconceptualizing empirical management and social science*. SAGE Publications.

Hubbard, R., Parsa, R. A., & Luthy, M. R. (1997). The spread of statistical significance testing in psychology: The case of the *Journal of Applied Psychology*, 1917-1994. *Theory & Psychology*, *7*(4), 545–554. https://doi.org/10.1177/0959354397074006

Hubbard, R., Vetter, D. E., & Little, E. L. (1998). Replication in strategic management: Scientific testing for validity, generalizability, and usefulness. *Strategic Management Journal*, *19*(3), 243–254. https://doi.org/10.1002/(SICI)1097-0266(199803)19:3<243::AID-SMJ951>3.0.CO;2-0

Huber, J., Inoua, S., Kerschbamer, R., König-Kersting, C., Palan, S., & Smith, V. L. (2022). Nobel and novice: Author prominence affects peer review. *Proceedings of the National Academy of Sciences*, *119*(41), e2205779119. https://doi.org/10.1073/pnas.2205779119

Huisman, J., & Smits, J. (2017). Duration and quality of the peer review process: The author's perspective. *Scientometrics*, *113*(1), 633–650. https://doi.org/10.1007/s11192-017-2310-5

Husted, B. W., & de Jesus Salazar, J. (2006). Taking Friedman seriously: Maximizing profits and social performance. *Journal of Management Studies*, *43*(1), 75–91. https://doi.org/10.1111/j.1467-6486.2006.00583.x

Imbens, G. W., & Rubin, D. B. (2015). *Causal inference for statistics, social, and biomedical sciences: An introduction*. Cambridge University Press.

Ioannidis, J. P. A. (2006). Journals should publish all "null" results and should sparingly publish "positive" results. *Cancer Epidemiology, Biomarkers & Prevention*, *15*(1), 186–186. https://doi.org/10.1158/1055-9965.EPI-05-0921

Ioannidis, J. P. A. (2012). Why science is not necessarily self-correcting. *Perspectives on Psychological Science*, *7*(6), 645–654. https://doi.org/10.1177/1745691612464056

Ioannidis, J. P. A. (2016). The mass production of redundant, misleading, and conflicted systematic reviews and meta-analyses. *The Milbank Quarterly*, *94*(3), 485–514. https://doi.org/10.1111/1468-0009.12210

Ioannidis, J. P. A., Stanley, T. D., & Doucouliagos, H. (2017). The power of bias in economics research. *The Economic Journal*, *127*(605), F236–F265. https://doi.org/10.1111/ecoj.12461

Jackson, D. L., Gillaspy, J. A., & Purc-Stephenson, R. (2009). Reporting practices in confirmatory factor analysis: An overview and some recommendations. *Psychological Methods*, *14*(1), 6–23. https://doi.org/10.1037/a0014694

Jacobson, R. P., Marchiondo, L. A., Jacobson, K. J. L., & Hood, J. N. (2020). The synergistic effect of descriptive and injunctive norm perceptions on counterproductive work behaviors. *Journal of Business Ethics*, *162*(1), 191–209. https://doi.org/10.1007/s10551-018-3968-1

Jacowitz, K. E., & Kahneman, D. (1995). Measures of anchoring in estimation tasks. *Personality and Social Psychology Bulletin*, *21*(11), 1161–1166. https://doi.org/10.1177/01461672952111004

John, L. K., Loewenstein, G. F., & Prelec, D. (2012). Measuring the prevalence of questionable research practices with incentives for truth telling. *Psychological Science*, *23*(5), 524–532. https://doi.org/10.1177/0956797611430953

Johns, G. (2006). The essential impact of context on organizational behavior. *Academy of Management Review*, *31*(2), 386–408. https://doi.org/10.5465/AMR.2006.20208687

Johns, G. (2018). Advances in the treatment of context in organizational research. *Annual Review of Organizational Psychology and Organizational Behavior*, *5*(1), 21–46. https://doi.org/10.1146/annurev-orgpsych-032117-104406

Johnson, R., Watkinson, A., & Mabe, M. (2018). *The STM Report: An overview of scientific and scholarly publishing* (No. 5). STM: International Association of Scientific, Technical and Medical Publishers. https://www.stm-assoc.org/2018_10_04_STM_Report_2018.pdf

Joseph, D. L., Jin, J., Newman, D. A., & O'Boyle, E. H. (2015). Why does self-reported emotional intelligence predict job performance? A meta-analytic investigation of mixed EI. *Journal of Applied Psychology*, *100*(2), 298–342. https://doi.org/10.1037/a0037681

Judge, G., & Schechter, L. (2009). Detecting problems in survey data using Benford's law. *Journal of Human Resources*, *44*(1), 1–24. https://doi.org/10.3368/jhr.44.1.1

Jussim, L. J., Crawford, J. T., Anglin, S. M., Stevens, S. T., & Duarte, J. L. (2016). Interpretations and methods: Towards a more effectively self-correcting social psychology. *Journal of Experimental Social Psychology*, *66*, 116–133. https://doi.org/10.1016/j.jesp.2015.10.003

Kacperczyk, A., Beckman, C. M., & Moliterno, T. P. (2015). Disentangling risk and change: Internal and external social comparison in the mutual fund industry. *Administrative Science Quarterly*, *60*(2), 228–262. https://doi.org/10.1177/0001839214566297

Karhulahti, V.-M., & Backe, H.-J. (2021). Transparency of peer review: A semi-structured interview study with chief editors from social sciences and humanities. *Research Integrity and Peer Review*, *6*(1), 13. https://doi.org/10.1186/s41073-021-00116-4

Kehm, B. M. (2020). Global university rankings: Impacts and applications. In M. Biagioli & A. Lippman (Eds.), *Gaming the metrics: Misconduct and manipulation in academic research* (pp. 93–100). The MIT Press.

Kelley, T. L. (1927). *Interpretation of educational measurements*. World Book Company.

Kenny, D. A. (1979). *Correlation and causality*. Wiley-Interscience.

Kepes, S., Banks, G. C., & Oh, I.-S. (2014). Avoiding bias in publication bias research: The value of "null" findings. *Journal of Business and Psychology*, *29*(2), 183–203. https://doi.org/10.1007/s10869-012-9279-0

Kepes, S., Keener, S. K., McDaniel, M. A., & Hartman, N. S. (2022). Questionable research practices among researchers in the most research-productive management programs. *Journal of Organizational Behavior*, *43*(7), 1190–1208. https://doi.org/10.1002/job.2623

Kerr, N. L. (1998). HARKing: Hypothesizing after the results are known. *Personality and Social Psychology Review*, *2*(3), 196–217. https://doi.org/10.1207/s15327957pspr0203_4

Kidwell, M. C., Lazarevi⊠, L. B., Baranski, E. N., Hardwicke, T. E., Piechowski, S., Falkenberg, L.-S., Kennett, C., Slowik, A., Sonnleitner, C., Hess-Holden, C., Errington, T. M., Fiedler, S., & Nosek, B. A. (2016). Badges to acknowledge open practices: A simple, low-cost, effective method for increasing transparency. *PLOS Biology*, *14*(5), e1002456. https://doi.org/10.1371/journal.pbio.1002456

Kieser, A. (2010). Unternehmen Wissenschaft? *Leviathan*, *38*(3), 347–367. https://doi.org/10.1007/s11578-010-0093-7

Kieser, A., Nicolai, A., & Seidl, D. (2015). The practical relevance of management research: Turning the debate on relevance into a rigorous scientific research program. *Academy of Management Annals*, *9*(1), 143–233. https://doi.org/10.1080/19416520.2015.1011853

Kim, E., Cao, C., Liu, S., Wang, Y., & Dedrick, R. (2022). Testing measurement invariance over time with intensive longitudinal data and identifying a source of non-invariance. *Structural Equation Modeling: A Multidisciplinary Journal*, 1–19. Advance online publication. https://doi.org/10.1080/10705511.2022.2130331

Klein, R. A., Cook, C. L., Ebersole, C. R., Vitiello, C., Nosek, B. A., Hilgard, J., Ahn, P. H., Brady, A. J., Chartier, C. R., Christopherson, C. D., Clay, S., Collisson, B., Crawford, J. T., Cromar, R., Gardiner, G., Gosnell, C. L., Grahe, J., Hall, C., Howard, I., Joy-Gaba, J. A., … Ratliff, K. A. (2022). Many Labs 4: Failure to replicate mortality salience effect with and without original author involvement. *Collabra: Psychology*, *8*(1), 35271. https://doi.org/10.1525/collabra.35271

Klein, R. A., Ratliff, K. A., Vianello, M., Adams, R. B., Bahník, Š., Bernstein, M. J., Bocian, K., Brandt, M. J., Brooks, B., Brumbaugh, C. C., Cemalcilar, Z., Chandler, J. J., Cheong, W., Davis, W. E., Devos, T., Eisner, M., Frankowska, N., Furrow, D., Galliani, E. M., Hasselman, F., … Nosek, B. A. (2014). Investigating variation in replicability: A "Many Labs" replication project. *Social Psychology*, *45*(3), 142–152. https://doi.org/10.1027/1864-9335/a000178

Klein, R. A., Vianello, M., Hasselman, F., Adams, B. G., Adams, R. B., Alper, S., Aveyard, M., Axt, J. R., Babalola, M. T., Bahník, Š., Batra, R., Berkics, M., Bernstein, M. J., Berry, D. R., Bialobrzeska, O., Binan, E. D., Bocian, K., Brandt, M. J., Busching, R., Redei, A. C., Cai, H., … Nosek, B. A. (2018). Many Labs 2: Investigating variation in replicability across samples and settings. *Advances in Methods and Practices in Psychological Science*, *1*(4), 443–490. https://doi.org/10.1177/2515245918810225

Kline, R. B. (2013). *Beyond significance testing: Statistics reform in the behavioral sciences*. American Psychological Association. https://doi.org/10.1037/14136-01

Kline, R. B. (2016). *Principles and practice of structural equation modeling*. Guilford Press.

Kluger, A. N., & Tikochinsky, J. (2001). The error of accepting the "theoretical" null hypothesis: The rise, fall, and resurrection of commonsense hypotheses in psychology. *Psychological Bulletin*, *127*(3), 408–423. https://doi.org/10.1037/0033-2909.127.3.408

Koch, S. (1992). The nature and limits of psychological knowledge: Lessons of a century qua "science." In S. Koch & D. E. Leary (Eds.), *A century of psychology as science*. (pp. 75–97). American Psychological Association. https://doi.org/10.1037/10117-024

Kühberger, A., Fritz, A., & Scherndl, T. (2014). Publication bias in psychology: A diagnosis based on the correlation between effect size and sample size. *PLoS ONE*, *9*(9), e105825. https://doi.org/10.1371/journal.pone.0105825

Kuhn, T. S. (1996). *The structure of scientific revolutions* (3rd ed.). University of Chicago Press.

Kulikowski, K. (2022). For the public, it might be an evidence-based practice not to listen to I-O psychologists. *Industrial and Organizational Psychology*, *15*(2), 273–276. https://doi.org/10.1017/iop.2022.10

Laakso, M., & Björk, B.-C. (2022). Open access journal publishing in the business disciplines: A closer look at the low uptake and discipline-specific considerations. *Journal of Librarianship and Information Science*, *54*(2), 216–229. https://doi.org/10.1177/09610006211006769

Laitin, D. D., Miguel, E., Alrababa'h, A., Bogdanoski, A., Grant, S., Hoeberling, K., Hyunjung Mo, C., Moore, D. A., Vazire, S., Weinstein, J., & Williamson, S. (2021). Reporting all results efficiently: A RARE proposal to open up the file drawer. *Proceedings of the National Academy of Sciences*, *118*(52), e2106178118. https://doi.org/10.1073/pnas.2106178118

Lakatos, I. (1970). History of science and its rational reconstructions. *PSA: Proceedings of the Biennial Meeting of the Philosophy of Science Association*, *1970*, 91–136. https://doi.org/10.1086/psaprocbienmeetp.1970.495757

Lakens, D. (2023). Is my study useless? Why researchers need methodological review boards. *Nature*, *613*(7942), 9. https://doi.org/10.1038/d41586-022-04504-8

Lambert, L. S., & Newman, D. A. (2022). Construct development and validation in three practical steps: Recommendations for reviewers, editors, and authors. *Organizational Research Methods*, 109442812211153. Advance online publication. https://doi.org/10.1177/10944281221115374

Landers, R. N., & Behrend, T. S. (2015). An inconvenient truth: Arbitrary distinctions between organizational, mechanical turk, and other convenience samples. *Industrial and Organizational Psychology*, *8*(2), 142–164. https://doi.org/10.1017/iop.2015.13

Landis, R. S., James, L. R., Lance, C. E., Pierce, C. A., & Rogelberg, S. G. (2014). When is nothing something? Editorial for the null results special issue of *Journal of Business and Psychology*. *Journal of Business and Psychology*, *29*(2), 163–167. https://doi.org/10.1007/s10869-014-9347-8

Landy, J. F., Jia, M. L., Ding, I. L., Viganola, D., Tierney, W., Dreber, A., Johannesson, M., Pfeiffer, T., Ebersole, C. R., Gronau, Q. F., Ly, A., van den Bergh, D., Marsman, M., Derks, K., Wagenmakers, E.-J., Proctor, A., Bartels, D. M., Bauman, C. W., Brady, W. J., Cheung, F., … Uhlmann, E. L. (2020). Crowdsourcing hypothesis tests: Making transparent how design choices shape research results. *Psychological Bulletin*, *146*(5), 451–479. https://doi.org/10.1037/bul0000220

Lapinski, M. K., & Rimal, R. N. (2005). An explication of social norms. *Communication Theory*, *15*(2), 127–147. https://doi.org/10.1111/j.1468-2885.2005.tb00329.x

Larivière, V., Haustein, S., & Mongeon, P. (2015). The oligopoly of academic publishers in the digital era. *PLOS ONE*, *10*(6), e0127502. https://doi.org/10.1371/journal.pone.0127502

Laudan, L. (1981). *Science and hypothesis: Historical essays on scientific methodology*. Springer Science+Business Media.

LeBreton, J. M., Scherer, K. T., & James, L. R. (2014). Corrections for criterion reliability in validity generalization: A false prophet in a land of suspended judgment. *Industrial and Organizational Psychology*, *7*(4), 478–500. https://doi.org/10.1111/iops.12184

LeBreton, J. M., & Senter, J. L. (2007). Answers to 20 questions about interrater reliability and interrater agreement. *Organizational Research Methods*, *11*(4), 815–852. https://doi.org/10.1177/1094428106296642

Lewin, W. H. G. (2011). *For the love of physics: From the end of the rainbow to the edge of time—A journey through the wonders of physics*. Free Press.

Lewis, C. S. (2001). *The weight of glory: And other addresses*. HarperOne. (Original work published 1949)

Lewis, D. W. (2012). The inevitability of open access. *College & Research Libraries*, *73*(5), 493–506. https://doi.org/10.5860/crl-299

Liberate Science GmbH. (2023). *ResearchEquals.com*. https://www.researchequals.com/

Lindley, D. V. (2014). *Understanding uncertainty*. John Wiley & Sons.

Locke, E. A., & Latham, G. P. (2006). New directions in goal-setting theory. *Current Directions in Psychological Science*, *15*(5), 265–268. https://doi.org/10.1111/j.1467-8721.2006.00449.x

Logan, C. J. (2017). We can shift academic culture through publishing choices. *F1000Research*, *6*, 518. https://doi.org/10.12688/f1000research.11415.2

London, A. J., & Kimmelman, J. (2020). Against pandemic research exceptionalism. *Science*, *368*(6490), 476–477. https://doi.org/10.1126/science.abc1731

London, B. (2021). Reviewing peer review. *Journal of the American Heart Association*, *10*(15), e021475. https://doi.org/10.1161/JAHA.121.021475

Lyman, R. L. (2013). A three-decade history of the duration of peer review. *Journal of Scholarly Publishing*, *44*(3), 211–220. https://doi.org/10.3138/jsp.44.3.001

Lynøe, N., Jacobsson, L., & Lundgren, E. (1999). Fraud, misconduct or normal science in medical research—An empirical study of demarcation. *Journal of Medical Ethics*, *25*(6), 501–506. https://doi.org/10.1136/jme.25.6.501

Mackey, J. D., McAllister, C. P., Ellen, B. P., & Carson, J. E. (2021). A meta-analysis of interpersonal and organizational workplace deviance research. *Journal of Management*, *47*(3), 597–622. https://doi.org/10.1177/0149206319862612

Marchi, S. de, & Hamilton, J. T. (2006). Assessing the accuracy of self-reported data: An evaluation of the toxics release inventory. *Journal of Risk and Uncertainty*, *32*(1), 57–76. https://doi.org/10.1007/s10797-006-6666-3

Marshall, E. (2000). How prevalent is fraud? That's a million-dollar question. *Science*, *290*(5497), 1662–1663. https://doi.org/10.1126/science.290.5497.1662

Martone, M. E., Garcia-Castro, A., & VandenBos, G. R. (2018). Data sharing in psychology. *American Psychologist*, *73*(2), 111–125. https://doi.org/10.1037/amp0000242

Maslow, A. H. (1966). *The psychology of science: A reconnaissance*. Harper & Row.
Max-Planck-Gesellschaft. (2003, October 23). *Berlin declaration on open access to knowledge in the sciences and humanities*. https://openaccess.mpg.de/Berlin-Declaration
Maxwell, S. E., & Cole, D. A. (2007). Bias in cross-sectional analyses of longitudinal mediation. *Psychological Methods*, *12*(1), 23–44. https://doi.org/10.1037/1082-989X.12.1.23
McElreath, R. (2020). *Statistical rethinking: A Bayesian course with examples in R and Stan*. CRC Press.
McNeish, D. M. (2018). Thanks coefficient alpha, we'll take it from here. *Psychological Methods*, *23*(3), 412–433. https://doi.org/10.1037/met0000144
McShane, B. B., Gal, D., Gelman, A., Robert, C., & Tackett, J. L. (2019a). Abandon statistical significance. *The American Statistician*, *73*(Suppl 1), 235–245. https://doi.org/10.1080/00031305.2018.1527253
McShane, B. B., Tackett, J. L., Böckenholt, U., & Gelman, A. (2019b). Large-scale replication projects in contemporary psychological research. *The American Statistician*, *73*(Suppl 1), 99–105. https://doi.org/10.1080/00031305.2018.1505655
Meehl, P. E. (1967). Theory-testing in psychology and physics: A methodological paradox. *Philosophy of Science*, *34*(2), 103–115. https://doi.org/10.1086/288135
Meehl, P. E. (1978). Theoretical risks and tabular asterisks: Sir Karl, Sir Ronald, and the slow progress of soft psychology. *Journal of Consulting and Clinical Psychology*, *46*(4), 806–834. https://doi.org/10.1037//0022-006X.46.4.806
Meehl, P. E. (1990a). Why summaries of research on psychological theories are often uninterpretable. *Psychological Reports*, *66*(1), 195. https://doi.org/10.2466/PR0.66.1.195-244
Meehl, P. E. (1990b). Appraising and amending theories: The strategy of Lakatosian Defense and two principles that warrant it. *Psychological Inquiry*, *1*(2), 108–141. https://doi.org/10.1207/s15327965pli0102_1
Menkveld, A. J., Dreber, A., Holzmeister, F., Huber, J., Johanneson, M., Kirchler, M., Razen, M., Weitzel, U., Abad, D., Abudy, M. (Meni), Adrian, T., Ait-Sahalia, Y., Akmansoy, O., Alcock, J., Alexeev, V., Aloosh, A., Amato, L., Amaya, D., Angel, J. J., Bach, A., … Bao, L. (2021). Non-standard errors. *SSRN Electronic Journal*. https://doi.org/10.2139/ssrn.3961574
Merton, R. K. (1942). A note on science and democracy. *Journal of Legal and Political Sociology*, *1*(1 and 2), 115–126.
Merton, R. K. (1957). Priorities in scientific discovery: A chapter in the sociology of science. *American Sociological Review*, *22*(6), 635. https://doi.org/10.2307/2089193
Merton, R. K. (1968). The Matthew effect in science: The reward and communication systems of science are considered. *Science*, *159*(3810), 56–63. https://doi.org/10.1126/science.159.3810.56
Merton, R. K. (1973). *The sociology of science: Theoretical and empirical investigations*. University of Chicago Press.
Merton, R. K., & Barber, E. G. (2004). *The travels and adventures of serendipity: A study in historical semantics and the sociology of science*. Princeton University Press. (Original work published 1958)
Merton, R. K., & Barber, E. G. (2017). Sociological ambivalence. In A. T. Edward (Ed.), *Sociological theory, values, and sociocultural change* (pp. 91–120). Routledge. (Original work published 1963).
Micklethwait, J., & Wooldridge, A. (1997). *The witch doctors: What the management gurus are saying, why it matters and how to make sense of it*. Mandarin.
Mill, J. S. (1974). *A system of logic: Ratiocinative and inductive: Being a connected view of the principles of evidence and the methods of scientific investigation* (J. M. Robson, Ed.; Vol. 7). University of Toronto Press. (Original work published 1843)
Miller, C. C., & Bamberger, P. (2016). Exploring emergent and poorly understood phenomena in the strangest of places: The footprint of discovery in replications, meta-analyses, and null findings. *Academy of Management Discoveries*, *2*(4), 313–319. https://doi.org/10.5465/amd.2016.0115
Mitchell, T. R., & James, L. R. (2001). Building better theory: Time and the specification of when things happen. *Academy of Management Review*, *26*(4), 530. https://doi.org/10.2307/3560240
Mitroff, I. I. (1974). Norms and counter-norms in a select group of the Apollo moon scientists: A case study of the ambivalence of scientists. *American Sociological Review*, *39*(4), 579. https://doi.org/10.2307/2094423

Modecki, K. L., Low-Choy, S., Uink, B. N., Vernon, L., Correia, H., & Andrews, K. (2020). Tuning into the real effect of smartphone use on parenting: A multiverse analysis. *Journal of Child Psychology and Psychiatry*, *61*(8), 855–865. https://doi.org/10.1111/jcpp.13282

Molinié, A., & Bodenhausen, G. (2013). On toxic effects of scientific journals. *Journal of Biosciences*, *38*(2), 189–199. https://doi.org/10.1007/s12038-013-9328-5

Morgan, T. M., Krumholz, H. M., Lifton, R. P., & Spertus, J. A. (2007). Nonvalidation of reported genetic risk factors for acute coronary syndrome in a large-scale replication study. *JAMA*, *297*(14), 1551. https://doi.org/10.1001/jama.297.14.1551

Mulkay, M. J. (1976). Norms and ideology in science. *Social Science Information*, *15*(4–5), 637–656. https://doi.org/10.1177/053901847601500406

Mulkay, M. J. (1980). Interpretation and the use of rules: The case of the norms of science. *Transactions of the New York Academy of Sciences*, *39*(1 Series II), 111–125. https://doi.org/10.1111/j.2164-0947.1980.tb02772.x

Munafò, M. R., Nosek, B. A., Bishop, D. V. M., Button, K. S., Chambers, C. D., Percie du Sert, N., Simonsohn, U., Wagenmakers, E.-J., Ware, J. J., & Ioannidis, J. P. A. (2017). A manifesto for reproducible science. *Nature Human Behaviour*, *1*(1), 0021. https://doi.org/10.1038/s41562-016-0021

Münch, R. (2014). *Academic capitalism: Universities in the global struggle for excellence*. Routledge.

Münch, R. (2015). Science in the hands of strategic management: The metrification of scientific work and its impact on the evolution of knowledge. In I. M. Welpe, J. Wollersheim, S. Ringelhan, & M. Osterloh (Eds.), *Incentives and performance* (pp. 33–48). Springer. https://doi.org/10.1007/978-3-319-09785-5_3

Murphy, K. R., & Russell, C. J. (2017). Mend it or end it: Redirecting the search for interactions in the organizational sciences. *Organizational Research Methods*, *20*(4), 549–573. https://doi.org/10.1177/1094428115625322

Muthukrishna, M., & Henrich, J. (2019). A problem in theory. *Nature Human Behaviour*, *3*(3), 221–229. https://doi.org/10.1038/s41562-018-0522-1

National Science Foundation. (2015). *NSF's public access plan: Today's data, tomorrow's discoveries: Increasing access to the results of research funded by the National Science Foundation*. https://www.nsf.gov/pubs/2015/nsf15052/nsf15052.pdf

National Science Foundation (NSF). (2016). *Responsible Conduct of Research (RCR)*.

Neyman, J., & Pearson, E. S. (1933). The testing of statistical hypotheses in relation to probabilities a priori. *Mathematical Proceedings of the Cambridge Philosophical Society*, *29*(04), 492–510. https://doi.org/10.1017/S030500410001152X

Nickerson, R. S. (1998). Confirmation bias: A ubiquitous phenomenon in many guises. *Review of General Psychology*, *2*(2), 175–220. https://doi.org/10.1037/1089-2680.2.2.175

Nosek, B. A., Alter, G. C., Banks, G. C., Borsboom, D., Bowman, S. D., Breckler, S. J., Buck, S., Chambers, C. D., Chin, G., Christensen, G., Contestabile, M., Dafoe, A., Eich, E., Freese, J., Glennerster, R., Goroff, D., Green, D. P., Hesse, B. W., Humphreys, M., Ishiyama, J., … Yarkoni, T. (2015). Promoting an open research culture. *Science*, *348*(6242), 1422–1425. https://doi.org/10.1126/science.aab2374

Nosek, B. A., Ebersole, C. R., DeHaven, A. C., & Mellor, D. T. (2018). The preregistration revolution. *Proceedings of the National Academy of Sciences*, *115*(11), 2600–2606. https://doi.org/10.1073/pnas.1708274114

Nosek, B. A., Hardwicke, T. E., Moshontz, H., Allard, A., Corker, K. S., Dreber, A., Fidler, F., Hilgard, J., Kline Struhl, M., Nuijten, M. B., Rohrer, J. M., Romero, F., Scheel, A. M., Scherer, L. D., Schönbrodt, F. D., & Vazire, S. (2022). Replicability, robustness, and reproducibility in psychological science. *Annual Review of Psychology*, *73*(1), 719–748. https://doi.org/10.1146/annurev-psych-020821-114157

Nosek, B. A., & Lakens, D. (2014). Registered reports: A method to increase the credibility of published results. *Social Psychology*, *45*(3), 137–141. https://doi.org/10.1027/1864-9335/a000192

Nosek, B. A., Spies, J. R., & Motyl, M. (2012). Scientific utopia II: Restructuring incentives and practices to promote truth over publishability. *Perspectives on Psychological Science*, *7*(6), 615–631. https://doi.org/10.1177/1745691612459058

Nunnally, J. C. (1975). Psychometric theory—25 years ago and now. *Educational Researcher*, *4*(10), 7–21. https://doi.org/10.3102/0013189X004010007

Nunnally, J. C. (1978). *Psychometric theory* (2nd ed.). McGraw-Hill.

Nye, J., & Moul, C. (2007). The political economy of numbers: On the application of Benford's law to international macroeconomic statistics. *The B.E. Journal of Macroeconomics*, *7*(1). https://doi.org/10.2202/1935-1690.1449

Obels, P., Lakens, D., Coles, N. A., Gottfried, J., & Green, S. A. (2020). Analysis of open data and computational reproducibility in registered reports in psychology. *Advances in Methods and Practices in Psychological Science*, *3*(2), 229–237. https://doi.org/10.1177/2515245920918872

Oberauer, K., & Lewandowsky, S. (2019). Addressing the theory crisis in psychology. *Psychonomic Bulletin & Review*, *26*(5), 1596–1618. https://doi.org/10.3758/s13423-019-01645-2

O'Boyle, E. H., Banks, G. C., Carter, K., Walter, S. L., & Yuan, Z. (2019). A 20-year review of outcome reporting bias in moderated multiple regression. *Journal of Business and Psychology*, *34*(1), 19–37. https://doi.org/10.1007/s10869-018-9539-8

O'Boyle, E. H., Banks, G. C., & Gonzalez-Mulé, E. (2017). The Chrysalis effect: How ugly initial results metamorphosize into beautiful articles. *Journal of Management*, *43*(2), 376–399. https://doi.org/10.1177/0149206314527133

O'Boyle, E. H., & Götz, M. (2022). Questionable research practices. In L. J. Jussim, J. A. Krosnick, & S. T. Stevens (Eds.), *Research integrity: Best practices for the social and behavioral sciences* (pp. 260–294). Oxford University Press. https://doi.org/10.1093/oso/9780190938550.003.0010

O'Donnell, M., Dev, A. S., Antonoplis, S., Baum, S. M., Benedetti, A. H., Brown, N. D., Carrillo, B., Choi, A. L., Connor, P., Donnelly, K., Ellwood-Lowe, M. E., Foushee, R., Jansen, R., Jarvis, S. N., Lundell-Creagh, R., Ocampo, J. M., Okafor, G. N., Azad, Z. R., Rosenblum, M., Schatz, D., … Nelson, L. D. (2021). Empirical audit and review and an assessment of evidentiary value in research on the psychological consequences of scarcity. *Proceedings of the National Academy of Sciences*, *118*(44), e2103313118. https://doi.org/10.1073/pnas.2103313118

Oliu-Barton, M., Pradelski, B. S. R., Aghion, P., Artus, P., Kickbusch, I., Lazarus, J. V., Sridhar, D., & Vanderslott, S. (2021). SARS-CoV-2 elimination, not mitigation, creates best outcomes for health, the economy, and civil liberties. *The Lancet*, *397*(10291), 2234–2236. https://doi.org/10.1016/S0140-6736(21)00978-8

Open Science Collaboration. (2015). Estimating the reproducibility of psychological science. *Science*, *349*(6251), aac4716. https://doi.org/10.1126/science.aac4716

Oppenheimer, D. M., Meyvis, T., & Davidenko, N. (2009). Instructional manipulation checks: Detecting satisficing to increase statistical power. *Journal of Experimental Social Psychology*, *45*(4), 867–872. https://doi.org/10.1016/j.jesp.2009.03.009

Orben, A., & Lakens, D. (2020). Crud (re)defined. *Advances in Methods and Practices in Psychological Science*, *3*(2), 238–247. https://doi.org/10.1177/2515245920917961

Orlitzky, M. (2012). How can significance tests be deinstitutionalized? *Organizational Research Methods*, *15*(2), 199–228. https://doi.org/10.1177/1094428111428356

Ostroff, C. (2019). Contextualizing context in organizational research. In S. E. Humphrey & J. M. LeBreton (Eds.), *The handbook of multilevel theory, measurement, and analysis*. (pp. 39–65). American Psychological Association. https://doi.org/10.1037/0000115-003

Oxfam America. (2015). *Lives on the line: The human cost of cheap chicken*.

Park, M., Leahey, E., & Funk, R. J. (2023). Papers and patents are becoming less disruptive over time. *Nature*, *613*(7942), 138–144. https://doi.org/10.1038/s41586-022-05543-x

Parsons, S. (2022). Exploring reliability heterogeneity with multiverse analyses: Data processing decisions unpredictably influence measurement reliability. *Meta-Psychology*, *6*, 1-22. https://doi.org/10.15626/MP.2020.2577

Paterson, D. G., & Tinker, M. A. (1931). Studies of typographical factors influencing speed of reading. *Journal of Applied Psychology*, *15*(3), 241–247. https://doi.org/10.1037/h0074261

Pearson, K. (1911). *The grammar of science* (3rd ed.). Adam and Charles Black.

Peterson, R. A., & Kim, Y. (2013). On the relationship between coefficient alpha and composite reliability. *Journal of Applied Psychology*, *98*(1), 194–198. https://doi.org/10.1037/a0030767

Pfeffer, J. (1982). *Organizations and organization theory*. Pitman.

Pham, M. T., & Oh, T. T. (2021a). On not confusing the tree of trustworthy statistics with the greater forest of good science: A comment on Simmons et al.'s perspective on pre-registration. *Journal of Consumer Psychology*, *31*(1), 181–185. https://doi.org/10.1002/jcpy.1213

Pham, M. T., & Oh, T. T. (2021b). Preregistration is neither sufficient nor necessary for good science. *Journal of Consumer Psychology*, *31*(1), 163–176. https://doi.org/10.1002/jcpy.1209

Pinfield, S., Salter, J., & Bath, P. A. (2016). The "total cost of publication" in a hybrid open-access environment: Institutional approaches to funding journal article-processing charges in combination with subscriptions. *Journal of the Association for Information Science and Technology*, *67*(7), 1751–1766. https://doi.org/10.1002/asi.23446

Pittenger, D. J. (1993). The utility of the Myers-Briggs type indicator. *Review of Educational Research*, *63*(4), 467–488. https://doi.org/10.3102/00346543063004467

Pittenger, D. J. (2005). Cautionary comments regarding the Myers-Briggs type indicator. *Consulting Psychology Journal: Practice and Research*, *57*(3), 210–221. https://doi.org/10.1037/1065-9293.57.3.210

Piwowar, H. A., Day, R. S., & Fridsma, D. B. (2007). Sharing detailed research data is associated with increased citation rate. *PLoS ONE*, *2*(3), e308. https://doi.org/10.1371/journal.pone.0000308

Piwowar, H. A., Priem, J., Larivière, V., Alperin, J. P., Matthias, L., Norlander, B., Farley, A., West, J., & Haustein, S. (2018). The state of OA: A large-scale analysis of the prevalence and impact of open access articles. *PeerJ*, *6*, e4375. https://doi.org/10.7717/peerj.4375

Platt, J. R. (1964). Strong inference: Certain systematic methods of scientific thinking may produce much more rapid progress than others. *Science*, *146*(3642), 347–353. https://doi.org/10.1126/science.146.3642.347

Popper, K. R. (1963). *Conjectures and refutations: The growth of scientific knowledge*. Routledge.

Popper, K. R. (1983). *Realism and the aim of science*. Routledge. (Original work published 1956)

Popper, K. R. (2002). *The logic of scientific discovery*. Routledge. (Original work published 1959)

Price, L. R. (2017). *Psychometric methods: Theory into practice*. Guilford Press.

Prosser, A. M. B., Hamshaw, R. J. T., Meyer, J., Bagnall, R., Blackwood, L., Huysamen, M., Jordan, A., Vasileiou, K., & Walter, Z. (2022). When open data closes the door: A critical examination of the past, present and the potential future for open data guidelines in journals. *British Journal of Social Psychology*, bjso.12576. https://doi.org/10.1111/bjso.12576

Proulx, T., & Morey, R. D. (2021). Beyond statistical ritual: Theory in psychological science. *Perspectives on Psychological Science*, *16*(4), 671–681. https://doi.org/10.1177/17456916211017098

Purgar, M., Klanjscek, T., & Culina, A. (2022). Quantifying research waste in ecology. *Nature Ecology & Evolution*, *6*(9), 1390–1397. https://doi.org/10.1038/s41559-022-01820-0

Reynolds, K. J., Subašić, E., & Tindall, K. (2015). The problem of behaviour change: From social norms to an ingroup focus. *Social and Personality Psychology Compass*, *9*(1), 45–56. https://doi.org/10.1111/spc3.12155

Rhemtulla, M. (2016). Population performance of SEM parceling strategies under measurement and structural model misspecification. *Psychological Methods*, *21*(3), 348–368. https://doi.org/10.1037/met0000072

Rhemtulla, M., van Bork, R., & Borsboom, D. (2020). Worse than measurement error: Consequences of inappropriate latent variable measurement models. *Psychological Methods*, *25*(1), 30–45. https://doi.org/10.1037/met0000220

Richter, M. K. (1966). Revealed preference theory. *Econometrica*, *34*(3), 635. https://doi.org/10.2307/1909773

Rogelberg, S. G., King, E. B., & Alonso, A. (2022). How we can bring I-O psychology science and evidence-based practices to the public. *Industrial and Organizational Psychology*, *15*(2), 259–272. https://doi.org/10.1017/iop.2021.142

Roloff, J., & Zyphur, M. J. (2019). Null findings, replications and preregistered studies in business ethics research. *Journal of Business Ethics*, *160*(3), 609–619. https://doi.org/10.1007/s10551-018-3864-8

Romero, F., & Sprenger, J. (2021). Scientific self-correction: The Bayesian way. *Synthese*, *198*(S23), 5803–5823. https://doi.org/10.1007/s11229-020-02697-x

Rosen, C. C., Dimotakis, N., Cole, M. S., Taylor, S. G., Simon, L. S., Smith, T. A., & Reina, C. S. (2020). When challenges hinder: An investigation of when and how challenge stressors impact employee outcomes. *Journal of Applied Psychology*, *105*(10), 1181–1206. https://doi.org/10.1037/apl0000483

Roth, W.-M. (2002). Editorial power/authorial suffering. *Research in Science Education*, *32*(2), 215–240. https://doi.org/10.1023/A:1016030212572

Rothe, H. F., & Nye, C. T. (1958). Output rates among coil winders. *Journal of Applied Psychology*, *42*(3), 182–186. https://doi.org/10.1037/h0041121

Rynes, S. L., Colbert, A. E., & Brown, K. G. (2002). HR Professionals' beliefs about effective human resource practices: Correspondence between research and practice. *Human Resource Management*, *41*(2), 149–174. https://doi.org/10.1002/hrm.10029

Saitone, T. L., Aleks Schaefer, K., & Scheitrum, D. P. (2021). COVID-19 morbidity and mortality in U.S. meatpacking counties. *Food Policy*, *101*, 102072. https://doi.org/10.1016/j.foodpol.2021.102072

Saks, A. M. (1995). Longitudinal field investigation of the moderating and mediating effects of self-efficacy on the relationship between training and newcomer adjustment. *Journal of Applied Psychology*, *80*(2), 211–225. https://doi.org/10.1037/0021-9010.80.2.211

Salanova, M., Agut, S., & Peiró, J. M. (2005). Linking organizational resources and work engagement to employee performance and customer loyalty: The mediation of service climate. *Journal of Applied Psychology*, *90*(6), 1217–1227. https://doi.org/10.1037/0021-9010.90.6.1217

Salgado, J. F., & Moscoso, S. (2019). Meta-analysis of interrater reliability of supervisory performance ratings: Effects of appraisal purpose, scale type, and range restriction. *Frontiers in Psychology*, *10*, 2281. https://doi.org/10.3389/fpsyg.2019.02281

Sanders, K., van Riemsdijk, M., & Groen, B. (2008). The gap between research and practice: A replication study on the HR professionals' beliefs about effective human resource practices. *The International Journal of Human Resource Management*, *19*(10), 1976–1988. https://doi.org/10.1080/09585190802324304

Saylors, R., & Trafimow, D. (2021). Why the increasing use of complex causal models is a problem: On the danger sophisticated theoretical narratives pose to truth. *Organizational Research Methods*, *24*(3), 616–629. https://doi.org/10.1177/1094428119893452

Schäfer, T., & Schwarz, M. A. (2019). The meaningfulness of effect sizes in psychological research: Differences between sub-disciplines and the impact of potential biases. *Frontiers in Psychology*, *10*(April), 1–13. https://doi.org/10.3389/fpsyg.2019.00813

Schauer, J. M. (2022). Replicability and meta-analysis. In W. O'Donohue, A. Masuda, & S. Lilienfeld (Eds.), *Avoiding questionable research practices in applied psychology* (pp. 301–342). Springer. https://doi.org/10.1007/978-3-031-04968-2_14

Scheel, A. M., Schijen, M. R. M. J., & Lakens, D. (2021). An excess of positive results: Comparing the standard psychology literature with registered reports. *Advances in Methods and Practices in Psychological Science*, *4*(2), 251524592110074. https://doi.org/10.1177/25152459211007467

Schmidt, F. L. (1992). What do data really mean? Research findings, meta-analysis, and cumulative knowledge in psychology. *American Psychologist*, *47*(10), 1173–1181. https://doi.org/10.1037/0003-066X.47.10.1173

Schmitt, N. W., & Ali, A. A. (2015). The practical importance of measurement invariance. In C. E. Lance & R. J. Vandenberg (Eds.), *More statistical and methodological myths and urban legends* (pp. 327–346). Routledge.

Schmoch, U. (2015). The informative value of international university rankings: Some methodological remarks. In I. M. Welpe, J. Wollersheim, S. Ringelhan, & M. Osterloh (Eds.), *Incentives and performance* (pp. 141–154). Springer. https://doi.org/10.1007/978-3-319-09785-5_9

Schroter, S., Black, N., Evans, S., Godlee, F., Osorio, L., & Smith, R. (2008). What errors do peer reviewers detect, and does training improve their ability to detect them? *Journal of the Royal Society of Medicine*, *101*(10), 507–514. https://doi.org/10.1258/jrsm.2008.080062

Schweinsberg, M., Feldman, M., Staub, N., van den Akker, O. R., van Aert, R. C. M., van Assen, M. A. L. M., Liu, Y., Althoff, T., Heer, J., Kale, A., Mohamed, Z., Amireh, H., Venkatesh Prasad, V., Bernstein, A., Robinson, E., Snellman, K., Amy Sommer, S., Otner, S. M. G., Robinson, D., Madan, N., … Luis Uhlmann, E. (2021). Same data, different conclusions: Radical dispersion in empirical results when independent analysts operationalize and test the same hypothesis. *Organizational Behavior and Human Decision Processes*, *165*, 228–249. https://doi.org/10.1016/j.obhdp.2021.02.003

Scientific Pandemic Influenza Group on Modelling, Operational sub-group (SPI-M-O). (2020). *SPI-M-O: Consensus statement on COVID-19*. Scientific Advisory Group for Emergencies (SAGE). https://assets.publishing.service.gov.uk/government/uploads/system/uploads/attachment_data/file/931146/S0801_SAGE61_201007_SPI-M-O_Consensus_Statement.pdf

Serghiou, S., Contopoulos-Ioannidis, D. G., Boyack, K. W., Riedel, N., Wallach, J. D., & Ioannidis, J. P. A. (2021). Assessment of transparency indicators across the biomedical literature: How open is open? *PLOS Biology*, *19*(3), e3001107. https://doi.org/10.1371/journal.pbio.3001107

Shaffer, J. A., DeGeest, D. S., & Li, A. (2016). Tackling the problem of construct proliferation: A guide to assessing the discriminant validity of conceptually related constructs. *Organizational Research Methods*, *19*(1), 80–110. https://doi.org/10.1177/1094428115598239

Silberzahn, R., Uhlmann, E. L., Martin, D. P., Anselmi, P., Aust, F., Awtrey, E., Bahník, Š., Bai, F., Bannard, C., Bonnier, E., Carlsson, R., Cheung, F., Christensen, G., Clay, R., Craig, M. A., Dalla Rosa, A., Dam, L., Evans, M. H., Flores Cervantes, I., Fong, N., … Nosek, B. A. (2018). Many analysts, one data set: Making transparent how variations in analytic choices affect results. *Advances in Methods and Practices in Psychological Science*, *1*(3), 337–356. https://doi.org/10.1177/2515245917747646

Simmons, J. P., Nelson, L. D., & Simonsohn, U. (2011). False-positive psychology: Undisclosed flexibility in data collection and analysis allows presenting anything as significant. *Psychological Science*, *22*(11), 1359–1366. https://doi.org/10.1177/0956797611417632

Simmons, J. P., Nelson, L. D., & Simonsohn, U. (2021a). Pre-registration is a game changer. But, like random assignment, it is neither necessary nor sufficient for credible science. *Journal of Consumer Psychology*, *31*(1), 177–180. https://doi.org/10.1002/jcpy.1207

Simmons, J. P., Nelson, L. D., & Simonsohn, U. (2021b). Pre-registration: Why and how. *Journal of Consumer Psychology*, *31*(1), 151–162. https://doi.org/10.1002/jcpy.1208

Simonsohn, U., Simmons, J. P., & Nelson, L. D. (2022). *AsPredicted*. https://aspredicted.org/

Slavković, A., & Seeman, J. (2023). Statistical data privacy: A song of privacy and utility. *Annual Review of Statistics and Its Application*, *10*(1), 189–218. https://doi.org/10.1146/annurev-statistics-033121-112921

Smith, G. C. S., & Pell, J. P. (2003). Parachute use to prevent death and major trauma related to gravitational challenge: Systematic review of randomised controlled trials. *BMJ*, *327*(7429), 1459–1461. https://doi.org/10.1136/bmj.327.7429.1459

Smith, R. (2006). Peer review: A flawed process at the heart of science and journals. *Journal of the Royal Society of Medicine*, *99*(4), 178–182. https://doi.org/10.1177/014107680609900414

Soderberg, C. K. (2018). Using OSF to share data: A step-by-step guide. *Advances in Methods and Practices in Psychological Science*, *1*(1), 115–120. https://doi.org/10.1177/2515245918757689

Soderberg, C. K., Errington, T. M., Schiavone, S. R., Bottesini, J., Thorn, F. S., Vazire, S., Esterling, K. M., & Nosek, B. A. (2021). Initial evidence of research quality of registered reports compared with the standard publishing model. *Nature Human Behaviour*, *5*(8), 990–997. https://doi.org/10.1038/s41562-021-01142-4

Sotola, L. K. (2022). Garbage in, garbage out? Evaluating the evidentiary value of published meta-analyses using z-curve analysis. *Collabra: Psychology*, *8*(1), 32571. https://doi.org/10.1525/collabra.32571

Spearman, C. (1910). Correlation calculated from faulty data. *British Journal of Psychology*, *3*(3), 271–295. https://doi.org/10.1111/j.2044-8295.1910.tb00206.x

Spector, P. E. (2019). Do not cross me: Optimizing the use of cross-sectional designs. *Journal of Business and Psychology*, *34*(2), 125–137. https://doi.org/10.1007/s10869-018-09613-8

Spector, P. E. (2022, December 12). Theory is misused in organizational science. Paul Spector. https://paulspector.com/theory-is-misused-in-organizational-science/

Stanley, T. D., Carter, E. C., & Doucouliagos, H. (2018). What meta-analyses reveal about the replicability of psychological research. *Psychological Bulletin*, *144*(12), 1325–1346. https://doi.org/10.1037/bul0000169

Staw, B. M., & Ross, J. (1985). Stability in the midst of change: A dispositional approach to job attitudes. *Journal of Applied Psychology*, *70*(3), 469–480. https://doi.org/10.1037/0021-9010.70.3.469

Steegen, S., Tuerlinckx, F., Gelman, A., & Vanpaemel, W. (2016). Increasing transparency through a multiverse analysis. *Perspectives on Psychological Science*, *11*(5), 702–712. https://doi.org/10.1177/1745691616658637

Stefan, N. (2022). Metabolic disorders, COVID-19 and vaccine-breakthrough infections. *Nature Reviews Endocrinology*, *18*(2), 75–76. https://doi.org/10.1038/s41574-021-00608-9

Stein, R., & Swan, A. B. (2019). Evaluating the validity of Myers-Briggs type indicator theory: A teaching tool and window into intuitive psychology. *Social and Personality Psychology Compass*, *13*(2), e12434. https://doi.org/10.1111/spc3.12434

Steneck, N. H. (2006). Fostering integrity in research: Definitions, current knowledge, and future directions. *Science and Engineering Ethics*, *12*(1), 53–74. https://doi.org/10.1007/PL00022268

Stern, J., Arslan, R. C., Gerlach, T. M., & Penke, L. (2019). No robust evidence for cycle shifts in preferences for men's bodies in a multiverse analysis: A response to Gangestad, Dinh, Grebe, Del Giudice, and Emery Thompson (2019). *Evolution and Human Behavior*, *40*(6), 517–525. https://doi.org/10.1016/j.evolhumbehav.2019.08.005

Stewart, N., Ungemach, C., Harris, A. J. L., Bartels, D. M., Newell, B. R., Paolacci, G., & Chandler, J. J. (2015). The average laboratory samples a population of 7,300 Amazon Mechanical Turk workers. *Judgment and Decision Making*, *10*(5), 479–491.

STM. (2021). *STM global brief 2021: Economics & market size: An STM report supplement*. STM: International Association of Scientific, Technical and Medical Publishers. https://www.stm-assoc.org/2022_08_24_STM_White_Report_a4_v15.pdf

Stodden, V. (2015). Reproducing statistical results. *Annual Review of Statistics and Its Application*, *2*(1), 1–19. https://doi.org/10.1146/annurev-statistics-010814-020127

Stodden, V., Seiler, J., & Ma, Z. (2018). An empirical analysis of journal policy effectiveness for computational reproducibility. *Proceedings of the National Academy of Sciences*, *115*(11), 2584–2589. https://doi.org/10.1073/pnas.1708290115

Stroebe, W. (2019). What can we learn from Many Labs replications? *Basic and Applied Social Psychology*, *41*(2), 91–103. https://doi.org/10.1080/01973533.2019.1577736

Sutton, R. I., & Staw, B. M. (1995). What theory is not. *Administrative Science Quarterly*, *40*(3), 371. https://doi.org/10.2307/2393788

Swiss Academies of Arts and Sciences. (2021). *Code of conduct for scientific integrity*. Swiss Academies of Arts and Sciences.

Swiss National Science Foundation (SNSF). (2022). *Open access to publications*. Swiss National Science Foundation. https://www.snf.ch/en/VyUvGzptStOEpUoC/topic/undefined/en/VyUvGzptStOEpUoC/topic/

Tappin, D. C., Bentley, T. A., & Vitalis, A. (2008). The role of contextual factors for musculoskeletal disorders in the New Zealand meat processing industry. *Ergonomics*, *51*(10), 1576–1593. https://doi.org/10.1080/00140130802238630

Tennant, J. P., Dugan, J. M., Graziotin, D., Jacques, D. C., Waldner, F., Mietchen, D., Elkhatib, Y., B. Collister, L., Pikas, C. K., Crick, T., Masuzzo, P., Caravaggi, A., Berg, D. R., Niemeyer, K. E., Ross-Hellauer, T., Mannheimer, S., Rigling, L., Katz, D. S., Greshake Tzovaras, B., Pacheco-Mendoza, J., … Colomb, J. (2017). A multi-disciplinary perspective on emergent and future innovations in peer review. *F1000Research*, *6*, 1151. https://doi.org/10.12688/f1000research.12037.3

Thalmayer, A. G., Toscanelli, C., & Arnett, J. J. (2021). The neglected 95% revisited: Is American psychology becoming less American? *American Psychologist*, *76*(1), 116–129. https://doi.org/10.1037/amp0000622

Thorndike, E. L. (1904). *An introduction to the theory of mental and social measurements*. The Science Press.

Tihanyi, L. (2020). From "That's Interesting" to "That's Important." *Academy of Management Journal*, *63*(2), 329–331. https://doi.org/10.5465/amj.2020.4002

Timming, A. R., Farndale, E., Budhwar, P., & Wood, G. (2021). Editorial: What are registered reports and why are they important to the future of human resource management research? *Human Resource Management Journal*, *31*(3), 595–602. https://doi.org/10.1111/1748-8583.12359

Torka, A.-K., Mazei, J., Bosco, F. A., Cortina, J. M., Götz, M., Kepes, S., O'Boyle, E. H., & Hüffmeier, J. (2023). How well are open science practices implemented in industrial and organizational psychology and management? *European Journal of Work and Organizational Psychology*. Advance online publication. https://doi.org/10.1080/1359432X.2023.2206571

Toth, A. A., Banks, G. C., Mellor, D., O'Boyle, E. H., Dickson, A., Davis, D. J., DeHaven, A., Bochantin, J., & Borns, J. (2021). Study preregistration: An evaluation of a method for transparent reporting. *Journal of Business and Psychology*, *36*(4), 553–571. https://doi.org/10.1007/s10869-020-09695-3

Tourish, D. (2020). The triumph of nonsense in management studies. *Academy of Management Learning & Education*, *19*(1), 99–109. https://doi.org/10.5465/amle.2019.0255

TurkerView. (2023). *Queuebicle | TurkerView's MTurk workflow management application*. https://turkerview.com/qbc/

Tversky, A., & Kahneman, D. (1981). The framing of decisions and the psychology of choice. *Science*, *211*(4481), 453–458. https://doi.org/10.1126/science.7455683

Ucci, M. A., D'Antonio, F., & Berghella, V. (2022). Double- vs single-blind peer review effect on acceptance rates: A systematic review and meta-analysis of randomized trials. *American Journal of Obstetrics & Gynecology MFM*, *4*(4), 100645. https://doi.org/10.1016/j.ajogmf.2022.100645

U.S. Department of Health & Human Services. (2022, August 29). *When and how to comply | public access*. NIH Public Access Policy. https://publicaccess.nih.gov/

Van De Ven, A. H., & Johnson, P. E. (2006). Knowledge for Theory and Practice. *Academy of Management Review*, *31*(4), 802–821. https://doi.org/10.5465/amr.2006.22527385

van Dijk, H., & van Zelst, M. (2020). Comfortably numb? Researchers' satisfaction with the publication system and a proposal for radical change. *Publications*, *8*(1), 14. https://doi.org/10.3390/publications8010014

Van Noorden, R. (2013). Open access: The true cost of science publishing. *Nature*, *495*(7442), 426–429. https://doi.org/10.1038/495426a

van Zwet, E. W., & Cator, E. A. (2021). The significance filter, the winner's curse and the need to shrink. *Statistica Neerlandica*, *75*(4), 437–452. https://doi.org/10.1111/stan.12241

Vanpaemel, W., Vermorgen, M., Deriemaecker, L., & Storms, G. (2015). Are we wasting a good crisis? The availability of psychological research data after the storm. *Collabra*, *1*(1), 1–5. https://doi.org/10.1525/collabra.13

Vazire, S. (2022). Let's peer review peer review. In L. J. Jussim, J. A. Krosnick, & S. T. Stevens (Eds.), *Research integrity: Best practices for the social and behavioral sciences* (pp. 357–369). Oxford University Press. https://doi.org/10.1093/oso/9780190938550.003.0014

Vazire, S., Schiavone, S. R., & Bottesini, J. G. (2022). Credibility beyond replicability: Improving the four validities in psychological science. *Current Directions in Psychological Science*, *31*(2), 162–168. https://doi.org/10.1177/09637214211067779

Vicente-Saez, R., & Martinez-Fuentes, C. (2018). Open science now: A systematic literature review for an integrated definition. *Journal of Business Research*, *88*(January), 428–436. https://doi.org/10.1016/j.jbusres.2017.12.043

Viswesvaran, C., Ones, D. S., & Schmidt, F. L. (1996). Comparative analysis of the reliability of job performance ratings. *Journal of Applied Psychology*, *81*(5), 557–574. https://doi.org/10.1037/0021-9010.81.5.557

von Neumann, J., & Morgenstern, O. (2007). *Theory of games and economic behavior* (60th Anniversary Edition). Princeton University Press.

Vosgerau, J., Simonsohn, U., Nelson, L. D., & Simmons, J. P. (2019). 99% impossible: A valid, or falsifiable, internal meta-analysis. *Journal of Experimental Psychology: General*, *148*(9), 1628–1639. https://doi.org/10.1037/xge0000663

Voslinsky, A., & Azar, O. H. (2021). Incentives in experimental economics. *Journal of Behavioral and Experimental Economics*, *93*, 101706. https://doi.org/10.1016/j.socec.2021.101706

Wagenmakers, E.-J., Wetzels, R., Borsboom, D., & van der Maas, H. L. J. (2011). Why psychologists must change the way they analyze their data: The case of psi: Comment on Bem (2011). *Journal of Personality and Social Psychology*, *100*(3), 426–432. https://doi.org/10.1037/a0022790

Wagenmakers, E.-J., Wetzels, R., Borsboom, D., van der Maas, H. L. J., & Kievit, R. A. (2012). An agenda for purely confirmatory research. *Perspectives on Psychological Science*, *7*(6), 632–638. https://doi.org/10.1177/1745691612463078

Wallace, W. A., & Ollivere, B. (2022). How open access publishing developed in the 2010s and the potential for publishing misconduct. In J. Faintuch & S. Faintuch (Eds.), *Integrity of scientific research: Fraud, misconduct and fake news in the academic, medical and social environment* (pp. 509–514). Springer. https://doi.org/10.1007/978-3-030-99680-2_50

Ward, M. K., & Meade, A. W. (2023). Dealing with careless responding in survey data: Prevention, identification, and recommended best practices. *Annual Review of Psychology*, *74*(1), annurev-psych-040422-045007. https://doi.org/10.1146/annurev-psych-040422-045007

Wason, P. C. (1960). On the failure to eliminate hypotheses in a conceptual task. *Quarterly Journal of Experimental Psychology*, *12*(3), 129–140. https://doi.org/10.1080/17470216008416717

Wason, P. C., & Johnson-Laird, P. N. (1972). *Psychology of reasoning: Structure and content*. Harvard University Press.

Wasserstein, R. L., & Lazar, N. A. (2016). The ASA statement on *p*-values: Context, process, and purpose. *The American Statistician*, *70*(2), 129–133. https://doi.org/10.1080/00031305.2016.1154108

Webb, M. A., & Tangney, J. P. (2022). Too good to be true: Bots and bad data from Mechanical Turk. *Perspectives on Psychological Science*, 174569162211200. https://doi.org/10.1177/17456916221120027

Weick, K. E. (1995). What theory is not, theorizing is. *Administrative Science Quarterly*, *40*(3), 385. https://doi.org/10.2307/2393789

Wellcome Trust. (2012, June 28). *Wellcome Trust strengthens its open access policy*. Wellcome. https://wellcome.org/press-release/wellcome-trust-strengthens-its-open-access-policy

Wetzel, E., & Roberts, B. W. (2020). Commentary on Hussey and Hughes (2020): Hidden invalidity among 15 commonly used measures in social and personality psychology. *Advances in Methods and Practices in Psychological Science*, *3*(4), 505–508. https://doi.org/10.1177/2515245920957618

Wicherts, J. M., Klein, R. A., Swaans, S. H. F., Maassen, E., Stoevenbelt, A. H., Peeters, V. H. B. T. G., de Jonge, M., & Rüffer, F. (2022). How to protect privacy in open data. *Nature Human Behaviour*, *6*(12), 1603–1605. https://doi.org/10.1038/s41562-022-01481-w

Wigboldus, D. H. J., & Dotsch, R. (2016). Encourage playing with data and discourage questionable reporting practices. *Psychometrika*, *81*(1), 27–32. https://doi.org/10.1007/s11336-015-9445-1

Wolins, L. (1962). Responsibility for raw data. *American Psychologist*, *17*(9), 657–658. https://doi.org/10.1037/h0038819

Woo, S. E., Keith, M., & Thornton, M. A. (2015). Amazon Mechanical Turk for industrial and organizational psychology: Advantages, challenges, and practical recommendations. *Industrial and Organizational Psychology*, *8*(2), 171–179. https://doi.org/10.1017/iop.2015.21

Wouters, P. (2020). The mismeasurement of quality and impact. In M. Biagioli & A. Lippman (Eds.), *Gaming the metrics: Misconduct and manipulation in academic research* (pp. 67–75). The MIT Press.

Xie, Y., Wang, K., & Kong, Y. (2021). Prevalence of research misconduct and questionable research practices: A systematic review and meta-analysis. *Science and Engineering Ethics*, *27*(4), 41. https://doi.org/10.1007/s11948-021-00314-9

Yan, T. (2021). Consequences of asking sensitive questions in surveys. *Annual Review of Statistics and Its Application*, *8*(1), 109–127. https://doi.org/10.1146/annurev-statistics-040720-033353

Yankelovich, D. (1972). *Corporate priorities: A continuing study of the new demands on business*.

Yip, J. A., & Schweitzer, M. E. (2022). Norms for behavioral change (NBC) model: How injunctive norms and enforcement shift descriptive norms in science. *Organizational Behavior and Human Decision Processes*, *168*, 104109. https://doi.org/10.1016/j.obhdp.2021.104109

Zhou, H., & Fishbach, A. (2016). The pitfall of experimenting on the web: How unattended selective attrition leads to surprising (yet false) research conclusions. *Journal of Personality and Social Psychology*, *111*(4), 493–504. https://doi.org/10.1037/pspa0000056

Ziliak, S. T., & McCloskey, D. N. (2008). *The cult of statistical significance: How the standard error costs us jobs, justice, and lives*. University of Michigan Press.

CHAPTER 3

RETAINING SELF-INITIATED EXPATRIATES: SYSTEMATIC REVIEWS AND MANAGERIAL PRACTICES

Caleb Lugar, Jeremy D. Meuser, Milorad M. Novicevic, Paul D. Johnson, Anthony P. Ammeter and Chad P. Diaz II

ABSTRACT

In this chapter, the authors examined expatriates that self-initiate their international work for personal reasons and the factors that affect their departure from an organization. The authors conducted a systematic review of self-initiated expatriation (SIE) and its definitions in order to propose an integrated definition of SIE and model its nomological network. In addition, the authors construct a roadmap for future research directions in the SIE domain. Finally, using a qualitative research design, the authors studied the organizational practices designed to reduce SIE turnover in an exemplary multinational organization. Overall, our contributions are enhanced clarity of the SIE construct and the theorized practice of SIE retention.

Keywords: Expatriate; international; self-initiative; adjustment; embeddedness; retention

Research in Personnel and Human Resources Management, Volume 41, 93–125

Published under exclusive licence by Emerald Publishing Limited
ISSN: 0742-7301/doi:10.1108/S0742-730120230000041005

INTRODUCTION

Traditionally, multinational organizations have attempted to meet their staffing needs by sourcing talent internally through time-bound and tailored international relocation packages for their employees that promote work abroad – with the assumption that they would thereafter either return to their home-country organization or be transferred to another host-country subsidiary (Edström & Galbraith, 1977). These internal employees are typically persuaded to accept these temporary assignments with the enticing associated monetary and career incentives that they perceive would help them achieve their desired professional goals (Linder, 2019). The employees that accept these offers are referred to as company-transferred or *assigned* expatriates (AEs). However, the reliance on AEs has proven inadequate in emerging markets that have challenged organizations to identify new sources of globally mobile talent. In particular, the increase in demand for globally mobile employees willing and able to serve in a sustained manner has forced multinational organizations to tap into new talent pools (Doherty, 2013; Gunz & Peiperl, 2007; Guthridge et al., 2008).

SIEs are employees who originate their international relocation on their own (Haslberger & Vaiman, 2013). They are distinct from AEs in that SIEs self-initiate their search for international employment opportunities for personal reasons. Additionally, SIEs typically possess higher levels of education and have a greater intent to return to their home countries at some point in the future (Al Ariss et al., 2012; Haak-Saheem & Brewster, 2017).

Our goal for this article is to capture the views of subsidiary managers about factors that influence organizational practices for SIE retention. We have taken a broad approach toward achieving this goal by reviewing previous SIE research to highlight the strengths and weaknesses of the literature, proposing an integrated definition of the SIE construct, and synthesizing a model of SIE and its nomological network. Second, we review self-initiated expatriation and SIE turnover. Third, we evaluate the future research directions in previous research to construct a roadmap for the development of SIE research. Finally, we examine the views of subsidiary managers in a multinational organization to propose a model of SIE turnover. In conclusion, we outline the contributions, practical implications, and limitations of this article. Overall, our contributions enhance the understanding of SIE retention (Post et al., 2020) and provide a rich canvas for future research directions.

DEFINING SIE: A SYSTEMATIC APPROACH

Despite growth in the study of SIE, the primary barrier to its theoretical development has been the lack of consensus among researchers on the definition of SIEs (Biemann & Andresen, 2010). Mobile workers increasingly contribute to cross-border business activities of multinational enterprises (Bonache et al., 2020) and over the last 25 years SIEs have emerged as an important form of global workers (Shaffer et al., 2012), making it imperative to find a shared understanding and clear definition of the SIE construct to advance theory around it

(Podsakoff et al., 2016; Whetton, 1989) and to address common construct clarity issues organizational scholars have struggled with (e.g., Shaffer et al., 2016; Wayne et al., 2007).

To address this issue, we develop a formal definition by analyzing how the definitional elements of the SIE concept have changed in and across the different stages of the SIE definition's evolution. We employ distributional concept analysis (de Bolla et al., 2019), a method used by scholars to clarify constructs with "messy" definitions. As will be described, our analyses measure the co-occurrences of words across definitions over time to identify the key terms that have overlapped and thus reflect the convergence of the definition. Importantly, this allows us to uncover systematically how SIE scholars have been developing their conceptualization of this distinct type of expatriation.

Origins of the Definition of SIE

SIE research originated from Inkson et al.'s (1997) seminal study of the overseas experiences (OE) of young people traveling from New Zealand to the United Kingdom and other developed countries for leisure, internships, and working vacations. These educated young people in New Zealand viewed the OE as "a rite of passage, a symbol of adulthood, a social norm, a source of pride, and an experience which provides common conversational currency among those who take it" (Inkson & Myers, 2003, p. 171). This form of SIE "is in essence a local expression of the 'backpacker culture' increasingly in evidence among young people from countries around the world" (Inkson & Myers, 2003, p. 172). Although OE is a form of SIE, SIE is broader, making both this term and definition inappropriate to describe SIEs. Building on the OE concept, Suutari and Brewster (2000) introduced a compound term "self-initiated foreign work experience," which was the first to include the term "work" in their conceptualization of self-initiated international workers. The following year, Bhuian et al. (2001) introduced "contractual employment" in their definition of self-initiated overseas expatriates. The proliferation of terms for SIE was resolved in 2010 when researchers reached a consensus to use the term "Self-initiated Expatriate" for this group of expatriates (Doherty, 2013).

Despite the agreement on the term to describe the phenomena, there was no consensus on which definitional elements should be included in the definition of SIEs. Subsequent failed attempts to formalize the SIE definition (Arp et al., 2013) influenced Doherty et al. (2013) to concede "we do not purport to have a prescriptive definition of SIE." In other words, these failures have left SIE researchers with an undefined term for the phenomenon that they study, which is a clear obstacle to advancing SIE theory (Cerdin & Selmer, 2014).

Reviewing Past Proposed Definitions

To conduct a comprehensive review of the SIE literature, we searched for the term "self-initiated expatriate" and 11 variations[1] of the term in the SCOPUS database as well as EBSCOhost, ProQuest, and PsycINFO databases to identify the relevant articles. This search returned 316 unique articles. As some of these articles did not explicitly provide a definition for SIE, we removed them from our analyses. This removal resulted in 150 definitions of SIEs from 186 published articles from 1997 to 2020 (the complete list of articles and original SIE definitions containing these elements are available from the lead author upon request). From this array of SIE definitions, we extracted 35 definitional elements with their frequencies of use.

A review by Cerdin and Selmer (2014) identified inconsistencies across previously proposed SIE definitions and accentuated the need for both SIE construct clarity and narrowing the number of definitional elements. The authors proposed the following four critical elements of an SIE definition, "(a) self-initiated international relocation, (b) regular employment (intentions), (c) intentions of a temporary stay, and (d) skilled/professional qualifications" (p. 1294). We compared these four critical elements to the 35 definitional elements contained in the 150 definitions with SIE definitions that we selected and found that only a small percentage of articles cited temporary stay (5%) and skilled professional (8%) as requirements to be included in a definition of SIEs. We also found that Cerdin and Selmer (2014) did not include the following two specific elements that several other authors found critically important: (1) not transferred or not assigned by their organization (at 34% and reflecting the very essence of SIE, in our view) and (2) self-funded relocation (22%). We did find commonality for the definitional elements referring to the following terms: international (58%), work (52%), self-initiation (43%), and relocation (32%).

We also identified that the act of self-initiation is not included in more than half of the SIE definitions, possibly because those SIE researchers believed that adding this element is redundant because it is already contained in the compound term "self-initiated expatriate" (Hussain et al., 2019; Selmer & Lauring, 2010; Tharenou & Caulfield 2010). Other SIE researchers argue for an explicit inclusion of this term in the SIE definition (Cerdin & Selmer, 2014; Makkonen, 2016; Vaiman et al., 2015). This definitional disagreement about the elements of SIE illustrates the fragmentation of definitions and the related lack of construct clarity in this nascent domain of expatriation research and the need to revisit the definition of SIEs using a systematic approach.

IDENTIFYING DEFINITIONAL CONFOUNDS IN THE SIE NOMOLOGICAL NETWORK

Our review identified another latent issue revealing that some of these definitional elements confounded SIE antecedents, moderators, and/or outcomes with the definition of SIE itself. To address these latent deficiencies, we arranged these elements into the nomological network of the SIE definition (see Fig. 1) based on the following two widely accepted criteria: (1) the SIE phenomenon should be defined accurately without making any tautological statements (Antonakis et al., 2016, p. 301) and (2) the antecedents and outcomes of the SIE construct should not be used to define the construct itself (MacKenzie, 2003). The purpose of creating this nomological network is to identify the inputs that are crucial to develop a unifying definition of the SIE construct and to parse the confounding antecedents, moderators, and outcomes related to the SIE construct.

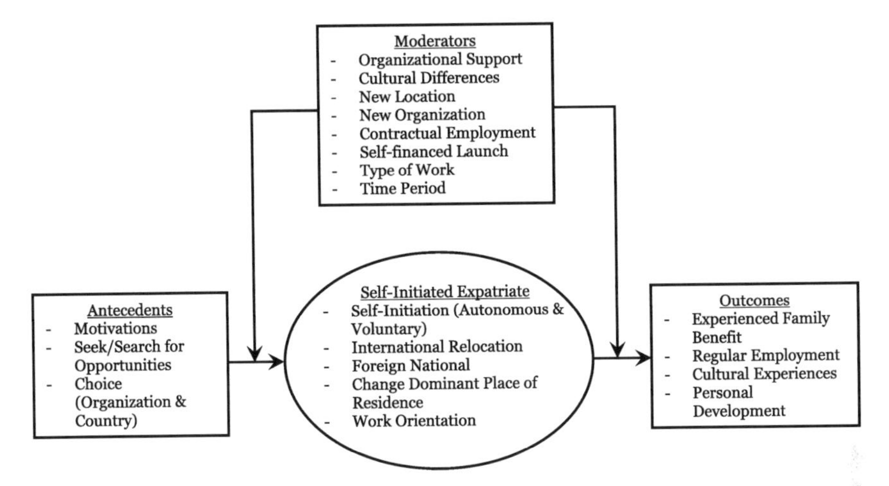

Fig. 1. Nomological Network of SIE Definition.

Antecedents

Antecedents commonly included in SIE definitions include motivations that are either work-related (i.e., career development – Jannesari & Sullivan, 2019; protean career – Cao et al., 2013; improved employment opportunities in the foreign country – Presbitero & Quita, 2017), tourism oriented (i.e., cultural experiences, travel, and exploration; Hussain et al., 2019; Peiperl et al., 2014; Selmer et al., 2018) or related to perceived personal development (e.g., learning a language; exposure to culture). These motivations, which are antecedents because they precede and inspire an individual's international relocation, are neither exclusive to SIEs (e.g., career development and protean careers can manifest in employees' home countries) nor homogenous in their nature (SIEs are idiosyncratically motivated to engage in a SIE experience). Therefore, motivations cannot be elements of a SIE definition.

Moderators

Several studies included in the SIE definition variables that moderate the relationship between SIEs and various antecedents and outcomes. For example, organizational support (or its absence) is frequently cited as a definitional element of SIE; however, there are multiple issues associated with using organizational support as a definitional element for SIEs. First, there are not only various forms of support provided by an organization to SIEs but also varying degrees of these forms of support. Some SIEs are provided with predeparture training, moving allowances, and pre-arranged mentors to help them adjust in the new foreign country, organization, and culture. In contrast, other SIEs, specifically those who self-finance their international move, are not provided with any special treatment or assistance in their new endeavor. Second, organizational support theoretically moderates the relationships between both antecedents and SIE variables and SIE variables and outcomes. For example, the level of organizational support provided by the organization moderates the decision of an individual who is motivated by career development to become a SIE. An internal dialogue such as, "Will this organization provide support through the socialization, training, and mentoring necessary to advance my career?" influences the individual's decision to become a SIE. Other examples of organizational support include language training or company-sponsored childcare. Therefore, it is more appropriate to think of organizational support as a continuous moderator for both antecedents and outcomes of SIE.

Other moderators which were included in previous definitions are: (1) significant cultural difference between host country (i.e., a US native initiating a work role in Canada is still a SIE); (2) contractual employment (SIE experiences can be carefully planned or improvised; they can be gig or contractual); (3) employment in a new organization (one can initiate a SIE experience within an organization currently employing them); (4) the type of work performed (we argue any kind of job or career can involve self-initiation in a foreign context); (5) defined contract length or open-ended duration. These are moderators of both the decision to undertake the SIE experience and the outcomes of that experience.

Outcomes

Some SIE definitions conflate the outcomes of the SIE experience with its definition. For example, an SIE experience may be beneficial (Pieperl et al., 2014) or detrimental to a family (Richardson & McKenna, 2006). SIE may result in regular employment better than the opportunities available in the home country. Further, the actual cultural experiences and actual personal development may vary from person to person as experiences are uniquely individual. These potential outcomes of an SIE experience should not be confounded with the SIE construct definition itself.

THE EVOLUTION OF THE SIE DEFINITION

As an alternative method to a manual top-down approach that we used to uncover SIE definitional elements, we also use distributional concept analysis for discerning the structure of this concept. This method tracks the history of concepts by creating a measure of lexical co-occurrences contained in the constellation of definitions by focusing on the diachronic analysis of word distributions seeking to reveal the underlying structure of the SIE concept over different time periods (de Bolla et al., 2019). The measure of the co-occurrences of words across definitions helps identify the key terms that, over time, have been components of SIE. As the definition of SIE evolved during the past two decades of SIE research, so has the constellation of words that comprise it. Importantly, the extent of the overlap between terms revealed by the lexical computation method and the SIE definitional elements reflects the convergence of our proposed definition. This structural approach to the convergence of the SIE definition reveals new ways of knowing the past and the present of the SIE concept in comparison to the extant ways found in the literature. The approach reveals how the terms, which express the SIE concept in a meaningful way, have changed in and across the different stages of the SIE definition's evolution, thus uncovering how SIE scholars have been developing their thinking about this distinct type of expatriation. The higher the level of overlap with respect to commonalities in the SIE definitions, the more relevant it is to a revised SIE definition.

To conduct this analysis, we collected the 150 SIE definitions from the 186 articles included in our systematic review of SIE definitions and classified the definitions into three historical periods based on their year of publication. The first embryonic period of SIE research contained studies that were published from 1997 through 2013. This nascent period in the development of the SIE research ended with the publication of the first special issue of the SIE phenomenon in *Career Development International* in 2013 (Doherty et al., 2013). The second growth period of the SIE research continued from 2014 to 2017, while the third covers the years of research since 2017.

We subsequently cleaned the corpus of each definition, removed all punctuation, and used the results of a distributional probability factor analysis Python script (de Bolla et al., 2019) to produce a list of lexical co-associations in the constellations of SIE definitions. We conducted this analysis for each of the three historical periods of SIE studies to compare and contrast the primary co-associations contained in the periodic lexical profiles to each other with the goal to uncover changes in the words reflecting SIE definitional elements over time, as detailed in Table 1. To assess which words were being used most often, the 10 most common co-occurrences in each of the three time periods became the focus. Due to an equal number of co-occurrences in the 10th paring, we included the top 11 words with co-occurrences in the second and third time periods.

For the first time period of the SIE research (1997–2013), a total of 1,084 lexical co-occurrences were uncovered in the constellation of SIE definitions consisting of 380 different word pairs (33% of the total number of co-occurrences in all SIE definitions included at least one of these words). For example, the word "career" appeared along with the word "development" five times among the definitions. Additionally, the words "experiences" and "pursue" each appeared four times with the word "career." Furthermore, 11 words appeared 31 times with the word "career" in the definitions of SIEs.

For the second time period (2014–2017), a total of 1,136 lexical co-occurrences were uncovered in the constellation of SIE definitions consisting of 436 different word pairs. The 11 top terms were included in the co-occurrences of 458 pairs, which made up 40% of all co-occurrences. Changes between periods 1 and 2 suggest that SIE researchers realized that contractual employment was not necessary to be an SIE and that SIEs expatriated to places that were not necessarily "overseas" but rather "international." The percent of total co-occurrences in which the top terms were included increased from 33% in period 1 to 40% in period 2, suggesting an increase in SIE definition agreement among SIE researchers.

In the third time period (2018–2020), a total of 477 lexical co-occurrences were uncovered in the constellation of SIE definitions consisting of 206 different word

Table 1. Changes in SIE Verbal Constellations Over Time.

Changes in SIE Verbal Constellation Over Time											
Phase 1 (1997–2013)					Phase 2 (2014–2017)					Phase 3 (2018–2020)	
Row Labels	Sum of Occurrences	From Phase 1 to Phase 2			Row Labels	Sum of Occurrences	From Phase 2 to Phase 3			Row Labels	Sum of Occurrences
Career	31	Continue	Drop	Added	Country	81	Continue	Drop	Added	Abroad	27
Contractual	31	Country	Career	International	Employment	28	Individual	Country	Abroad	Career	17
Country	53	Employment	Contractual	Relocation	Hired	32	Organization	Employment	Career	Decide	19
Employment	26	Hired	Overseas	Stay	Individuals	55	Without	Hired	Decided	Expatriation	20
Hired	32	Individual	Parent	Temporary	International	30	Work	International	Expatriation	Individuals	43
Individual	51	Organization	Transferred	Without	Organization	35		Stay	Initiative	Initiative	14
Organization	41			Work	Relocation	28		Temporary	Move	Move	20
Overseas	35				Stay	37			Support	Organization	14
Parent	30				Temporary	53				Support	17
Transferred	30				Without	33				Without	18
Grand Total	360				Work	46				Work	27
					Grand Total	458				Grand Total	236

Note: Terms are listed in alphabetical order.

pairs. The top 11 words were included in the co-occurrences of 236 pairs, which made up 49% of all co-occurrences. Changes between periods 2 and 3 suggest that SIE researchers recognized the duration of the SIE experience was not core to the SIE concept and emphasized that self-initiation is a key part of the SIE definition. The fact that the top words in each time period are increasingly represented in the total number of co-occurrences suggests that SIE researchers are very gradually approaching consensus in understanding of how SIEs should be defined.

Defining SIE

We used our assessments of the historical evolution of the SIE concept to propose a definition of SIEs synthesized from the nomological network of SIE definitions. Using distributional concept analysis, we parsed common definitional elements into a nomological network to propose the following concise definition:

> Self-initiated expatriates are individuals who agentically originate an international change in their dominant place of residence for the purpose of work outside of their home country.

Our proposed definition corresponds with the historical conceptualization, as shown in Table 2. Specifically, in the first period, three elements that align with our proposed definition, in the second period, there are five points of alignment, and in the third period, all seven elements are in alignment (see Table 2). Our methods converge on a concise definition we propose is supported by the literature and represents an explication of the gradual evolution of the literature. We believe that this definition can serve as the foundation for scale development and future SIE research.

In the following section, we provide a systematic review of SIE studies to develop integrated pictorial representations of the nomological network of the SIE construct.

Review of Quantitative SIE Studies

We conducted a systematic literature review of SIE studies published between 1997 and November 2019 based on the search using the terms listed above. The search produced 875 total documents. After sorting for documents written in English, eliminating duplicate documents that had been identified across multiple

Table 2. Historical SIE Definition Development.

Our Proposed Definition	First Period	Second Period	Third Period
Foreign National	Individual	Individual	Expatriation
Agentically			Decide
Self-initiate			Initiative
International	Overseas	International	Abroad
Change		Relocation	Move
Dominant place of residence		Stay	Move
Purpose of work	Employment	Work	Work

databases, removing dissertations, book chapters, conference papers, books, and documents that were not published in peer-reviewed journals, we ended with 164 quantitative and qualitative studies that were published as articles in peer-reviewed journals. We sorted the articles which were found through our search into quantitative (71) and qualitative/conceptual (93) types. For this section, we focus only on quantitative. We coded them based on the level of analysis examined in the studies and based on the theoretical frame applied to synthesize a model that depicts the nomological network in the SIE literature. To capture the evolution of the SIE research over time, we divided up the total number of articles into three time periods reflecting the nascent stage (the first time period or Phase 1: 1997–2013), growth stage (the second time period or Phase 2: 2014–2017), and the recent maturing stage (the third time period or Phase 3: 2018–2020).

The studies in Phase 1 of the SIE research evolution focused mainly on the examination of individual-level antecedents and their outcomes. These studies relied heavily upon correlational analysis which revealed the relationships between individual-level constructs such as motivations, expatriate type (AE vs. SIE), demographic variables, and experiences with outcome variables such as job satisfaction, adjustment, turnover intentions, motivations for expatriation, and mobility patterns.

In Phase 2 of the SIE research evolution, researchers continued to conduct studies examining the relationships between individual-level antecedents such as perceived organizational support, boundaryless mindset, personality variables, while including intrapersonal and interpersonal variables that were related to outcome variables such as retention, well-being, performance (job, task, teaching, and research), and adjustment (general, cultural, job, work, interaction, etc.). In this Phase 2, researchers introduced a number of national-level antecedent variables such as concentration of talent, cultural novelty, cultural value distance, and the extent of political/economic globalization. The increased complexity of study designs and analytical methods employed in this Phase 2 is evidenced by the growing use of mediating variables such as career satisfaction, organizational commitment, trust motivation, social integration, learning speed, and psychological availability.

Phase 3 of the SIE research evolution contains studies in which individual-level constructs continue to dominate the preferred level of interest for antecedents. However, SIE motivations are no longer included in the studies, as researchers have shifted their attention to the relationship between antecedents related to personal characteristics (age, education, gender, and marital status), experiences, and skills, and outcome variables such as career capital, boundary spanning, and engagement. Moreover, four studies included the new mediators of job insecurity, perceived employability, social capital, psychological availability, and psychological needs satisfaction.

Review of Qualitative SIE Research

Using the selection criterion for a systematic review described in the review of quantitative research, we identified 93 qualitative SIE articles with the potential to be included in this review. As the primary aim of this qualitative review was to understand what researchers had learned empirically from studying SIEs, we removed 12 articles that did not report the analysis of primary data. Additionally, we removed articles from the set due to their conceptual (15), editorial (3), or unrelated (7) nature. We thus identified a final set of 56 appropriate qualitative empirical studies.

Upon further analysis of the selected SIE qualitative articles, we found that 44% of them did not employ a guiding theory used for framing the study, while only 11% of them specified the use of grounded theory. Eight of the studies utilized one of the career theories (career capital theory, career construction theory, and contemporary career theory), whereas seven of the studies utilized different social theories (social capital theory, social exchange theory, social identity theory, social learning theory, and social network theory). Several other theories were used in individual studies (i.e., conservation of resource theory, consumer decision-making theory, cultural theory, human capital theory, migration theory, PE-fit theory, psychological contract theory, self-categorization theory, systems theory, theory of vocational adjustment, and theory of work adjustment). The fact that nearly half of the selected qualitative SIE studies lack theoretical grounding reflects the lack of consensus among the SIE researchers about which dominant theories should guide the research of SIEs, suggesting that the research of the SIE phenomenon is still in the nascent stage of its development.

While most qualitative SIE studies lacked a guiding theory, they did cover a broad range of topics. The most common topic addressed in the SIE studies was the careers of SIEs, as 30% of the articles focused on career development, career capital, and career success. The next most common topic, addressed in 18% of the articles, was SIE adjustment. While 16% of the articles focused on the topic of motivation for SIE relocation, the topics of identity or identity disclosure, SIE employment considerations, and expatriate types/typologies were addressed in 5% of the articles. Two articles each were published on psychological contract, relocation decision-making, social networks, and transition; while one article was published on each of the following topics: attitude, connections, cross-cultural self-preparation, development, PE fit, global talent management, justice, knowledge transfer, mobility, onboarding, performance management, repatriation, work-life balance, and international relocation strategy.

REVIEW OF SUGGESTED FUTURE DIRECTIONS FOR SIE RESEARCH

Overall, our results suggest that it is not only the definition of SIE that is fragmented but also the future research directions as well. Our review examined SIE-related antecedents, mediators, moderators, boundary conditions, and outcomes of SIE over the past 23 years. However, we also categorized the proposed future research in these articles into six different areas: methodological, intrapersonal, interpersonal, organizational, contextual, and other aspects. In the first category, the articles suggest that future SIE researchers should design studies that support sound *methodological* practices. At a basic level, the pool of participants included in SIE studies should be carefully selected and described so that comparisons can be made across studies. Multilevel studies that consider micro, meso, and macro factors would be of significant value to the SIE literature as well as studies that incorporate field experimental and longitudinal designs.

The second category is *intrapersonal* phenomena consisting of seven sub-domains. First, future studies should focus on demographic and experiential markers that might influence SIEs differentially such as SIEs with varied characteristics such as gender, race, ethnicity, previous foreign work experience, and educational levels. The second sub-domain involves the motivations that drive SIEs to undertake international positions, particularly how motivations change or stay the same over time, how the process through which motivations to engage in SIE come to fruition, and how the opportunity to choose a country of interest and pursue a protean career influences SIE motivation.

The third sub-domain relates to mobility intentions and behaviors including intent to return, intent to turn over, intent to repatriate, intent to move out of the host country, intentions to stay, and willingness to engage in SIE again. Understanding the mobility of SIE and their various intentions is of great importance to both researchers and managers of multinational organizations. Fourth is the psychological impact of the SIE's career. Particularly relevant are the factors related to SIE career satisfaction, commitment, and success as well as the factors related to their career anchors, boundaryless career perspective, development, experience, and outcomes.

The fifth sub-domain relates to the psychological comfort and affect that SIEs feel and exhibit toward their job, organization, community, and host culture. Specifically, psychological issues related to adjustment, acculturation, engagement, attitudes, and satisfaction should be further explored. Sixth is how the perceptions of the multinational organization influence SIEs. In particular, future studies should examine how the concepts of organizational identification, perceived organizational support, the psychological contract, and perceived work/life balance influence SIEs' cognitions and emotions. Seventh relates to the personal aspects of work abroad, including perceived performance, commitment, creativity, cross-cultural psychological capital, dual country identity, experiential learning, psychological dynamics, receptivity, subjective career experience, subjective career success, embeddedness, and psychological effects of perceived underemployment.

The third broad category of future SIE studies addresses *interpersonal* issues that impact SIEs and the individuals with whom they interact such as AEs, migrants, and host-country nationals. Particularly relevant is the impact that immediate and extended family have on SIEs adjustment and support. Furthermore, the SIEs' relationships inside and outside their work and expatriate communities could be fruitful grounds for research.

The fourth broad category for future SIE studies involves inquiry into the multinational *organizations* that employ this group of individuals. The first sub-domain of interest relates to human resource practices such as cultural training, recruiting, retention, selection, and both voluntary and involuntary turnover.

The second relates to organizational perceptions of SIEs in terms of their employability, managerial reception of SIEs, contribution of SIEs to organizational-level human capital, economic impact of SIEs, the view of SIEs as strategic resources, and the strategic fit of SIEs. Third is the organizational characteristics and desired outcomes of organizations that employ SIEs. Specifically, future studies should consider individual, team, unit, and organizational outcomes related to the employment of SIEs as well as organizational characteristics such as cultural diversity, entrepreneurial initiatives, and performance goals. The final subject of interest regarding multinational organizations is the relationship between the organization and the SIE. For example, future studies should examine the impact of organizational support for SIEs through logistical and financial aid and the impact of leadership through leader–member exchange or managerial intervention on SIEs' physical, emotional, and psychological health.

The fifth broad category of future SIE studies is related to *contextual* variables such as cultural distance between home and host countries, immigration policies, host-country perceptions of SIEs, national stage of globalization, and structural barriers. Also, global shocks such as a pandemic or economic disruption can impact SIEs and their organizations as well as the acceptance of different forms and means of international virtual work made possible through technological developments. Therefore, the suggestion is that SIE researchers should conduct future studies in new contexts and under varying conditions to better understand the impact of contextual influences on SIEs and their employing organizations.

The final category of future SIE studies includes a variety of *other* suggestions that have been brought up in the SIE literature. For example, SIE researchers should design future studies to examine SIE job search, SIE responses to job relocation offers, as well as the opt-out strategies and predeparture orientation that may shed light on their turnover patterns. In addition, understanding SIEs' social networks, social support, and how they might transition from AE to SIE to migrant (or some other combination) would also provide novel insights. Finally, the review of SIE experiences upon repatriation and re-expatriation has garnered little attention in the literature to date.

In sum, we have outlined multiple promising avenues for future research in the SIE domain that fall under the categories of methodology, intrapersonal, interpersonal, organizational, contextual, and other. However, we recognize that this field of inquiry has just begun its third decade, and therefore the phenomenon of SIE is likely to continue to grow for the foreseeable future.

REVIEW OF SIE RETENTION

In the following sections, we narrow our review to include only the qualitative SIE studies that include constructs of managerial importance for SIE retention, specifically those found as significant in the review of quantitative studies – SIE adjustment, embeddedness, and retention. These factors are crucial for the *organization's perceptions of SIE employability*, which include organizationally relevant factors that contribute to perceptions of SIE employability such as the pursuit of new business opportunities, rapid growth, global ambition, organizational maturity (Kumar & Chhokar, 2019), strategic goals regarding localization, attrition rate of local employees, the need for contemporary experiences and methods, and moral/ethical business decision considerations (Makkonen, 2017), which are the primary area of research. This focus also includes contextual factors such as person-environment fit (Makkonen, 2015), the increased importance of the local market area, cultural and language factors, the balance of supply and demand of local talent, and the degree of appreciation of Western education and qualifications (Makkonen, 2017). Finally, it includes human and social capital, career identity, and personal adaptability at the individual level.

Another area of interest is the relationship between SIE employment and the subsequent *organizationally perceived outcomes and onboarding activities*. After interviewing 24 SIE human resource managers, recruitment consultants, and managers in China, Makkonen (2017) identified both positive and negative outcomes of organizational importance related to the employment of SIEs. The positive outcomes included increased organizational effectiveness and performance, compliance with moral and ethical standards, and a mutually beneficial relationship. Additionally, Arp (2013) found that organizational growth was a positive outcome of SIE employment. The negative outcomes of SIE employment reported in the studies were the inability to contribute to organizational performance, issues with work efficiency, high levels of attrition, organizational friction and imbalance, and financial risks and wasted resources (Makkonen, 2017). Also, Guðmundsdóttir and Lundbergsdóttir (2016), who interviewed seven directors, managers, counselors, and consultants in a Nordic corporation to study the onboarding process and experience of SIE employees, found three positive factors related to onboarding – the provision of a mentor, incorporation of the spouse into the onboarding process, and the integration of non-work-related knowledge sharing.

A further area encompassed the *organizational global talent management strategies* used by organizations that employ SIEs. Farndale et al. (2014) interviewed 16 general managers and human resource specialists to assess the goals that influence strategies among multinational corporations. The assessed organizational-level goals were business control, client demands, and economic considerations; individual-level goals included personal development, career development, family considerations, and overseas work experience. The authors suggested that multinational organizations should balance organizational and individual SIE goals to implement global talent management practices that are mutually beneficial (Farndale et al., 2014).

Richardson and McKenna (2014) introduced a special case of an SIE that they labeled as the *Organizational SIE*. The Organizational SIE refers to individual SIEs that self-initiate transfer from one country to another country while staying employed within the same multinational organization. While SIEs have traditionally been defined as those who join a new organization, Organizational SIEs are defined as those who remain in the same multinational organization throughout the transitions in their employment. The authors found that Organizational SIEs relied on their professional networks which allowed them to move internationally within the same organization. The employment of Organizational SIEs benefits the organization by creating business opportunities, facilitating new market entry, engaging in knowledge sharing, increasing connectivity, and increasing communication throughout the organization (Richardson & McKenna, 2014).

Finally, the *likelihood of a foreign executive in a local organization (FELO)* in a multinational corporation is another area of interest for researchers. Arp (2013) examined the likelihood of the appointment of a FELO by interviewing 46 foreign executives and 25 local peers located in Malaysia. The author identified the following orientations in the organizational typology: pragmatic-oriented organizations, global/local action-oriented organizations, and nationalistic/nepotistic/ethnocentric-oriented organizations. The orientations identified in the FELO typology included the global executive nomad, innate identity, entrepreneurial innovator, and localized. The authors proposed that the likelihood of a FELO appointment is dependent on the match between the individual-level FELO type and the organizational-level typological orientation (Arp, 2013). In sum, the seven SIE qualitative articles, in which the organizational factors were considered, produced five themes. In the next section, we will further narrow our focus by reviewing past qualitative SIE studies that have examined adjustment, embeddedness, and retention.

REVIEW OF QUALITATIVE STUDIES ON SIE ADJUSTMENT, EMBEDDEDNESS, AND RETENTION

We found 13 qualitative SIE studies involving adjustment at the individual level. In addition to the three common adjustment types (general, work, and interaction) proposed by Black et al. (1991), four other adjustment types were addressed (adjustment in attitude, emotional adjustment, cultural adjustment, and pressure for subjective adjustment).

General adjustment was the most commonly examined adjustment type as it was included in nine out of the 13 studies. Individual-level factors related to general adjustment included loneliness (Beitin, 2012), language ability (Beitin, 2012; Farcas & Goncalves, 2019; Harry et al., 2019; Richardson & Ng, 2019; van Bakel & Salzbrenner, 2019), relationship building (Beitin, 2012; Farcas & Goncalves, 2019), use of personal networks (Araujo et al., 2014), freedom of choice (Farcas et al., 2019; Schreuders-van den Bergh & Plessis, 2016), self-efficacy (Agha Alikhani, 2017), social reinforcement/interactions (Agha-Alikhani, 2017; Farcas & Goncalves, 2019; Schreuders-van den Bergh & Plessis, 2016), tenure (Agha-Alikhani, 2017), cultural experiences (Farcas & Goncalves, 2019; Harry et al., 2019; Richardson & Ng, 2019), identifying cultural similarities (Danisman, 2017), satisfaction with accommodations (Farcas & Goncalves, 2019), ancestral ties to host country (Richardson & Ng, 2019), realistic expectations (Farcas & Goncalves, 2019), previous international experience (Farcas & Goncalves, 2019), and personality (Farcas & Goncalves, 2019). Two studies reported that attitude toward host culture (Danisman, 2017) and upward learning spirals (Schreuders-van den Bergh & Plessis, 2016) mediate between individual-level factors and general adjustment. Additionally, Langinier and Froehlicher (2018) found that the relationship between social engagement and general adjustment at the individual level is moderated by macro-level factors, such as proportion of internationals, importance of national/international communities, need to speak the language, and the international corporate cultures.

In addition to the individual-level factors reported to influence general adjustment, organizational and contextual-level factors were also reported as significant. At the organizational level, the management style utilized by the host-country organization influenced the SIEs general adjustment (van Bakel & Salzbrenner, 2019). At the contextual level, Beitin (2012) reported that significant events of global scope such as the World Trade Center attacks on September 11, impacted the general adjustment of some SIEs. Furthermore, host-country nationals with negative attitudes toward foreigners also impacted the general adjustment of SIEs (Farcas & Goncalves, 2019).

Researchers reported several individual-level factors related to *work* adjustment. These factors included the use of personal networks (Araujo et al., 2014), language ability (Farcas & Goncalves, 2019; Richardson & Ng, 2019), relationship building (Farcas & Goncalves, 2012), autonomy (Farcas et al., 2012), social interactions (Farcas et al., 2012), cultural experiences (Farcas et al., 2012; Richardson & Ng, 2019), realistic expectations (Farcas et al., 2012), previous international experiences (Farcas et al., 2012), and ancestral ties to the host country (Richardson & Ng, 2019). *Interaction* adjustment was impacted by the same factors with the exception of the ancestral ties. However, interaction adjustment was also influenced by xenophobic attacks and cases when host-country nationals were unwilling to communicate with expatriates (Harry et al., 2019). Despotovic et al. (2015) found that SIEs who engage in cross-cultural self-preparation report to experience a greater adjustment in attitudes toward their context in their new location. Agha-Alikhani (2018) reported that SIEs with longer tenure felt higher levels of pressure for subjective adjustment. Farcas and Goncalves (2019) posited that individual-level factors such as language ability, relationship building, autonomy, social interactions, satisfaction with accommodations, realistic expectations, previous international experience, and personality influence emotional adjustment. The final type of adjustment, *cultural* adjustment, is reported to be influenced by social engagement (Clark & Altman, 2016), identification with host culture (Farcas & Goncalves, 2017), satisfaction with accommodations (Farcas et al., 2017; Richardson & Ng, 2019), and previous international experience (Richardson & Ng, 2019). Furthermore, cultural adjustment can be mediated by mutual support and networking within the expat community (Clark & Altman, 2016).

Four qualitative SIE research studies included elements of fit, sacrifice, or links, which are the three dimensions of *embeddedness* (Farndale et al., 2014; Makkonen, 2015; Miralles-Vazquez & McGaughey, 2015; Richardson & McKenna, 2014). Richardson and McKenna (2014) found that Organizational SIEs utilized their links in their home-country organization to help facilitate their expatriation. Once these SIEs arrive in their host country they begin establishing new links that help them to become embedded in their new context. The individual-level outcomes associated with the accumulation of host-country organizational links included increased performance, skills, experience, learning, professional development opportunities, repatriation support, further expatriate opportunities, and a negative impact on home-country links (Richardson & McKenna, 2014).

Organizational-level outcomes associated with embeddedness due to links included increased organizational performance, organizational learning, new business opportunities, knowledge sharing, and the facilitation of international collaboration (Miralles-Varquez & McGaughey, 2015; Richardson & McKenna, 2014). Farndale et al. (2014) posited that an organizational outcome due to the sacrifice dimension of embeddedness included influence on global talent management strategies. Makkonen (2015) found that the fit dimension of embeddedness at the job, group, organization, and cultural levels impacted how organizations perceive the employability of SIEs.

The *retention* of SIEs was comprehensively addressed by Arp (2013) in the article "Typologies: What types of foreign executives are appointed by local organizations and what types of organizations appoint them?" In this study, the author interviewed 46 foreign executives and 25 host-country nationals from Malaysia. This data analysis yielded two typologies. The first typology included three types of local organizations, namely nationalistic, pragmatic, and global mindset. The second typology included four types of FELOs including global executive nomads, innate identity FELOs, entrepreneurial innovator FELOs, and localized FELOs. Regarding tenure, the author found that the FELOs tenure in the local organization was largely dependent on the type of FELO category in which they fall.

The shortest tenure is reported for *global executive* FELOs because they are "appointed for specific expertise and hard skills, to be replaced by local successors" (Arp, 2013, p. 178). The second type of FELOs, the *innate identity* FELOs, is expected to complete a medium-length tenure in the local organization, as they are appointed based on the appropriateness of their characteristics. The third type of FELOs, *entrepreneurial innovator* FELOs, is also expected to complete a medium-length tenure with the local organization, as they have the "ability to translate a foreign concept into genuine innovation in the host-country context" and discover new business opportunities (Arp, 2013, p. 180). The final type of FELOs, the *localized* FELOs, is expected to complete a very long tenure in the local organization because they have developed a "third-cultureness" which is "a unique supranational stance on socio-economic issues combined with deep understanding of, and emotional involvement with, their host-country environment" (Arp, 2013, p. 181). Arp's (2013) study is the only qualitative study that examines SIE tenure in multinational organizations.

A SYSTEMATIC STUDY OF ORGANIZATIONAL PRACTICES FOR RETAINING SIE

While individual-level research of SIEs has grown over the last 25 years, we know very little how to theorize the practices that multinational organizations introduce for the retention of their SIE employees. Based on the insights that we derived from our systematic reviews, we designed a study to evaluate the factors and the related organizational practices that could potentially influence SIE retention in their multinational organization. We used abductive theorization to frame practice theory and employed a qualitative design to conduct interviews with a multinational organization's subsidiary managers to capture their views of the factors that influence SIE retention.

Practice Theory as Theoretical Foundation

Central to our research is that the activities, procedures, and policies used by organizations for SIE retention are driven by the view of SIEs as resources that have meaningful value for the organization (Feldman, 2004). In our study, we use the lens of practice theory (Feldman & Worline, 2016) to uncover how SIE practices have unfolded in a multinational organization, focusing on addressing the factors that are likely to increase SIE retention. In particular, theorizing these practices involved tying them to theoretical "drivers" derived from the questions that subsidiary managers ask based on their practical knowledge – with the intent to implement the related practices that would retain SIEs. In other words, our theorizing of SIE retention practices incorporated managerial knowledge about the likely responses to the factors influencing SIE retention which are critical for the development of organizational "practice wisdom" (Thompson, 2017, p. 25).

The practical wisdom of retaining SIEs requires refraining from prescribing SIE retention practices before identifying the elements of the managers' knowledge about SIE retention and assessing how to tailor this practical knowledge to the theory that supports the implemented solution for the SIE retention problem. In our case, theorizing SIE retention practices – procedures, activities, and policies – means aligning them to the underlying theoretical drivers of adjustment, embeddedness, and retention (Stepney & Thompson, 2021).

QUALITATIVE DESIGN OF OUR STUDY

To implement the qualitative design of our study, we developed and administered an interview protocol with questions focused on the factors that the findings from the systematic reviews indicated to influence SIE retention (i.e., adjustment, embeddedness, and cross-cultural adjustment). Our primary research goal was to understand how the relevant retention practices unfolded to address these factors. We utilized purposive sampling when interviewing our sample ($n = 10$) of subsidiary unit managers/directors who worked in our focal multinational organization. Eight interviewees were male and the age of the interviewees ranged from 42 to 67 years. All interviewed managers held the highest country-level position (Director) at the time of our interviews, but several of them had previously held other managerial positions such as lead teacher, principal, and global vice president from 6 to 24 years. The average number of years of their experience managing SIEs was 11.7 years, their average organizational tenure was 12.5 years, and their average expatriate tenure was 15.6 years. These interviewees lived in up to four different countries throughout their SIE tenure. Each interview lasted an average of 76 minutes, yielding a transcription averaging around 10,000 words and analytic memos averaging 14 pages.

Following Miralles-Vazquez and McGaughey's (2015) suggestions for the sampling and analysis in this study, we did not pursue either theoretical saturation (i.e., to continue the collection and analysis of data to the point where no new themes or insights are uncovered) or data saturation (i.e., to continue interviewing until the data set is complete, with redundancy and replication indicating the saturation point) because we maintain that the findings of this study are suggestive in the form of principles rather than as conclusive as predictions. In the following section, we present the results of our analysis of the transcribed interviews and describe the subsidiary managers' views of the personal, relational, and contextual factors that may influence the relationship between adjustment, embeddedness, and retention of SIEs. We classified these factors as either facilitating, hindering, or with a mixed effect.

MANAGERIAL VIEW OF THE FACTORS INFLUENCING RELATIONSHIPS BETWEEN SIE ADJUSTMENT, EMBEDDEDNESS, AND RETENTION

When the subsidiary managers were asked about the factors that might influence SIE adjustment, embeddedness, and retention, they claimed, or indicated, the primacy of different factors. While 28% of the respondents claimed that *personal* factors primarily influenced embeddedness and retention, 43% claimed the primary influence of *interpersonal* factors, and 29% claimed the primacy of *contextual* factors. In the following sections, we describe in detail how managers view that personal, interpersonal, and contextual factors may either facilitate or hinder the adjustment, embeddedness, and retention of SIEs.

Personal Factors That Managers Believe Facilitate SIE Adjustment, Embeddedness, and Retention

Managers claimed that four personal factors contributed to the adjustment, embeddedness, and retention of SIEs in their multinational organization. These factors included SIE's abilities, actions, mentality, and speed to adjust. The first factor, *ability*, refers to the extent to which SIEs are able to focus on their job tasks and use the host-country language. These abilities are likely to facilitate adjustment, embeddedness, and retention of SIEs. For example, Burch[2] said, "The ability to adjust, yes, the willingness to adjust absolutely will affect if they will be embedded or not." The second personal factor refers to the specific *actions* that SIEs undertake to adjust. Respondents identified specific personal actions that the adjusted SIEs take, and which seem to facilitate their embeddedness and retention. Those SIEs "talk to people," "learn the language," "go outside," "jump in," and "start working." Tedrick explained,

> If they cannot adjust … If they don't feel like you can go to people and talk to people through that adjustment period, and they are just having difficulty adjusting to the culture, the country, the school … I don't think they would feel part of the team. As a result, they wouldn't be as embedded and they wouldn't be as likely to sign on for another contract.

Similarly, Paulos asserted,

> You have got to learn the language and learn the culture, you don't have to master it, but you have to go outside. Really work hard at the relationships. Really work hard at friendships with colleagues. Have to make some friends outside of school. Being flexible. Getting to know people.

The third personal factor that managers perceived to contribute to SIE adjustment, embeddedness, and retention is the SIE's *mentality* (i.e., frame of mind) characterized by flexibility, acceptance, and willingness to embrace the local culture. According to Diab,

> If everyone else in the community has accepted a certain way of doing things and a certain set of values and embraced the culture, but you have not, I do not see how you can become embedded.

The fourth personal factor refers to the *speed of adjustment*. As respondents pointed out, experienced SIEs commonly become embedded more quickly because they feel comfortable in their professional role. For example, Jeter explained,

> It happens much quicker, because they adjust quicker, they are not all flumexed [*sic.*] … it just makes them move to the embedded stage much faster because, mainly, they are focusing on teaching and the adjustments that are happening at school.

In sum, subsidiary managers agree that the high levels of these four personal factors are likely to influence SIEs to become adjusted, embedded and remain employed within their multinational organization.

Personal Factors That Inhibit SIE Adjustment, Embeddedness, and Retention

Respondents identified three personal factors that inhibit the adjustment, embeddedness and retention of SIEs: (1) the SIEs' inability to change, (2) their rigid mentality, and (3) their stressful psychological reactions. *Inability to change* inhibits the adjustment, embeddedness, and retention of SIEs because it prevents them from making necessary adjustments in the new environment. As Diab explained, "If you can't make the adjustments, you are not going to be able to become embedded." *Rigid mentality* refers to SIE thinking patterns that are characterized by resistance to change and unpliable expectations. According to Kevin,

> Some things that are normally expected, do not exist in the new school. For example, we had one teacher, when he came there was a grey area and it was an unexpected thing that he couldn't get over and he ended up not being able to stay.

The SIE's propensity to exhibit *stressful psychological reaction* is the third personal factor that managers viewed to inhibit SIE adjustment and embeddedness and thus engender their turnover intentions. Jeter explained,

> When you bring in a 20-year experienced teacher, the only thing he or she worries about, for the most part, is how to live in [foreign country], and they can make that adjustment fairly quickly. The other person has double the issues and double the stress in their lives.

Personal Factors With a Mixed Impact on SIE Adjustment, Embeddedness, and Retention

Managers responding to our question – how the professional tenure of SIEs impacted their retention at the subsidiary level – argued that the occupationally embedded SIEs are retained when the subsidiary managers are *meeting the specific needs* of these experienced SIEs. For example, Jeter stated that experienced SIEs, "Need incentives that can look like a lot of different things." Similarly, Elisha said that, "More experienced teachers may be at a different stage of life and have different needs." Abigail added, "Longevity is really based on whether they have the resources they need to be comfortable."

However, some managers viewed *previous experience* of SIEs as a latent liability that sometimes might impede their adjustment, embeddedness, and retention because some SIEs might have developed undesirable behaviors. For example, Michelle claimed,

> If there is a large adjustment, it is more likely that the experienced teacher will not become embedded. They have the confidence to go and work somewhere else … they might think 'I am too old for this, I have too much experience for this, I have done it this way and I am not willing to change now ….'

Therefore, subsidiary managers view the previous experience as a personal factor with a mixed impact on SIE adjustment, embeddedness and retention of SIEs.

Interpersonal Factors Influencing SIE Adjustment, Embeddedness, and Retention

The interviewed respondents claimed that interpersonal factors could have a mixed impact on the SIE adjustment, embeddedness, and retention. The first interpersonal factor that they mentioned is the SIEs' *ingroup/outgroup classification* of their colleagues. In contrast to outgroup SIEs who are on the "outer edge," ingroup SIEs who feel "a part" of the local group will more likely become adjusted and embedded in the organization and the local community. Tedrick pointed out,

> Yes, because if you cannot adjust, then you feel on the outer edge and you don't feel a part … and I don't think they would feel part of the team. As a result, they wouldn't be as embedded and they wouldn't be as likely to sign on for another contract or to be embedded.

The second interpersonal factor is the *depth of relationships* that SIEs have with others in the local community. Diab asserted that SIEs who do not adjust,

> […] will not be able to have the depth of relationship with their colleagues, students, or local community. Without that depth of relationship, the chance for embeddedness is simply not there. I do not see how you could do it.

The third interpersonal factor involves the *normative expectations* that are commonly imposed upon the SIEs by the local community. These expectations are often crucial for the SIEs to feel comfortable working in the organization. This is parallel to our previous personal factor of willingness to embrace aspects of the culture an individual is in, and we find the same quote applies as it indicates the influence of the community:

> If everyone else in the community has accepted a certain way of doing things and a certain set of values and embraced the culture, if you have not, I do not see how you can become embedded … the chance for embeddedness is simply not there.

CONTEXTUAL FACTORS IMPACTING ADJUSTMENT, EMBEDDEDNESS, AND RETENTION

The most critical contextual factors are related to SIE family needs because the subsidiary managers in this multinational organization perceive that these SIE needs should be met with priority, particularly to retain their occupationally embedded SIEs. The interviewees articulated six contextual factors related to meeting SIE family needs: *family member conditions*, *family events*, *familial environment*, *family benefits*, *family resources*, and *family health*. The first factor was related to family member *conditions* such as the employment potential for the SIE's spouse or the extent of the children's adaptation to the new environment. Paulos pointed out, "Their spouse is in a job in the community and they get to stay in a job and have fulfillment in their career." Judah added that SIEs leave because "Their kids might not be adapting."

The second contextual factor associated with the family needs of SIEs is related to significant family *events* such as marriage. Jeter argued,

> Other reasons have nothing to do with the school, they have family issues or they are looking to repatriate to the States or wherever they are from … or they get married. Actually here, that has been a bigger issue here than anything because we have a lot of single female teachers and they get married.

The third factor is the need for a *familial environment*, which is characterized by a shared sense of family atmosphere in the organization and the community. For example, Kevin stated,

> A lot of experienced teachers have been here from the beginning and the foundational purpose and family atmosphere is a lot of why the long term teachers and administrators are still here.

Abigail explained this sense of purpose,

> People stay because we have a familial community. People here do connect, when you ask the students, the caring community is what they say, and the teachers feel the same way.

The fourth contextual factor revolves around family *benefits* such as free tuition for children and the ease of transfer from one subsidiary of the multinational organization to another. Paulos argued that, "If they have families, they like putting their kids through school with free tuition and they recognize the importance of that for their kids' education." When addressing the desire for some families to move from one location to another, Paulos added, "For some people that are more nomadic, that is a big draw to the network, to be able to see more than just one country or two."

The fifth contextual factor involves *resources needed to support the family* such as the related financial compensation and housing arrangements. Elisha observed, "Typically, experienced teachers are at the stage of life where they need more financial security … [w]e have people who leave our organization because of limited resources." In addition, Abigail added, "I find, in Japan, if people have the resources they need, mainly money, you know housing and things like that, they are content." The sixth contextual factor related to family needs is associated with family *health*. Having their health insurance needs covered appropriately by the organization as well as being able to receive quality treatments in the host country are important factors influencing SIE retention. Abigail commented, "We have had some with health problems and they needed to go home to get services that they can't get here in Japan." Paulos added, "We have good health insurance, and that definitely helps out for people who are established." Overall, managers perceived that these six contextual factors related to meeting family needs should be given priority to retain SIEs.

ALIGNMENT BETWEEN ORGANIZATIONAL PRACTICES AND THE FACTORS INFLUENCING SIE ADJUSTMENT, EMBEDDEDNESS, AND RETENTION

Subsidiary managers were asked what practices their multinational organizations used or should use, to improve SIE retention by meeting the SIE needs and addressing other factors that influence SIE adjustment. To engage in "theorizing [these] practices" (Feldman & Worline, 2016), three co-authors of this article examined all interviewee responses and coded them in terms of their alignment with the previously identified personal, interpersonal, and contextual factors. The multinational organization has, over time, developed multiple practices to address the factors that could positively impact SIE adjustment, embeddedness, and retention.

Organizational policies outlining the provision of health insurance, competitive salaries, and other benefits were found aligned with the SIEs family health and resource needs. For example, Michelle stated,

> From a financial and benefit perspective, you get money towards retirement and that is tied to policy … experienced teachers start thinking about whether they need to go back to establish social security. From a benefit perspective, we try to validate their need to advance their education and retirement.

Additionally, the coders cited organizational procedures and actions such as providing counseling and hosting activities as ways in which SIE's family environmental and conditional needs were met. For illustration, Judah explained, "We celebrate birthdays and look out for what is going on in people's lives.

Celebrations and building community at this school is important to meet the needs of families."

The practice of recommending social outlets was introduced to promote SIE engagement in community activities. While the organizational policy outlining the assignment of a mentor was adopted to promote a healthy psychological mentality. A procedure put in place to promote the speed of adjustment was to share information. Tedrick explained,

> We offer new teacher orientation right when teachers hit the ground and it shares all sorts of information about the country and the school, we really want to lay that out as quickly as possible and share that information to help them.

Several actions that the multinational organization took were aimed at influencing the interpersonal factors that contribute to SIE adjustment, embeddedness, and retention. These organizational actions, which included bringing people together physically, developing a strong culture, and highlighting incentives, were aligned with the interpersonal factors of the SIEs such as belonging to the group, achieving deeper relationships, and managing internal and external expectations. In this regard, Michelle commented, "Where they feel comfortable and they develop a deeper relationship with someone at all stages of life. I think that is helpful." Overall, the multinational organization's practices were principally aligned with the factors that could influence SIE retention.

Summary of the Findings of Our Qualitative Study

The intense competitive global landscape in the twenty-first century forces multinational organizations to increasingly draw from the limited talent pool of SIEs with the aim to meet their human capital needs. A major related challenge that multinational organizations face is SIE retention. In our systematic review of qualitative SIE studies, we identified the five themes (employment, organizational SIE, talent management strategies, FELO appointment, and perceptions of SIE employability) related to SIE retention. While previous researchers have reported the significant role of adjustment and embeddedness in the retention of SIEs examined at the individual level (Hussain & Deery, 2018; Ren et al., 2014), we introduced the managerial perspective on the factors of organizational relevance that influence retention of SIEs in multinational organizations. Specifically, using a qualitative research design, we have identified concrete policies, procedures, and practices that managers in multinational organizations can incorporate to retain SIEs by addressing the needs critical for their adjustment and embeddedness.

Our study has unique methodological and theoretical contributions. Methodologically, this is one of the rare studies based on interviews of unit managers in the international business domain. Theoretically, this is the first empirical study in international business that is grounded in the theoretical conceptualization of "theorizing practice." Theorizing practice is crucial for understanding the need for social order in multinational organizations that are attempting to infuse coherence and reflexivity in their diverse cross-border activities. This approach accentuates the role of managers in SIE activities, procedures, and policies and aligning them with the related behaviors of organizational members. Also, with this study, we respond to Knight et al.'s (2021) call for "... greater methodological triangulation ... to optimize outcomes in scholarly research, in both exploratory and confirmatory research, to produce rigorous and reliable theory" (p. 2). In addition, following the suggestion by Reuber and Fischer (2021), we examine an exemplary case of a multinational organization employing SIE's to demonstrate how a "small-N research design" advocated by Jonsson and Foss (2011) can be productively used for theorization.

To summarize, our findings indicate that managers view the components of SIE embeddedness as highly relevant for SIE retention. Specifically, we found that the managers' view is that SIEs who are tenured and embedded in their occupation (i.e., educational professionals) are more likely to be embedded in the organization and retained by the organization.

This is illustrated by the following statement of a manager who addressed the ability of occupationally embedded SIEs to become organizationally embedded:

> It happens much quicker ... it just makes them move to the (organizationally) embedded stage must faster because, mainly, they are focusing on teaching and the adjustments that are happening at school ... Experience with things like parent-teacher conferences and things that could be stressful, they are comfortable with all of that, so they become part of the community quickly. They also jump in there and start doing all of these things that make them an integral part of the community quickly.

We also found that the relationship between occupational embeddedness and organizational embeddedness is conditioned by the SIEs' ability to adjust to the new culture (i.e., cross-cultural adjustment). In other words, those SIEs that are more capable of adjusting to the new cultural environment are more likely to be organizationally embedded and retained. This is depicted by the following comment of a manager, "If there is a large adjustment, it is more likely that the experienced teacher will not become embedded." Another manager explained that if the SIE,

> [...] cannot adjust, then they feel on the outer edge and they don't feel a part ... and I don't think they would feel part of the team. As a result, they wouldn't be as embedded and they wouldn't be as likely to sign on for another contract or to be embedded.

DISCUSSION

In the intense competitive global landscape in the twenty-first century, multinational organizations increasingly draw candidates from the limited talent pool of SIEs and develop appropriate practices to retain them. We designed this study using the insights from our systematic reviews, the theoretical frame of practice theory, and a qualitative approach to examine the managerial views of the factors that influence how well organizational practices address the needs critical for SIE adjustment, embeddedness, and retention. Our findings from the systematic reviews indicated that SIE adjustment, their occupational embeddedness, and their organizational embeddedness were potentially relevant to their retention. This finding guided our design of the qualitative study in which we interviewed subsidiary managers to assess their views of the practices that are likely to ensure that SIEs are retained by the organization once the influential factors are addressed.

Our focal organization implemented policies, procedures, and actions to address the retention of its SIEs. In particular, the organization and the subsidiary managers focused on enhancing the embeddedness of SIEs and their families through social support and resource allocation. Managers shared information, hosted activities, and created a welcoming culture for newly hired SIEs. When faced with a new environment, these actions worked to create a comfortable workplace. To further allay SIE fears and generate interest, the organization created policies and practices that provided benefits in the form of insurance, counseling, and interesting locations. These actions furthered embeddedness by creating feelings of safety in an unfamiliar – but novel – environment.

Practical Implications

The actions of the managers of our focal organization generally align with the recommended actions of human resource experts regarding the retention of expatriates. Regardless of their status (AE or SIE), helping expatriates adjust to their new jobs, country, and culture encourages embeddedness in their new venture (Black et al., 1991). While objective forms of adjustment (i.e., task performance) are important, for retention purposes subjective forms of adjustment (i.e., job satisfaction) take prominence. This is particularly the case for SIEs who have no previous connection with the organization to establish embeddedness, self-manage their careers, and are often motivated to move abroad to explore and undergo novel life experiences (Doherty, 2012).

Despite the importance of the job itself for a salary and for providing purpose, it is not the primary cause of SIE expatriation. As a result, the model for retention of SIEs places increased importance on those non-employment-related factors. Retention literature often points to the importance of traditional job satisfaction factors in preserving hired talent. However, while factors such as increased compensation and rewards, training and development, and alignment with organizational goals and values are relevant, they do not hold the same relevance as they might with AEs because SIEs are highly agentic and operate willingly with regard to their intrinsic motivations. If organizations are going to attempt to retain SIEs, then they must assist in activating those intrinsic motivators (Mayrhofer et al., 2008). The internal motivators most commonly referred to by SIEs include improved career prospects, financial benefits, personal development opportunities, and valued cultural experiences (Suutari et al., 2018).

SIEs seeking improved career prospects do so in pursuit of opportunities for work experiences unavailable in their own countries at their career level. The need for worker talent in organizations abroad provides openings that need to be filled from the global labor market due to local labor scarcity or constraints. When the organization searches for skilled indigenous talent in the local market, they are required to cast a broader net looking for talent. This may include candidates less skilled in the task, but more culturally acclimated due to the soft skills they possess in the international context (Kealey et al., 2005). Candidates can also be more skilled and looking for a change in the host country. Regardless of skill level, opportunistic SIE with the desire to work abroad may achieve a career path previously unavailable if they stayed in their home country.

Managers in organizations that recruit globally can use the broader labor market to increase their organizational talent. For low skill positions, managers need to understand the position they're hiring and the *basic* skills (task or cultural) required for the position. By acknowledging the soft skills required for the global hire in addition to the basic skills, the manager broadens the talent pool available. This robust talent pool requires more effort to evaluate, but a willingness to use alternative skill sets provides access to previously untapped talent. Further, giving an opportunity to an underskilled expatriate can encourage feelings of normative commitment in the employee (Meyer & Allen, 1991). As a result of attaining a position that they may not have otherwise been able to attain, the expatriate may feel an obligation to stay with the organization beyond that provided by other factors.

In contrast, overskilled candidates are opportunities for managers to hire talent that the local labor market cannot provide. The overskilled SIEs decision to take work abroad has little to do with the work itself. Rather, it is an opportunity to self-manage their career while experiencing their new home. This group of SIEs in particular is difficult to manage and retain due to their desirable skill set and lack of embeddedness with the organization (Sullivan & Arthur, 2006). One possible path forward, particularly with those organizations with an ideological mission, is to search for SIEs whose values align with those of the organization. Previous research provides evidence that value fit between multinational organizations and their employees positively influences retention (Presbitero et al., 2016).

An extension of the work opportunities in a new country is the financial benefits associated with employment abroad. Remuneration and other forms of compensation to the expatriate potentially exceed that available to the employee who does not work abroad. This potential excess is demonstrated in two modes. The first is one in which the total compensation in the new country exceeds that available in the expatriate's home country based on the labor market, exchange rates, or other factors. The other mode is one in which despite equivalent compensation, the cost of living is lower in the new country. This mode can include numerous cost factors such as rent, food, or taxes. Maybe more important to the SIE, however, are non-monetary factors such as healthcare, vacation, and valuable cultural experiences. Regardless of whether the compensation benefits come from the revenue or cost to the expatriate, the manager must be aware of these motivating factors for each expatriate because the continuance commitment associated with total compensation (Meyer & Allen, 1991) is only as persistent as the next position or location with a better cost/benefit ratio. This is particularly relevant to SIE because they have already showed the willingness and ability to act on their own motives because of their desire for mobility.

Potentially the most salient of the motives for SIEs to move abroad is the desire to develop personally. SIEs tend to act with little planning in their decision to move abroad because of their desire for adventure, a significant change to their lives, and the benefits of working abroad for their families (Richardson &

Mallon, 2005). SIEs who move for these reasons tend to respond to the features and qualities of a region or country. There is a romance to leaving a life behind to live in another country which elicits an emotional reaction that can be difficult to deny for some. For example, SIE has been described as a liberating experience from pressing mid-life issues for women over 50 years old (Myers et al., 2017). Novelty in a person's experiences triggers positive emotions "…in contexts appraised as safe and as offering novelty, change, and a sense of possibility" (Fredrickson, 1998). The novelty of a new country and culture encourages personal growth that is promoted by positive emotions. This potentially results in an effective commitment to the organization which helps with the retention of talent.

However, in Fredrickson's definition of novelty, it is noted that the environment must be perceived as safe by the SIE. This is a path forward for managers in organizations. Providing training, development, and social support to the SIE as they acculturate to their new environment helps increase feelings of safety. Acculturation takes several forms, so the opportunities for managers to provide that support are many. Emotional acculturation which assists SIEs in adapting their emotional intelligence abilities to a new culture potentially decreases social detachment from the local environment (Leersnyder et al., 2013) and increases the likelihood of social network embeddedness to help increase retention. By helping SIEs adjust their emotional regulation in the face of new expectations about emotions, managers not only help employees adapt but also create employees who are more capable of interacting with the culture in the new host country.

Beyond emotional acculturation are the many other forms of adaptation important for retention for organizations. SIE adjustment to the local culture has been found to relate positively to their language proficiency (Peltokorpi, 2008), potentially due to their personal investment before their move to learn the language of their new location. Once the SIE is in the host country, it is too late for that initial form of commitment, but the manager can still encourage it by providing opportunities for training in the new language. As well, by understanding and using the host-country language, the SIE feels safer and more capable to interact with the local population.

Although it is important for SIEs themselves to adjust to the host country, it is potentially more important for the family of the SIE to experience the same kind of adjustment (Schoepp & Forstenlechner, 2010). A family consisting of the SIE, spouse, and children contain a number of stakeholders that are relevant to the decision to stay in the host country. Helping the family adjust to their new environment through socialization increases the likelihood of retention by removing a source of concern in the SIE's life (Van der Laken et al., 2019). Managers then should consider a holistic approach to retention and include the entire family in their efforts. Helping families find housing, enroll children in schooling, navigate a healthcare system, find transportation, learn a new language, acculturate emotionally, and create valued cultural experiences are all things that are important to enable effective adaptation (Richardson & Zikic, 2007).

All that said, there is a subpopulation of SIEs for whom these factors are subverted to the potential experiences of living and working abroad, particularly in young workers. These SIEs are difficult to retain. They're typically somewhat unskilled, have few social ties to embed them in a particular location, and seek the adventure of global travel. They are also willing to take positions below their skill level to obtain these experiences, which suggests that they are unlikely to view economic factors as important. Thus, while affective commitment to the organization is possible, any form of normative or continuance commitment is unlikely. When the novelty of the situation wears off and the resulting positive emotions disappear, so does the affective commitment. Thus, these young, globally mobile workers are difficult to retain. In these cases, it may be helpful for the SIE to develop a relational psychological contract with the organization instead of simply a transactional contract (Chen & Shaffer, 2017). Hussain and Deery (2018) suggest helping SIEs to develop strong relationships and interpersonal ties at work through carefully considered team composition, social support, and socialization opportunities to help with the retention of SIEs.

The final motivation for SIEs to work abroad is for valued cultural experiences. Although there is not a great deal that managers can do to provide those experiences, they can certainly provide the opportunity for employees to discover them on their own. Providing time for holidays, compensation levels that allow exploration, and flexibility in location choice (if possible) can be attractive benefits for SIEs.

Limitations

Several limitations, which are inherently present in this complex type of research, are also present in this study. The limitation common to all qualitative studies is the subjectivity inherent to the processes of data collection through interviews and a high level of researchers' involvement in the analysis (Stake, 2010). Additionally, our selection of participants in the qualitative study did not guarantee that the subjective judgments, expressed by the managers in the small sample size, were representative of all subsidiary managers (Hayes, 2020).

CONCLUSION

Using a qualitative research design, we examined the organizational perspective on the SIE retention and identified the factors and the related practices that subsidiary managers believe influence the SIE embeddedness, adjustment, and retention in their multinational organization. Using this methodological approach, grounded in practice theory, we analyzed the transcribed interviews of the subsidiary managers and the multinational organization's policy documentation. The result of employing this approach allowed a deeper understanding of the managerial perspective on SIE retention, particularly in terms of the practices that could increase it.

NOTES

1. Self initiated expatriate, self-initiated expatriation, self initiated expatriation, self propelled expatriation, self propelled expatriate, self directed expatriate, self directed

expatriation, self initiated foreign workers, self initiated foreign employee, self initiated corporate employee, and self initiated corporate expatriate.

2. Respondents have been given generic names.

REFERENCES

Agha-Alikhani, B. (2018). Adjustment in international work contexts: Insights from self-initiated expatriates in academia. *Thunderbird International Business Review*, *60*(6), 837–849.

Al Ariss, A., Koall, I., Ozbilgin, M., Suutari, V., Cao, L., Hirschi, A., & Deller, J. (2012). Self-initiated expatriates and their career success. *Journal of Management Development*, *31*(2), 159–172.

Antonakis, J., Bastardoz, N., Jacquart, P., & Shamir, B. (2016). Charisma: An ill-defined and ill-measured gift. *Annual Review of Organizational Psychology and Organizational Behavior*, *3*, 293–319.

Araujo, B. V. B., Teixeira, M. L. M., Cruz, P. D., & Malini, E. (2014). Understanding the adaptation of organisational and self-initiated expatriates in the context of Brazilian culture. *The International Journal of Human Resource Management*, *25*(18), 2489–2509.

Arp, F. (2013). Typologies: What types of foreign executives are appointed by local organisations and what types of organisations appoint them? *German Journal of Human Resource Management*, *27*(3), 167–194.

Arp, F., Hutchings, K., & Smith, W. A. (2013). Foreign executives in local organisations. *Journal of Global Mobility*, *1*(3), 312–335.

Beitin, B. K. (2012). Syrian self-initiated expatriates: Emotional connections from abroad. *International Migration*, *50*(6), 1–17.

Bhuian, S. N., Al-Shammari, E. S., & Jefri, O. A. (2001). Work-related attitudes and job characteristics of expatriates in Saudi Arabia. *Thunderbird International Business Review*, *43*(1), 21–32.

Biemann, T., & Andresen, M. (2010). Self-initiated foreign expatriates versus assigned expatriates. *Journal of Managerial Psychology*, *25*(4), 430–448.

Black, J. S., Mendenhall, M., & Oddou, G. (1991). Toward a comprehensive model of international adjustment: An integration of multiple theoretical perspectives. *Academy of Management Review*, *16*(2), 291–317.

Bonache, J., Brewster, C., & Froese, F. J. (Eds.). (2020). *Global mobility and the management of expatriates*. Cambridge University Press.

Cao, L., Hirschi, A., & Deller, J. (2013). The positive effects of a protean career attitude for self-initiated expatriates: Cultural adjustment as a mediator. *Career Development International*, *18*(1), 56–77.

Cerdin, J. L., & Selmer, J. (2014). Who is a self-initiated expatriate? Towards conceptual clarity of a common notion. *The International Journal of Human Resource Management*, *25*(9), 1281–1301.

Chen, Y. P., & Shaffer, M. A. (2017). The influences of perceived organizational support and motivation on self-initiated expatriates' organizational and community embeddedness. *Journal of World Business*, *52*(2), 197–208.

Clark, D., & Altman, Y. (2016). In the age of 'liquid modernity': Self-initiated expatriates in Crete, their multi-generational families and the community. *The International Journal of Human Resource Management*, *27*(7), 729–743.

Danisman, S. (2017). Attitudes towards culture in the new home: Self-initiated expatriate academics in Turkey. *British Journal of Middle Eastern Studies*, *44*(1), 1–29.

de Bolla, P. D., Jones, E., Nulty, P., Recchia, G., & Regan, J. (2019). Distributional concept analysis: A computational model for history of concepts. *Contributions to the History of Concepts*, *14*(1), L66–L92.

Despotovic, W. V., Hutchings, K., & McPhail, R. (2015). Cross-cultural self-preparation of Australian self-initiated expatriates for working and living in South Korea: 'Stumped like a bonsai: A show of what could have been'. *Asia Pacific Journal of Human Resources*, *53*(2), 241–259.

Doherty, N. (2013). Understanding the self-initiated expatriate: A review and directions for future research. *International Journal of Management Reviews*, *15*(4), 447–469.

Doherty, N., Richardson, J., & Thorn, K. (2013). Self-initiated expatriation and self-initiated expatriates. *Career Development International*, *18*(1), 97–112.

Edström, A., & Galbraith, J. R. (1977). Transfer of managers as a coordination and control strategy in multinational organizations. *Administrative Science Quarterly*, *22*(2), 248–263.

Farcas, D., & Goncalves, M. (2017). Motivations and cross-cultural adaptation of self-initiated expatriates, assigned expatriates, and immigrant workers: The case of Portuguese migrant workers in the United Kingdom. *Journal of Cross-Cultural Psychology*, *48*(7), 1028–1051.

Farcas, D., & Gonçalves, M. (2019). A grounded theory approach to understand the Portuguese emerging adult self-initiated expatriates' cross-cultural adaptation in the United Kingdom. *Journal of Global Mobility: The Home of Expatriate Management Research*, *7*(1), 27–48.

Farndale, E., Pai, A., Sparrow, P., & Scullion, H. (2014). Balancing individual and organizational goals in global talent management: A mutual-benefits perspective. *Journal of World Business*, *49*(2), 204–214.

Feldman, M. S. (2004). Resources in emerging structures and processes of change. *Organization Science*, *15*(3), 295–309.

Feldman, M., & Worline, M. (2016). The practicality of practice theory. *Academy of Management Learning & Education*, *15*(2), 304–324.

Fredrickson, B. L. (1998). What good are positive emotions? *Review of General Psychology*, *2*(3), 300.

Guðmundsdóttir, S., & Lundbergsdóttir, L. M. (2016). Onboarding self-initiated expatriates. *Journal of Workplace Learning*, 28(8), 510–518.

Gunz, H. P., & Peiperl, M. (2007). *Handbook of career studies*. SAGE publications.

Guthridge, M., Komm, A. B., & Lawson, E. (2008). Making talent a strategic priority. *McKinsey Quarterly*, *1*, 48.

Haak-Saheem, W., & Brewster, C. (2017). 'Hidden' expatriates: International mobility in the United Arab Emirates as a challenge to current understanding of expatriation. *Human Resource Management Journal*, *27*(3), 423–439.

Harry, T. T., Dodd, N., & Chinyamurindi, W. (2019). Telling tales: Using narratives and story-telling to understand the challenges faced by a sample of self-initiated expatriates in South Africa. *Journal of Global Mobility*, *7*(1), 64–87.

Haslberger, A., & Vaiman, V. (2013). Self-initiated expatriates: A neglected source of the global talent flow. In V. Vaiman & A. Haslberger (Eds.), *Talent management of self-initiated expatriates* (pp. 1–15). Palgrave Macmillan.

Hayes, S. L. (2020). *The influence of organizational culture on the performance of small, private nonprofit colleges and universities: An explanatory sequential mixed-methods study*. Ph.D. thesis, Caldwell University.

Hussain, T., & Deery, S. (2018). Why do self-initiated expatriates quit their jobs: The role of job embeddedness and shocks in explaining turnover intentions. *International Business Review*, *27*(1), 281–288.

Hussain, T., Iren, P., & Rice, J. (2019). Determinants of innovative behaviors among self-initiated expatriates. *Personnel Review*, *49*(2), 349–369.

Inkson, K., Arthur, M. B., Pringle, J., & Barry, S. (1997). Expatriate assignment versus overseas experience: Contrasting models of international human resource development. *Journal of world business*, *32*(4), 351–368.

Inkson, K., & Myers, B. A. (2003). "The big OE": Self-directed travel and career development. *Career Development International*, *8*(4), 170–181.

Jannesari, M., & Sullivan, S. E. 2019. Career adaptability and the success of self-initiated expatriates in China. *Career Development International*, *24*(4), 331–349.

Jonsson, A, & Foss, N. (2011). International expansion through flexible replication; Learning from the internationalization experience of IKEA. *Journal of International Business Studies*, *44*, 1079–1102.

Kealey, D. J., Protheroe, D. R., MacDonald, D., & Vulpe, T. (2005). Re-examining the role of training in contributing to international project success: A literature review and an outline of a new model training program. *International Journal of Intercultural Relations*, *29*(3), 289–316.

Knight, G., Chidlow, A., & Minbaeva, D. (2022). Methodological fit for empirical research in international business: A contingency framework. *Journal of International Business Studies*, *53*(1), 1–14.

Kumar, R., & Chhokar, J. (2019). Self-initiated expatriates in the local organizations of developing countries. *Management Decision*, *57*(4), 1659–1674.

Langinier, H., & Froehlicher, T. (2018). Context matters: Expatriates' adjustment and contact with host country nationals in Luxembourg. *Thunderbird International Business Review*, *60*(1), 105–119.

Leersnyder, J., Boiger, M., & Mesquita, B. (2013). Cultural regulation of emotion: Individual, relational, and structural sources. *Frontiers in Psychology*, *4*, 55.

Linder, C. (2019). Expatriates' motivations for going abroad. *Employee Relations: The International Journal*, *41*(1), 552–570.

MacKenzie, S. B. (2003). The dangers of poor construct conceptualization. *Journal of the Academy of Marketing Science*, *31*(3), 323–326.

Makkonen, P. (2016). Employer perceptions of self-initiated expatriate employability in China. *Journal of Global Mobility*, *3*(3), 303–330.

Makkonen, P. (2017). The employability of newcomer self-initiated expatriates in China: An employers' perspective. *Asia Pacific Journal of Human Resources*, *55*(4), 498–515.

Mayrhofer, W., Sparrow, P., & Zimmermann, A. (2008). Modern forms of international working. In *International human resource management* (pp. 241–261). Routledge.

Meyer, J. P., & Allen, N. J. (1991). A three-component conceptualization of organizational commitment. *Human Resource Management Review*, *1*(1), 61–89.

Miralles-Vazquez, L., & McGaughey, S. L. (2015). Non-traditional international assignments, knowledge and innovation: An exploratory study of women's experiences. *Prometheus*, *33*(3), 277–303.

Myers, B., Inkson, K., & Pringle, J. K. (2017). Self-initiated expatriation (SIE) by older women: An exploratory study. *Journal of Global Mobility*, *5*(2), 158–173.

Peiperl, M., Levy, O., & Sorell, M. (2014). Cross-border mobility of self-initiated and organizational expatriates: Evidence from large-scale data on work histories. *International Studies of Management & Organization*, *44*(3), 44–65.

Peltokorpi, V. (2008). Cross-cultural adjustment of expatriates in Japan. *The International Journal of Human Resource Management*, *19*(9), 1588–1606.

Podsakoff, P. M., MacKenzie, S. B., & Podsakoff, N. P. (2016). Recommendations for creating better concept definitions in the organizational, behavioral, and social sciences. *Organizational Research Methods*, *19*(2), 159–203.

Post, C., Sarala, R., Gatrell, C., & Prescott, J. E. (2020). Advancing theory with review articles. *Journal of Management Studies*, *57*(2), 351–376.

Presbitero, A., & Quita, C. (2017). Expatriate career intentions: Links to career adaptability and cultural intelligence. *Journal of Vocational Behavior*, *98*, 118–126.

Presbitero, A., Roxas, B., & Chadee, D. (2016). Looking beyond HRM practices in enhancing employee retention in BPOs: focus on employee–organisation value fit. *The International Journal of Human Resource Management*, *27*(6), 635–652.

Ren, H., Shaffer, M. A., Harrison, D. A., Fu, C. K., & Fodchuk, K. M. (2014). Reactive adjustment or proactive embedding? Multistudy, multiwave evidence for dual pathways to expatriate retention. *Personnel Psychology*, *67*(1), 203–239.

Reuber, A. R., & Fischer, E. (2021). Putting qualitative international business research in context(s). *Journal of International Business Studies*, 53, 27–38.

Richardson, C., & Ng, K. H. (2019). No place like home? Self-initiated expatriates in their ancestral homeland. *Asia Pacific Journal of Human Resources*, *59*(3), 506–528.

Richardson, J., & Mallon, M. (2005). Career interrupted? The case of the self-directed expatriate. *Journal of World Business*, *40*(4), 409–420.

Richardson, J., & McKenna, S. (2006). Exploring relationships with home and host countries. Cross Cultural Management: *An International Journal*, *13*(1), 6–22.

Richardson, J., & McKenna, S. (2014). Towards an understanding of social networks among organizational self-initiated expatriates: A qualitative case study of a professional services firm. *The International Journal of Human Resource Management*, *25*(19), 2627–2643.

Richardson, J., & Zikic, J. (2007). The darker side of an international academic career. *Career Development International*, *12*(2), 164–186.

Schoepp, K., & Forstenlechner, I. (2010). The role of family considerations in an expatriate majority environment. *Team Performance Management: An International Journal*, *16*(5/6), 309–323.

Schreuders-van den Bergh, R., & Du Plessis, Y. (2016). Exploring the role of motivational cultural intelligence in SIE women's adjustment. *Journal of Global Mobility*, 4(2), 131–148.

Selmer, J., & Lauring, J. (2010). Self-initiated academic expatriates: Inherent demographics and reasons to expatriate. *European Management Review*, *7*(3), 169–179.

Selmer, J., McNulty, Y., Lauring, J., & Vance, C. (2018). Who is an expat-preneur? Toward a better understanding of a key talent sector supporting international entrepreneurship. *Journal of International Entrepreneurship*, *16*(2), 134–149.

Shaffer, J. A., DeGeest, D., & Li, A. (2016). Tackling the problem of construct proliferation: A guide to assessing the discriminant validity of conceptually related constructs. *Organizational Research Methods*, *19*(1), 80–110.

Shaffer, M. A., Kraimer, M. L., Chen, Y. P., & Bolino, M. C. (2012). Choices, challenges, and career consequences of global work experiences: A review and future agenda. *Journal of Management*, *38*(4), 1282–1327.

Stake, R. E. (2010). The point of triangulation. *Journal of Nursing Scholarship*, *33*(3), 254–256.

Stepney, P., & Thompson, N. (2021). Isn't it time to start "theorising practice" rather than trying to "apply theory to practice"? Reconsidering our approach to the relationship between theory and practice. *Practice*, *33*(2), 149–163.

Sullivan, S. E., & Arthur, M. B. (2006). The evolution of the boundaryless career concept: Examining physical and psychological mobility. *Journal of Vocational Behavior*, *69*(1), 19–29.

Suutari, V., & Brewster, C. (2000). Making their own way: International experience through self-initiated foreign assignments. *Journal of World Business*, *35*(4), 417–436.

Suutari V., Brewster C., & Dickmann M. (2018). Contrasting assigned expatriates and self-initiated expatriates: A review of extant research and a future research agenda. In M. Dickmann, V. Suutari, & O. Wurtz (Eds.), *The management of global careers* (pp. 63–89). Palgrave Macmillan. https://doi.org/10.1007/978-3-319-76529-7_3

Tharenou, P., & Caulfield, N. (2010). Will I stay or will I go? Explaining repatriation by self-initiated expatriates. *Academy of Management Journal*, *53*(5), 1009–1028.

Thompson, N. (2017). *Theorizing practice* (2nd ed.). Palgrave.

Vaiman, V., Haslberger, A., & Vance, C. M. 2015. Recognizing the important role of self-initiated expatriates in effective global talent management. *Human Resource Management Review*, *25*(3), 280–286.

van Bakel, M., & Salzbrenner, S. (2019). Going abroad to play: Motivations, challenges, and support of sports expatriates. *Thunderbird International Business Review*, *61*(3), 505–517.

Van der Laken, P. A., Van Engen, M. L., Van Veldhoven, M. J. P. M., & Paauwe, J. (2019). Fostering expatriate success: A meta-analysis of the differential benefits of social support. *Human Resource Management Review*, *29*(4), 100679.

Wayne, J. H., Grzywacz, J. G., Carlson, D. S., & Kacmar, K. M. (2007). Work-family facilitation: A theoretical explanation and model of primary antecedents and consequences. *Human Resource Management Review*, *17*, 63–76.

Whetton, D. A. (1989). What constitutes a theoretical contribution? *The Academy of Management Review*, *14*(4), 490–495.

CHAPTER 4

A THEORY OF PROFESSIONAL TOUCHING BEHAVIOR IN ORGANIZATIONS: IMPLICATIONS FOR HUMAN RESOURCE SCHOLARS AND PRACTITIONERS

Pok Man Tang, Anthony C. Klotz, Joel Koopman, Elijah X. M. Wee and Yizhen Lu

ABSTRACT

Professional touching behavior (PTB), defined as intentional touching behavior that occurs between organizational members and that falls within the boundaries of appropriateness and professionalism in the workplace, *is prevalent in organizations. Scholars from multiple disciplines, including human resources researchers, have acknowledged the importance of physical contact for facilitating interpersonal communication and relationship-building. However, PTB may not only elicit positive reactions from those who receive it but also negative reactions as well, with implications for social dynamics in organizations. PTB can, on the one hand, fulfill employees' desires for interpersonal connection; at the same time, such physical contact at work can represent a threat to employees' health. To explain the nature and implications of these divergent effects of receiving PTB, the authors draw upon sociometer theory and behavioral immune system (BIS) theory to model the* emotional, cognitive, *and* physiological *processes via which, and the conditions under which, receiving such behavior will result in socially functional responses and prompt subsequent prosocial behavior, and when PTB will be perceived as a health risk*

Research in Personnel and Human Resources Management, Volume 41, 127–159

Published under exclusive licence by Emerald Publishing Limited
ISSN: 0742-7301/doi:10.1108/S0742-730120230000041006

and prompt withdrawal behavior. The theoretical framework of this chapter expands our conceptual understanding of the consequences of interpersonal physical contact at work and has important human resources management (HRM) implications for organizational managers.

Keywords: Emotions; well-being; interpersonal behavior; professional touching; sociometer; behavioral immune system

Touch is arguably the most foundational and powerful form of communication that humans possess. Indeed, in our species' evolution, interpersonal communication via touch preceded the development of verbal and written modalities (Burgoon et al., 1996). Touch is also the first sense that human fetuses develop and the most developed sense that we have when we are born (Field, 2001). As such, it plays an outsized role in our initial communication with other humans and the external world (Hertenstein et al., 2006). Beyond infancy, touch remains perhaps the most intense form of human communication, in part because of its ability to elicit emotional and cognitive reactions "at times more powerful than language" (Gallace & Spence, 2010, p. 247). Although not as frequently used throughout one's lifespan as verbal and written forms of communication (e.g., Hatwell et al., 2003), the impact of touch on human social interactions is nonetheless profound, including that which occurs in the work domain (Fuller, Simmering, Marler, Cox & Bennett, 2011; Simmering et al., 2013).

Within organizations, in particular, employees often use this age-old form of physical communication – touching – in their daily interactions with one another (Fuller et al., 2011). This is for good reason, as touch is one of the most powerful ways to get others' attention (Field, 2001). In addition, touch can complement and amplify the strength of other commonly used forms of communication such as verbal exchanges and written messages (e.g., Frank, 1957; Geldard, 2012; Hertenstein et al., 2006). The impact of touch has been shown in prior research which indicates that this form of communication accounts for more than half of the variability of people's responses to one another during interpersonal interactions (Mechrabian, 1981). The reason that humans are more sensitive to touch (physical contact) compared to other forms of interactions has been articulated by evolutionary and developmental psychologists, who explain that the association between touch and a sense of (inter)personal attachment and social connection is likely developed through childhood interactions with our primary caregivers (Bowlby, 2008).

The importance of touch in the work domain is evidenced by the many ways it is used by workers in contemporary organizations. In the workplace, prototypical forms of work-based touch communication include handshakes to communicate greetings (e.g., Stewart et al., 2008), taps on the shoulder to signal interruptions (e.g., Blanchard & Johnson, 1983; Field, 2001; Todd, 2019), nudges to get someone's attention (Jones & Yarbrough, 1985), or pats on the back to signify a job well done (Fuller et al., 2011). As these examples illustrate, touching is a prevalent means via which employees communicate social information in the course of their work.

Although it serves important social functions at work, touch-based communication can also cause problems in the workplace. In particular, it is one of the primary ways in which infections spread in workplaces (Thomas & Kim, 2021; Yeager, 2020). For employees returning to work in the wake of the COVID-19 pandemic, there is a heightened sense of risk associated with touching, and both employees and organizational managers are seeking ways to reduce physical contact (e.g., Katila et al., 2020). Indeed, the potential health risk associated with touch-based communication may be more acute in the workplace than in other settings, given that employees sometimes attend work when they are sick (Dew et al., 2005; Gosselin et al., 2013; Johns, 2010), that the closed, indoor environments typifying many workplaces facilitate the spread of sickness (Bain & Baldry, 1995), and that worker hygiene practices are often lax (e.g., employees commonly do not wash their hands after shaking hands or eating lunch, thereby increasing the likelihood of disease transmission; Zivich et al., 2018). Together, the social signals conveyed by such behavior occur in tandem with health risks, raising the question of when and why employees will respond positively versus negatively to touch. Addressing this question not only can shed light on how employees react to this enduring form of communication but also, as importantly, can indicate whether touch should have a role in the workplace going forward, especially given that HRM scholars and practitioners are increasingly concerned about the role that physical contact plays at work.

The aforementioned social and health-related consequences of touching align with two evolutionarily developed systems that provide insight into the process of how employees (and potentially managers) may respond to physical contact at work. First, people possess an internal regulation system termed the sociometer to detect social signals (Leary & Baumeister, 2000). This system, which operates outside of conscious awareness, helps people understand the meaning conveyed by the behavior of other individuals (e.g., Borenzweig, 1983; Kneidinger et al., 2001; Stier & Hall, 1984). Specifically, touching often conveys information to recipients regarding their relational standing and relational value in social settings including organizations (Leary, 2005, 2011). From an interpersonal standpoint, professional or work-related touching behaviors thus provide social information that informs employees of their social worth in the workplace.

In addition to this social system, individuals possess an infection-detection system that operates as a dormant alarm in people's minds, sounding when physical contact creates the risk of detrimental consequences to one's health (Schaller, 2015; Schaller & Park, 2011). This BIS exists because in general, many common infectious diseases spread via physical contact with other people (Li et al., 2020; Phan et al., 2020). Depending on the circumstances surrounding physical contact, this system will signal when touch is regarded as "infection-connoting stimuli" (Murray & Schaller, 2016, p. 83). In the workplace, this means that professional touching can potentially signal an infection risk to receivers, thereby eliciting a series of defensive responses. As such, the socially functional effects of touching are counterbalanced by an immunological response that sometimes labels touching behavior as aversive for organizational members, especially for the recipients.

In this monograph, we draw upon insights from sociometer theory (Leary, 2005, 2011; Leary & Baumeister, 2000) and BIS theory (Murray & Schaller, 2016; Schaller, 2015; Schaller & Park, 2011) to develop a dual appraisal-based framework that describes the consequences of receiving coworkers' professional or work-related touching behavior (see Fig. 1). To begin, we propose a construct which we label PTB – defined as *intentional touching behavior between organizational members that falls within the boundaries of appropriateness and professionalism in the workplace*.[1]

From here, we theorize how recipients experience PTB through the lens of two evolutionarily developed systems that provide insight into how people respond to PTB in the workplace. First, guided by sociometer and BIS theory, we theorize that following physical contact during work interactions (i.e., professional touching), recipients undergo a primary appraisal process to determine whether such behavior has implications for their positive relational value at work (i.e., whether touch is socially beneficial), as well as whether there are implications for risk of infection (i.e., whether touch is a health concern). To present a balanced view of the consequences of professional touching at work, we integrate these two systems and situate them within the work context to develop a comprehensive theory of professional touching that explains how organizational members appraise and react to coworkers' touching behavior at work. Then, to reconcile the tensions between these two perspectives, we build a theory related to how personal, relational, and situational factors (i.e., recipients' personal comfort with touch, the quality of recipients' relationship with the other party in the interaction, and the norms related to touching in the given situation) should shape the extent to which the sociometer system versus the BIS guides employee responses to PTB.

We go on to propose that when the appraisal of professional touching leads to activation of the sociometer system, it should inform an immediate series of emotional (i.e., pride), cognitive (i.e., self-esteem), and physiological (i.e., oxytocin secretion) responses, which in turn affect recipients' behaviors (i.e., prosocial). Alternatively, when professional touching causes the activation of the BIS, it should inform a very different series of emotional (i.e., disgust), cognitive (i.e., threat), physiological (i.e., cytokines secretion), and behavioral (i.e., withdrawal) responses. We then explain how these secondary appraisals help recipients of professional touching further evaluate the appropriateness of the primary appraisal and its coinciding responses. Here, we describe how both sociometer-based personal (i.e., need for belonging) and contextual (i.e., organizational political climate) factors as well as BIS-based personal (i.e., need for healthiness) and contextual (i.e., organizational hygienic climate) factors will shape employees' responses to PTB.

By building theory on how professional touching affects those who receive it, this monograph meaningfully extends our understanding of a ubiquitous workplace behavior that is under more scrutiny than ever. By describing the consequences of PTB from a joint evolutionary lens – through our incorporation of

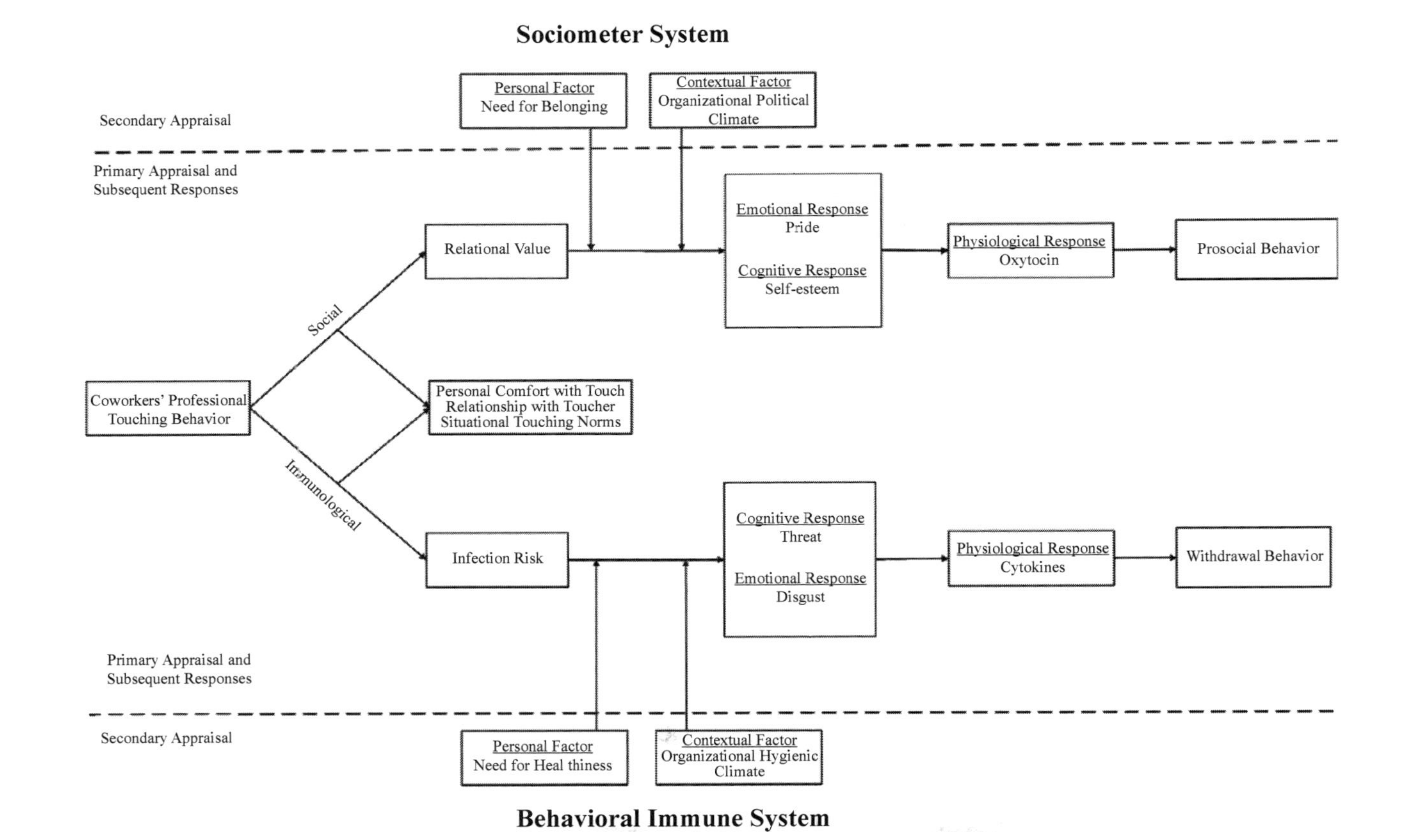

Fig. 1. A Theory of PTB From the Perspective of Recipient Employees in Organization.

insights from both sociometer and BIS theory – our model explains the contrasting potential consequences of this behavior. Because of the disparate reactions that touch can elicit, understanding when, why, and for whom each system will operate is of critical importance to understand the role of touch in the post-pandemic workplace (for both employees and human resources managers). By elucidating the existence and unpacking the operation and consequences of these two perspectives, we respond to calls from organizational scholars to address "the lack of understanding regarding a recipient's responses" to touching behavior during work interactions (Fuller et al., 2011, p. 2).

Second, our integrated appraisal-based framework contributes to sociometer theory and BIS theory simultaneously. Our work enriches sociometer theory by theorizing that workplace touching can convey social signals that reflect employees' relational value in the workplace. By viewing touching at work through the lens of sociometer theory, our work extends the predictive power of this theory by broadening the interpersonal behavior that one's sociometer can detect rather than limiting it to social rejection or inclusion (Liu & Zhang, 2016). In addition, our theorizing contributes to the behavioral immunology literature by explaining the role that appraisal processes play in the BIS (Schaller, 2015). Specifically, we extend BIS theory by applying it to a specific behavior (i.e., touching) and context (i.e., work) and explaining how activation of this system can lead to employee withdrawal. Ultimately, these two distinct systems shed light on the emotional, cognitive, physiological, and behavioral consequences of interpersonal physical contact in the workplace.

Finally, by unpacking the roles that personal and contextual factors play in how employees respond to professional touching, we explain not only *how* such touching affects employee behavior, but also *when* the social (i.e., sociometer) versus the immunological (i.e., BIS) response system will be activated. Overall, this integrated framework answers the question of *why*, *when*, and *for whom*, PTB impacts employee behavior in organizations (Whetten, 1989). To conclude, the theory that we develop and present in this monograph provides crucial insights for both HRM scholars and managers to better understand how employees in the post-pandemic world would react to others' PTB at work. In sum, it is our intention for this monograph to raise more questions than answers to advance needed scholarship in this space and push HRM managers to set clearer boundaries about PTB at work.

PTB IN ORGANIZATIONS

As mentioned earlier, touching is one of the oldest forms of communication (Knapp, 1980) and it remains a common aspect of communication among organizational members (Heaphy, 2007). However, as Marler et al. (2011, p. 145) noted, "the literature on interpersonal touch in the workplace is scant" and somewhat scattered (Fuller et al., 2011). Thus, an important precursor to our theorizing involves establishing conceptual boundaries around our phenomenon of interest and situating our framework within this literature.

As previously noted and defined, the focus of our monograph is on what we refer to as PTB. To explain, touching that occurs in the workplace can be received as either appropriate or inappropriate both in the eyes of the receiver and in relation to organizational norms and policies. Our focus is on touch that would normally be considered context-appropriate by both the receiver and the organization. Defined this way, PTB is intended to connect with prior touching and communication research which has focused on touch as a means of transmitting both social and work-related messages during interactions in organizations (e.g., Blanchard & Johnson, 1983; Crusco & Wetzel, 1984; Stewart et al., 2008). This conceptualization firmly excludes the body of research on what would widely be considered context-inappropriate touching (e.g., sexual harassment and interpersonal deviance). Because those types of touching are almost universally experienced negatively (Dunlop & Lee, 2003; Morrow et al., 1994; Woolum et al., 2017) and further are fundamentally norm-violating (e.g., Robinson & Bennett, 1995) and potentially illegal, they lie beyond the scope of our theorizing.

PTB can occur in many forms across different circumstances during the course of work (e.g., high-fives, light touches on the hand or shoulder; Hall & Friedman, 1999; Simmering et al., 2013). These touching behaviors often occur as employees work on tasks together, try to persuade one another of their perspective, and both celebrate accomplishments and bemoan failures (e.g., Hornik, 1992; Marler et al., 2011). While the exact form of touch and the context in which it occurs may vary, a commonality is that employees often use touching behavior to amplify the strength of messages they convey during work-related interactions (e.g., Field, 2001; Fuller et al., 2011). In this way, professional touch is not only regarded as a communication-based conduit to facilitate the achievement of work goals but also as important indicator for employees' social relationships at work (Heaphy, 2017). Toward this end, scholars have theorized that PTB is a type of social ritual in the workplace that transcends other non-verbal forms of communication (e.g., gestures or facial expressions) by sending relatively complex messages that facilitate goal-pursuit processes (Schroeder et al., 2019).

Although PTB is defined as context-appropriate, this does not mean that a given instance is necessarily interpreted favorably. Given the subtlety of touch, and the diversity of messages that can be embedded in it, recipients have the potential to experience a wide range of responses. While in many cases it may be welcomed given its role in conveying social acknowledgment and support (e.g., Goldman & Fordyce, 1983; Heaphy, 2017; Todd, 2019), if those more primitive areas of our brain interpret it as a potential threat, then it is possible for touch to lead to a variety of negative response. This makes clear that the ultimate message conveyed by touch is heavily dependent "on the meaning and evaluation inferred by the recipient" (Whitcher & Fisher, 1979, p. 88). To more thoroughly understand how employees will respond to PTB, it is thus necessary to elucidate the processes through which recipients attribute meaning to coworkers' PTB (Fisher et al., 1976).

As interpersonal physical contact facilitates the fulfillment of humans' basic need to develop and maintain social closeness with others (Davis, 1999; Montagu, 1972), touching can convey important social information to individuals, that is, touch may contain signals suggesting the quality of social connections and the recipients' social worth (Graham et al., 1991; Hertenstein et al., 2006). Within the context of organizations, then, receiving PTB should trigger employees to interpret what such behavior signals about their social standing in the workplace (Leary et al., 1998). At the same time, since our brains evolved to be wary of the potential dangers associated with physical contact, touching can also activate people's infection-detection systems (Schaller, 2015). As such, this primitive area of our brain can appraise PTB from colleagues as a potential source of disease (Salathé et al., 2010; Zhao et al., 2019). With this conceptualization of PTB, we next describe the consequences of receiving this type of interpersonal contact at work via both the socially functional lens of sociometer theory and the immunological lens of BIS.

PRIMARY APPRAISAL OF PTB: BENEFIT VERSUS HARM

As articulated earlier, PTB can activate up to two evolutionarily developed systems (i.e., sociometer and BIS). Next, we describe these two systems, and precisely why and how they will shape employee responses to PTB, in detail.

Sociometer Perspective on PTB

Over millennia, humans have evolved to send and receive social signals during interactions for the purpose of survival (Leary, 2010). Through this process, human beings have developed "an internal monitor of the degree to which one is valued as a relational partner" (Leary & Baumeister, 2000, p. 2). This internal monitor is referred to as the sociometer, which is at the core of a regulatory system that continuously detects and appraises social signals from other individuals in social settings such as coworkers in organizations (i.e., the sociometer system; Baumeister & Leary, 1995; Leary, 2005). When functioning properly, this system guides individuals to appropriately adjust their social behavior in response to the appraisals of these signals from the external environment (Leary, 2011). More specifically, when an employee's sociometer system registers behavior from a coworker that signals that the employee is "valued as a relational partner" (e.g., by receiving help; Leary & Baumeister, 2000, p. 2), it responds by triggering a self-evaluative process to determine appropriate behavioral responses. In the instance of receiving social support from a coworker, for instance, employees may respond by engaging in more affiliative behaviors to maintain their positive self-appraisals. In other words, employees' sociometers help them gain and preserve a desired level of relational value in social settings (Liu & Zhang, 2016).

According to sociometer theory, in addition to overt verbal messages, others' non-verbal behavior during interpersonal interactions serve important social functions (Denissen et al., 2008). For example, when a coworker touches a colleague on the shoulder, it can convey social acceptance from the toucher (Gallace & Spence, 2010), while an encouraging pat from a peer can signal cooperation and friendship from others at work (Heaphy, 2017; Kraus et al., 2010). In this way, the sociometer system shapes how employees appraise and respond to social signals conveyed by coworkers' PTB and regulates employees' subsequent psychological, physiological, and behavioral responses such that they are appropriate for the situation (Baumeister & Leary, 1995; Leary et al., 1995; Schilpzand et al., 2016).

Inherent in people's sociometer is a dual appraisal process that helps individuals detect and interpret social signals from others (Leary & Baumeister, 2000). The first appraisal is automatic (Lazarus, 1991, 2001; Leary, 2005). Upon experiencing an event, people instantly assess the relevance and significance of this stimulus – whether or not it is socially beneficial (Lazarus, 1991). Given that PTB plays a crucial role in conveying social signals, recipients of PTB will promptly evaluate whether such behavior represents a positive or negative social signal about their interpersonal relationships in the workplace (Fuller et al., 2011; Heaphy, 2017). This primary appraisal process helps recipients to quickly determine what such behavior from coworkers' means in terms of their current relational value both in the specific relationship and at work more broadly (Leary, 2005; Leary & Baumeister, 2000; Leary & Downs, 1995; Puranik et al., 2019). In essence, this automatic appraisal process provides an immediate assessment of coworkers' PTB, and what such behavior means about recipients' social worth in the eyes of coworkers (Lazarus, 1991; Leary & Baumeister, 2000).

Because PTB is limited to touching that is considered appropriate for the work context by both the receiver and the organization, this form of interpersonal contact should often be appraised as a form of social validation, support, and acknowledgment (Fuller et al., 2011; Heaphy, 2007; Leary & Baumeister, 2000). In support of this notion, research indicates that PTB serves as an indicator of one's social approval in the workplace (Montagu, 1972). For example, a gentle touch from a colleague can signal one's positive connection to others in the workplace (Sin & Koole, 2013). In addition, PTB in the form of high-fives or pats on the shoulder can convey acceptance and support to recipients (Hertenstein et al., 2006; Jones & Yarbrough, 1985; Leary, 2011). As such, physical contact-based behaviors can provide instantaneous self-evaluative information and feedback to recipients (Marler et al., 2011), regarding their social standing at work (e.g., Lamothe, 2018; von Mohr et al., 2017; Williams & Bargh, 2008). PTB can thus provide positive social feedback by conveying to employees that they are valued by others in the workplace (Simmering et al., 2013). In sum, based on sociometer theory, recipients detect the social signals encapsulated in coworkers' PTB, which in turn convey to recipients that they are valuable organizational members (Leary, 2005, 2011; Leary & Baumeister, 2000).

> *P1*. PTB positively relates to recipients' appraisals of their relational value in their workplace.

BIS Perspective on PTB

In addition to triggering a sociometer-based appraisal process, PTB has the potential to simultaneously activate another system within humans, one that is focused on defending against potential health risks. To understand why PTB may trigger such a defense system, it is important to consider that human beings evolved alongside infections and diseases (Ewald, 1995; Wolfe et al., 2007). Over tens of thousands of years of interactions with pathogens (i.e., any form of microbe that can trigger one's immune system, including bacteria and viruses; Casadevall & Pirofski, 2002), humans developed a unique psycho-immunological system that coordinates a series of disease-avoidance responses to health threats (Barreiro & Quintana-Murci, 2010). This BIS "comprises psychological processes that infer infection risk from perceptual cues, and that respond to these perceptual cues through the activation of aversive emotions, cognitions and behavioral impulses" (Schaller, 2011, p. 3418). Essentially, the BIS acts as the "first line of defense against contamination" and protects human beings from potential health-related risks (Terrizzi et al., 2013, p. 99). The BIS contains multiple mechanisms to detect the presence of pathogens during interpersonal encounters and to help individuals avoid further direct contact with these pathogens (Schaller & Park, 2011). As such, some BIS scholars conceptualize this system as a type of proactive defense, the main purpose of which is to enhance the survival of human beings (Schaller & Duncan, 2007). In this way, the BIS serves to direct behavior to avoid infection in the first place rather than relying solely on the reactive internal immunological system to deal with infections once they are present (Murray & Schaller, 2016; Schaller, 2015; Schaller & Park, 2011).

According to BIS theory, humans' BIS includes a primary appraisal mechanism that determines how individuals interpret potential sources of infection with which they come into contact on a daily basis (i.e., infection risk or not; Murray & Schaller, 2016). During the primary appraisal process, individuals immediately and subjectively evaluate the likelihood of getting sick due to exposure to the infection risk after interpersonal encounters involving physical contact (Schaller & Park, 2011). Moreover, the BIS is sensitive to the existence of any health-related information that is available and relevant to making this risk assessment during interactions with others (Murray & Schaller, 2016). Specifically, the BIS is "sensitive to perceptual cues indicating that pathogens may be present" (Schaller & Park, 2011, p. 99). The implication is that this system should appraise these cues as potential health risks. In workplaces, such cues are often present. As described earlier, physical contact is a common means via which infections spread (e.g., Nicolaides et al., 2020; Worboys, 2000), it is not uncommon for employees to come to work while ill (e.g., Dew et al., 2005; Gosselin et al., 2013), and much of work takes place in closed, indoor settings which facilitate the transmission of illnesses (e.g., Bain & Baldry, 1995). For these reasons, when an employee touches a fellow colleague, the receivers' BIS will likely appraise such behavior as a potential infection risk rather than as a benign event (Schaller, 2011).

> *P2*. PTB positively relates to recipients' appraisals of their infection risk in their workplace.

Relational Value (Sociometer) and Infection Risk (BIS): The Influence of Personal, Relational, and Contextual Factors

We have thus far described how the sociometer and BIS prompt employees to appraise coworkers' PTB in two fundamentally different ways. In doing so, we have treated all episodes of PTB equally. In reality, PTB may occur in various forms across different work settings. In terms of the extent to which employees appraise PTB as a potential benefit versus a source of potential harm, the primary set of determinants should involve the considerations relevant to the recipient at three different levels namely personal, relational, and situational.

First, at the personal level, the recipient's personal comfort with touch should play a crucial role in affecting the outcome of primary appraisal among these individuals. This comfort can be defined as individuals' dispositional perspective of touching (physical) behavior as an acceptable form of interpersonal exchange (e.g., Burleson et al., 2019; Clark & Reis, 1988). When employees on the receiving end of PTB have higher levels of personal comfort with touch, they are more likely to see PTB as a legitimate and credible way of conveying social support, understanding, and caring in the workplace (Sahi et al., 2021). In other words, workers who are comfortable with touch should be very likely to view PTB positively, as a signal of their importance in their relationship(s) and as a meaningful way for maintaining social bonding, as opposed to something threatening (Schirmer et al., 2015). To this point, scholars from other disciplines such as consumer psychology have similarly highlighted that individuals' level of comfort with "intentional interpersonal touch from or to another person" positively relates to the extent to which they attach relational value to such behavior (Webb & Peck, 2015, p. 62). Taken altogether, employees' personal comfort with touch should influence the likelihood that upon receipt of PTB, they appraise such behavior as a relational endorsement rather than a threat to their well-being.

> *P3a.* Personal comfort with touch will influence recipients' appraisals of PTB such that recipients will be more likely to appraise PTB as a source of relational value (rather than infection risk) when their personal comfort with touch is high.

Second, at the relational level, the interpersonal connection between those who engage in PTB and those who receive it should play a meaningful role in determining whether recipients will appraise such behavior as a positive signal of their relational value versus a potential threat to their physical well-being. Relationship psychologists have suggested that relational closeness (e.g., in a romantic relationship) between the individuals involved in an episode involving touch positively relates to whether recipients view the touching as appropriate behavior (Remland & Jones, 2022). Further, communication and anthropology scholars converge in their explanations that to the degree that recipients of PTB have close and intimate relationships with the person who initiates touching, recipients are inclined to experience touch as not only non-intrusive and meaningful but also as an effective communication gesture (Devito et al., 2000; Koeppel et al., 1993). Finally, ethnomethodologists have also argued that the relationship quality between those who give and receive touch is one of the most important factors that determine the legitimacy of such behavior in interpersonal encounters (Cekaite & Mondada, 2020). Applying this concept to the workplace and organizational literature, it thus stands to reasons that whether they receive PTB from a coworker (high relationship quality with peers; Farmer et al., 2015) or a supervisor (high relationship quality with the leader; Schriesheim et al., 1999), how recipients appraise the behavior will be strongly shaped by their relationship quality with the other individual. More specifically, PTB from a coworker or supervisor with whom an employee has a strong relationship should be more likely to be experienced as a social endorsement of their relational value at work than when it comes from an organizational member with whom they do not share a particularly close relationship. In these latter cases, PTB is more likely to be appraised more negatively, including as a health risk.

P3b. Relationship quality will influence recipients' appraisals of PTB such that recipients will be more likely to appraise PTB as a source of relational value (rather than infection risk) when their relationship quality with the person engaging in PTB is high.

Third, at a higher, situational level, norms within organizations, professions, and industries likely also play a vital role in affecting the primary appraisal process among PTB recipients. For example, "human touch" has been proposed as a normative behavior during the service delivery process (Solnet et al., 2019, p. 392); thus, employees within this section are more likely to see PTB as an appropriate means of communicating work-related messages among coworkers and to customers. Professional service settings can also be ones in which PTB is viewed as necessary for professionals to carry out their basic job functions. Interestingly, this includes healthcare settings (e.g., nursing; Routasalo, 1999). For example, when medical team members work alongside one another together in an emergency room to save a patient, initiating and receiving PTB may be critical to effectively carry out necessary medical procedures. As these examples illustrate, there are industries and professional situations in which recipients are likely to view PTB as an integral part of their jobs and their social connections to their colleagues and customers. This can be contrasted with industries or occupations that potentially in which PTB is not necessary for the job such as educational settings (e.g., Reilly et al., 1986). In such situations, PTB is more likely to be viewed by recipients an unneeded infection risk or a health threat in the form of sexual harassment and interpersonal teasing (Lipson, 2001). Overall, norms associated with different professional situations (e.g., industry and profession) should play a meaningful role in determining the appropriateness of PTB from the perspective of recipients (Hedlin et al., 2019).

P3c. Norms relevant to the context in which PTB occurs will influence recipients' appraisals of PTB such that they will be more likely to appraise PTB as a source of relational value (rather than infection risk) when PTB is normative for the professional context in which it takes place.

Now that we have described how and when employees will appraise PTB as a source of relational value versus and infection risk, we delve more deeply into the sociometer and BIS-based consequences of these appraisals. To do so, we first explicate the primary set of *emotional*, *cognitive*, *physiological*, and *behavioral* responses that occur when recipients appraise PTB as a source of relational value.

THE SOCIALLY FUNCTIONAL PERSPECTIVE: SOCIOMETER THEORY

Subsequent Sociometer-based Responses

Socio-emotional Response

According to sociometer theory, when employees' social standing is affirmed via positive social evaluation by others, such as in response to PTB, they should experience positive self-evaluative emotions (Tracy & Robins, 2007). That is, receiving PTB from coworkers should convey to receivers the achievement of a positive self-representation in the work setting as well as the maintenance of desirable social connections and relationships with others (i.e., heightened relational value), which should make receivers feel positively toward themselves (Robins et al., 2007; Tangney et al., 1989). Regarding what particular self-focused emotion should result from favorable appraisals about one's relational value, emotion theorists have specifically posited that pride is commonly experienced in response to others' behavioral signals of one's social acceptability (Tangney et al., 2007; Tracy & Robins, 2004; Tracy et al., 2007). Following this, when employees experience heightened relational value as a result of receiving PTB, their primary emotional reaction should be pride.

> *P4.* As a result of PTB being appraised as a benefit to recipients' relational value, they will experience the emotion of pride.

Socio-cognitive Response

Per sociometer theory, the primary appraisal process and emotional response (i.e., pride) converge to provide crucial social information to recipients' sociometer, which subsequently regulates one's cognitive self-evaluation, and more specifically, the global judgment of one's self in the workplace (Denissen et al., 2008; Leary, 2011; Liu & Zhang, 2016). In this way, the sociometer system transforms the validation by others conveyed by PTB into a positive primary appraisal of one's relational value at work, leading to feelings of pride. Such positive self-appraisal, according to sociometer theorists (e.g., Leary, 2005), should then drive elevated self-esteem, defined as a person's appraisal of their relational value (Leary & Baumeister, 2000). Indeed, researchers have noted that the positive, self-evaluative nature of pride at work should elicit positive cognitive self-appraisals in employees because pride is reflective of how much employees are able to achieve at work (e.g., Chen et al., 2004; So et al., 2015); therefore, feelings of pride often relate to subsequent positive evaluations about oneself in the form of heightened self-esteem (e.g., Williams & Desteno, 2008). When PTB is appraised as a positive indication of recipients' relational value and triggers feelings of pride, then recipients should experience a boost in self-esteem due to the pride of being socially acknowledged (Robins et al., 2007; Simmering et al., 2013). Taken together, the emotional response of pride stemming from PTB should lead recipients to view themselves more favorably.

P5. The emotion of pride stemming from the receipt of PTB will lead to elevated self-esteem in recipients.

Socio-physiological Response

Although sociometer theory primarily deals with individuals' emotional and cognitive responses to social cues, research in other domains suggest that a third, physiological-based response will take place during the primary appraisal of PTB. To this point, prior physiological research indicates that the social signals conveyed by touching behavior can play a crucial role in facilitating the secretion of oxytocin (e.g., Uvnäs-Moberg, 1998), a hormone that promotes prosocial behaviors in individuals (e.g., Leng et al., 2005). In particular, this line of research has shown that social cues from others provide self-evaluation information for individuals, and when this information is positive, an array of neural impulses is sent to the hypothalamus region of the brain, which is responsible for oxytocin secretion (i.e., hypothalamus; Renaud & Bourquet, 1991). In other words, the favorable appraisal of social signals from others facilitates the secretion of oxytocin in the receiving individuals (e.g., Ellingsen et al., 2014; Light et al., 2005; Lund et al., 2002). Applied to the receipt of PTB specifically, when recipients of PTB experience pride (i.e., a positive self-evaluative emotion) and self-esteem (i.e., a positive self-appraisal cognition), the recognition of these positive self-evaluations by the social regions of recipients' brains should send neural impulses to the hypothalamus (Sabatier et al., 2007), triggering the nervous system to release oxytocin into the bloodstream (Leng et al., 2005).

P6. The receipt of PTB will indirectly lead to the secretion of oxytocin in recipients, via elevated pride and self-esteem.

Socio-behavioral Response

Sociometer theory posits that the primary appraisal in response to social signals from the external environment ultimately affects people's behavior such that they maintain a desired level of relational value (Leary, 2005; Leary et al., 1995). Most commonly, emotional and cognitive responses to social signals prompt individuals to engage in behaviors that further promote their social acceptance (e.g., positive deeds; Schilpzand & Huang, 2018; Schilpzand et al., 2016). Beyond how pride and self-esteem may lead employees to engage in positive social behavior following PTB, research on the effects of oxytocin suggests that one form of behavior is especially likely to follow PTB when it is appraised as a source of relational value. That is, oxytocin promotes prosociality among individuals (Lim & Young, 2006) in that its release activates specific brain regions and the part of the nervous system that are responsible for coordinating prosocial behavior (Swanson & Kuypers, 1980). Indeed, scholars regard oxytocin as "a facilitator of sociality" (Yamasue et al., 2012, p. 14110) that promotes and regulates humans' prosocial behavior (Bartz et al., 2011; Hammock & Young, 2006), and empirical research has shown that oxytocin in individuals' bloodstream positively relates to prosocial behavior (e.g., Bosch & Young, 2018; Carter et al., 1992). The release of oxytocin in response to PTB, then, should lead to prosocial behavior in recipients (e.g., Bartz et al., 2011; Feldman, 2012), meaning that the sociometer-based process following the receipt of PTB should leave employees neurophysiologically primed to behave prosocially.

> *P7.* The increased pride and self-esteem caused by the receipt of PTB will indirectly lead to recipient prosocial behavior via the physiological response of increased oxytocin secretion.

Having delineated the sociometer-based response process to the receipt of PTB, we now turn to BIS to explicate how the appraisal of PTB as a health risk should lead to a different emotional, cognitive, physiological, and behavioral response process.

THE IMMUNOLOGICAL PERSPECTIVE: BIS THEORY

Subsequent BIS-based Responses

Immuno-emotional Response

The central tenet of BIS theory is that the primary appraisal of infection risk leads to an emotional response that directs subsequent disease-avoidance responses (Murray & Schaller, 2016; Schaller, 2014). Following this, BIS theory posits that one particular affective response – disgust – is activated in response to the detection of potential infection risks (Ackerman et al., 2018; Schaller, 2015). Disgust, which is associated with feelings of contamination and impurity, evolved from a primitive affective response aimed at expelling contaminated oral stimuli (Rozin & Fallon, 1987; Rozin et al., 2008). In modern humanity, disgust continues to inform individuals of the possible contamination of food, but it also signals the possible presence of many health-related risks (Oum et al., 2011).

Researchers have pinpointed the central role of disgust in the BIS (Curtis et al., 2011; Lieberman & Patrick, 2014; Peng et al., 2013) and shown that disease-connoting stimuli specifically trigger disgust, as opposed to other possible emotional reactions (Tybur et al., 2013). Given the potential for PTB to transmit illness between employees at work, recipients are likely to appraise such interpersonal encounters as creating potential for such transmission, thereby triggering the BIS-based "emotional experience of disgust" (Schaller, 2011, p. 3419). Therefore, in the workplace, when a recipient appraises PTB as an infection risk, it should elicit disgust.

> *P8.* As a result of PTB being appraised as an infection risk to recipients, they will experience the emotion of disgust.

Immuno-cognitive Response

BIS theory indicates that when people experience disgust after appraising a cue as disease-connoting, they then experience threat cognitions associated with the potential of experiencing harm to one's health (Curtis et al., 2011). Specifically, the experience of disgust increases individuals' awareness of diseasing-connoting cues (e.g., Ackerman et al., 2009; Olatunji et al., 2009), which thus causes feelings of being threatened (Curis et al., 2004). In other words, disgust heightens people's sense of vulnerability to contagious disease and triggers defense-based cognitions (i.e., threat; Davey, 2011). As a result, when individuals experience the emotion of disgust (e.g., in response to a coworker's PTB), they should also tend to exaggerate the presence of other sources of disgust from their short-term memory, which will heighten feelings of vulnerability (i.e., threat) (Schaller, 2011, 2015). In the case of receiving PTB from a coworker, the emotional response of disgust will likely amplify recipients' sensitivity and correspondingly their perceptions of vulnerability (Rouel et al., 2018), which combined should manifest in cognitions of threat.

P9. The emotion of disgust stemming from the receipt of PTB will lead to elevated threat perceptions in recipients.

Immuno-physiological Response

BIS theory not only focuses on the psycho-cognitive responses to appraisals of infection risk but also it concurrently indicates a physiological mechanism that prompts subsequent disease-avoidant behavioral responses (Murray & Schaller, 2016). Per BIS theory, the emotional and cognitive responses (i.e., disgust and threat perceptions) resulting from the primary appraisal contribute to a specific physiological response in individuals (Larson, 2002) – the production of cytokines from immune cells (Dantzer & Kelley, 2007). Cytokines are a special type of immunological protein that directs the body to prepare for disease-avoidant actions physiologically and behaviorally (Dantzer et al., 1998). When the BIS appraises stimuli as disease-connoting, the resulting emotional and cognitive responses activate individuals' immunological systems (Schaller et al., 2010). This physiological activation directs white-blood cells (i.e., a typical type of immune cells) to release cytokines. In the context of the workplace, then, the experience of disgust and threat stemming from the receipt of PTB should initiate a BIS-based physiological reaction in the form of the release of cytokines.

P10. The receipt of PTB will indirectly lead to the release of cytokines, via elevated disgust and threat perceptions.

Immuno-behavioral Response

According to BIS theory, the cytokines released by the immunological system in response to a potential infection risk (Clark & Fessler, 2015) will be detected in the bloodstream by receptors in humans' endocrine systems, which will then send neural signals to the brain that an avoidance-based behavioral response is needed (Larson, 2002). In response to these neural signals, impulses are sent to multiple organs and systems (e.g., muscular and cardiovascular systems) to cease physical and social activities to conserve resources (Hart, 1988). In other words, cytokines-driven brain signals prompt individuals to reduce all forms of behavioral activities, especially those requiring large amounts of energy (Larson & Dunn, 2001; Schaller et al., 2010).

In the context of work, then, cytokines secretion stemming from the receipt of PTB should reduce employees' engagement in resource-depleting activities (Aubert, 1999; Dantzer et al., 1999; Schaller et al., 2010). This reduction in engagement often takes the form of avoidance-oriented behavior, namely withdrawal (Eder & Eisenberger, 2008). Therefore, when cytokines are released in response to the disgust and threat triggered by receiving PTB, they should cause employees to withdraw from activities such as work tasks and social engagement with coworkers. Meanwhile, per BIS theory, these employees should also prepare themselves to fight against any potential pathogen through ceasing all unnecessary forms of physical activity or behavior at work to spare resources (Kent et al., 1992). As such, the conclusion of the BIS-based process stemming from the receipt of PTB should be withdrawal, which serves the purpose of behaviorally protecting the employee from further immunological risk (Kelley et al., 2003).

> *P11.* The increased disgust and threat perceptions caused by the receipt of PTB will indirectly lead to recipient withdrawal behavior via the physiological response of increased cytokines.

SECONDARY APPRAISAL OF PTB

Both sociometer theory and BIS theory suggest that in parallel with this primary appraisal is a second appraisal process that shapes individuals' perceptions of the appropriateness of their primary appraisal (Lazarus, 1991, 2001). Specifically, as people undergo the emotional, cognitive, and physiological responses described above, they simultaneously consider the appropriateness of such responses for themselves and their situation and adjust these responses accordingly. As we describe next, in the case of receiving PTB at work, this secondary appraisal process will influence the strength of employees' primary appraisals of PTB and their associated responses.

Sociometer-based Secondary Appraisal of PTB

Secondary appraisals begin with a person-based process that is geared "towards confirming" the primary appraisal based on one's personal characteristics (Li et al., 2019, p. 365). Relevant to sociometer theory, individuals differ in terms of their need for belonging – how much they desire social validation and acceptance from others (Leary, 2021). Moreover, the extent to which individuals experience a need for belonging relates to how strongly they react to the presence or absence of positive social information from others (e.g., Baumeister et al., 2007). As such, the degree to which people harbor a need for belonging should shape the effect of PTB on the relational value derived from receiving such behavior and thus the subsequent pride and self-esteem it elicits.

Individuals high in the need for belonging are sensitive to social signals with regards to their social acceptance across social settings (Pickett et al., 2004), whereas individuals low in the need for belonging exhibit relatively little concern about signals related to their interpersonal relationships (Baumeister & Leary, 1995). Therefore, employees high in need for belonging should be particularly responsive to the primary appraisal of coworkers' PTB because they are predisposed to value social connections to, and relationships with, others (Leary & Kelly, 2009). In contrast, because employees low in need for belonging are less motivated by interpersonal acceptance, they should be less affected by the social signals associated with PTB. Overall, individuals with high levels of need for belonging should be more likely to confirm and evaluate their primary appraisal as accurate, which should strengthen the pride and self-esteem they experience following PTB.

> *P12*. The relationships between the appraisal of PTB as a benefit to their relational value and subsequent pride and self-esteem will be stronger for recipients who are high in need for belonging, than for those who are low in need for belonging.

Furthermore, appraisal theorists propose that individuals go through a context-based process in the secondary appraisal by evaluating the relevance of their responses to the primary appraisal in a more cognitively effortful manner (Lazarus, 1991, 2001). In the case of the sociometer-based responses to PTB, this means that recipients will further evaluate whether the primary appraisal is socially favorable or not to them (Lazarus & Smith, 1988). In this secondary process, one contextual factor – organizational political climate – should be particularly relevant in shaping employees' sociometer-based reactions to PTB. Political climate refers to the shared belief among organizational members how much the work environment is characterized by political behavior (Andrews & Kacmar, 2001). Because political behavior is inherently social, the organizational political climate within which PTB occurs should affect the extent to which recipients appraise such behavior as socially beneficial. In a highly political climate, organizational members tend to be driven by self-interest (Rosen et al., 2014); therefore, even when coworkers exhibit intentional and appropriate physical contact that conveys positive social signals, recipients are likely to regard PTB as politically motivated and self-serving. Prior research has shown that when recipients of ostensibly positive behavior attribute it to political motives, they respond less positively (Ferris et al., 1995). Likewise, when recipients of PTB attribute the positive interpersonal contact to political motives, it is unlikely they will also feel that the PTB is a positive signal of their relational value. On the contrary, employees working in less political climates should see PTB from coworkers as a genuine and authentic means to establish social connections instead of attributing it to self-interest. In this way, organizational political climate should heighten the extent to which the recipients of PTB view such behavior as politically motivated rather than as a genuine, social-oriented act aimed at developing relationships.

P13. The relationships between recipients' appraisals of PTB as a benefit to their relational value and their subsequent pride and self-esteem will be weaker in high political climates compared to low political climates.

BIS-based Secondary Appraisal of PTB

As noted earlier, secondary appraisal usually begins with a person-based process that is geared toward confirming the primary appraisal (Li et al., 2019). Specific to BIS theory, individuals' need for healthiness should play a prominent role in shaping this confirmation process. Individuals high in need for healthiness possess a strong inclination to avoid sources of potential infection (Haselton & Nettle, 2006). These individuals are exceedingly sensitive to the risk of infection and they tend to overgeneralize the cues associated with infection risk (Park et al., 2007). In the parlance of BIS theory, then, employees high in need for healthiness are predisposed to broadly perceive superficial cues, including the receipt of PTB, as disease-connoting (Murray & Schaller, 2016). These individuals tend to perceive the risk of infection as relatively high in most of their interpersonal encounters and appraise physical contact during these interactions as key pathways of contagion (Schaller, 2015). In contrast, individuals low in need for healthiness are less sensitive toward the existence of disease-connoting cues or behavior because these individuals are not particularly alert in protecting themselves against pathogens. Hence, relative to employees who are low in need for healthiness, recipients of PTB, who are high in need for healthiness are more likely to confirm and evaluate their primary appraisal of PTB as an infection risk as accurate, which should strengthen their responses of disgust and threat.

P14: The relationships between the appraisal of PTB as an infection risk and subsequent disgust and threat perceptions will be stronger for recipients who are high in need for healthiness, than for those who are low in need for healthiness.

As part of the secondary appraisal, the appropriateness of the primary appraisal and corresponding responses will also be informed by the context in which it takes place (Lazarus, 1991, 2001). Therefore, recipients of PTB should consider the context in which PTB occurs when assessing the accuracy of their primary appraisal of the behavior as a risk of infection (Lazarus & Smith, 1988). Given that BIS theory deals with limiting individuals' exposure to infection risks (Ackerman et al., 2018), one contextual factor that deals with mitigating that same risk – organizational hygienic climate should be especially relevant. Organizational hygienic climate refers to shared values and beliefs among organizational members regarding the importance of maintaining high levels of personal hygiene at work (Story et al., 2008). Increasingly, organizational researchers have discussed the importance of health-focused organizational climates for the sake of employees' occupational health (e.g., Arbogast et al., 2016; Kim et al., 2021; Sonnentag et al., 2017). Due to this importance, the extent to which an organization possesses a hygienic climate should influence recipients' perceptions of the accuracy of their primary appraisal of PTB as a health risk. In organizations with strong hygienic climates, hygiene-specific guidelines are often reiterated by managers, thereby fostering adherence with such guidelines among employees (e.g., Daugherty et al., 2012). As a result, employees working in strong, compared to weak, organizational hygienic climates tend to be more vigilant about, and sensitive to, the health-related implications of physical contact or interpersonal encounters that potentially expose them to infection risks (Yuan et al., 2009). Plus, to the extent that an organization emphasizes the importance of personal hygiene at work, employees tend to be more aware of the infection potential represented by interpersonal contact with coworkers (e.g., Thompson & Rew, 2015). Following from the above, when recipients of PTB work in an organization with strong hygienic climate, they should react more negatively to such behavior and thus are more likely to confirm their primary appraisal of PTB as a risk to their health. As a result, it should strengthen their emotional response of disgust and cognitive response of threat.

P15. The relationships between recipients' appraisals of PTB as an infection risk and their subsequent disgust and threat perceptions will be stronger in high hygienic organizational climates compared to low hygienic climates.

DISCUSSION

Touch is a fundamental form of interpersonal communication, the receipt of which has important social and physiological effects (Davis, 1999; Knapp, 1980) that shape humans' emotions, cognitions, physiology, and behavior. In the workplace, PTB remains a ubiquitous form of communication that has the strength to convey messages in a way that other mediums cannot (e.g., Lynn et al., 1998; Stier & Hall, 1984). Because of the prevalence and strength of PTB, its effects in the workplace are complex; it can be a very effective and positive form of communication, but it can also be a source of extreme discomfort and disgust for recipients. The importance of the effects of touch in the workplace is increasing even more in the wake of the pandemic and the widespread shift to remote work arrangements that preclude this form of communication. And yet HRM scholars' understanding of the consequences of this behavior is limited. Thus, there is a pressing need to disentangle and build theory regarding the potential effects of receiving PTB from colleagues at work (Fuller et al., 2011; Marler et al., 2011).

In order to close this science/practice gap (Ferris et al., 1999) between our academic understanding of the effects of PTB and the reality that HR professionals are increasingly have to deal with the complexity of it in the workplace, we focused on two systems that humans possess that shape how they respond to PTB (i.e., sociometer and BIS). Despite sharing similar evolutionary roots, their co-existence creates tensions when considered in the context of the workplace. On the one hand, from a sociometer (i.e., social-functional) perspective, PTB sends social signals to recipients that can be used to evaluate their relational value in the workplace, which subsequently triggers a series of responses that ultimately prompt recipients of PTB to enact prosocial behavior. On the other hand, from a BIS (i.e., psycho-immunological) perspective, PTB represents a potential disease-connoting stimulus which triggers recipients' evaluation of their infection risk in the workplace, initiating a series of responses that ultimately prompts recipients of PTB to engage in withdrawal behavior (Murray & Schaller, 2016; Schaller, 2015). To provide guidance regarding which of the two systems will play a leading role in shaping employee responses to PTB, we explained the personal, relative, and situational factors that will trigger whether PTB is appraised as a source of relational value versus a health risk.

The result of our theorizing is a model and set of propositions that we believe are useful for informing HR scholars and practitioners as to the complex dynamics stemming from PTB. In particular, for HRM and/or organizational researchers interested in topics pertaining to physical contact at work (e.g., Fuller et al., 2011; Heaphy, 2017), we show two theoretically grounded paths via which the receipt of such behavior can either be positive or negative. In doing so, we not only expand out theoretical knowledge of this phenomenon but also lay the groundwork for empirical work that tests and extends our propositions. Our theorizing is equally important for HRM practitioners, for whom PTB presents particularly thorny issues. For those who see little harm in it, our model makes a clear and strong case for the physiological, mental, and behavioral damage that touching can cause. For others who may feel that touching has no place in modern work settings, we show how and why its elimination would likely weaken the social fabric of the organization. Overall, it is our hope that by providing such a thorough and grounded explanation for PTB's effects, both academic and practitioner conversations about this phenomenon will be richer, more evidence-based, and more effective when it comes to understanding PTB's place in organizational communication.

Intended Contributions

Our model integrates the central tenets of sociometer theory and BIS theory to build new theory that elucidates how PTB at work affects organizational members. By doing so, we contribute to research on touching behavior, sociometer theory, and BIS theory in the organizational literature. First, by delineating *when* and *for whom* the sociometer- and BIS-based responses to PTB may be more salient, we provide a thorough account of the consequences of interpersonal touching at work. More specifically, our theory takes a balanced perspective in shedding light on *why* and *how* PTB affects recipients' engagement in prosocial and withdrawal behaviors, and in doing so, it offers novel insights regarding the consequences of work-related physical contacts in the workplace. As we alluded to earlier, humans possess two evolutionarily developed systems (i.e., sociometer and BIS) to interpret others' social behavior, which when considered in tandem, create potential tension regarding the impact of PTB at work on recipients. Our theory not only acknowledges the role of these two systems when it comes to receiving PTB but also helps reconcile such potential tensions by identifying the personal, relational, and situational factors that influence the strength of recipients' sociometer-based versus BIS-based responses to PTB. In doing so, our theory heeds call to address "the lack of understanding regarding a recipient's responses" to PTB in the workplace (Fuller et al., 2011, p. 2).

Second, in using sociometer theory to guide our theorizing related to the social implications of PTB, our integrated framework broadens the scope of sociometer theory in the organizational literature. Although organizational scholars have used sociometer theory to explain how employees may react to coworkers' (anti) social behavior, scant attention has been given to the processes (i.e., emotional, cognitive, physiological, and behavioral reactions) that unfold when employees' sociometers detect these social signals from coworkers (Schilpzand et al., 2016). In addition, by viewing PTB through the lens of sociometer theory, this monograph enriches sociometer theory by extending the interpersonal behavior that employees' sociometer can detect and react to rather than limiting it to social rejection or inclusion (Leary & Baumeister, 2000).

Third, our model extends BIS theory by applying it to the organizational context (i.e., receiving PTB at work), and in doing so uncovering the series of responses that ultimately lead to the enactment of withdrawal behavior. In addition, our model directly responds to calls from BIS theorists to develop theory that disentangles "the appraisal (process) of infection risk" in individuals' BIS (Schaller, 2015, p. 219). By doing so, it deepens scholars' understanding regarding the triggering process (i.e., appraisal) that leads to the series of responses in an individual's BIS (Murray & Schaller, 2016) upon receiving a stimulus. Moreover, our model illuminates the complete BIS-based set of responses (i.e., emotional, cognitive, physiological, and behavioral) that can be triggered by a particular behavior (i.e., PTB). In doing so, we move beyond extant BIS research that has predominantly focused on single psychological or behavioral responses to infection-connotating stimuli (e.g., Eskine et al., 2011; Miller & Maner, 2012; Young et al., 2011).

Fourth and finally, the current monograph joins and extends emerging conversations regarding the importance of taking multidisciplinary approaches to more thoroughly understand the mechanisms through which different types of employee behavior affect recipients (e.g., Glomb et al., 2011; Reina et al., 2015). Specifically, this paper moved beyond useful but common affective and cognitive mechanisms and examined PTB from a neuro-biological perspective (e.g., Field, 2010). In doing so, our theorizing illuminates the usefulness of adopting the lenses of occupational health and social connectedness at work to understand the socio-physiological consequences of employee behavior (e.g., Leary, 2005; Sonnentag et al., 2017), instead of only the cognitive and affective effects. This model should thus serve as further evidence of the value of looking outside of the organizational literature when trying to understand organizational phenomena.

Directions for Future HRM and Organizational Research

Beyond enhancing HRM scholars' and managers' understanding about how employees react to coworkers' PTB, our theorizing opens new avenues for future research. First, this monograph provides a guiding framework for scholars to empirically examine the two distinct systems that are activated by receiving PTB at work. To do this, researchers will need to validate or adapt measures to assess the frequency of receiving PTB from coworkers during a particular period of time and the appraisal of relational value and infection risk. Regarding these empirical examinations, we would also like to call researchers' attention to potential boundary conditions (i.e., the need preferences of individuals and the climates of organizations) of the two pathways developed in our model.

Second, methodologies based in neuroscience have been increasingly common in organizational and HRM research because these approaches help uncover the neuro-physiological mechanisms of workplace phenomena (Waldman et al., 2019). These approaches would also be useful for examining the neuro-physiological mechanisms that we predicted are triggered by PTB. For example, future research may employ methods using functional magnetic resonance imaging to examine employees' brain regions that are responsible for the release of oxytocin or cytokines upon receiving PTB in the workplace. By doing so, future research can test the neural mechanisms that underlie the physiological responses that we propose in our model. In another example, researchers can use less intrusive physiological approaches to assess hormone (e.g., oxytocin) levels in recipients of PTB, such as by collecting and analyzing their saliva (Huffmeijer et al., 2012).

Third, although there are psychometrically sound measures to assess interpersonal touching behavior (e.g., Fuller et al., 2011; Jones & Brown, 1996), these measures are largely subjective (e.g., perceived frequency of coworkers' touching during work-related interactions). Therefore, we encourage future HRM research to adopt mixed-method approaches (i.e., assessing PTB in a field study using subjective measures as well as manipulating PTB in an experiment setting) and consider operationalizations that objectively capture the receipt of PTB. To the later point, future research may consider using skin pressure sensor to detect the intensity and frequency of PTB (e.g., Someya et al., 2004). Specifically, this physiological instrument can measure touch input from others on a focal employee's skin and transform it into objective data that indicates the depth and frequency of touch receipt during work interactions (Nittala et al., 2018).

Fourth, as recent psychology research explicitly highlights, "an individual's power or status" can directly influence whether PTB will be appraised in a favorable manner or not (Schirmer et al., 2022, p. 2). To this end, we encourage researchers to consider how recipients' reactions to PTB will be shaped by the status of the other party. From the perspective of sociometer theory, employees are primed to detect any social information encapsulated in colleagues' PTB (Leary & Baumeister, 2000). Thus, it is possible that when an organizational member who is respected and possesses prestige in the workplace (i.e., high status) engages in PTB, recipients' sociometers are likely to appraise such PTB as a potential source of enhancement to their own social standing in the workplace (Earley, 1999; Yu et al., 2019). Put differently, when a coworker who initiates PTB has high workplace status, such contact will likely be seen by recipients as a signal of social acknowledgment (e.g., Schirmer & Adolphs, 2017). Meanwhile, from the perspective of BIS theory, employees continuously scan for any infection-connotating clues that accompany colleagues' behaviors (e.g., Schaller, 2015). Researchers have found that one important cue that aids in determining the likelihood of others' disease-carrying potential is those individuals' social status (Murray & Schaller, 2016). In particular, the protection mechanism to broadly detect any possible infection-connotating clues that is inherent in people's BIS is sensitive to contact with people with lower social status (e.g., Makhanova et al., 2015; Miller & Maner, 2012). This helps to explain why prior research in health and clinical psychology has consistently shown that to the extent that people have low status, they are more likely to be seen as potential disease carriers (e.g., Adler et al., 2000; Krantz & McCeney, 2002; Mirowsky & Ross, 2017). Relative to that from high status coworkers, employees should thus appraise PTB from lower workplace status organizational members as a potential health risk (e.g., Murray & Schaller, 2016), prompting further BIS activation. All in all, we encourage future research to take status into consideration while dissecting the reactions of the PTB recipients.

Fifth, while the primary focus of this monograph is to develop a theory of recipients' sociometer- and BIS-based reactions to PTB at work, we encourage future research to delve into the role that social comparison might play in this dual appraisal model. Per social comparison theory, it is possible that employees might compare their receipt of PTB with their peers (Suls & Wheeler, 2012). Following the predictions from social comparison theorists, when the PTB recipients engage in downward social comparisons (comparing themselves with the peers who have not received PTB), the sociometer system should be more activated (Smith, 2000) and they should experience strong feelings of pride. That said, when the PTB recipients engage in upward social comparisons (comparing themselves with colleagues who receive high levels of PTB), they might view themselves as missing out on the relational value signaled by PTB and thus potentially experience the emotion of envy or resentment. As these propositions suggest, we feel that there is a promising research avenue for HRM researchers to consider the direction (upward vs. downward) of social comparison while examining the dynamics of how employees respond to PTB.

Finally, regarding the measurement of our proposed moderators, our model opens new avenues for future research to develop and validate measurement scales in assessing employees' shared perceptions of organizational hygienic climate, which may concurrently advance the occupational health literature (e.g., Sonnentag et al., 2017; Wałaszek et al., 2017). Meanwhile, with regard to the characteristics of the person who initiates PTB, we primarily focused on the personal, relational, as well as contextual factors, based on their theoretical relevance to both sociometer theory and BIS theory. However, there may be additional characteristics of those who engage in PTB that influence how recipients react to such behavior. For example, the interpersonal perceptions of the person who initiates PTB (i.e., warmth and competence; Fiske et al., 2007) may affect the activation of the sociometer and BIS in the recipients of PTB. It is possible that when PTB is initiated by someone perceived to be warm, recipients' sociometers may react more strongly due to stronger signals of intimacy and social closeness (Cuddy et al., 2008). Accordingly, future studies should more fully explore how individual differences of the employee who initiates PTB may influence how employees respond to such behavior.

CONCLUSION

Despite being as important as it has ever been in the work domain, the topic of touch has been left largely untouched by organizational researchers. Perhaps because of the intimacy associated with this form of communication, touch can be a sensitive subject, but that cannot deter HRM practitioners or researchers from giving PTB the degree of examination that it warrants. In this monograph, we put this fundamental form of human communication back in the theoretical spotlight by developing a conceptual model that explains the nature of PTB and unpacks the complex paths via which it can cause employees on the receiving end of it to either become better organizational citizens or to recede from engagement in the firm. Overall, we hope that this expansion of our understanding of the consequences of PTB in organizations jump starts new research and new conversations among and between HRM academics and practitioners that yield additional insights into this emerging yet often neglected phenomenon in the workplace.

NOTE

1. Importantly, we note that this definition excludes one impactful form of touch in the work domain – that which is involved in some incidents of sexual harassment (e.g., Fitzgerald & Cortina, 2018). We have taken the appropriateness of such behavior into consideration while developing the boundary conditions for the primary appraisal process (*P3a–c*). However, a more complete treatment of this form of touch at work is beyond the scope of this paper and has been extensively reviewed in recent articles (e.g., Konard & Gutek, 1986; Lee & Guerrero, 2001).

REFERENCES

Ackerman, J. M., Becker, D. V., Mortensen, C. R., Sasaki, T., Neuberg, S. L., & Kenrick, D. T. (2009). A pox on the mind: Disjunction of attention and memory in the processing of physical disfigurement. *Journal of Experimental Social Psychology*, *45*(3), 478–485.

Ackerman, J. M., Hill, S. E., & Murray, D. R. (2018). The behavioral immune system: Current concerns and future directions. *Social and Personality Psychology Compass*, *12*(2), 57–70.

Adler, N. E., Epel, E. S., Castellazzo, G., & Ickovics, J. R. (2000). Relationship of subjective and objective social status with psychological and physiological functioning: Preliminary data in healthy, White women. *Health Psychology*, *19*(6), 586–592.

Andrews, M. C., & Kacmar, K. M. (2001). Discriminating among organizational politics, justice, and support. *Journal of Organizational Behavior: The International Journal of Industrial, Occupational and Organizational Psychology and Behavior*, *22*(4), 347–366.

Arbogast, J. W., Moore-Schiltz, L., Jarvis, W. R., Harpster-Hagen, A., Hughes, J., & Parker, A. (2016). Impact of a comprehensive workplace hand hygiene program on employer health care insurance claims and costs, absenteeism, and employee perceptions and practices. *Journal of Occupational and Environmental Medicine*, *58*(6), e231–e240.

Aubert, A. (1999). Sickness and behaviour in animals: A motivational perspective. *Neuroscience & Biobehavioral Reviews*, *23*(7), 1029–1036.

Bain, P., & Baldry, C. (1995). Sickness and control in the office—The sick building syndrome. *New Technology, Work and Employment*, *10*(1), 19–31.

Barreiro, L. B., & Quintana-Murci, L. (2010). From evolutionary genetics to human immunology: How selection shapes host defence genes. *Nature Reviews Genetics*, *11*(1), 17–30.

Bartz, J. A., Zaki, J., Bolger, N., & Ochsner, K. N. (2011). Social effects of oxytocin in humans: Context and person matter. *Trends in Cognitive Sciences*, *15*(7), 301–309.

Baumeister, R. F., Brewer, L. E., Tice, D. M., & Twenge, J. M. (2007). Thwarting the need to belong: Understanding the interpersonal and inner effects of social exclusion. *Social and Personality Psychology Compass*, *1*(1), 506–520.

Baumeister, R. F., & Leary, M. R. (1995). The need to belong: Desire for interpersonal attachments as a fundamental human motivation. *Psychological Bulletin*, *117*(3), 497.

Blanchard, K., & Johnson, S. (1983). The one-minute manager. *Cornell Hotel and Restaurant Administration Quarterly*, *23*(4), 39–41.

Borenzweig, H. (1983). Touching in clinical social work. *Social Casework*, *64*(4), 238–242.

Bosch, O. J., & Young, L. J. (2018). Oxytocin and social relationships: From attachment to bond disruption. *Current Topics in Behavioral Neurosciences*, *35*, 97–117.

Bowlby, J. (2008). *A secure base: Parent-child attachment and healthy human development*. Basic Books.

Burgoon, J. K., Buller, D. B., & Woodall, W. G. (1996). *Nonverbal communication: The unspoken dialogue* (2nd ed.). McGraw-Hill.

Burleson, M. H., Roberts, N. A., Coon, D. W., & Soto, J. A. (2019). Perceived cultural acceptability and comfort with affectionate touch: Differences between Mexican Americans and European Americans. *Journal of Social and Personal Relationships*, *36*(3), 1000–1022.

Carter, C. S., Williams, J. R., Witt, D. M., & Insel, T. R. (1992). Oxytocin and social bonding. *Annals of the New York Academy of Sciences*, *652*(1), 204–211.

Casadevall, A., & Pirofski, L.-A. (2002). What is a pathogen? *Annals of Medicine*, *34*(1), 2–4.

Cekaite, A., & Mondada, L. (2020). Towards an interactional approach to touch in social encounters. In A. Cekaite & L. Mondada (Eds.), *Touch in social interaction: Touch, language and body* (pp. 1–26). Routledge.

Chen, G., Gully, S. M., & Eden, D. (2004). General self-efficacy and self-esteem: Toward theoretical and empirical distinction between correlated self-evaluations. *Journal of Organizational Behavior*, *25*(3), 375–395.

Clark, J. A., & Fessler, D. M. (2015). The role of disgust in norms, and of norms in disgust research: Why liberals shouldn't be morally disgusted by moral disgust. *Topoi*, *34*(2), 483–498.

Clark, M. S., & Reis, H. T. (1988). Interpersonal processes in close relationships. *Annual Review of Psychology*, *39*, 609–672.

Crusco, A. H., & Wetzel, C. G. (1984). The Midas touch: The effects of interpersonal touch on restaurant tipping. *Personality and Social Psychology Bulletin*, *10*(4), 512–517.

Cuddy, A. J., Fiske, S. T., & Glick, P. (2008). Warmth and competence as universal dimensions of social perception: The stereotype content model and the BIAS map. *Advances in Experimental Social Psychology*, *40*, 61–149.

Curtis, V., De Barra, M., & Aunger, R. (2011). Disgust as an adaptive system for disease avoidance behaviour. *Philosophical Transactions of the Royal Society B: Biological Sciences*, *366*(1563), 389–401.

Dantzer, R., Bluthé, R.-M., Layé, S., Bret-Dibat, J.-L., Parnet, P., & Kelley, K. W. (1998). Cytokines and sickness behavior. *Annals of the New York Academy of Sciences*, *840*(1), 586–590.

Dantzer, R., & Kelley, K. W. (2007). Twenty years of research on cytokine-induced sickness behavior. *Brain, Behavior, and Immunity*, *21*(2), 153–160.

Dantzer, R., Wollman, E., Vitkovic, L., & Yirmiya, R. (1999). Cytokines and depression: Fortuitous or causative association? *Molecular Psychiatry*, *4*(4), 328–332.

Daugherty, E. L., Paine, L. A., Maragakis, L. L., Sexton, J. B., & Rand, C. S. (2012). Safety culture and hand hygiene: Linking attitudes to behavior. *Infection Control & Hospital Epidemiology*, *33*(12), 1280–1282.

Davey, G. C. (2011). Disgust: The disease-avoidance emotion and its dysfunctions. *Philosophical Transactions of the Royal Society B: Biological Sciences*, *366*(1583), 3453–3465.

Davis, P. (1999). *The power of touch: The basis for survival, health, intimacy, and emotional well-being!* Hay House, Inc.

Denissen, J. J., Penke, L., Schmitt, D. P., & Van Aken, M. A. (2008). Self-esteem reactions to social interactions: Evidence for sociometer mechanisms across days, people, and nations. *Journal of Personality and Social Psychology*, *95*(1), 181.

DeVito, J. A., O'Rourke, S., & O'Neill, L. (2000). *Human communication*. Longman.

Dew, K., Keefe, V., & Small, K. (2005). 'Choosing' to work when sick: Workplace presenteeism. *Social Science & Medicine*, *60*(10), 2273–2282.
Dunlop, P. D., & Lee, K. (2004). Workplace deviance, organizational citizenship behavior, and business unit performance: The bad apples do spoil the whole barrel. *Journal of Organizational Behavior: The International Journal of Industrial, Occupational and Organizational Psychology and Behavior*, *25*(1), 67–80.
Earley, P. C. (1999). Playing follow the leader: Status-determining traits in relation to collective efficacy across cultures. *Organizational Behavior and Human Decision Processes*, *80*(3), 192–212.
Eder, P., & Eisenberger, R. (2008). Perceived organizational support: Reducing the negative influence of coworker withdrawal behavior. *Journal of Management*, *34*(1), 55–68.
Ellingsen, D.-M., Wessberg, J., Chelnokova, O., Olausson, H., Laeng, B., & Leknes, S. (2014). In touch with your emotions: Oxytocin and touch change social impressions while others' facial expressions can alter touch. *Psychoneuroendocrinology*, *39*, 11–20.
Eskine, K. J., Kacinik, N. A., & Prinz, J. J. (2011). A bad taste in the mouth: Gustatory disgust influences moral judgment. *Psychological Science*, *22*(3), 295–299.
Ewald, P. W. (1995). The evolution of virulence: A unifying link between parasitology and ecology. *The Journal of Parasitology*, *81*(5), 659–669.
Farmer, S. M., Van Dyne, L., & Kamdar, D. (2015). The contextualized self: How team–member exchange leads to coworker identification and helping OCB. *Journal of Applied Psychology*, *100*(2), 583.
Feldman, R. (2012). Oxytocin and social affiliation in humans. *Hormones and Behavior*, *61*(3), 380–391.
Ferris, G., Bhawuk, D., Fedor, D., & Judge, T. (1995). Organizational politics and citizenship: Attributions of intentionality and construct definition. In M. J. Martinko (Ed.), *Attribution theory: An organizational perspective*. Routledge.
Ferris, G. R., Hochwarter, W. A., Buckley, M. R., Harrell-Cook, G., & Frink, D. D. (1999). Human resources management: Some new directions. *Journal of Management*, *25*(3), 385–415.
Field, T. (2001). Chronic maternal depression affects infants, newborns and the foetus. In S. Goodman (Ed.), *Children of depressed parents: Alternative pathways & risk for psychopathology* (pp. 174–186). Lawrence Erlbaum.
Field, T. (2010). Touch for socioemotional and physical well-being: A review. *Developmental review*, *30*(4), 367–383.
Fisher, J. D., Rytting, M., & Heslin, R. (1976). Hands touching hands: Affective and evaluative effects of an interpersonal touch. *Sociometry*, *39*(4), 416–421.
Fiske, S. T., Cuddy, A. J., & Glick, P. (2007). Universal dimensions of social cognition: Warmth and competence. *Trends in Cognitive Sciences*, *11*(2), 77–83.
Fitzgerald, L. F., & Cortina, L. M. (2018). Sexual harassment in work organizations: A view from the 21st century. In C. B. Travis, J. W. White, A. Rutherford, W. S. Williams, S. L. Cook, & K. F. Wyche (Eds.), *APA handbook of the psychology of women: Perspectives on women's private and public lives* (Vol. 2, pp. 215–234). American Psychological Association.
Frank, L. K. (1957). Tactile communication. *Genetic Psychology Monographs*, *56*, 209–225.
Fuller, B., Simmering, M. J., Marler, L. E., Cox, S. S., Bennett, R. J., & Cheramie, R. A. (2011). Exploring touch as a positive workplace behavior. *Human Relations*, *64*(2), 231–256.
Gallace, A., & Spence, C. (2010). The science of interpersonal touch: An overview. *Neuroscience & Biobehavioral Reviews*, *34*(2), 246–259.
Geldard, F. A. (2012). Sensory communication. In W. A. Rosenblith (Ed.), *Cutaneous channels of communication* (1st ed., pp. 73–87). Wiley.
Glomb, T. M., Duffy, M. K., Bono, J. E., & Yang, T. (2011). Mindfulness at work. *Research in Personnel and Human Resource Management, 30*, 115–157. doi: 10.1108/S0742-7301(2011)0000030005.
Goldman, M., & Fordyce, J. (1983). Prosocial behavior as affected by eye contact, touch, and voice expression. *The Journal of Social Psychology*, *121*(1), 125–129.
Gosselin, E., Lemyre, L., & Corneil, W. (2013). Presenteeism and absenteeism: Differentiated understanding of related phenomena. *Journal of Occupational Health Psychology*, *18*(1), 75–86.
Graham, G. H., Unruh, J., & Jennings, P. (1991). The impact of nonverbal communication in organizations: A survey of perceptions. *The Journal of Business Communication (1973)*, *28*(1), 45–62.

Hall, J. A., & Friedman, G. B. (1999). Status, gender, and nonverbal behavior: A study of structured interactions between employees of a company. *Personality and Social Psychology Bulletin*, *25*(9), 1082–1091.

Hammock, E. A., & Young, L. J. (2006). Oxytocin, vasopressin and pair bonding: Implications for autism. *Philosophical Transactions of the Royal Society B: Biological Sciences*, *361*(1476), 2187–2198.

Hart, B. L. (1988). Biological basis of the behavior of sick animals. *Neuroscience & Biobehavioral Reviews*, *12*(2), 123–137.

Haselton, M., & Nettle, D. (2006). The paranoid optimist: An integrative evolutionary model of cognitive biases. *Personality and Social Psychology Review*, *10*, 47–66.

Hatwell, Y., Streri, A., & Gentaz, E. (2003). *Touching for knowing: Cognitive psychology of haptic manual perception* (Vol. 53). John Benjamins Publishing.

Heaphy, E. D. (2017). Bodily insights: Three lenses on positive organizational relationships. In J. E. Dutton & B. R. Ragins (Eds.), *Exploring positive relationships at work: Building a theoretical and research foundation* (pp. 47–72). Psychology Press.

Hedlin, M., Åberg, M., & Johansson, C. (2019). Too much, too little: Preschool teachers' perceptions of the boundaries of adequate touching. *Pedagogy, Culture & Society*, *27*(3), 485–502.

Hertenstein, M. J., Verkamp, J. M., Kerestes, A. M., & Holmes, R. M. (2006). The communicative functions of touch in humans, nonhuman primates, and rats: A review and synthesis of the empirical research. *Genetic, Social, and General Psychology Monographs*, *132*(1), 5–94.

Hornik, J. (1992). Tactile stimulation and consumer response. *Journal of Consumer Research*, *19*(3), 449–458.

Huffmeijer, R., Alink, L. R., Tops, M., Grewen, K. M., Light, K. C., Bakermans-Kranenburg, M. J., & van Ijzendoom, M. H. (2012). Salivary levels of oxytocin remain elevated for more than two hours after intranasal oxytocin administration. *Neuroendocrinol Lett*, *33*, 21–25.

Johns, G. (2010). Presenteeism in the workplace: A review and research agenda. *Journal of Organizational Behavior*, *31*(4), 519–542.

Jones, S. E., & Brown, B. C. (1996). Touch attitudes and behaviors, recollections of early childhood touch, and social self-confidence. *Journal of Nonverbal Behavior*, *20*(3), 147–163.

Jones, S. E., & Yarbrough, A. E. (1985). A naturalistic study of the meanings of touch. *Communications Monographs*, *52*(1), 19–56.

Katila, J., Gan, Y., & Goodwin, M. H. (2020). Interaction rituals and 'social distancing': New haptic trajectories and touching from a distance in the time of COVID-19. *Discourse Studies*, *22*(4), 418–440.

Kelley, K. W., Bluthé, R.-M., Dantzer, R., Zhou, J.-H., Shen, W.-H., Johnson, R. W., & Broussard, S. R. (2003). Cytokine-induced sickness behavior. *Brain, Behavior, and Immunity*, *17*(1), 112–118.

Kent, S., Bluthé, R.-M., Kelley, K. W., & Dantzer, R. (1992). Sickness behavior as a new target for drug development. *Trends in Pharmacological Sciences*, *13*, 24–28.

Kim, S., Cho, S., & Park, Y. (2021). Daily microbreaks in a self-regulatory resources lens: Perceived health climate as a contextual moderator via microbreak autonomy. *Journal of Applied Psychology*, 107(1), 60–77.

Knapp, M. (1980). *Essentials of nonverbal communication*. Holt, Rinehart & Winston.

Kneidinger, L. M., Maple, T. L., & Tross, S. A. (2001). Touching behavior in sport: Functional components, analysis of sex differences, and ethological considerations. *Journal of Nonverbal Behavior*, *25*(1), 43–62.

Koeppel, L. B., Montagne-Miller, Y., O'Hair, D., & Cody, M. J. (1993). Friendly? flirting? wrong? In P. J. Kalbfleisch (Ed.), *Interpersonal communication: Evolving interpersonal relationships* (pp. 13–32). Hillsdale, NJ: Lawrence Erlbaum.

Krantz, D. S., & McCeney, M. K. (2002). Effects of psychological and social factors on organic disease: A critical assessment of research on coronary heart disease. *Annual Review of Psychology*, *53*(1), 341–369.

Kraus, M. W., Huang, C., & Keltner, D. (2010). Tactile communication, cooperation, and performance: An ethological study of the NBA. *Emotion*, *10*(5), 745–749.

Lamothe, C. (2018, January 3). Let's touch: Why physical connection between human beings matters. *The Guardian*. https://www.theguardian.com/society/2018/jan/03/lets-touch-why-physical-connection-between-human-beings-matters

Larson, S. J. (2002). Behavioral and motivational effects of immune-system activation. *The Journal of General Psychology*, *129*(4), 401–414.

Larson, S. J., & Dunn, A. J. (2001). Behavioral effects of cytokines. *Brain, Behavior, and Immunity*, *15*(4), 371–387.

Lazarus, R. S. (1991). Cognition and motivation in emotion. *American Psychologist*, *46*(4), 352–367.

Lazarus, R. S. (2001). Relational meaning and discrete emotions. In K. R. Scherer, A. Schorr, & T. Johnstone (Eds.), *Appraisal processes in emotion: Theory, methods, research* (pp. 37–67). Oxford University Press.

Lazarus, R. S., & Smith, C. A. (1988). Knowledge and appraisal in the cognition—Emotion relationship. *Cognition & Emotion*, *2*(4), 281–300.

Leary, M. R. (2005). Sociometer theory and the pursuit of relational value: Getting to the root of self-esteem. *European Review of Social Psychology*, *16*(1), 75–111.

Leary, M. R. (2010). Affiliation, acceptance, and belonging. In S. T. Fiske, D. T. Gilbert, & G. Lindzey (Eds.), *Handbook of social psychology* (Vol. 2, pp. 864–897). John Wiley & Sons.

Leary, M. R. (2011). Sociometer theory. In P. A. Van Lange, A. W. Kruglanski, & E. T. Higgins (Eds.), *Handbook of theories of social psychology* (Vol. 2, pp, 141–159). SAGE Publications.

Leary, M. R. (2021). The need to belong, the sociometer, and the pursuit of relational value: Unfinished business. *Self and Identity*, *20*(1), 126–143.

Leary, M. R., & Baumeister, R. F. (2000). The nature and function of self-esteem: Sociometer theory. *Advances in Experimental Social Psychology*, *32*, 1–62.

Leary, M. R., & Downs, D. L. (1995). Interpersonal functions of the self-esteem motive. In M. Kernis (Ed.), *Efficacy, agency, and self-esteem* (pp. 123–144). Plenum.

Leary, M. R., Haupt, A. L., Strausser, K. S., & Chokel, J. T. (1998). Calibrating the sociometer: The relationship between interpersonal appraisals and the state self-esteem. *Journal of Personality and Social Psychology*, *74*(5), 1290–1299.

Leary, M. R., & Kelly, K. M. (2009). Belonging motivation. In M. R. Leary & R. H. Hoyle (Eds.), *Handbook of individual differences in social behavior* (pp. 400–409). Guilford Press.

Leary, M. R., Tambor, E. S., Terdal, S. K., & Downs, D. L. (1995). Self-esteem as an interpersonal monitor: The sociometer hypothesis. *Journal of Personality and Social Psychology*, *68*(3), 518–530.

Lee, J. W., & Guerrero, L. K. (2001). Types of touch in cross-sex relationships between coworkers: Perceptions of relational and emotional messages, inappropriateness, and sexual harassment. *Journal of Applied Communication Research*, *29*(3), 197–220.

Leng, G., Caquineau, C., & Sabatier, N. (2005). Regulation of oxytocin secretion. *Vitamins & Hormones*, *71*, 27–58.

Li, Q., Guan, X., Wu, P., Wang, X., Zhou, L., Tong, Y., Ren, R., Leung, K. S. M., Lau, E. H. Y., Wong, J. Y., Xing, X., & Xiang, N. (2020). Early transmission dynamics in Wuhan, China, of novel coronavirus-infected pneumonia. *New England Journal of Medicine*, *382*, 1199–1207.

Li, X., McAllister, D. J., Ilies, R., & Gloor, J. L. (2019). Schadenfreude: A counternormative observer response to workplace mistreatment. *Academy of Management Review*, *44*(2), 360–376.

Lieberman, D., & Patrick, C. (2014). Are the behavioral immune system and pathogen disgust identical? *Evolutionary Behavioral Sciences*, *8*(4), 244–250.

Light, K. C., Grewen, K. M., & Amico, J. A. (2005). More frequent partner hugs and higher oxytocin levels are linked to lower blood pressure and heart rate in premenopausal women. *Biological Psychology*, *69*(1), 5–21.

Lim, M. M., & Young, L. J. (2006). Neuropeptidergic regulation of affiliative behavior and social bonding in animals. *Hormones and Behavior*, *50*(4), 506–517.

Lipson, J. (2001). *Hostile hallways: Bullying, teasing, and sexual harassment in school.* AAUW Educational Foundation.

Liu, S., & Zhang, L. (2016). Sociometer theory. *Encyclopedia of evolutionary psychological science*, 1–4.

Lund, I., Yu, L.-C., Uvnas-Moberg, K., Wang, J., Yu, C., Kurosawa, M., Agren, G., Rosén, A., Lekman, M., & Lundeberg, T. (2002). Repeated massage-like stimulation induces long-term effects on nociception: Contribution of oxytocinergic mechanisms. *European Journal of Neuroscience*, *16*(2), 330–338.

Lynn, M., Le, J.-M., & Sherwyn, D. S. (1998). Reach out and touch your customers. *Cornell Hotel and Restaurant Administration Quarterly*, *39*(3), 60–65.

Makhanova, A., Miller, S. L., & Maner, J. K. (2015). Germs and the out-group: Chronic and situational disease concerns affect intergroup categorization. *Evolutionary Behavioral Sciences*, *9*(1), 8–19.

Marler, L. E., Cox, S. S., Simmering, M. J., Bennett, R. J., & Fuller, J. B. (2011). Exploring the role of touch and apologies in forgiveness of workplace offenses. *Journal of Managerial Issues*, *23*, 144–163.

Mehrabian, A. (1981). *Silent messages* (2nd ed.). Wadsworth.

Miller, S. L., & Maner, J. K. (2012). Overperceiving disease cues: The basic cognition of the behavioral immune system. *Journal of Personality and Social Psychology*, *102*(6), 1198–1213.

Mirowsky, J., & Ross, C. E. (2017). *Education, social status, and health*. Routledge.

Montagu, A. (1972). *Touching, the human significance of the skin*. Perennial Library.

Morrow, P. C., McElroy, J. C., & Phillips, C. M. (1994). Sexual harassment behaviors and work related perceptions and attitudes. *Journal of Vocational Behavior*, *45*(3), 295–309.

Murray, D. R., & Schaller, M. (2016). The behavioral immune system: Implications for social cognition, social interaction, and social influence. *Advances in Experimental Social Psychology*, *53*, 75–129.

Nicolaides, C., Avraam, D., Cueto-Felgueroso, L., González, M. C., & Juanes, R. (2020). Hand-hygiene mitigation strategies against global disease spreading through the air transportation network. *Risk Analysis*, *40*(4), 723–740.

Nittala, A. S., Withana, A., Pourjafarian, N., & Steimle, J. (2018). Multi-touch skin: A thin and flexible multi-touch sensor for on-skin input. In *Proceedings of the 2018 CHI conference on human factors in computing systems* (pp. 1–12). Association for Computing Machinery.

Olatunji, B. O., Wolitzky-Taylor, K. B., Willems, J., Lohr, J. M., & Armstrong, T. (2009). Differential habituation of fear and disgust during repeated exposure to threat-relevant stimukellyin contamination-based OCD: An analogue study. *Journal of Anxiety Disorders*, *23*(1), 118–123.

Oum, R. E., Lieberman, D., & Aylward, A. (2011). A feel for disgust: Tactile cues to pathogen presence. *Cognition and Emotion*, *25*(4), 717–725.

Park, J. H., Schaller, M., & Crandall, C. S. (2007). Pathogen-avoidance mechanisms and the stigmatization of obese people. *Evolution and Human Behavior*, *28*(6), 410–414.

Peng, M., Chang, L., & Zhou, R. (2013). Physiological and behavioral responses to strangers compared to friends as a source of disgust. *Evolution and Human Behavior*, *34*(2), 94–98.

Phan, L. T., Nguyen, Thuong V, Luong, Q. C., Nguyen, T. V., Nguyen, H. T., Le, H. Q., Nguyen, T. T., Cao, T. M., & Pham, Q. D. (2020). Importation and human-to-human transmission of a novel coronavirus in Vietnam. *New England Journal of Medicine*, *382*(9), 872–874.

Pickett, C. L., Gardner, W. L., & Knowles, M. (2004). Getting a cue: The need to belong and enhanced sensitivity to social cues. *Personality and Social Psychology Bulletin*, *30*(9), 1095–1107.

Puranik, H., Koopman, J., Vough, H. C., & Gamache, D. L. (2019). They want what I've got (I think): The causes and consequences of attributing coworker behavior to envy. *Academy of Management Review*, *44*(2), 424–449.

Remland, M. S., & Jones, T. S. (2022). The functions and consequences of interpersonal touch in close relationships. In *Nonverbal communication in close relationships: What words don't tell us* (pp. 307–339). Cham: Springer International Publishing.

Renaud, L. P., & Bourquet, C. W. (1991). Neurophysiology and neuropharmacology of hypothalamic magnocellular neurons secreting vasopressin and oxytocin. *Progress in Neurobiology*, *36*(2), 131–169.

Reilly, M. E., Lott, B., & Gallogly, S. M. (1986). Sexual harassment of university students. *Sex Roles*, *15*, 333–358.

Reina, C. S., Peterson, S. J., & Waldman, D. A. (2015). Neuroscience as a basis for understanding emotions and affect in organizations. In D. A. Waldmann & P. A. Balthazard (Eds.), *Organizational neuroscience* (Vol. 7, pp. 213–232). Bingley: Emerald Group Publishing Limited.

Robins, R. W., Noftle, E. E., & Tracy, J. L. (2007). Assessing self-conscious emotions: A review of self-report and nonverbal measures. In J. L. Tracy, R. W. Robins, & J. P. Tangney (Eds.), *The self-conscious emotions: Theory and research* (pp. 443–467). Guilford Press.

Robinson, S. L., & Bennett, R. J. (1995). A typology of deviant workplace behaviors: A multidimensional scaling study. *Academy of Management Journal*, *38*(2), 555–572.

Rosen, C. C., Ferris, D. L., Brown, D. J., Chen, Y., & Yan, M. (2014). Perceptions of organizational politics: A need satisfaction paradigm. *Organization Science*, *25*(4), 1026–1055.

Rouel, M., Stevenson, R. J., & Smith, E. (2018). Predicting contamination aversion using implicit and explicit measures of disgust and threat overestimation. *Behaviour Change*, *35*(1), 22–38.

Routasalo, P. (1999). Physical touch in nursing studies: a literature review. *Journal of Advanced Nursing*, *30*(4), 843–850.

Rozin, P., & Fallon, A. E. (1987). A perspective on disgust. *Psychological Review*, *94*(1), 23–41.

Rozin, P., Haidt, J., & McCauley, C. R. (2008). Disgust. In M. Lewis & J. M. Haviland-Jones (Eds.), *Handbook of emotions* (2nd ed., pp. 637–653). Guilford Press.

Sabatier, N., Rowe, I., & Leng, G. (2007). Central release of oxytocin and the ventromedial hypothalamus. *Biochemical Society Transactions*, *35*(5), 1247–1251.

Sahi, R. S., Dieffenbach, M. C., Gan, S., Lee, M., Hazlett, L. I., Burns, S. M., Lieberman, M. D., Shamay-tsoory, S., & Eisenberger, N. I. (2021). The comfort in touch: Immediate and lasting effects of handholding on emotional pain. *PloS one*, *16*(2), e0246753.

Salathé, M., Kazandjieva, M., Lee, J. W., Levis, P., Feldman, M. W., & Jones, J. H. (2010). A high-resolution human contact network for infectious disease transmission. *Proceedings of the National Academy of Sciences*, *107*(51), 22020–22025.

Schaller, M. (2011). The behavioural immune system and the psychology of human sociality. *Philosophical Transactions of the Royal Society B: Biological Sciences*, *366*(1583), 3418–3426.

Schaller, M. (2014). When and how disgust is and is not implicated in the behavioral immune system. *Evolutionary Behavioral Sciences*, *8*(4), 251–256.

Schaller, M. (2015). The behavioral immune system. In D. M. Buss (Ed.), *The handbook of evolutionary psychology, Volume 1: Foundation* (pp. 206–224). John Wiley & Sons.

Schaller, M., & Duncan, L. A. (2007). The behavioral immune system: Its evolution and social psychological implications. In J. P. Forgas, M. G. Haselton, & W. von Hippel (Eds.), *Evolution and the social mind: Evolutionary psychology and social cognition* (pp. 293–307). Psychology Press.

Schaller, M., Miller, G. E., Gervais, W. M., Yager, S., & Chen, E. (2010). Mere visual perception of other people's disease symptoms facilitates a more aggressive immune response. *Psychological Science*, *21*(5), 649–652.

Schaller, M., & Park, J. H. (2011). The behavioral immune system (and why it matters). *Current Directions in Psychological Science*, *20*(2), 99–103.

Schilpzand, P., & Huang, L. (2018). When and how experienced incivility dissuades proactive performance: An integration of sociometer and self-identity orientation perspectives. *Journal of Applied Psychology*, *103*(8), 828–841.

Schilpzand, P., Leavitt, K., & Lim, S. (2016). Incivility hates company: Shared incivility attenuates rumination, stress, and psychological withdrawal by reducing self-blame. *Organizational Behavior and Human Decision Processes*, *133*, 33–44.

Schirmer, A., & Adolphs, R. (2017). Emotion perception from face, voice, and touch: Comparisons and convergence. *Trends in Cognitive Sciences*, *21*(3), 216–228.

Schirmer, A., Cham, C., Zhao, Z., & Croy, I. (2022, June 29). What makes touch comfortable? An examination of touch giving and receiving in two cultures. *Personality and Social Psychology Bulletin*. https://doi.org/10.1177/01461672221105966

Schirmer, A., Reece, C., Zhao, C., Ng, E., Wu, E., & Yen, S.-C. (2015). Reach out to one and you reach out to many: Social touch affects third-party observers. *British Journal of Psychology*, *106*(1), 107–132.

Schroeder, J., Risen, J. L., Gino, F., & Norton, M. I. (2019). Handshaking promotes deal-making by signaling cooperative intent. *Journal of Personality and Social Psychology*, *116*(5), 743.

Schriesheim, C. A., Castro, S. L., & Cogliser, C. C. (1999). Leader-member exchange (LMX) research: A comprehensive review of theory, measurement, and data-analytic practices. *The Leadership Quarterly*, *10*(1), 63–113.

Simmering, M. J., Fuller, J. B., Marler, L. E., Cox, S. S., & Bennett, R. J. (2013). Tactile interaction norms and positive workplace touch. *Journal of Managerial Issues*, *29*(4), 132–153.

Sin, M. T. A., & Koole, S. L. (2013). That human touch that means so much: Exploring the tactile dimension of social life. *Mind Magazine*, *2*, 17.

Smith, R. H. (2000). Assimilative and contrastive emotional reactions to upward and downward social comparisons. In J. Suls & L. Wheeler (Eds.), *Handbook of social comparison: Theory and research* (pp. 173–200). Kluwer Academic Publishers.

So, J., Achar, C., Han, D., Agrawal, N., Duhachek, A., & Maheswaran, D. (2015). The psychology of appraisal: Specific emotions and decision-making. *Journal of Consumer Psychology*, *25*(3): 359–371.

Someya, T., Sekitani, T., Iba, S., Kato, Y., Kawaguchi, H., & Sakurai, T. (2004). A large-area, flexible pressure sensor matrix with organic field-effect transistors for artificial skin applications. *Proceedings of the National Academy of Sciences*, *101*(27), 9966–9970.

Sonnentag, S., Pundt, A., & Venz, L. (2017). Distal and proximal predictors of snacking at work: A daily-survey study. *Journal of Applied Psychology*, *102*(2), 151–162.

Solnet, D., Subramony, M., Ford, R. C., Golubovskaya, M., Kang, H. J., & Hancer, M. (2019). Leveraging human touch in service interactions: Lessons from hospitality. *Journal of Service Management*, *30*(3), 392–409.

Stewart, G. L., Dustin, S. L., Barrick, M. R., & Darnold, T. C. (2008). Exploring the handshake in employment interviews. *Journal of Applied Psychology*, *93*(5), 1139–1146.

Stier, D. S., & Hall, J. A. (1984). Gender differences in touch: An empirical and theoretical review. *Journal of Personality and Social Psychology*, *47*(2), 440–459.

Story, M., Kaphingst, K. M., Robinson-O'Brien, R., & Glanz, K. (2008). Creating healthy food and eating environments: Policy and environmental approaches. *Annual Review of Public Health*, *29*, 253–272.

Suls, J., & Wheeler, L. (2012). Social comparison theory. *Handbook of Theories of Social Psychology*, *1*, 460–482.

Swanson, L., & Kuypers, H. (1980). The paraventricular nucleus of the hypothalamus: Cytoarchitectonic subdivisions and organization of projections to the pituitary, dorsal vagal complex, and spinal cord as demonstrated by retrograde fluorescence double-labeling methods. *Journal of Comparative Neurology*, *194*(3), 555–570.

Tangney, J. P., Dearing, R. L., Wagner, P. E., & Gramzow, R. (1989). *Test of self-conscious affect-3*. George Mason University.

Tangney, J. P., Stuewig, J., & Mashek, D. J. (2007). What's moral about the self-conscious emotions. In J. L. Tracy, R. W. Robins, & J. P. Tangney (Eds.), *The self-conscious emotions: Theory and research* (pp. 21–37). Guilford Press.

Terrizzi, J. A. Jr, Shook, N. J., & McDaniel, M. A. (2013). The behavioral immune system and social conservatism: A meta-analysis. *Evolution and Human Behavior*, *34*(2), 99–108.

Thomas, P. A., & Kim, S. (2021). Lost touch? Implications of physical touch for physical health. *The Journals of Gerontology: Series B*, *76*(3), e111–e115.

Thompson, S. J., & Rew, L. (2015). The Healthy Workplace Project: Results of a hygiene-based approach to employee wellness. *American Journal of Health Promotion*, *29*(5), 339–341.

Todd, S. (2019, April 16). The new guidelines for touching at work. *Quartz at Work*. https://qz.com/work/1595463/is-it-okay-to-hug-a-co-worker-a-guide-to-respecting-boundaries/.

Tracy, J. L., & Robins, R. W. (2004). Putting the self into self-conscious emotions: A theoretical model. *Psychological Inquiry*, *15*(2), 103–125.

Tracy, J. L., & Robins, R. W. (2007). The nature of pride. In J. L. Tracy, R. W. Robins, & J. P. Tangney (Eds.), *The self-conscious emotions: Theory and research* (pp. 263–282). Guilford Press.

Tracy, J. L., Robins, R. W., & Tangney, J. P. (2007). *The self-conscious emotions: Theory and research*. Guilford Press.

Tybur, J. M., Lieberman, D., Kurzban, R., & DeScioli, P. (2013). Disgust: Evolved function and structure. *Psychological Review*, *120*(1), 65–84.

Uvnäs-Moberg, K. (1998). Oxytocin may mediate the benefits of positive social interaction and emotions. *Psychoneuroendocrinology*, *23*(8), 819–835.

von Mohr, M., Kirsch, L. P., & Fotopoulou, A. (2017). The soothing function of touch: Affective touch reduces feelings of social exclusion. *Scientific Reports*, *7*(1), 1–9.

Wałaszek, M., Kołpa, M., Wolak, Z., Różańska, A., & Wójkowska-Mach, J. (2017). Poor hand hygiene procedure compliance among polish medical students and physicians—The result of an ineffective education basis or the impact of organizational culture? *International Journal of Environmental Research and Public Health*, *14*(9), 1026.

Waldman, D. A., Wang, D., & Fenters, V. (2019). The added value of neuroscience methods in organizational research. *Organizational Research Methods*, *22*(1), 223–249.

Webb, A., & Peck, J. (2015). Individual differences in interpersonal touch: On the development, validation, and use of the "comfort with interpersonal touch" (CIT) scale. *Journal of Consumer Psychology*, *25*(1), 60–77.

Whetten, D. A. (1989). What constitutes a theoretical contribution? *Academy of Management Review*, *14*(4), 490–495.

Whitcher, S. J., & Fisher, J. D. (1979). Multidimensional reaction to therapeutic touch in a hospital setting. *Journal of Personality and Social Psychology*, *37*(1), 87.

Williams, L. A., & DeSteno, D. (2008). Pride and perseverance: The motivational role of pride. *Journal of Personality and Social Psychology*, *94*(6), 1007–1017.

Williams, L. E., & Bargh, J. A. (2008). Experiencing physical warmth promotes interpersonal warmth. *Science*, *322*(5901), 606–607.

Wolfe, N. D., Dunavan, C. P., & Diamond, J. (2007). Origins of major human infectious diseases. *Nature*, *447*(7142), 279–283.

Woolum, A., Foulk, T., Lanaj, K., & Erez, A. (2017). Rude color glasses: The contaminating effects of witnessed morning rudeness on perceptions and behaviors throughout the workday. *Journal of Applied Psychology*, *102*(12), 1658–1672.

Worboys, M. (2000) *Spreading germs: Disease theories and medical practice in Britain, 1865–1900*. Cambridge University Press.

Yamasue, H., Yee, J. R., Hurlemann, R., Rilling, J. K., Chen, F. S., Meyer-Lindenberg, A., & Tost, H. (2012). Integrative approaches utilizing oxytocin to enhance prosocial behavior: From animal and human social behavior to autistic social dysfunction. *Journal of Neuroscience*, *32*(41), 14109–14117a.

Yeager, A. (2020, May 19) Losing touch: Another drawback of the COVID-19 pandemic. *The Scientist*. https://www.the-scientist.com/news-opinion/losing-touch-another-drawback-of-the-COVID19-pandemic-67542.

Young, S. G., Sacco, D. F., & Hugenberg, K. (2011) Vulnerability to disease is associated with a domain-specific preference for symmetrical faces relative to symmetrical non-face stimuli. *European Journal of Social Psychology*, *41*(5), 558–563.

Yu, A., Hays, N. A., & Zhao, E. Y. (2019) Development of a bipartite measure of social hierarchy: The perceived power and perceived status scales. *Organizational Behavior and Human Decision Processes*, *152*, 84–104.

Yuan, C., Dembry, L., Higa, B., Fu, M., Wang, H., et al. (2009) Perceptions of hand hygiene practices in China. *Journal of Hospital Infection*, *71*(2), 157–162.

Zhao, P., Chan, P.-T., Gao, Y., Lai, H.-W., Zhang, T., et al. (2019) Physical factors that affect microbial transfer during surface touch. *Building and Environment*, *158*, 28–38.

Zivich, P. N., Gancz, A. S., & Aiello, A. E. (2018) Effect of hand hygiene on infectious diseases in the office workplace: A systematic review. *American Journal of Infection Control*, *46*(4), 448–455.

CHAPTER 5

LOOKING BACK TO MOVE FORWARD: A 20-YEAR OVERVIEW AND AN INTEGRATED MODEL OF HUMAN RESOURCE PROCESS RESEARCH

Karin Sanders, Rebecca Hewett and Huadong Yang

ABSTRACT

Human resource (HR) process research emerged as a response to questions about how (bundles of) HR practices related to organizational outcomes. The goal of HR process research is to explain variability in employee and organization outcomes by focusing on how HR practices are intended (adopted) by senior managers, the way that these HR practices are implemented and communicated by line managers, and how employees perceive, understand, and attribute these HR practices. In the first part of this chapter, we present a review of 20 years of HR process research from the start, to how it developed, and is now maturing. Within the body of HR process research, several different research theoretical streams have emerged, which are largely studied in isolation without benefiting from each other. Therefore, in the second part of this chapter, we draw on previous work to propose a staged process model in which we integrate the different research streams of HR process research, recognizing contingencies in the model. This leads us to an agenda for future research and practical implications in the final part of the chapter.

Keywords: Employees' perceptions of HR practices; HR attributions; HR implementation; HR process research; HRM system strength; intended HR practices

Research in Personnel and Human Resources Management, Volume 41, 161–197

Published under exclusive licence by Emerald Publishing Limited
ISSN: 0742-7301/doi:10.1108/S0742-730120230000041007

INTRODUCTION

There is a long-standing tradition in (strategic) human resource management (HRM) research to examine the effects of HR practices on organizational performance (Boon et al., 2019; Combs et al., 2006; Huselid, 1995; Jiang et al., 2012). To understand the so-called "black box" between HRM and performance (Purcell et al., 2003; Wright & Gardner, 2003), scholars have focused primarily on relationships between the content of individual HR practices – such as recruitment and selection, training and development, performance appraisal, remuneration, and rewards – and different organizational outcomes such as profit, revenue, and turnover of the organization. Recognizing that individual HR practices are likely interdependent on each other (Delery, 1998), research has also focused on the implications of combinations of individual HR practices, also called bundles or systems of HR practices, such as high-performance work systems (HPWS; Appelbaum et al., 2000) or high-commitment HR practices (Collins & Smith, 2006).

The relationship between (bundles of) HR practices and organizational performance has traditionally been explained with theoretical frameworks at the organizational level (see Bednall et al., 2022). For instance, the resource-based view of the firm (Wright & McMahan, 2011) assumes that bundles of HR practices support firm performance by attracting, developing, and retaining top-performing employees whose skills and contributions align with the strategy of the organization. This enabled scholars to demonstrate that bundles of HR practices are related to organizational outcomes which can help organizations become more effective and achieve a competitive advantage (Jiang et al., 2012). While strategic HRM scholars have often assumed that these bundles of HR practices are also beneficial for employee outcomes, empirical studies indicate that this is not always the case (Jensen et al., 2013; Kroon et al., 2009), which suggests that there is variability between individuals and organizational units in the effectiveness of HR practices, and that some HR practices which are designed to increase organizational performance may, at times, do so at the expense of individual employees (e.g., increasing job demands).

This growing evidence that even in the same organization, employees can perceive and respond to HR practices differently led to new theoretical developments. For instance, some variability in employee outcomes can be explained by how bundles of HR practices are communicated in the organization (Den Hartog et al., 2013) and by how employees interpret and understand these bundles of HR practices (Nishii et al., 2008). Building on these ideas, some HRM scholars have (re)framed the HRM-performance relationship as a communication challenge. This has led, over the past two decades, to increased attention on the "HR process," suggesting that how HRM is communicated, received, and understood shapes employee outcomes (see Bowen & Ostroff, 2004; Guest, 2021; Hewett et al., 2018; Nishii et al., 2008; Ostroff & Bowen, 2016; Sanders et al., 2014, 2021; Wang et al., 2020). The goal of HR process research is to explain variability in employee outcomes by focusing on how HR practices are intended (adopted) by senior managers, how they are implemented and communicated by line managers, and how employees perceive, understand, and attribute these HR practices (Nishii & Wright, 2008; Sanders et al., 2021a; Wright & Nishii, 2013).

In the first part of this chapter, we present a 20-year overview of HR process research in three stages. We first discuss the origins of the HR process approach including the (staged) process model of strategic HRM proposed by Wright and Nishii (2013[1]), and two research frameworks which further elaborate the core elements of the process model: the strength of the HRM system (Bowen & Ostroff, 2004) and HR attributions. Second, building on this body of work, researchers started to test and replicate the hypotheses and propositions of these "early years" papers. This is reflected in a growing body of empirical research and the publication of three special issues: one in *Human Resource Management* (Sanders et al., 2014), one on HR attributions in *Human Resource Management Journal* (Sanders et al., 2021b), and one focusing on evidence from Asia in *Asian-Pacific Journal of HR* (Sanders et al., 2022). We call this stage "the development of the HR process research."

The third stage of HR process research can be seen as the "maturing of the HR process field," which is reflected in growing meta-review and critical discussion of the body of work. For instance, in 2016, after winning the *Academy of Management Review*'s Decade Award, Ostroff and Bowen reflected on their HRM system strength model; Hewett et al. (2018) reviewed the growth of attributional perspectives in the HR process research; Wang et al. (2020) published a review on the "what," "why," and "how" of employees' perceptions of HR practices; a handbook on HR process research brought together different perspectives (Sanders et al., 2021a, 2021b); and the first meta-analysis on perceived HRM system strength[2] research was published (Bednall et al., 2022). The maturing of this body of work is reflected in a quote from Patrick Wright in the handbook on HR process research: "While the issues and debates around the content of HR practices have not ebbed, today more attention focuses on the processes through which these practices work." While we discuss the important publications and events in the development and maturing stages of HR process research, we do not aim to provide a complete review of all the work related to this research but rather a helicopter view for scholars new to HR process research or more experienced researchers to take a step back.

While the different streams of HR process research reviewed in the first part of our chapter are maturing, they still operate mainly in silos with limited interconnection. We argue that this is a missed opportunity in making progress in the field of HR process research. Therefore, in the second part of this chapter, we propose a process model which incorporates theories of HRM system strength and HR attributions, which dominate the HR process research (Sanders, 2022; Sanders et al., 2021a, 2021b), and focus on the core elements of the staged process model. In addition, one of the weaknesses of the research streams within the HR process research is an unanswered question about the universality of HR process models across organizational or national contexts (see Bednall et al., 2022; Farndale & Sanders, 2017; Sanders et al., 2021a, 2021b). Therefore, we consider these contingencies in our revised staged process model. In the final part of this chapter

(Part 3), we discuss future research related to our revised staged proposed model and the practical implications of HR process research.

PART I. THE START OF HR PROCESS RESEARCH

In this chapter, we draw on three articles that have particularly influenced the theoretical basis of HR process research: (a) Wright and Nishii's (2013) theoretical chapter "Variability within Organizations: Implications for Strategic Human Resource Management," (b) Bowen and Ostroff's (2004) theory paper "Understanding HRM-Firm Performance Linkages: The Role of the 'Strength' of the HRM System," and (c) Nishii et al.'s (2008) conceptual and empirical paper, "Employee Attributions of the 'why' of HR practices: Their Effects on Employee Attitudes and Behavior." In the following sections, we introduce these three papers and consider their impact on HR process research.

Wright & Nishii's HR Process Model

Wright and Nishii's (2013) process model of strategic HRM is inspired by the reflection that existing, content-based approaches did not adequately explain variation in the relationship between bundles of HR practices and organizational performance. They argue that variability within organizations provides important and interesting insights into the role of HR practices concerning individual-, group-, and organizational-level outcomes (see Fig. 1). The main argument in their process model is that the desired outcomes of HR practices as designed and adopted by management (referred to as *intended* HR practices) may be diluted, or changed, by the way that practices are implemented by managers (*actual* HR practices), which shapes how practices are *perceived* by employees.

There are three key implications of Wright and Nishii's (2013) chapter. First, the HR practices intended by organizational decision-makers are filtered through line managers, who are responsible for "bringing practices to life" (Purcell &

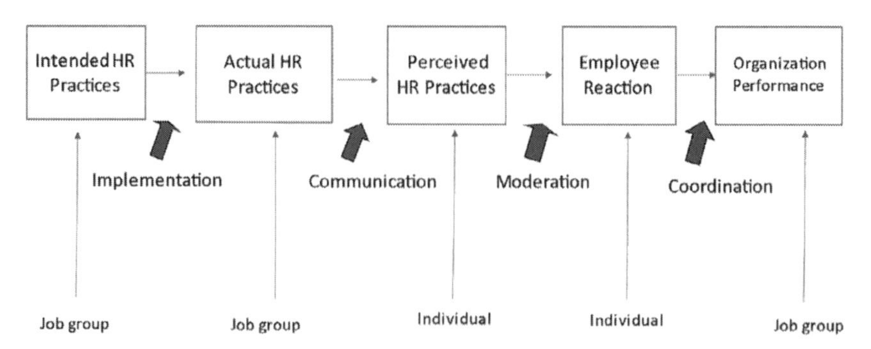

Fig. 1. The Process Model of SHRM (Adopted From Nishii & Wright, 2008, p. 7).
Source: Nishii and Wright (2008, p. 7).

Hutchinson, 2007, p. 16; see also Guest, 2021). This can explain the variability between organizational units in how HR practices are experienced by groups of employees. The relationship between intended and actual HR practices is then moderated by factors such as line managers' leadership style (Daniel, 1985), personalities and behaviors (Schneider & Reichers, 1983). Other moderating effects at the group level on the relationship between actual HR and employees' perceptions include social interaction and common experiences among members of the group (James et al., 1988; Kozlowski & Hattrup, 1992).

The second implication is that there is a difference between the HR system objectively stated in policies and procedures (HR content) and the subjective experience of the HR system by individuals or groups of employees. This draws on a core principle of psychological climate research (James et al., 1990; Schneider, 1987): it is people's subjective perceptions that drive behavior rather than objective characteristics of the environment. When Nishii and Wright (2006) published their first working paper the small body of HR research which explicitly addressed employees' perceptions of HR practices often confounded perceptions with objective characteristics rather than recognizing these as meaningfully different constructs.

The third implication is that the way that employees perceive HR practices influences their attitudinal and behavioral responses to the practices. This draws on theories of social cognition, which suggest that employees attach different meanings to social stimuli based on the frameworks that they use to make sense of social information (Fiske & Taylor, 1991). It means that, even if employees perceive bundles of HR practices in their organization in a similar way, they will not always respond consistently. Individuals' responses are shaped by their motivations (Locke & Latham, 1990), past experiences (Rousseau, 2001), demographic background (Cox, 1993), values (Judge & Bretz, 1992), and personalities (Hough & Schneider, 1996). Nishii and Wright (2008) therefore argue that it is important to understand the relationship between employees' perceptions and their responses and to consider the factors which moderate this relationship when explaining the overarching relationship between bundles of HR practices and organizational performance.

Bowen and Ostroff's HRM System Strength

In their *Academy of Management Review* paper and based on the work of Ferris et al. (1999), and their earlier chapter on multilevel research in organizations (Ostroff & Bowen, 2000), Bowen and Ostroff (2004) explain the process by which employees make sense of HR practices within an organization by drawing on the co-variation principle of Kelley's (1967, 1973) attribution theory as their organizing framework. The co-variation principle suggests that, when people observe behaviors or events, they draw on multiple instances of the behavior or event across both time and situations to interpret its meaning. As such, they employ a co-variation principle to determine the cause of the behaviors or events based on three features: distinctiveness, consistency, and consensus. Distinctiveness refers to the extent to which the event or behavior "stands out" in its environment, thereby capturing the attention and arousing the interest of observers (Kelley, 1967, p. 102). Consistency refers to similarity across time and modality. If the behaviors or events are the same across situations, observers perceive the situation as consistent. Consensus is the similarity of behaviors across observers. If many observers perceive the situation in the same way, the consensus is high.

The first implication of the HRM system strength model is that it provides a theoretically grounded explanation for "the features of an HR system that send signals to employees that allow them to understand the desired and appropriate responses and form a collective sense of what is expected" (Bowen & Ostroff, 2004, p. 204), which describes when and how individual perceptions of HR practices can be shared among employees. HRM system strength (the meta-features of distinctiveness, consistency, and consensus of the HR system) therefore explains how HR as a system "can contribute to organizational performance by motivating employees to adopt desired attitudes and behaviors that, in the collective, help to achieve the organization's strategic goals" (p. 204).

The second implication of this model is in providing a theoretical basis to examine the strength of the HRM system. Bowen and Ostroff (2004) used the three meta-features of distinctiveness, consistency, and consensus as an organizing framework for nine specific characteristics relevant to the HR system. Distinctiveness comprises visibility, understandability of HR practices, the relevance of HR practices to strategic and individual goal achievement, and legitimacy of the authority of the HR function. Consistency includes instrumentality by establishing an unambiguous perceived cause-effect relationship between the HRM system's desired content-focused behaviors and associated employee consequences; validity, in terms of consistency between the intentions and the reality of the practice and alignment (vertical and horizontal); and stability over time. Consensus is composed of agreement among message senders and fairness of practices. These features and meta-features work in concert to deliver HR messages. Based on the co-variation model of attribution theory (Kelley, 1967, 1973), when employees perceive HR as highly distinctive, highly consistent, and highly consensual, they attribute HR to the entity (management as representatives of the organization) so they understand what is expected from them (see also Sanders & Yang, 2016).

Finally, HRM system strength needs to be interpreted as a collective process; an indication of the psychological climate relating to the HR system. This collective process explains the emergence of a shared understanding of what is valued, expected, and rewarded in the organization. Bowen and Ostroff (2004) argue that organizational climate only emerges from individual perceptions of HR practices when HRM system strength is high (i.e., when employees perceive HR practices as distinctive, consistent, and consensual) because a strong system ensures shared perceptions. Conversely, when HRM system strength is low, individual perceptions of HR practices (psychological climate) tend to be idiosyncratic. Furthermore, a strong organizational climate will influence employees' attitudes and behaviors in a positive way as it is clear to employees what to do.

Nishii et al.'s HR Attributions

Nishii et al.'s (2008) model of HR attributions explains how the relationship between bundles of HR practices and organizational performance-related outcomes is filtered through employees' beliefs about the intentions of their organization when designing and implementing HR practices. Their model draws on Heider (1958) and Weiner's (1979, 1985a, 1985b, 1986, 2008, 2018) theories of causal attribution, which suggest that individuals form explanations (attributions) for their own behavior and the behavior of others to enhance their ability to understand, predict, and control their environment (Wong & Weiner, 1981). A key dimension of Heider's (1985, 1986) attribution theory is the locus of causality, which concerns whether an individual considers the cause of behavior or an event to be internal (i.e., generated by the person) or external (i.e., generated by the situation). Drawing on this principle, Koys (1988) was the first to argue that employees can make an internal attribution if HR activities appear to be freely chosen by the organization ("out of a spirit of justice" or "to attract and retain employees") rather than forced by external pressures ("encourage individual or organizational performance" or "to comply with government relations"). The empirical results of Koys' exploratory research indicate that, while internal explanations are positively related to employees' commitment, external explanations are not.

Nishii et al. (2008) built on the work of Koys (1988) to propose a more systematic model of HR attributions. They define HR attributions as the beliefs that employees form about the intentions of management to design and implement HR practices. On the one hand, employees may believe that an HR practice is designed to comply with external factors such as trade union pressure. On the other hand, internal attributions are the beliefs that the actions of the organization are due to factors over which management has control. Nishii et al. (2008) argue that internal attributions are more complex than external attributions and, therefore, organize internal attributions along two dimensions: (1) the extent to which the (internal) attributions represent business goals versus employee-oriented goals underlying HR practices (based on research from the likes of Lepak et al., 2002; Osterman, 1994); and (2) whether a practice is designed to engender commitment or enforce control, which is based on a distinction highlighted by Arthur (1994). By crossing these two dimensions, Nishii et al. (2008) identify four types of internal HR attributions: service quality, employee wellbeing, cost reduction, and employee exploitation.

Using data from 4,500 employees and 1,100 department managers from a service firm, Nishii et al. (2008) found support for their theory that employees make varying attributions for the same HR practice. Their results indicate that these HR attributions are differentially associated with employee commitment and satisfaction. Specifically, the attributions that HR practices motivated by an organization's concern for enhancing service quality or employee wellbeing (commitment attributions) are positively related to employee commitment and satisfaction whereas attributions focused on reducing costs and exploiting employees (control attributions) are negatively associated with these attitudes. External attributions involving union compliance were not significantly related to these theoretical outcomes. They further found that these attitudinal outcomes were related to different dimensions of employee organization citizenship behaviors, which were in turn related to customer satisfaction at the group level.

The HR attributions model contributes, first, to our understanding of variability in individuals' responses to the same HR practices. By drawing on principles of attribution theory from social psychology (e.g., Heider, 1958; Weiner, 1985a, 1985b), the HR attributions model provides a theoretically grounded explanation for variability at the individual level. As the role of attributions in social life is well-established – both theoretically and empirically – it provided a much-needed organizing framework for the growing body of work on employee perceptions of HR practices. Second, the dimensional structure of Nishii et al.'s (2008) model provides a generalizable model to understand how bundles of HR practices, or individual HR practices, are interpreted by employees and the implications of this interpretation for outcomes at the individual, group, and organizational level. This model also offers a springboard for research to examine how these attributions are shaped by stimuli from the environment around employees (e.g., their manager, colleagues, and communication processes) and employees' internal schema (e.g., personality, prior experiences, and values).

THE DEVELOPMENT OF HR PROCESS RESEARCH

The three papers introduced in the previous section (Bowen & Ostroff, 2004; Nishii et al., 2008; Wright & Nishii, 2013) provided fuel for the fire for the new sub-field of strategic HRM research and have inspired scholars to dig further into the "black box" between (bundles of) HR practices and performance. The process model provides a broader guiding framework on which the HRM system strength and HR attributions theories elaborate. Despite the fact that these seminal papers are highly cited in the (HR) management literature, the number of empirical studies that tested the different models are relatively low. For instance, Bowen and Ostroff's paper (2004) is cited 1,711 times (Web of Science, January 2023) yet the meta-analysis of Bednall et al. (2021) reported 42 empirical papers on this topic; Nishii et al. (2008) is cited 766 times (Web of Science, January 2023) but in her review of the HR attribution research, Hewett (2021) found 17 empirical papers and, applying slightly different parameters, Hu and Oh (2022) identified 34 empirical papers that tested Nishii et al.'s model.

Empirical Shift: From Content to Process

In 2014, the first special issue on HR process research, entitled "Is the HRM Process Important?" was published (Sanders et al., 2014). In their editorial, Sanders et al. (2014) content analyzed all submissions for the special issue and concluded that they all examined perceptions of and attributions about HRM. Even when HRM practices seem to be central in the article, the authors were mainly focused on the perceptions that employees hold about such practices. This indicated that the process view of HRM at that time was strongly built on the intermediate and/or direct role of employees' attributions and perceptions of their organization. This special issue on the HR process research contained articles from two research streams: the process model (Nishii & Wright, 2008; Wright & Nishii, 2013) and HRM system strength (Bowen & Ostroff, 2004). While work on HR attributions is mentioned in the introduction of the special issue, no articles in this special issue focused on this research stream, which was slower to take off (Hewett et al., 2018).

Reflective of a shift in theory from the content of HR systems to the process between practices and organizational performance, most of the articles in the 2014 special issue contained both perspectives. For example. Aksoy and Bayazit (2014) adopted Bowen and Ostroff's (2004) HRM system strength model and tested it within the context of a management-by-objectives (MBO) system. Sumelius et al. (2014) likewise brought together the content and process perspective to address the question "What determines employee perceptions of HRM process features?" Their study aimed to explore influences on employee perceptions of the visibility, validity, procedural, and distributive justice of performance appraisal in subsidiaries of multinational corporations and at what levels these influences reside. Katou et al. (2014) investigated the impact of an HRM system (integrating both the content and process of HR practices) on organizational performance through collective employee reactions. Finally, Piening et al. (2014) focused on empirically examining the gap between intended and implemented HR practices, drawing on the work of Wright and Nishii (2013).

From HRM System Strength to Perceived HRM System Strength

One trend which is evident in the early years after the publication of Bowen and Ostroff's (2004) article is a shift regarding the level of analysis from organizational climate (shared perceptions), which was the focus of their theory, to individual perceptions of the meta-features of HRM system strength (distinctiveness, consistency, and consensus), as discussed by Ostroff and Bowen (2016). Sanders et al. (2008) were one of the first to test the HRM system strength framework, in a study among employees, line managers, and HR managers working in four hospitals in the Netherlands. They examined distinctiveness, consistency and consensus as the main effects, and shared perceptions of high-commitment HRM (organizational climate) as a mediator in the relationship between HRM system strength and affective commitment. They found that organizational climate did not mediate the relationship between HRM system strength and affective commitment as expected; instead, organizational climate moderated the relationship between individual perceptions of consistency and affective commitment. This study was replicated by Li et al. (2011), who examined how individual perceptions of HRM system strength and organizational climate were associated with hotel employees' work satisfaction, vigor, and intention to quit in the Chinese context. The distinctiveness of HRM system strength was found to be related to the three employee work attitudes. In addition, they found that organizational climate strengthened the positive relationship between consensus and work satisfaction and the negative relationship between consensus and intention to quit. Similarly, Aksoy and

Bayazit (2014) included both (the shared perceptions of) HRM system strength and organizational climate in their research and found that HRM system strength was related to organizational climate. Other studies examined the effects of perceived HRM system strength on the individual level (Bednall & Sanders, 2017; Bednall et al., 2014, 2017; Frenkel et al., 2012a, 2012b, 2013; Frenkel & Yu, 2011).

This theoretical shift from climate to perceptions is also reflected in the measurement of perceived HRM system strength. Independently, teams from Belgium (Delmotte et al., 2012) and Portugal (Coelho et al., 2012) conducted several studies to develop measurements of perceptions of HRM system strength. Although these measures contain some similarities they also highlight differences. While Delmotte et al. (2012) found more than nine features in their factor structure, Coelho et al. (2012) found only one. In a later meta-analysis, Bednall et al. (2022) found that the most frequently used scale to measure perceived HRM system strength is that of Delmotte et al. (2012). Together, this body of work highlights a theoretical and empirical shift toward individual perceptions of the strength of the HR system.

Empirical Development of the HR Attributions Model

Despite the slow start most of the more recent empirical research on the HR process has been based on Nishii et al.'s (2008) model (Hewett et al., 2018). Much of the early research inspired by Nishii et al.'s study represents a replication of their model with differential outcomes and serves to elaborate the nomological net of HR attributions (Hewett, 2021). For example, multiple studies have found that commitment (service quality and employee wellbeing) attributions are positively related to affective commitment (Fontinha et al., 2012; Khan & Tang, 2016; Van De Voorde & Beijer, 2015), job satisfaction (Tandung, 2016; Valizade et al., 2016), performance-related outcomes (Chen & Wang, 2014; Yang & Arthur, 2019) and negatively related to intention to quit (Lee et al., 2019), thus supporting the findings of Nishii et al. (2008). Additionally, control (cost reduction and employee exploitation) attributions have been related to stress-related outcomes such as work overload, emotional exhaustion, and burnout (Shantz et al., 2016; Van De Voorde & Beijer, 2015; Wang et al., 2020).

A smaller number of studies examined theoretical antecedents to HR attributions, in particular high-performance work practices (HPWPs; Van De Voorde & Beijer, 2015; Sanders et al., 2021a, 2021b). For example, Van de Voorde and Beijer (2015) found that the presence of HPWPs, as rated by unit managers, was positively related to commitment attributions from employees. In a vignette-based experimental study in combination with a cross-sectional survey, Sanders et al. (2021a, 2021b) found that employees' perceptions of HPWPs were positively related to service-quality attributions and negatively related to cost-reduction attributions. Hewett et al. (2019) applied Kelley and Michela 1980s principles of information (perceptions of distributive and procedural fairness), beliefs (organizational cynicism), and motivation (perceived relevance) as the antecedents of HR attributions to study the purpose of workload models for academic faculty in the UK. They found that fairness and cynicism were more important for the formation of internal attributions of commitment than for cost-reduction or exploitation attributions. Two of these studies also considered the interactions between various antecedents to explain HR attributions: Sanders et al. (2021a, 2021b) examined the moderating effect of the power-distance-orientation and found that the relationships between HPWP and HR attributions (service-quality and cost-reduction attributions) were stronger for employees with a low-level of power-distance-orientation, indicating that individuals who rely less on managers to shape their interpretations are more likely to perceive HPWP as it was intended. Hewett et al. (2019) found an interaction between organizational cynicism and perceptions of distributive fairness in predicting HR attributions, such that the perceptions of distributive fairness buffered the relationship between cynicism and control-focused attributions.

The steady growth of research applying the HR attributions framework is reflected in a special issue in the *Human Resource Management Journal* (Sanders et al., 2021b). Papers in this special issue served to further present some important empirical and theoretical questions about the HR attributions framework. For example, Montag-Smit and Smit (2021) demonstrated the value of the framework for understanding responses to specific HR practices. They examined the relationship between three dimensions of pay secrecy policies (i.e., distributive nondisclosure, communication restriction, and procedural nondisclosure) and employee trust in management, finding that HR attributions mediated the relationships between pay secrecy and trust in management. They also found that employee preferences for sharing pay information moderated some of these relationships; those unwilling to share personal pay information did not make negative attributions of secretive distributive pay policies. However, employees with a preference for disclosure concluded that pay secrecy had more malevolent intentions. Their novel contribution lies in their focus on the specific HR practice of pay secrecy and on the role of trust as an outcome. Alfes et al. (2021) considered, for the first time, how different HR attributions combine, recognizing that attributions are unlikely to be independent (Hewett, 2021). They found that a combination of wellbeing and exploitation attributions, which they call performance attribution, mediated the relationship between HPWPs and employee engagement. Fan et al. (2021) likewise furthered our understanding of the multilevel nature of attributions by examining the effect of team-level HR attributions. They found that transformational leadership moderated the relationship between team-level commitment attributions and team performance.

HR Process Research Goes Global: Evidence From Asia

In their 2022 special issue, Sanders et al. highlight that most HR research has been undertaken in Western, developed countries and generalized to contexts such as Asia-Pacific countries (De Cieri et al., 2021). This is important because evidence suggests that the Asia-Pacific region is a challenging and dynamic context for management research (Rowley, 2017) and evidence has emerged of low external validity of management constructs in general to Asian-Pacific countries (Zhao et al., 2020). Neglecting important contextual considerations such as institutional factors and societal norms that may be unique and require an understanding of the local contexts in Asia-Pacific countries (Bhagat et al., 2010), may therefore hide important theoretical and empirical challenges.

Babar et al. (2022) aimed to create new knowledge regarding the boundaries of perceived HRM system strength based on the co-variation principle and drawing on the job-demands-resource model. Employees' religiosity, defined as an individual's religious beliefs and values that keep them motivated in their work practices (Lynn et al., 2009), was found to be a boundary condition of the moderating effect of perceived HRM system strength in the relationship between performance appraisal quality (clarity, regularity, and openness) and employees' proficient, adaptive, and proactive performance. The findings of this two-wave, multiactor study in Pakistan highlighted that the relationship between performance appraisal quality and employee performance is strongest when it is embedded within a strong HR system (high-perceived HRM system strength) and low religiosity, or in low perceived HRM system strength and high religiosity conditions, suggesting a compensation effect between perceived HRM system strength and employees' religiosity.

Jiang et al. (2022) presented a cross-level moderated mediation model arguing that, although many studies investigated the effects of HR practices on employee performance, it is unknown how top managers' beliefs about HR importance influence HRM effectiveness at the departmental level. Based on the upper echelon's theory, these authors empirically tested a trickle-down effect of top managers' belief in HR importance on employee performance. The results from a cross-level analysis among Chinese top managers, department supervisors, and employees suggested that top managers' belief in HRM importance was positively related to HRM competence, which, in turn, mediated the relationship between HRM importance at the firm level and HRM effectiveness at the departmental level: the effectiveness of HRM as evaluated by department supervisors had a significantly positive relationship with employees' perceived HR practices, and the effectiveness of HRM as evaluated by department supervisors was indirectly related to employees' performance through their perceived HR practices.

MATURING OF HR PROCESS RESEARCH

The maturity of this body of work is reflected in several review papers (Hewett et al., 2018; Hu & Oh, 2022; Ostroff & Bowen, 2016; Wang et al., 2020), book chapters (featured in the edited book by Sanders et al., 2021a), and meta-analyses (Bednall et al., 2022) and has taken a high-level view of HR process research. These reviews not only summarized previous research but also introduced new lines of enquiry based on critical questions about the application and development of these streams of research. These publications indicate that HR process research is maturing. In this section, we consider the key conclusions and remaining questions arising from these reviews.

Reflecting on the Strength of HRM System Research

In 2016, Ostroff and Bowen were invited to write a reflection on their decade award from *Academy of Management Review*, recognizing the contribution of their HRM system strength theory to management scholarship. Their review focused on how the construct of HRM system strength has been used in the subsequent years and linked this construct to related areas and topics such as strategic HRM, HRM architecture, social psychological constructs, and organizational climate. In this reflection article, they highlighted a significant difference between their theoretical model and its interpretation by many empirical researchers (as discussed in the section in this chapter on the development of HR process research). Bowen and Ostroff introduced HRM system strength as an organizational-level construct that explains how the use of HR practices creates unambiguous messages about the broader culture, climate, priorities, and values of an organization to its employees and work units. Most empirical studies, however, have interpreted the construct of HRM system strength in terms of employee perceptions of distinctiveness, consistency, and consensus and measured and examined its effects at the individual level by using the scales developed by Delmotte et al. (2012), Coelho et al. (2012), and others (see Bednall et al., 2022).

Although Ostroff and Bowen (2016) agreed that this perceived HRM system strength is a "meaningful construct" (p. 198), it is different from their original idea. Following Delmotte et al. (2012), Ostroff and Bowen see "perceptions of HRM system strength" "as an appropriate label for these idiosyncratic perceptions since they reflect processing of the social context that can, in turn, influence individual responses" (p. 198). Theories like social exchange (Thibaut & Kelley, 1959) and social information processing (Salancik & Pfeffer, 1978) seem to be well suited to explain the consequences of these perceptions of HRM system strength. As we highlighted earlier, most of these studies indicate that there is indeed a positive relationship between perceptions of HRM system strength and individual outcomes such as affective commitment, job satisfaction, knowledge sharing, informal learning outcomes, innovation, and identification and a negative relationship with negative emotions, burnout, and turnover (intentions). In this way, Ostroff and Bowen (2016) argue that perceptions of HRM system strength highlight that within-unit and within-organization variability as explained by Wright and Nishii (2013) can be linked to individual outcomes.

Reflecting this trend in how HRM system strength has been applied (as a perception rather than climate-level construct), Bednall et al.'s (2022) meta-analysis of 42 studies (comprising 65 samples and 29,444 unique participants) on perceived HRM system strength compared two competing hypotheses regarding the moderating or mediating effect of employee perceptions of HRM system strength on the relationship between bundles of HR practices and employee outcomes. Based on signaling theory (Connelly et al., 2011), these authors hypothesized that perceived HRM system strength acts as a mediator. On the other hand, based on the co-variation principle of attribution theory (Kelley, 1967, 1973), they alternatively hypothesized that perceived HRM system strength acts as a moderator. The results from this meta-analysis supported the mediating effect of perceived HRM system strength in the relationship between (bundles of) HR practices and employee and organizational outcomes.

Bednall et al.'s (2022) meta-analysis provide some directions for future HR process research, that is, perceived HRM system strength transfers (mediates) the effects of (bundles of) HR practices on employee outcomes instead of being independent of them and act as a moderator. Even when accounting for study characteristics, such as the operationalization of perceived HRM system strength, study design (cross-sectional versus longitudinal or experimental designs), industry, sampling strategy, and publication status, these authors detected a consistent pattern of the mediating effect of perceived HRM system strength and an inconsistent pattern regarding the moderating effect of perceived HRM system strength.

These conclusions should, however, be considered in light of concerns about measurement and validity highlighted by multiple authors (Hewett et al., 2018; Ostroff & Bowen, 2016; Sanders et al., 2021a, 2021b). For example, Sanders et al. (2021a) content analyzed 41 empirical research papers, including 19 peer-reviewed journal articles, seven working papers, six dissertations, and nine conference papers, and highlighted several empirical concerns regarding several types of validity which limit the conclusions drawn by this body of work. First, concerning the fit between the measures and the underlying constructs they are designed to represent. From the 41 studies in their content analysis, Sanders et al. identified 22 (61%) which included data regarding perceived HRM system strength and outcomes from the same source (employees), raising concerns about construct validity. Second, it is a perennial concern about the extent to which causal conclusions can be drawn from studies on perceived HRM system strength (issues also discussed by Hewett et al., 2018; Wang et al., 2020). Twenty-eight articles out of the 41 (68%) in the Sanders et al.'s (2021a) review relied on cross-sectional research designs (including some two-wave studies) with only one experimental study (Sanders & Yang, 2016). The majority of studies also focused only on the individual or employee level (69%), without paying attention to the team or organization level. Overall, the conclusion from the authors is that the validity of perceived HRM system strength research can be further improved through the adoption of research designs that permit stronger conclusions about causality. Increasing the validity is important to address challenging problems and produce findings that contribute to a robust body of knowledge (Bainbridge et al., 2017) and can be used by practitioners to pursue evidence-based management (Barends & Rousseau, 2018).

A Critical Look at HR Attributions Research

In a critical review of HR attributions research, Hewett (2021) reviewed 17 empirical and conceptual papers as the basis of an agenda for future research. The analysis focused on three areas: (a) the positioning of HR attributions in the HR process chain, (b) the dimensional structure of HR attributions, and (c) the context of HR attributions concerning specific HR practices. The first issue relates to the extent to which attributions are distinct from more general perceptions (Beijer et al., 2021). In the second issue, Hewett highlighted some inconsistencies in how the dimensions of HR attributions have been operationalized and potential overlaps in the definition and measurement of performance-related attributions.

For example, while Nishii et al. (2008) used the term "employee exploitation" to describe the control-based, employee-focused attributions, van der Voorde and Beijer (2015) labeled the same survey items as a performance attribution which taps into the commitment-based, employee-focused attribution. The final issue relates to the extent to which attributions should be considered in the context of specific practices, building on a small number of studies that examine specific HR attributions (e.g., Hewett et al., 2019; Montag-Smith & Smit, 2020). Here, Hewett concludes that more consideration should be given to context and meso- and macro-level influences on attribution formation.

The maturing of HR attributions research has seen several similar discussions about the generalizability of the attribution framework based on concerns about inconsistencies in empirical studies (see also Hewett et al., 2018). This has led to suggestions that HR attributions should be integrated with other theoretical perspectives to both test the boundaries of the theory and explain more of the HR process. Given the theoretical basis of the HR attribution framework, Hewett et al. (2018, 2019, 2021) have also called for research to "better integrate HR attributions both with existing, more established, HR theories and by drawing inspiration from the expansive body of work on attributions in the social sciences" (Hewett et al., 2019, p. 29) that helps to explain how attributions are formed and shaped individuals' understanding of their environment.

An attempt to integrate HR attributions with other established theories can be seen in the recent review by Hu and Oh (2022) in a chapter in *Research in Personnel and Human Resource Management*. These authors discussed the "why" and "how" of HR practices presented a critical review of the antecedents and consequences of employee HR attribution research. They concluded that notwithstanding several narrative reviews (e.g., Hewett, 2021; Wang et al., 2020) an overarching theory-driven, multilevel framework that helps to guide the antecedents and outcomes of employee HR attributions has been under-developed. They address this research gap by drawing on signaling theory (Connelly et al., 2011). In this, they highlight the signaler (line and HR managers), signal (HR practices content, HRM strength, HR salience, and message medium), and characteristics of the receiver (workplace experience, personality, and identity) as well as the signaling environment as the antecedents of employee HR attributions. On the side of the outcomes, they cluster individual and collective attitudes and wellbeing.

Finally, reflecting on the findings of their empirical conclusions about the important role of external HR attributions, Hewett et al. (2019) suggest an alternative dimensional structure for HR attributions. These authors propose a continuum ranging from more organization-centric (exploitation attributions) to more employee-centric (commitment attributions, employee wellbeing, and service quality), while cost-saving attributions are more ambiguous. Further, they suggest that this continuum applies to both internal and external attributions. Although this revised framework is yet to be empirically tested, it highlights a potential need to re-evaluate Nishii et al.'s (2008) typology and in general, more research to establish the consistency of the dimensional structure of the framework (Hewett, 2021).

PART II. A REVISED PROCESS MODEL: INCORPORATING HRM SYSTEM STRENGTH AND HR ATTRIBUTIONS

From our 20-year review in Part 1, it is clear that scholars have started to ask more critical questions about how the different theories and perspectives can add to our knowledge about the HR process. One of the recurring themes focuses on how these related perspectives can be brought together to enrich our understanding of the HR process. How, for example, do HR attributions and (perceived) HRM system strength work in concert to help us understand the various stages in the process model of Wright and Nishii (2013)? How are HR attributions informed by (perceived) HRM system strength or how is (perceived) HRM system strength further shaped by HR attributions? Inspired by the need to provide a more coherent explanation that cuts across the different streams of research, we propose an integrated model to understand the HR process. Before we present the integrated model, we review some previous studies that aim to connect the concepts of (perceived) HRM system strength and HR attributions.

Existing Research to Connect the (Perceived) HRM System Strength With HR Attribution Concepts

There have been some attempts to directly integrate the concepts of HRM system strength and HR attributions. For example, based on a review of 65 papers on the HR process from the lens of attribution theories, Hewett et al. (2018) proposed different pathways to bring these streams together. Most relevant to this chapter is their discussion about how HRM system strength and HR attributions might interact. One option is a cross-level interaction of which employee HR attributions might moderate their response to climate-level HRM system strength. Alternatively, a group-level interaction in which HRM system strength moderates the relationship between collective HR attributions and group-level outcomes. They conclude that more empirical research is needed to examine these interactions and that there may be multiple ways that HRM system strength and HR attributions relate to one another. They also call for researchers to pay attention to “the levels” that these two concepts represent explaining that “the two processes proposed above explain, respectively, consistency [system strength] and variability [attributions] in how individuals respond to HR practices” (p. 113).

Li’s (2021) work shows another example of how these two concepts can be integrated. Li applied the elaboration likelihood model (ELM) to explain that HR professionals can be seen as the center of communication flows from management to employees. Based on the ELM, Li argued that HR attributions can be viewed as the central route relating to communication quality, while perceived HR credibility (i.e., the extent to which HR professionals are perceived as credible by employees) can be viewed as a peripheral route related to communication source credibility. Li contended that the perceptions of HRM system strength can improve both routes and, ultimately, alter employees’ general attitudes at work. However, Li acknowledges that more research on the combination of perceived HRM system strength and the ELM of information influence is needed.

Along with these two theoretical and conceptual works, some empirical studies have also been conducted to connect (perceived) HRM system strength with HR attributions. For instance, Katou et al. (2021) proposed and tested an integrated multilevel framework to examine the relationship between HRM content and organizational performance through the serial mediating mechanisms of HRM system strength, line manager HR implementation, and employee HR attributions. Using a sample of Greek private organizations with data from senior managers, line managers, and employees, they concluded that: (1) HRM system strength mediates the relationship between HRM content and line manager HR implementation; (2) line manager HR implementation mediates the relationship between HRM system strength and employee HR attributions; and (3) employee HR attributions mediate the relationship between line manager HR implementation and organizational performance. In the same special issue, Guest et al. (2021) applied signaling theory (Connelly et al., 2011) to position HRM system strength (indicated by agreement in HR practices between managers and employees) as a moderator to the relationship between HR practices implemented by managers and HR attributions made by employees. Using a sample of banking firms in Portugal, they found that implemented HR practices were attributed as commitment-focused in a strong HR system (high agreement in HR practices between managers and employees).

Finally, Hu and Oh (2022) posited that HRM system strength moderates the relationship between individual HR attributions and collective outcomes by fostering three emergent enabling states – cognitive states, behavioral processes, and affective states (Ployhart & Moliterno, 2011). They argue that a strong HRM system (high distinctiveness, consistency, and consensus) may fulfill these three emergent states leading to a shared commitment-focused HR attribution and ultimately a collective effort to improve team performance.

Overall, given the different studies, we can conclude that there is no clear theoretical direction and consistent evidence for how the different streams of HR process research, particularly how the two concepts of (perceived) HRM system strength and HR attributions should be integrated. The integration is important because it helps to identify the uniqueness of each construct and clarifies different parts of the HR process (Wang et al., 2020).

Introducing a Revised HR Process Model

We take Wright and Nishii's (2013) staged process model as the starting point for our revised process model, recognizing that intended HR practices as designed by HR management are implemented (primarily) by line managers to bring these practices to life, which then informs employees' perceptions of these practices, and leads to outcomes at the individual, group, and organizational levels. We elaborate on this existing process model in several ways. First, we suggest that (perceived) HRM system strength (Bowen & Ostroff, 2004) and HR attributions

(Nishii et al., 2008) can be integrated into this model to better explain the interconnections between the different stages and the roles that different actors play. Second, we draw on Kelley and Michela's (1980) work on attribution formation as the underlying framework to suggest various moderators at the different stages of the model. Third, we draw on the contingency, or best-fit, perspective (Delery & Doty, 1996; Rabl et al., 2014) to argue that the effectiveness of perceptions, understanding, and attributions of HR practices are likely to vary across contexts, especially across national cultures (Farndale & Sanders, 2017). Finally, while Wright and Nishii (2013) already positioned their staged process model as a multilevel model, we elaborate on this and explain mechanisms at different levels on the relationship between intended HR at the organization level on the one hand and outcomes at different levels on the other. Our proposed model is presented in Fig. 2.

Connecting HRM System Strength

Although there have been some attempts to integrate HRM system strength and HR attributions, there is no consistency in how these are theoretically positioned. For example, some have argued that (perceived) HRM system strength should be seen as a moderator between intended HR practices and individuals' HR attributions (Hewett et al., 2018), while other researchers argue that (perceived) HRM system strength should be considered as a moderator between actual HR practices implemented by line managers or the HR department and employee HR attributions (Guest et al., 2021; Li, 2021), or alternatively as a mediator between the content of the HR systems and line managers' implementation (Katou et al., 2021). These approaches assume that HRM system strength operates at the level of intended HR practices. In other words, HRM practices themselves signal system strength. Here, we take a different approach.

We suggest that HRM system strength can be integrated into the HR process model to explain actual HR practices as defined by Wright and Nishii (2013) instead of intended practices at the organizational level. Wright and Nishii suggest that actual HR practices are those implemented at the unit level (often by

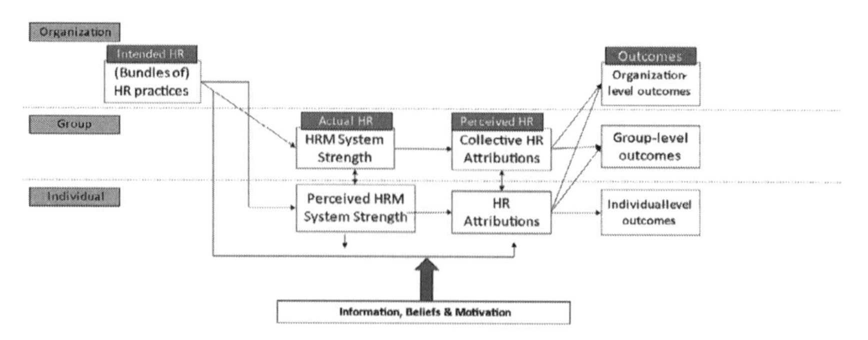

Fig. 2. A Revised Staged Process Model of SHRM.

line managers) which conveys information about HR practices to employees. This is therefore closely aligned to the HRM system strength construct as introduced by Bowen and Ostroff (2004, p. 204): "the features of an HR system that send signals to employees that allow them to understand the desired and appropriate responses and form a collective sense of what is expected." Aligning HRM system strength with actual HR practices recognizes that HR practices, in themselves, do not send out signals about what is expected, valued, and rewarded by an organization. Rather, these signals are sent out through the HRM implementation process. For example, a written policy document sends no signals until it is communicated to employees or put to use in some way (Hewett & Shantz, 2021).

Positioning HRM system strength as an indicator of actual HR practices allows us to argue that HRM system strength should be considered at both the group and the individual level in the HR process model. This is aligned with the empirical work we reviewed earlier, which has demonstrated that both individual and collective perceptions of HRM system strength are meaningful and conceptually distinct. Based on a review of HR research drawing on attribution theories, Hewett et al. (2018) reflected that individual-level perceptions of HRM system strength explain the variance between employees' responses to HR practices, whereas group-level HRM system strength mainly explains within-unit consistency and between-unit variance. This again highlights that both individual and collective perceptions of HRM system strength are informative.

A second implication is that perceptions of HRM system strength can be considered as interactive across levels. To explain this, we draw on research on composition and compilation (Kozlowski & Klein, 2000) to elaborate on the process through which perceived HRM system strength manifests at the higher level. The composition process pays attention to the emergence or manifestation of HRM system strength which arises from the similarity, consensus or sharedness among individual employees' perceptions of HRM system strength within a group or unit. For example, it is likely that team members share perceptions regarding the meta-features of distinctiveness, consistency, and/or consensus, and these similar perceptions may manifest at the higher level as team-level HRM system strength. The compilation process explains how higher-level HRM system strength evolves through the configurations of heterogeneity and variability of perceived HRM system strength. Compilation pays attention to dissimilarity, dissensus, or disagreement among individual members' perceptions of HRM system strength within group or unit. For instance, in one group there is a large difference regarding members' perceptions of HRM system strength; in another group, this difference can be small. When the differences are used to configure perceived HRM system strength, the compilation process occurs. HRM system strength then emerges based on the (dis)similarity of perceived HRM system strength across members within a unit, group or organization (Fulmer & Ostroff, 2016; Kozlowski & Chao, 2018).

Aligning HRM system strength to actual HR practices also feeds back to Bowen and Ostroff's (2004) framework by providing a guide for relevant antecedents. Bowen and Ostroff (2004; see also Ostroff & Bowen, 2016) largely remain silent about the antecedents of HRM system strength. By placing the construct of HRM system strength in the staged process model, the intended HR practices adopted by an organization will appear as one of the antecedents that influence the way that actors shape actual HR practices. The study of Katou et al. (2021), discussed earlier, shows some support for this line of reasoning.

Connecting HR Attributions

We bring HR attributions to the next stage of the HR process to explain perceived HR practices. As we discussed earlier in the chapter, there is a growing and consistent body of work which supports the theory that HR attributions shape individuals' responses to HR practices (Hewett, 2021; Hewett et al., 2018; Wang et al., 2020). The HR attribution framework provides a theoretically grounded model of employee perceptions beyond other descriptive and evaluative measures, which are more indicative of employees' general satisfaction and may be heavily influenced by affective experiences (Beijer et al., 2021). The positioning of HR attributions as a perception is supported by research on social information processing (Salancik & Pfeffer, 1978), which suggests that individuals understand their environment in three stages: "selection," "organization," and "interpretation and judgement" (Fiske & Taylor, 1991). The "selection" stage involves choosing stimuli, cues, and signals to which individuals pay attention. In the "organization" stage, individuals assign new information to familiar categories. In the HR process model, these first two stages concern employee perceptions of the actual HR practices. In the final stage of "interpretation and judgment," individuals translate the organized information and give meaning to the information and make judgments about this information. The stage of interpretation and judgment is also called "attribution" (Kelley, 1973).

Similar to the HRM system strength stage, we argue that HR attributions should be considered at both the individual and the group level as both add different explanations to the relationships between HRM system strength and outcomes. While Wright and Nishii (2013) mention that "considerable variation can occur at this [individual] level due to both variations in the actual HR practices (which would likely cause valid variance in perceived HR practices) and variation in the schemas that individuals employ in perceiving and interpreting HR-related information" (p. 102), they do not elaborate further on employees' perceptions of HR practices neither do they differentiate between the two levels of employees' perceptions.

The implication of placing HR attributions both at the group and the individual level in the "perceived HR practices" box is that HRM system strength is seen as directly antecedent to HR attributions. If HR information stands out, is consistent across time, and is agreed by different actors, employees will attribute their intentions in the way expected by management, and less variation will occur between actual HR practices indicated by the signals sent by the HRM system strength and perceived HR practices indicated by HR attributions. Several empirical studies support this line of reasoning. For example, recent research from Meier-Barthold et al. (2022) suggests that individuals' HR attributions are directly shaped by the extent to which HR management provides clear and unambiguous messages about HR practices (indicating a strong HRM system). They investigated the variability in HR attributions among employees and the organizational factors that influence this variability. Using signaling theory and the concept of situational strength, these authors argue that employees' HR attributions vary less when signals sent by HR management are unambiguous and the conveyed information is consistent. In an online scenario-based experiment they found that HRM system strength significantly explained variability in (some) HR attributions among employees. A similar line of reasoning can be found by Van de Voorde and Beijer (2015) and Sanders et al. (2021c).

With HR attributions positioned in the stage of perceived HR, this naturally flows to outcomes. While there is consistent evidence that employees' HR attributions relate to various attitudinal and behavioral outcomes at the individual level (Hewett et al., 2018), a smaller number of papers have examined HR attributions at the group or team level (Guest et al., 2021; Katou et al., 2021) and organizational level (Guest et al., 2021; Nishii et al., 2008). Furthermore, there is a small amount of research that shared attributions at the team level are also important for group-level outcomes (Fan et al., 2021; Guest et al., 2021; Nishii et al., 2008).

A Framework of Moderators

The second part of our revised model aims to provide a theory-driven account of the factors which moderate the different stages of the HR process. Wright and Nishii (2013) highlighted that there are moderators in their theoretical staged process model. For example, they consider "communication" as a moderator for "the linkage between the actual HR practices and the perceived HR practices [which] represents the communication challenge" (p. 105). In addition, they mention schema and cognitive processes including the psychological contract (Rousseau, 2001) and social information processing (Salancik & Pfeffer, 1978) as potentially important moderators. For instance, Wright and Nishii suggest that individuals' past experiences of organizations which exploited them shape their cognitive schema, which can influence the relationship between actual and perceived HR practices. What this lacks, though, is an organizing framework, which we offer here.

We draw on the theoretical framework of Kelley and Michela (1980) as a guiding principle. This framework connects the co-variation model of attribution theory (Kelley, 1967, 1973) to causal attribution theory (Weiner, 1979). Thus, it offers various factors as the antecedents of causal attributions. Kelley and Michela (1980) argued that individuals draw on three sources when forming causal attributions. The first source is information about a stimulus including its features and the environmental context in which it exists. The second source refers to general beliefs about the causes and effects of the stimulus, which are based on prior and ongoing experiences (Jones & Davis, 1965). As they are formed over time and repeated experience, beliefs are more stable than information. The final source is individuals' motivation to make attributions. The motivation element is aligned with the "salience" of the stimuli, which determines if employees are attuned to HR practices in their understanding of their work situation (Garg et al., 2021). This aligns with Bowen and Ostroff's (2004, p. 197) suggestion that none of the relationships

> between HR and performance will manifest unless the practices are salient across employees so that they collectively come to know what the practices are and develop a shared understanding of the practices and their foci.

This could relate to specific HR practices, for example, whether they are seen as personally relevant (e.g., in the case of some diversity practices; Nishii et al., 2018) or more broadly to how employees see their employment. Employees who see their job mainly as a way to earn a living and feel less connected to their organization might be less sensitive in trying to understand the reason behind HR practices, for instance.

We suggest that Kelley and Michela's (1980) framework can be used to explain moderators to both the path between intended HR practices and HRM system strength and between HRM system strength and HR attributions (Fig. 2).

In Table 1 we provide some examples of moderators (based on the Kelley and Michela [1980] model) to the relationships between intended HR practices and HRM system strength and between HRM system strength and HR attributions. At the first stage, there is evidence, for example, that line managers' willingness (motivation) to engage in HR practices shapes their HR-related behavior (Bos-Nehles et al., 2013; Op de Beeck et al., 2016), and that they are motivated to implement HR practices when they feel the practices enable them to be more effective in their job (Kuvaas et al., 2016). Research also suggests that stable beliefs shape the way that practices are enacted such as stereotypical views (Leisink & Knies, 2011), prioritizing the importance of their HR role (Shipton et al., 2016), the values that managers hold (Arthur et al., 2016) and trust in senior management (Farndale & Kelliher, 2013).

Finally, the individuals responsible for enacting HR practices use information such as their organization's intentions (Hewett & Shantz, 2023), the extent to which they have clear information about their HR role (Gilbert et al., 2011; Kuvaas et al., 2016), and information about top manager support for HR practices (Stirpe et al., 2013), as well as factual information such as workforce diversity (Everly & Schwarz, 2015), to decide which practices to implement and how to implement them. Although these studies did not directly examine these factors as moderators between intended practices and (perceived) HRM system strength as we suggest in our model, they do support the fact that these variables inform implementation behavior, and as manager implementation and system strength are entwined (Gilbert et al., 2015) they would support our proposition.

On the path between HRM system strength and HR attributions, Hewett et al. (2019) explicitly made use of Kelley and Michela's (1980) framework to argue that HR attributions are influenced by information (in their study: perceptions of distributive and procedural fairness), beliefs (organizational cynicism), and motivation (perceived relevance). In their study, they did not explicitly measure HRM system strength but were focusing on a salient HR practice (workload models) so an interaction with the strength of this practice may be inferred. Additional

Table 1. Examples of Moderators in the Revised HR Process Model.

	Moderators: Intended HR Practices > HRM System Strength	Moderators: HRM System Strength > HR Attributions
Information	Implementer's[a] perception of: • Utility of the HR practice • Fairness of the practice • Content clarity of HR practices • Procedural clarity regarding how to implement the practice successfully (role or task clarity)	Employees' perception of: • Utility of the HR practice • Fairness of the practice • Content clarity of HR practice • Procedure clarity of HR practices
	Implementer's available time to implement practices (e.g., task allocation)	
	Implementer's involvements of implementing HR practices	
Beliefs	Implementer's perception of: • Senior decision-makers' intentions (HR attributions toward senior managers) • Competence of HR department (or those designing the practice) • General perception of senior decision-makers (e.g., cynicism)	Employees' perception of: • Implementer's intentions (HR attributions toward implementer) • Competence of implementer of HR practice • General perceptions of implementer (e.g., cynicism) • Relationship with implementer (e.g., leader-member exchange)
	Implementer's management philosophy (e.g., strength of bottom line mentality; Babalola et al., 2020)	Employee's general philosophy toward work (e.g., bottom line mentality)
Motivation	Implementer's willingness to engage effort in the HR practice	Personal relevance of the HR practice
	Personal relevance (or perceived relevance to employees) of the HR practice	Employees' personal value orientation
	Role identity (e.g., does the implementer associate with their role as an implementer of HR practices)	Employees' goal orientation (performance oriented or learning/ development oriented)
	Implementer's personal value orientation	

[a]We refer here to "implementer" recognizing that line managers are not always responsible for implementing HR practices (e.g., in project-based organizations; Keegan & Den Hartog, 2019).

empirical research would also support this moderation. For example, employees' attributions about the intention of pay secrecy/transparency is informed by their preference for pay secrecy (Montag-Smit & Smit, 2020) which is a more stable belief; the role of communication processes as suggested by Wright and Nishii (2013) and empirically supported by Den Hartog et al. (2013) are mechanisms for information provision; and individuals are motivated to form perceptions of HR practices when they consider them personally relevant (as discussed in the review of diversity management practices by Nishii et al., 2018).

A Contingency-based Process Model

So far, the question of whether HR process research is more universalistic or more contingent on context is mainly ignored in empirical studies. While there are some theoretical discussions (Farndale & Sanders, 2017; Hewett, 2021; Sanders et al., 2021a, 2021b, 2022; Wang et al., 2020) and some empirical studies regarding the influence of national culture on perceived HRM system strength (Sanders et al., 2018), none of them has been solidly empirically tested (Bednall et al., 2022; Sanders & Bednall, 2022).

Our suggestion that the stages in the HR process are moderated by motivation, information, and, particularly, beliefs justifies why the HR process may be more contingent on macro context, such as national culture. Newman and Nollen (1996) emphasize that "national culture is a central organizing principle of employees' understanding of work, their approach to it, and how they expect to be treated" (p. 755). Research supports this idea that culture can influence how employees make sense of their environment and respond to signals (Fiske & Taylor, 1991; Sanders et al., 2014). For instance, in-group collectivism, defined as the degree to which individuals express pride, loyalty, and cohesiveness in their organizations or families (House et al., 2004), explains the attributional differences between West European and East Asian cultures (Hofstede, 1980, 1984). Western European cultures are in general more individualistic and people in such cultures tend to attribute behaviors and performances to dispositional or internal attributes. By contrast, East Asian cultures are generally more collectivistic and people in East Asian cultures tend to pay more attention to contextual or external attributes to explain behaviors and performance (e.g., Chiang & Birtch, 2007; Morris & Peng, 1994).

The best-fit argument is central to a contingency-based model. For instance, when applying a best-fit argument, Rabl et al. (2014; see also Newman & Nollen, 1996) argue that the use of HPWS fits better with an individualistic culture than a collectivistic culture, as people in individualistic cultures tend to focus more on rationality (House et al., 2004), which can be translated to a greater extent into ability, skills, and performance. Recently, Sanders et al. (2022) elaborated this best-fit argument to explain how the relationships between bundles of HR practices and perceived HRM system strength and between perceived HRM system strength and employee outcomes (discretionary behaviors and wellbeing) are contingent on the cultural value dimension of tightness-looseness, which is referred to as "the strength of social norms and the degree of sanctioning within societies" (Gelfand et al., 2006, p. 1226, 2011).

Together, this supports our argument that contextual factors, such as national culture, shape individuals' beliefs, the information they receive about HR practices, and their motivation concerning salience and interpretation of practices. This, then, in turn, moderates the stages of the HR process model.

PART III. FUTURE CHALLENGES AND PRACTICAL IMPLICATIONS

In this final section, we build on our review of 20 years of HR process research, which led to our revised HR process model, as the basis of an agenda for future research. While our review has highlighted the progress made in understanding the different stages in the so-called HR process between HR practices and organizational performance, it is also clear that many questions remain, and progress has been incremental in some areas. In Part 1 we already mentioned the differences between the popularity of the seminal papers in terms of citations and the relatively low number of empirical papers that aimed to test the models. Among the most obvious reasons why the number of empirical studies in the HR attributions and HRM system strength research streams to date is relatively low is the complexity of these frameworks (both theory and research methodology) and the number of resources necessary to study multilevel relationships (Beletskiy, 2011; Guest, 2011; Sanders & Yang, 2016). In this section, we highlight some areas which require further exploration but also call researchers to "think outside the box" on this topic. This raises new methodological challenges so after our theoretical questions, we highlight some methodological implications before moving on to what practitioners can learn from this body of work.

Future Research: Theoretical Questions

In this section, we discuss the following four theoretical questions and challenges that in our view should be central in future research regarding the HR process: (1) considering the HR process as a whole instead of isolated small elements of the HR process, (2) questions around HRM system strength and HR attribution across different levels of analysis, (3) questions around multiple actors to take into account in the different stages of the HR process, and (4) the importance of systematic research on context and moderators.

First, more integrated research including as many elements as possible of the revised model will lead to more progress in our understanding of the HR process. HR process research has mainly focused on employee-level outcomes when considering the consequences of perceived HRM system strength and HR attributions (Hewett et al., 2018; Wang et al., 2020) but remains relatively silent about the relationships between intended HR practices, (perceived) HRM system strength, HR attributions, and the effects on group and organizational level outcomes. By taking the whole revised process model, including outcomes on the group and organizational levels into account, more progress will be made, and a connection can be made with other strategic HRM research.

Second, we emphasize the importance of further research on HRM system strength and HR attributions across multiple levels of analysis. Important questions to answer here are: Are perceptions of HRM system strength and HR attributions at the employee-level the same as the aggregated constructs as collective HRM strength and collective HR attributions at the group or organizational level? How do HRM system strength and HR attributions at different levels interact with and influence each other? What are the antecedents and effects of HRM system strength and HR attributions at different levels? Recent empirical work mentioned earlier in this chapter by Meier-Barthold et al. (2022) is an example which addresses some of these questions. They investigated variability in HR attributions among employees and how organizational factors influenced this variability. Hewett et al. (2018) likewise provided some steppingstones to explore the relationships between HRM system strength and HR attributions at different levels when they discussed some options for how HRM system strength and HR attributions might interact. For instance, employees' HR attributions might moderate their response to climate-level HRM system strength (cross-level interaction), or HRM system strength at the group or organizational level might moderate the relationship between collective HR attributions and group-level outcomes (higher-order interaction). Finally, the theoretical and empirical work on composition and compilation processes can be helpful to explore the relationships between HRM system strength and HR attributions at different levels (Fulmer & Ostroff, 2016; Kozlowski & Chao, 2018; Kozlowski & Klein, 2000).

Third, although there is growing recognition that the assumptions that senior managers always define the intentions of HR practices and that line managers always implement HR practices are untenable (Hewett & Shantz, 2021; Kehoe & Wright, 2013), the majority of research on HR process is still based on these assumptions. Our revised model highlights that multiple actors can be involved in the HR process at different levels (e.g., individual versus collective sensemaking; see also Bos-Nehles et al., 2021) and at different stages. For instance, line managers and employees can be involved in the design of HR practices (Hewett & Shantz, 2021), senior managers and HR professionals are also recipients of these practices, employees may implement practices themselves (e.g., Keegan & Den Hartog, 2019), and multiple actors can shape the adoption of HR practices (e.g., influencing senior managers to adopt more sustainability-focused HR practices). More (theoretical) research is needed to explore the influence and interaction of multiple actors in the different stages of the revised process model.

Finally, future systematic research is needed to examine the extent to which the HR process is universal or contextual, inspired by the contingency model and best-fit model (see Rabl et al., 2014). Future research could consider the influence of other contextual variables. For instance, in addition to the cultural differences at the country level, contexts might also refer to employee differences at the individual level as it can be assumed that understanding (perceived HRM system strength) and attribution of the work environment is not only influenced by work-related factors (e.g., intended HR) and factors outside the work environment (e.g., home-life, social media, and social comparison to friends and family). Future research can better recognize that employees do not enter the workplace as a blank slate; they bring with them their past experiences, values, and beliefs that are formed as a result of how they have grown up and currently live and work (Lupu et al., 2018; Marquis & Tilcsik, 2013; Thornton et al., 2012) which can shape their evaluation of HR practices (Aktas et al., 2017; Heavey, 2012). Kitt and Sanders (2022) systematically reviewed 19 empirical studies that investigated the role of "imprinting factors" in HR process research. Imprinting factors include hereditary, familial and parental influences, individual differences, non-work contextual factors, and cultural beliefs that can affect the way employees understand and attribute HRM in their organization. These scholars concluded that non-work-related factors play an important role in explaining employees' perceived HRM system strength and HR attributions.

Yet, despite the understanding that these factors are important for explaining why employees have different reactions to bundles of HR practices, this body of work lacks a consistent and coherent theoretical and conceptual framework that explains the mechanisms through which these factors exert their effects. More research to include these factors in the staged process model is needed in future research.

Future Research: Methodological Challenges

The three main methodological implications of our review (aligned to calls made by others; Hewett et al., 2018; Ostroff & Bowen, 2016; Sanders et al., 2021a, 2021b; Wang et al., 2020) are (1) the need for more consideration of the construct definition of the different constructs in the revised process model, (2) the levels of analysis, and (3) matching research design to research questions.

While most reviews (Hewett, 2021; Ostroff & Bowen, 2016; Sanders et al., 2021a; Wang et al., 2020) conclude that new, revised, and more comprehensive measurements are needed to measure (perceived) HRM system strength, HR process researchers continue to use measures which are questionable in terms of reliability and validity and are mainly limited to one level of analysis. Part of these reliability and validity issues are caused by a lack of a clear construct definition. Ostroff and Bowen (2016) argue that as long as scholars use different conceptualizations for the same constructs and use different measurements to measure these constructs progress in the HR process field is limited. We, therefore, call for more research on methodology issues in HRM system strength research. In this, following Ostroff and Bowen (2016), we call for alternative – if possible, more objective – ways to measure constructs at different levels. For instance, it is questionable whether surveys among employees, HR managers, and line managers are the most suitable way to capture HRM system strength at the group or organizational level. So far, only a few studies measured HRM system strength at a higher level (e.g., Cunha & Cunha, 2009; Guest et al., 2022; Katou et al., 2014), and measures are not consistent. To understand more how senior, line, and HR managers share information and employ HRM system strength in their communication with their employees, Sanders et al. (2020) coded emails that were sent from senior management over 12 weeks during the first wave of the COVID-19 pandemic from 39 universities in 16 countries. The emails that were sent from vice-chancellors, deans, and heads of schools were coded in terms of distinctiveness (standing out, understandability, and relevance), consistency (across multiple messages) and consensus (same message from different senders). In this project, 41 coders were involved, and the focus was on explaining under which circumstances vice-chancellors, deans and heads of schools employ HRM system strength in their communication with employees. A similar line of reasoning can be argued for the construct definition and measurement of the proposed alternative dimensional structure for HR attributions from more organization-centric (exploitation attributions) to more employee-centric (commitment attributions, employee wellbeing, and service quality), while cost-saving attributions are more ambiguous for both internal and external attributions as proposed by Hewett et al. (2019; see also Hewett, 2021), and the need to re-evaluate Nishii et al.'s

(2008) typology. Like our call for more objective measures to assess HRM system strength at different levels, we also call for more objective measures for (collective) HR attributions. In addition, new measures can be designed that combine HRM system strength and HR attribution in the communication from the line and HR managers to their employees.

Finally, we call for better consideration of the alignment between research designs and research questions. This can for instance by applying multiple methods to test the model. Given the fact that both Kelley's (1967, 1973) and Weiner's (1958, 1985a, 1985b) work have been tested with experimental methods, the HR process field needs to consider continuing this tradition along with using quantitative questionnaire surveys. In addition, composition and compilation issues about perceived HRM system strength to team or organizational HRM system strength, and HR attributions at the employee level to collective HR attributions at the group or organizational level can be studied via qualitative interviews, observations, or ethnographic research. New contexts (e.g., gig work, algorithmic management, or self-managing organizations) may require more fundamental, inductive qualitative research to move beyond incremental theory development. It would also be beneficial to look outside of the HR process field for inspiration to adjacent fields such as social psychology (from which both HRM system strength and HR attributions theory are derived) but also fields which address complex processes (e.g., operations management), the role of technology in HR processes (e.g., human-computer interaction), or understanding more about the role of multiple stakeholders in HR processes (e.g., sustainability research).

In our theoretical and methodological agenda for future HR process research, we understand that we call for more ambitious radical, long-term, high-risk research. This may not be appealing for researchers focused on a PhD trajectory or staff in tenure and/or promotion tracks where the need for fast research outputs are highly salient (Lin & Sanders, 2014). The current reward structures for receiving promotion and tenure at (high-ranked) universities do not seem to motivate radical, long-term, high-risk research, but seem to motivate incremental, low-risk, and short-term research, with negative consequences for the progress in a field. However, more long-term international collaboration across research teams and specialisms can be considered for more progress in the HR process research.

Practical Implications of HR Process to HR Professionals and Managers

A good understanding of the HR process is useful and helpful for HR practitioners and managers alike. Here we focus on two important features of the HR process – multiactor involvement and psychological attributions – to discuss their practical implications. Both the original HR process model (Wright & Nishii, 2013) as described in Part I and the revised HR process model as proposed in Part II have acknowledged and highlighted that multiple actors (e.g., top managers, line managers, HR professionals, and employees) are involved in the HRM process within organizations. With this piece of information in mind, HR professionals should not only pay attention to the content of HRM, such as how to design HR strategy and how to set up HR policies and regulations but also take account of the interests and motivations of each party involved in the HR process. For instance, HR professionals need to think about how to motivate line managers to implement HR strategy and policies, how to effectively communicate HR strategy and policies to employees, and how to facilitate employees to make better sense of HR strategy and policies. With this mindset of approaching HRM, HR professionals may consider HRM as a process of branding internal clients and communicating or even negotiating HR strategy and policies between the parties involved. They can learn from and collaborate with the colleagues in marketing and communication departments about how to communicate the core messages by creating a strong HRM climate to make sure HR content can achieve its intended purpose.

As multiple actors participate in the HR process, HR professionals need to realize that there are differences in terms of perceiving and understanding HR content (i.e., strategy or policies and regulations). For instance, although line managers are considered an agent of management, they will have their own concerns or interests regarding HR strategy and policies, which may be different from the concerns or interests of top managers and frontline workers. From an HR process viewpoint, these disagreements represent reality rather than rhetoric. HR professionals need to communicate and negotiate these different perceptions and understandings to achieve a win–win outcome for all parties. For instance, they can take a top-down approach to strengthen HR signals sent from the top management by creating high-level HRM system strength and facilitating commitment-based HR attributions among employees. They can also take a bottom-up approach to employee sensemaking about HR strategy and policies, which develops an alternative path for communicating HR content. Often, these two approaches can take place simultaneously. To some extent, it is better to consider this process as a two-way communication or a management-employee negotiation facilitated by HR professionals. On this point, the HR process provides HR professionals with some new roles and functions in the management of people.

HRM system strength and HR attributions are placed at the center of the revised HR process model. One of the key features of these two concepts is that they highlight the importance of psychological attributions about HR in shaping employee behavior, which has practical implications to HR professionals and managers. To some extent, the process of psychological attribution is part of employees' sensemaking about HR and it places employees, rather than HR strategy and policies, at the center of people management. Complementing the resource-based view (Wright et al., 2001), the HR process approach reminds HR professionals and managers that employees are the focus of HRM. Moreover, the process of psychological attribution can take place at the individual level and at the collective level. HR professionals need to understand how individual employees make sense of HR as well as being sensitive to how collective sensemaking works. A practical recommendation to monitor employee psychological attributions of HR is to include measures of HR attributions in employee surveys. This can provide data for management to understand the missing link between HR practices and employee outcomes. Meanwhile, it will also serve as a feedback loop for HR professionals and managers to reflect on the HR strategy and policies and understand how some HR policies lose their meaning in the process of reaching employees. In short, the HR process once again echoes the viewpoint that employees' subjective and subtle experiences of HRM are as important as explicitly articulated HR strategy and policies to employee and organizational outcomes.

NOTES

1. In this chapter, we primarily refer to the chapter of Wright and Nishii (2013) as this is the most elaborate explanation of the model but acknowledge the earlier working paper of Nishii and Wright (2008) and the chapter of Wright and Nishii (2008).

2. While different terms are used to describe (perceived) HR(M) (system) strength in the publications reviewed in the chapter, we follow the original term Bowen and Ostroff (2004) introduced – "HRM system strength" – for consistency.

REFERENCES

Aksoy, E., & Bayazit, M. (2014). The relationships between MBO system strength and goal-climate quality and strength. *Human Resource Management*, *53*(4), 505–525.

Aktas, M., Farndale, E., & Gelfand, M. (2017). The influence of culture on the strength of HRM systems. In *Academy of management proceedings* (Vol. 2014, p. 11489). Academy of Management. https://doi.org/10.5465/ambpp.2014.11489abstract

Alfes, K., Veld, M., & Furstenberg, N. (2021). The relationship between perceived high-performance work systems, combinations of human resource well-being and human resource performance attributions. *Human Resource Management Journal*, *31*(3), 729–752.

Appelbaum, E., Bailey, T., Berg, P., Kalleberg, A. L., & Bailey, T. A. (2000). *Manufacturing advantage: Why high-performance work systems pay off*. Cornell University Press.

Arthur, J. B. (1994). Effects of human resource systems on manufacturing performance and turnover. *Academy of Management Journal*, *37*(3), 670–687.

Babalola, M. T., Greenbaum, R. L., Amarnani, R. K., Shoss, M. K., Deng, Y., Garba, O. A., & Guo, L. (2020). A business frame perspective on why perceptions of top management's bottom-line mentality result in employees' good and bad behaviors. *Personnel Psychology*, *73*(1), 19–41.

Babar, S., Obaid, A., Sanders, K., & Tariq, H. (2022). Faith in religion matters to HR strength, performance appraisal quality and employee performance. *Asian Pacific Journal of HR*, *60*(4), 788–813.

Bainbridge, H., Sanders, K., Cogin, J., & Lin, V. (2017). The pervasiveness and trajectory of methodological choices: A 20-year review of human resource management research. *Human Resource Management*, *56*(6), 887–913.

Barends, E., & Rousseau, D. M. (2018). *Evidence-based management—How to use evidence to make better organizational decisions*. Kogan Page.

Bednall, T. C., & Sanders, K. (2017). Do opportunities for formal learning stimulate follow-up participation in informal learning? A three-wave study. *Human Resource Management*, *56*(5), 803–820.

Bednall, T. C., Sanders, K., & Runhaar, P. (2014). Stimulating informal learning activities through perceptions of performance appraisal quality and human resource management system strength: A two-wave study. *Academy of Management Learning and Education*, *13*(1), 45–61.

Bednall, T. C., Sanders, K., & Yang, H. (2022). A meta-analysis on employee perceptions of human resource strength: Examining the mediating versus moderating hypotheses. *Human Resource Management*, *61*(1), 5–21.

Beijer, S., Peccei, R., van Veldhoven, M., & Paauwe, J. (2021). The turn to employees in the measurement of human resource practices: A critical review and proposed way forward. *Human Resource Management Journal*, *31*, 1–17.

Beletskiy, A. (2011). *Factors affecting employees' perceptions of the performance appraisal process*. Master's thesis. Hanken School of Economics, Department of Management and Organisation, Helsinki.

Bhagat R., McDevitt, A., & McDevitt, I. (2010). On improving the robustness of Asian management theories: Theoretical anchors in the era of globalization. *Asia Pacific Journal of Management*, *27*(2), 179–192.

Boon, C., Den Hartog, D. N., & Lepak, D. P. (2019). A systematic review of human resource management and their measurement. *Journal of Management*, *45*(6), 2498–2537.

Bos-Nehles, A., Trullen, J., & Valverde, M. (2021). HRM system strength implementation: A multi-actor process perspective. In K. Sanders, H. Yang, & C. Patel (Eds.), *Handbook on HR process research* (pp. 99–114). Edward Elgar.

Bos-Nehles, A. C., Van Riemsdijk, M. J., & Looise, J. K. (2013). Employee perceptions of line management performance: Applying the AMO theory to explain the effectiveness of line managers' HRM implementation. *Human Resource Management*, *52*(6), 861–877.

Bowen, D. E., & Ostroff, C. (2004). Understanding HRM–firm performance linkages: The role of the "strength" of the HRM system. *Academy of Management Review*, *29*(2), 203–221.

Chen, D., & Wang, Z. (2014). The effects of human resource attributions on employee outcomes during organizational change. *Social Behavior and Personality: An International Journal*, *42*(9), 1431–1444.

Chiang, F. F. T., & Birth, T. A. (2007). Examining the perceived causes of successful employee performance: An East-West comparison. *International Journal of HRM*, *18*(2), 232–248.

Coelho, J. P., Cunha, R. C., Gomes, J. F. S., & Correia, A. G. (2012). Developing and validating a measure of the strength of the HRM system: Operationalizing the construct and relationship among its dimensions. *Journal of Industrial Engineering and Management*, *8*(4), 1069–1086

Collins, C. J., & Smith, K. G. (2006). Knowledge exchange and combination: The role of human resource practices in the performance of high technology firms. *Academy of Management Journal*, *49*(3), 544–560. https://doi.org/10.5465/amj.2006.21794671

Combs, J., Liu, Y., Hall, A., & Ketchen, D. (2006). How much do high-performance work practices matter? A meta-analysis of their effects on organizational performance. *Personnel Psychology*, *59*, 501–528.

Connelly, B. L., Certo, S. T., Ireland, R. D., & Reutzel, C. R. (2011). Signaling theory: A review and assessment. *Journal of Management*, *37*(1), 39–67.

Cox, T. (1993). *Cultural diversity in organizations: Theory, research and practice*. Berrett-Koehler.

Cunha, R., & Cunha, M. P. (2009). Impact of strategy, strength of the HRM system and HRM bundles on organizational performance. *Problems and Perspectives in Management*, *7*(1), 57–69.

Daniel, T. L. (1985). Managerial behaviors: Their relationships to perceived organizational climate in high-technology company. *Group & Organization Studies*, *10*(4), 413–428.

De Cieri, H., Sanders, K., & Lin, V. C. H. (2022). International and comparative human resource management: An Asia-Pacific perspective. *Asian Pacific Journal of Human Resources*, *60*(1), 116–145.

Delery, J. E. (1998). Issues of fit in strategic human resource management: Implications for research. *Human resource Management Review*, *8*, 289–309.

Delmotte, J., De Winne, S., & Sels, L. (2012). Towards an assessment of perceived HRM system strength. Scale development and validation. *International Journal of Human Resource Management*, *23*, 1481–1506.

Den Hartog, D. N., Boon, C., Verburg, R. M., & Croon, M. A. (2013). HRM, communication, satisfaction, and perceived performance: A cross-level test. *Journal of Management*, *39*(6), 1637–1665.

Everly, B. A., & Schwarz, J. L. (2015). Predictors of the adoption of LGBT-friendly HR policies. *Human Resource Management*, *54*(2), 367–384.

Fan, D., Huang, Y., & Timming, A. (2021). Team-level human resource attributions and performance. *Human Resource Management Journal*, *31*(3), 753–774.

Farndale, E., & Kelliher, C. (2013). Implementing performance appraisal: Exploring the employee experience. *Human Resource Management*, *52*, 879–897.

Farndale, E., & Sanders, K. (2017). Conceptualizing HRM system strength through a cross-cultural lens. *International Journal of Human Resource Management*, *28*(1), 132–148.

Ferris, G. R., Hochwarter, W. A., Buckley, M. R., Harrell-Cook, G., & Frink, D. D. (1999). Human resource management: Some new directions. *Journal of Management*, *25*, 385–415.

Fiske, S. T., & Taylor, S. E. (1991). *McGraw-Hill series in social psychology. Social cognition* (2nd ed.). McGraw-Hill Book Company.

Fontinha, R., José Chambel, M., & De Cuyper, N. (2012). HR attributions and the dual commitment of outsourced IT workers. *Personnel Review*, *41*(6), 832–848.

Frenkel, S. J., Li, M., & Restubog, S. L. D. (2012a). Management, organizational justice and emotional exhaustion among Chinese migrant workers: Evidence from two manufacturing firms. *British Journal of Industrial Relations*, *50*(1), 121–147.

Frenkel, S. J., Restubog, S. L. D., & Bednall, T. C. (2012b). How employee perceptions of HR policy and practice influence discretionary work effort and co-worker assistance: Evidence from two organizations. *International Journal of Human Resource Management*, *23*(20), 4193–4210.

Frenkel, S. J., Sanders, K., & Bednall, T. C. (2013). Employee perceptions of management relations as influences on job satisfaction and quit intentions. *Asia Pacific Journal of Management*, *30*(1), 7–29.

Frenkel, S. J., & Yu, C. (2011). Managing co-worker assistance through identification. *Human Performance*, *24*, 387–404.

Fulmer, C. A., & Ostroff, C. (2016). Convergence and emergence in organizations: An integrative framework and review. *Journal of Organizational Behavior*, *37*(S1), S122–S145.

Garg, S., Jiang, K., & Lepak, D. P. (2021). HR practice salience: Explaining variance in employee reactions to HR practices. *International Journal of Human Resource Management*, *32*, 512–542.

Gelfand, M. J., Nishi, L. H., & Raver, J. L. (2006). On the nature and importance of the cultural tightness-looseness. *Journal of Applied Psychology*, *91*, 1225–1244.

Gelfand, M. J., Raver, J. L., Nishi, L., Leslie, L. M., Lun, J., Lim, B. C., Duan, L., Almaliach, A., Ang, S., Arnadottir, J., Aycan, Z., Boehnke, K., Boski, P., Cabecinhas, R., Chan, D., Chhokar, J., D'Amato, A., Ferrer, M., Fischlmayr, I. C., … Yamaguchi, S. (2011). Differences between tight and loose cultures: A 33-nation study. *Science*, *332*(6033), 1100–1104.

Gilbert, C., De Winne, S. & Sels, L. (2011). The influence of line managers and HR department on employees' affective commitment. *The International Journal of Human Resource Management*, *22*(8), 1618–1637. https://doi.org/10.1080/09585192.2011.56564

Guest, D. (2021). The role of line managers in the HRM process. In K. Sanders, H. Yang, & C. Patel (Eds.), *Handbook on HR process research* (pp. 177–193). Edward Elgar.

Guest, D. E. (2011). Human resource management and performance: Still searching for some answers. *Human Resource Management Journal*, *21*, 3–13.

Guest, D., Sanders, K., Rodrigues, R., & Oliveira, T. (2021). Signally theory as a framework for analysing HRM processes and integrating HR attribution theories: A conceptual and empirical analysis. *Human Resource Management Journal*, *31*(3), 796–818.

Heavey, A. (2012). *Unpacking HR attributions: An examination of potential predictors of HR attributions, trends over time, and the moderating role of HR information sources*. Cornell University.

Heider, F. (1958). *The psychology of interpersonal relations*. Wiley.

Hewett, R. (2021). HR attributions: A critical review and research agenda. In K. Sanders, H. Yang, & C. Patel (Eds.), *Handbook on HR process research* (pp. 7–26). Edward Elgar.

Hewett, R., & Shantz, A. (2021). A theory of HR co-creation. *Human Resource Management Review*, *31*, 17.

Hewett, R., Shantz, A., & Mundy, J. (2019). Information, beliefs, and motivation: The antecedents to human resource attributions. *Journal of Organizational Behavior*, *40*(5), 570–586.

Hewett, R., Shantz, A., Mundy, J., & Alfes, K. (2018). Attribution theories in human management research: A review and research agenda. *International Journal of Human Resource Management*, *29*(1), 87–126.

Hofstede, G. (1980). *Culture's consequences: International differences in work-related values*. Sage Publications.

Hofstede, G. (1984). The cultural relativity of the quality of life concept. *Academy of Management Review*, *9*, 389–398.

Hough, L. M., & Schneider, R. J. (1996). Personality traits, taxonomies, and applications in organizations. In M. Kevin (Ed.), *Individual differences and behavior in organization* (pp. 31–88). Jossey-Bass Publishers.

House, R. J., Hanges, P. J., Javidan, M., Dorfman, P. W., & Gupta, V. (2004). *Culture, leadership, and organizations: The GLOBE study of 62 societies*. Sage.

Hu, D., & Oh, I.-S. (2022). The "Why" and "How" of human resource (HR) practices: A critical review of the antecedents and consequences of employee HR attributions research. In M. R. Buckley, A. R. Wheeler, J. E. Baur, & J. R. B. Halbesleben (Eds.), *Research in personnel and human resources management* (Vol. 40, pp. 157–204). Emerald Publishing Limited.

Huselid, M. (1995). The impact of human resource management practices on turnover, productivity, and corporate financial performance. *The Academy of Management Journal*, *38*(3), 635–672. http://www.jstor.org/stable/256741

James, L. R., James, L. A., & Ashe, D. K. (1990). The meaning of organizations: The role of cognition and values. In B. Schneider (Ed.), *Organizational climate and culture*. Jossey-Bass Publishers.

James, L. R., Joyce, W. F., & Slocum, J. W. (1988). Organizations do not cognize. *Academy of Management Review*, *13*(1), 129–132.

Jensen, J. M., Patel, P. C., & Messersmith, J. G. (2013). High-performance work systems and job control: Consequences for anxiety, role overload, and turnover intentions. *Journal of Management*, *39*(6), 1699–1724.

Jiang, J., Li, S., & Zhu, W. (2022). The trickle-down effect of managers' belief in the importance of human resource management practices on employee performance: Evidence from China. *Asian Pacific Journal of HR*, *60*(4), 763–781.

Jiang, K., Lepak, D. P., Hu, J., & Baer, J. C. (2012). How does human resource management influence organizational outcomes? A metaanalytic investigation of mediating mechanisms. *Academy of Management Journal*, *55*(6), 1264–1294.

Jones, E. E., & Davis, K. E. (1965). From acts to dispositions the attribution process in person perception. *Advances in Experimental Social Psychology*, *2*, 219–266.

Judge, T. A., & Bretz, R. D. (1992). Effects of work values on job choice decisions. *Journal of Applied Psychology*, *77*(3), 261.

Katou, A. A, Budhwar, P. S., & Patel, C. (2014). Content vs process in the HRM–performance relationship: An empirical examination. *Human Resource Management*, *53*, 527–544.

Katou, A., Budhwar, P. S., & Patel, C. (2021). Line manager implementation and employee HR attributions mediating mechanisms in the HRM system–organizational performance relationship. A multilevel and multipath study. *Human Resource Management Journal*, *31*(3), 775–795.

Keegan, A., & den Hartog, D. (2019). Doing it for themselves? Performance appraisal in project-based organisations, the role of employees, and challenges to theory. *Human Resource Management Journal*, *29*(2), 217–237. https://doi.org/10.1111/1748-8583.1221

Kehoe, R., & Wright, P. (2013). The impact of high-performance human resource practices on employees' attitudes and behaviors. *Journal of Management*, *39*(2), 366–391.

Kelley, H. H. (1967). Attribution theory in social psychology. In D. Levine (Ed.), *Nebraska symposium on motivation* (pp. 192–238). University of Nebraska Press.

Kelley, H. H. (1973). The processes of causal attribution. *American Psychologist*, *28*(2), 107–128.

Kelley, H. H., & Michela, J. L. (1980). Attribution theory and research. *Annual Review of Psychology*, *31*(1), 457–501.

Khan, S. A., & Tang, J. (2016). The paradox of human resource analytics: Being mindful of employees. *Journal of General Management*, *42*(2), 57–66.

Kitt, A., & Sanders, K. (2022). Imprinting in HR process research: A systematic review and integrative conceptual model. *International Journal of HRM*. https://doi.org/10.1080/09585192.2022.2131457

Koys, D. J. (1988). Human resource management and a culture of respect: Effects on employees' organizational commitment. *Employee Responsibilities and Rights Journal*, *1*, 57–68.

Kozlowski, S. W., & Chao, G. T. (2018). Unpacking team process dynamics and emergent phenomena: Challenges, conceptual advances, and innovative methods. *American Psychologist*, *73*(4), 576.

Kozlowski, S. W., & Klein, K. J. (2000). A multilevel approach to theory and research in organizations: Contextual, temporal, and emergent processes. In K. J. Klein & S. W. Kozlowski (Eds.), *Multilevel theory, research and methods in organizations: Foundations, extensions, and new directions* (pp. 3–90). Jossey-Bass.

Kozlowski, S. W. J., & Hattrup, K. (1992). A disagreement about within-group agreement: Disentangling issues of consistency and consensus. *Journal of Applied Psychology*, *77*(2), 161–167.

Kroon, B., van de Voorde, K., & van Veldhoven, M. (2009). Cross-level effects of high-performance work practices on burnout: Two counteracting mediating mechanisms compared. *Personnel Review*, *38*(5), 509–525.

Kuvaas, B., Buch, R., Gagne, M., Dysvik, A., & Forest, J. (2016). Do you get what you pay for? Sales incentives and implications for motivation and changes in turnover intention and work effort. *Motivation and Emotion*, *40*(5), 667–680.

Lee, M. Y., & Edmondson, A. C. (2017). Self-managing organizations: Exploring the limits of less-hierarchical organizing. *Research in Organizational Behavior*, *37*, 35–58.

Lee, B. Y., Kim, T.-Y., Gong, Y., & Zheng, X. (2019). Employee well-being attribution and job change intentions: The moderating effect of task idiosyncratic deals. *Human Resource Management*, *59*(4), 327–338.

Leisink, P. L., & Knies, E. (2011). Line managers' support for older workers. *The International Journal of Human Resource Management*, *22*(9), 1902–1917.

Lepak, D. P., Taylor, M. S., Tekleab, A., & Marrone, J. (2002). Firms' use of high investment HR systems to manage employees for competitive advantage: Differential use and implications for performance. Presented at the Annual Meeting for the Academy of Management, Denver, CO.

Li, X. (2021). Putting perceived HR credibility into the HRM process picture: Insights from the elaboration likelihood model. In K. Sanders, H. Yang, & C. Patel (Eds.), *Handbook on HR research* (pp. 83–98). Edwards Elgar.

Li, X., Frenkel, S. J., & Sanders, K. (2011). Strategic HRM as process: How HR system and organizational climate strength influence Chinese employee attitudes. *International Journal of Human Resource Management*, *22*(9), 1825–1842.

Lin, C.-H. V., & Sanders, K. (2014). HR research methods: Where we are and where we need to go. In K. Sanders, J. A. Cogin, & H. T. J. Bainbridge (Eds.), *Research methods for human resource management* (pp. 136–154). Routledge Taylor & Frances Group.

Locke, E., & Latham, G. (1990). *A theory of goal setting and task performance*. Prentice Hall.

Lupu, I., Spence, C., & Empson, L. (2018). When the past comes back to haunt you: The enduring influence of upbringing on the work–family decisions of professional parents. *Human Relations*, *71*(2), 155–181.

Lynn, M. L., Naughton, M. J., & VanderVeen, S. (2009). Faith in religion scale (FWS): Justification, development, and validation of a measure of Judaeo-Christian religion in the workplace. *Journal of Business Ethics*, *85*(2), 227–243.

Marquis, C., & Tilcsik, A. (2013). Imprinting: Toward a multilevel theory. *Academy of Management Annals*, *7*(1), 195–245. https://doi.org/10.5465/19416520.2013.766076

Meier-Barthold, M., Biemandn, T., & Alfes, K. (2022). Strong signals in HR management: How the configuration and strength of an HR system explain the variability in HR attributions. *Human Resource Management*. https://doi.org/10.1002/hrm.22146

Montag-Smit, T., & Smit, B. (2021). What are you hiding? Employee attributions for pay secrecy policies. *Human Resource Management Journal*, *31*(3), 704–728.

Morris, M. W., & Peng, K. (1984). Culture and cause: American and Chinese attribution for social and physical events. *Journal of Personality and Social Psychology*, *67*, 949–971.

Newman, K. L., & Nollen, S. D. (1996). Culture and congruence: The fit between management practices and national culture. *Journal of International Business Studies*, *27*, 753–779.

Nishii, L. H., Khattab, J., Shemla, M., & Paluch, R. M. (2018). A multi-level process model for understanding diversity practice effectiveness. *Academy of Management Annals*, *12*(1), 37–82.

Nishii, L. H., Lepak, D. P., & Schneider, B. (2008). Employee attributions of the "why" of HR practices: Their effects on employee attributions and behaviors, and customer satisfaction. *Personnel Psychology*, *61*(3), 503–545.

Nishii, L. H., & Wright, P. M. (2008). Variability within organizations: Implications for strategic human resources management. In D. B. Smith (Ed.), *The people make the place: Dynamic linkages between individuals and organizations* (pp. 225–248). Taylor & Francis Group/Lawrence Erlbaum Associates.

Op de Beeck, S., Wynen, J., & Hondeghem, A. (2016) HRM implementation by line managers: explaining the discrepancy in HR-line perceptions of HR devolution. *The International Journal of*

Human Resource Management, *27*(17), 1901–1919. https://doi.org/10.1080/09585192.2015.1088562

Osterman P. (1994). How common is workplace transformation and how adopts it? *Industrial and Labor Relations Review*, *47*, 173–188.

Ostroff, C., & Bowen, D. E. (2016). Reflections on the 2014 decade award: Is there strength in the construct of HR system strength? *Academy of Management Review*, *41*(2), 196–214.

Piening, E. P., Baluch, A. M., & Ridder, H.-G. (2014). Mind the intended-implemented gap: Understanding employees' perceptions of HRM. *Human Resource Management*, *53*(4), 545–567.

Ployhart, R. E., & Moliterno, T. P. (2011). Emergence of human capital resource: A multilevel model. *Academy of Management Review*, *36*(1), 127–150.

Purcell, J., & Hutchinson, S. (2007). Front-line managers as agents in the HRM–performance causal chain: Theory, analysis and evidence. *Human Resource Management Journal*, *17*(1), 3–20.

Purcell, J., Kinnie, N., Hutchinson, S., Rayton, B., & Swart, J. (2003). *Understanding the people and performance link: Unlocking the black box*. Chartered Institute of Personnel and Development.

Rabl, T., Jayasinghe, M., Gerhart, B., & Kühlmann, T. M. (2014). A meta-analysis of country differences in the high-performance work system–business performance relationship: The roles of national culture and managerial discretion. *Journal of Applied Psychology*, *99*(6), 1011–1041. https://doi.org/10.1037/a0037712

Ribeiro, T. R., Coelho, J. P., & Gomes, J. F. S. (2011). HRM strength, situational strength and improvisation behavior. *Management Research*, *9*, 118–136.

Rousseau, D. M. (2001). Schema, promise, and mutuality: The building blocks of the psychological contract. *Journal of Occupational and Organizational Psychology*, *74*, 511–541.

Rowley C. (2017). Wither globalisation and convergence? Asian examples and future research. *Asia Pacific Business Review*, *23*(1), 1–9.

Salancik, G., & Pfeffer, J. (1978). A social information processing approach to job attitudes and task design. *Administrative Science Quarterly*, *23*(2), 224–253.

Sanders, K. (2022). The human resource management-outcomes relationship: An attributional HR process perspective. In *A research agenda for strategic human resource management* (pp. 45–65). Edward Elgar Publishing.

Sanders, K., & Bednall, T. C. (2022). Tightness-looseness and perceived HR strength research: Results from a meta-analysis. *Academy of management, annual meeting, proceedings*. https://doi.org/10.5465/AMBPP.2022.10909abstract

Sanders, K., Bednall, T. C., & Yang, H. (2021a). HR strength: Past, current and future research. In K. Sanders, H. Yang, & C. Patel (Eds.), *Handbook on HR process research* (pp. 27–45). Edward Elgar.

Sanders, K., Dorenbosch, L., & De Reuver, R. (2008). The impact of individual and shared employee perceptions of HRM on affective commitment: Considering climate strength. *Personnel Review*, *37(4)*, 412–425.

Sanders, K., Guest, D., & Rodrigues, R. (2021b). The role of HR attributions in the relationship between HRM and outcomes. *Human Resource Management Journal*, *31*(3), 694–703.

Sanders, K., Jorgensen, F., Shipton, H., Van Rossenberg, Y., Cunha, R., Li, X., Rodrigues, R., Wong, S. I., & Dysvik, A. (2018). Performance-based rewards and innovative behaviors. Human Resource Management, 57(6), 1455–1468.

Sanders, K., Nguyen, P. T., Bouckenooghe, D., Rafferty, A., & Schwarz, G. (2020). Unraveling the what and how of organizational communication to employees during the COVID-19 pandemic: Adopting an attributional lens. *Journal of Applied Behavioral Science*, *56*(3), 289–293.

Sanders, K., Shipton, H., & Gomes, J. F. S. (2014). Guest editors' introduction: Is the HRM process important? Past, current, and future challenges. *Human Resource Management*, *53*(4), 489–503.

Sanders, K., Song, L. J., Wang, Z., & Bednall, T. C. (2022). New frontiers in HR practices and HR processes: Evidence from Asia. *Asia Pacific Journal of Human Resources*, *60*(4), 703–720.

Sanders, K., & Yang, H. (2016). The HRM process approach: The influence of employees' attribution to explain the HRM–performance relationship. *Human Resource Management*, *55*, 201–217.

Sanders, K., Yang, H., & Li, X. (2021c). Quality enhancement or cost reduction? The influence of high-performance work systems and power distance orientation on employee human resource attributions. *The International Journal of Human Resource Management*, *32*(21), 4463–4490.

Sanders, K., Yang, H., & Patel, C. (Eds.). (2021b). *Handbook on HR process research*. Edward Elgar.

Schneider, B. (1987). The people make the place. *Personnel Psychology*, *28*, 447–479.

Schneider, B., & Reichers, A. E. (1983). On the etiology of climates. *Personnel Psychology*, *36*, 19–39.

Shantz, A., Arevshatian, L., Alfes, K., & Bailey, C. (2016). The effect of HRM attributions on emotional exhaustion and the mediating roles of job involvement and work overload. *Human Resource Management Journal*, *26*(2), 172–191.

Shipton, H. Sanders, K., Atkinson, C., & Frenkel, S. (2016). Sense-giving through HR roles: Line managers and employee commitment in health-care. *Human Resource Management Journal*, *26*, 29–45.

Sumelius, J., Bjorkman, I., Ehrnrooth, M., Makela, K., & Smale, A. (2014). What determines employee perceptions of HRM process features? The case of performance appraisal in MNC subsidiaries. *Human Resource Management*, *53*(4), 569–592.

Stirpe, L., Trullen, J., & Bonache, J. (2013). Factors helping the HR function gain greater acceptance for its proposals and innovations: Evidence from Spain. *The International Journal of Human Resource Management*, *24*(20), 3794–3811.

Tandung, J. C. (2016). The link between HR attributions and employees' turnover intentions. *Gadjah Mada International Journal of Business*, *18*(1), 55–69.

Thibaut, J. W., & Kelley, H. H. (1959). *The social psychology of groups*. Wiley.

Thornton, P., Lounsbury, M., & Ocasio, W. (2012). *The institutional logics perspective: A new approach to culture, structure and process*. Oxford University Press. https://doi.org/doi.org/10.3917/mana.155.0583

Valizade, D., Ogbonnaya, C., Tregaskis, O., & Forde, C. (2016). A mutual gains perspective on workplace partnership: Employee outcomes and the mediating role of the employment relations climate. *Human Resource Management Journal*, *26*(3), 351–368.

Van De Voorde, K., & Beijer, S. (2015). The role of employee HR attributions in the relationship between high-performance work systems and employee outcomes. *Human Resource Management Journal*, *25*(*1*), 62–78.

Wang, Y., Kim, S., Rafferty, A., & Sanders, K. (2020). Employee perceptions of HR practices: A critical review and future directions. *The International Journal of Human Resource Management*, *31*, 128–173.

Weiner, B. (1979). A theory of motivation for some classroom experiences. *Journal of Educational Psychology*, *71*(1), 3–25.

Weiner, B. (1985a). An attributional theory of achievement motivation and emotion. *Psychological Review*, *92*(4), 548–573.

Weiner, B. (1985b). "Spontaneous" causal thinking. *Psychological Bulletin*, *97*(1), 74.

Weiner, B. (1986). *An attributional theory of motivation and emotion*. Springer-Verlag. http://www.springer.com/gp/book/9781461293705

Weiner, B. (2008). Reflections on the history of attribution theory and research: People, personalities, publications, problems. *Social Psychology*, *39*(3), 151–156.

Weiner, B. (2018, March 16). *Keynote address*. The 3rd international symposium on attribution theory. Tallahassee, FL

Wong, P. T., & Weiner, B. (1981). When people ask 'why' questions, and the heuristics of attributional search. *Journal of Personality and Social Psychology*, *40*(4), 650–663. https://doi.org/10.1037/0022-3514.40.4.650.

Wright, P. M., Dunford, B. B., & Snell, S. A. (2001). Human resources and the resource based view of the firm. *Journal of Management*, *27*(6), 701–721.

Wright, P. M., & Gardner, T. M. (2003). The human resource-firm performance relationship: Methodological and theoretical challenges. In *The new workplace: A guide to the human impact of modern working practices* (pp. 311–328).

Wright, P. M., & McMahan, G. C. (2011). Theoretical perspectives for strategic human resource management. *Journal of Management*, *18*, 295–320.

Wright, P. M., & Nishii, L. H. (2013). Strategic HRM and organizational behavior: Integrating multiple levels of analysis. In D. E. Guest, J. Paauwe, & P. M. Wright (Eds.), *HRM and performance: Achievements and challenges* (p. 468). John Wiley & Sons, Inc.

Yang, J., & Arthur, J. B. (2019). Implementing commitment HR practices: Line manager attributions and employee reactions. *International Journal of Human Resource Management*. https://doi.org/10.1080/09585192.2019.1629986.

Zhao S., Liu, M., Zhu, C. J., & Liu, H. (2020). The role of leadership in human resource management: Perspectives and evidence from Asia Pacific. *Asia Pacific Business Review*. https://doi.org/10.1080/13602381.2020.1779496

CHAPTER 6

WORK-LIFE FLEXIBILITY POLICIES: MOVING FROM TRADITIONAL VIEWS TOWARD WORK-LIFE INTERSECTIONALITY CONSIDERATIONS*

Ellen Ernst Kossek, Brenda A. Lautsch, Matthew B. Perrigino, Jeffrey H. Greenhaus and Tarani J. Merriweather

ABSTRACT

Work-life flexibility policies (e.g., flextime, telework, part-time, right-to-disconnect, and leaves) are increasingly important to employers as productivity and well-being strategies. However, policies have not lived up to their potential. In this chapter, the authors argue for increased research attention to implementation and work-life intersectionality considerations influencing effectiveness. Drawing on a typology that conceptualizes flexibility policies as offering employees control across five dimensions of the work role boundary (temporal, spatial, size, permeability, and continuity), the authors develop a model identifying the multilevel moderators and mechanisms of boundary control shaping relationships between using flexibility and work and home performance. Next, the authors review this model with an intersectional lens. The authors direct scholars' attention to growing workforce diversity and increased variation in

*Kossek and Lautsch contributed equally to this manuscript in different ways and share first authorship.

Research in Personnel and Human Resources Management, Volume 41, 199–243

Published under exclusive licence by Emerald Publishing Limited
ISSN: 0742-7301/doi:10.1108/S0742-730120230000041008

flexibility policy experiences, particularly for individuals with higher work-life intersectionality, *which is defined as having multiple intersecting identities (e.g., gender, caregiving, and race), that are stigmatized, and link to having less access to and/or benefits from societal resources to support managing the work-life interface in a social context. Such an intersectional focus would address the important need to shift work-life and flexibility research from variable to person-centered approaches. The authors identify six research considerations on work-life intersectionality in order to illuminate how traditionally assumed work-life relationships need to be revisited to address growing variation in: access, needs, and preferences for work-life flexibility; work and nonwork experiences; and benefits from using flexibility policies. The authors hope that this chapter will spur a conversation on how the work-life interface and flexibility policy processes and outcomes may increasingly differ for individuals with higher work-life intersectionality compared to those with lower work-life intersectionality in the context of organizational and social systems that may perpetuate growing work-life and job inequality.*

Keywords: Work-life flexibility; flexibility policies; work-family conflict; work-life policies; intersectionality; work-life relationships

> Clearly, flex work is the new paradigm … So employers are shifting their focus away from "Why should we do this?" toward "How do we do this right?" (Leonard, SHRM, October 16, 2013)

Work-life flexibility policies such as telework, flextime, part-time work, and family leaves are experiencing heightened interest in research and practice. Experts continue to predict the availability of work-life flexibility policies will only rise in the future as the "new normal" (Kennedy, 2022). Three-fourths (75%) of office workers now choose their hybrid mix of remote and office work hours (Fleming, 2020), and more front-line workers can self-schedule (Kossek & Lee, 2020). With the rapid adoption of remote working in recent years, fueled by the COVID-19 pandemic, further growth of work-life flexibility policies has seemed unquestionable. Yet, companies from major banks to law firms and large organizations like J. P. Morgan have been calling workers back to the office and reducing telework options (Bundale, 2022; Kelly, 2022), suggesting that the perceived benefits of implementing flexibility practices may be in question, at least for employers. Companies also seem to face challenges in determining how to implement work-life flexibility in ways that support employees' careers and do not exacerbate inequality (Kossek & Lautsch, 2018). Fundamentally, we lack clear research and practical guidance on how employers can implement work-life flexibility in ways that enhance performance for all employees at both home and work, as research rarely finds dual benefits (Eddleston & Mulki, 2017). Meta-analytic reviews provide evidence that the effectiveness of flexibility policies in reducing work-family conflict is often more hyped than reality, showing stronger benefits for individuals with access to policies than through actual use (Allen et al., 2013).

In sum, whether and how individuals and organizations can fully and mutually benefit from work-life flexibility policies remains an open question. Recent reviews suggest a deeper understanding of linkages between work-life flexibility policies, boundary control, and implementation practices may provide a partial answer. Kossek et al. (2022) argue that whether and the extent to which work-life flexibility policies lead to positive work and nonwork outcomes may depend largely on the degree to which they provide control over the work role boundary. They suggest that work-life flexibility policies are not simply an assortment of discrete human resource programs but can be conceptualized as a means of enabling individuals to exert control over the work role boundary along five dimensions: temporal, spatial, size, permeability, and continuity. Further, they argue that how policies are implemented shape their implications for boundary control and associated outcomes, with implementation occurring across four stages (availability, access experiences, use, and outcomes) and multiple intersecting contexts (society, organization, workgroup, individual, and home).

The goal of this article is to present a model that extends this view of boundary control and implementation dynamics driving the outcomes of work-life flexibility policies to address several research gaps. First, we answer the call to develop a more nuanced view of moderators of implementation effectiveness (e.g., HR systems, group, individual, and home influences), which has been referred to as a "black box" of work-life policy implementation (Kossek et al., 2022). For example, we will argue that whether and how performance at work and home is enhanced by using flexibility is conditioned by the strength of the HR system, the supportiveness of the work-life culture, and the degree to which policies are customizable.

Second, while individuals' perceptions of boundary control over work role dimensions have been identified in reviews as an overarching mechanism linking policy use and outcomes, more nuanced work is needed to understand these processes. We highlight availability, reciprocity, and efficiency as distinct pathways through which control determines outcomes. We also focus on a dual agenda (Bailyn et al., 1997) view of examining how work-life flexibility policies may have mixed consequences for the work and nonwork domains. As Kossek et al. (2023) noted, there is a need to examine work and nonwork outcomes simultaneously as the work-life literature tends to focus on nonwork role benefits for the individual employee, often overlooking work effects, whereas other management fields such as leadership focus on the work role benefits and often overlook nonwork effects.

Third, we argue that work-life flexibility policies historically have been viewed in the work-life literature through what we refer to as a traditional work–nonwork theoretical lens: as organizational resources that through their mere availability and use, de facto, reduce conflict and buffer strain between work and nonwork roles, or facilitate their synthesis. These integrative general models of work-family conflict and enrichment processes comprise a valuable and widely used theoretical approach. Yet they have also been criticized as being overly focused on the ideas of individual choice in how work-family relationships are managed and on traditional and hetero-normal family structures (Özbilgin et al., 2011). Further, we argue that the work-family literature is largely underdeveloped in its integration of diversity in work-life experiences. Even when the most widely studied diversity variables such as gender or child- and older adult-care demands are included, researchers often overlook intersectional relationships between gender and other aspects of identity (e.g., race, etc.). By this, we mean that the prevailing work-life literature tends to treat measures of social categories such as gender and race as individual unique characteristics (Acker, 2006; Holvino, 2012 in Ruiz Castro & Holvino, 2016) rather than considering them as situated together within a social context and structures that shape their impact. We maintain that researchers must do a better job of looking at the employee as a "whole person" – how individual's lives at work and nonwork are interrelated and multiple nonwork identities and roles intersect – to better assess their human resource policy needs. In examining employees' lives holistically, we suggest that it is essential to examine the degree to which traditional relationships in the work-life literature may need to be reexamined through an intersectional lens. By *intersectional*, we mean how different combinations of race, gender, class, and other forms of identity highly relevant to how an employee may manage work-life relationships (e.g., also religion, sexuality, ability, immigration status, etc.) may differentially influence work-life dynamics toward some stigmatization, access to work-life resources and demands, as well as how it is shaped by social structures. Thus, as we elaborate in our definition below, work-life intersectionality refers to not merely the combining of two or more social identities in a relationship, but these identities are those that are generally stigmatized. The term "intersectional" has been used in this way in other subfields of the social sciences such as community and social psychology (e.g., Standley & Foster-Fishman, 2021). We expand on this definition below, focusing on work-life flexibility policies as an example of a work-life research stream that might benefit from integrating intersectional views into future research. This is an important gap to address as we believe the lack of attention to the growing diversity of the workforce regarding work-life issues may be one barrier to why work-life flexibility policies have not fully taken hold to more effectively balance employer and employee interests (Kossek & Thompson, 2016; Kossek et al., 2015).

CONTRIBUTIONS

First, there is a need for a more nuanced understanding of how understudied implementation moderators at various levels of analysis (e.g., individual, group, and organizational) lead to effectiveness on and off the job. Second, we shed light on the mechanisms (availability, reciprocity efficiency) by which control is linked to outcomes and add to the understanding of performance at work and home for a dual agenda, which is largely absent from the broader management flexibility literature. Third, adding an intersectionality lens to view work-life flexibility policies opens new avenues for work-life theorizing that moves the literature from a variable-centered approach (i.e., focusing on a single measure empirically and theoretically) to a person-centered approach (i.e., examining patterns of linked variables operating together as a whole) (Bergman & Magnusson, 1997). It may also help researchers understand the conditions under which using different types of flexibility leads to improved control and performance for some employees but less so for others including how aspects of the human resource systems and organizational cultures may need to be revised to support the effective use of work-life flexibility for many different types of workers. Our chapter aims to motivate researchers to examine interdependent clusters of personal characteristics pertaining to relevant work-life variables that operate simultaneously and that may alter the nature of work-life relationships. In doing so, we encourage researchers to examine how institutionalized "work-life privilege" (Kossek & Kelliher, 2022) and societal work-life intersectionality considerations – or the ability of some workers to have greater control over how they manage work-life relationships due to their hierarchical or labor market power and structural societal inequality – such as being a white male with a stay-at-home spouse – may alter assumed relationships between access and use of work-life flexibility policies and outcomes.

SUMMARY OF ARTICLE ORGANIZATION

In Part I, we first give an overview of the traditional work–nonwork lens on work-life flexibility policies and how using them may link to experiences of boundary control and performance. Then we introduce an intersectional work-life approach, contrasting traditional and intersectional approaches in Table 1. In Part II, we present our model of the traditional approach that examines general relationships between using work-life flexibility policies and performance via boundary control, varying mediating mechanisms, and implementation moderators.

Table 1. Comparison of Traditional and Intersectional Work-Life Views.

	Traditional Work-Family View (Part II)	Intersectional Work-Life View (Part III)
Theoretical Lenses	• Work-family conflict (Greenhaus & Beutell, 1985) • Work-family enrichment (Greenhaus & Powell, 2006) • Boundary management (Ashforth et al., 2000; Kossek & Lautsch, 2012; Kossek, Lautsch, & Eaton, 2006.) • Spillover (Edwards & Rothbard, 2000)	• Social justice (Rawls, 1971) • Social identity (Tajfel & Turner, 1979) • Multiple identities (Ramarajan, 2014) • Optimal distinctiveness (Brewer, 1991) • Inclusion (Shore et al., 2018)
Common Terminology	*Work-family* • "Not only nuclear families in which one or both parents work but also working teenagers; single working adults with siblings, parents, or other relations; and other persons who work and have immediate or extended families" (Edwards & Rothbard, 2000, p. 180)	*Work-life* or *work nonwork* • Includes nonwork-related considerations beyond family including education, friendships, and community involvement (Keeney et al., 2013, p. 221) • Captures "personal life" (Wilson & Baumann, 2015) and individuals without formal family-related responsibilities or demands (Casper et al., 2007b)

(*Continued*)

Table 1. (*Continued*)

	Traditional Work-Family View (Part II)	Intersectional Work-Life View (Part III)
Traditionally Studied Samples	*Traditional households with limited racial diversity* • Mostly white, married individuals with children (Casper et al., 2007a)	*Diverse, but more in conceptual than empirical research* • Although intersectionality involves wide-ranging diversity – including "minority, marginalized, and/or under-researched groups" (Beauregard et al., 2020, p. 465), recent critiques suggest that this is studied from a management standpoint more at a conceptual level than an empirical one (Hall et al., 2019)
Definitional Assumptions	• Having a career identity and a family identity of varying strengths (Lobel & St. Clair, 1992)	• Having multiple nonwork identities are assumed to be considered as an intersectional approach, but not necessarily sufficient for the assumed effects without consideration of stigmatized social identity and power dynamics (e.g., equal access to and opportunities to leverage resources to manage the work-life interface). (This paper: Kossek et al., 2023)
Level of Analysis	*Individual level* • Employee experiences and outcomes (e.g., work-family conflict, health, and well-being; Burrell et al., 2006)	*Multilevel* • Top-down macro-level influences including political influences, history, and gender norms (e.g., sexism and patriarchal influence; Crenshaw, 1989, 1991)
Analytical Approach	*Variable-centered approaches* • Consider how discreet individual attributes shape outcomes (Byron, 2005)	*Person-centered approaches* • Assume that clusters of work-nonwork-related attributes jointly operate to shape outcomes (Kossek, 2012)
Attention to Context	*Limited* • Focus on the role of supervision (Hammer et al., 2009; Kossek et al., 2023; Thomas & Ganster, 1995) and organizational culture (Thompson et al., 1999)	*Broader but incomplete* • Recognition that "historical and structural power relations are taken into account" but not fully integrated into intersectionality perspectives (Özbilgin et al., 2011, p. 180)
Opportunities	• Broaden context to address how individuals, workgroup, and organizational HR systems affect policy implementation • Assess mechanisms of control afforded through policies • (Simultaneous) consideration of both work and nonwork performance outcomes	• Integrate how institutions, power structures, and social intergroup dynamics shape policy implementation • Consider additional policy access and use barriers experienced by those with stigmatized, intersectional identities • Assess unique work and nonwork outcomes specific to those with stigmatized intersectional identities • Consider how intersectional stigmatized identities may have multiplicative effects that alter traditionally assumed dynamics of resources

In Part III, we examine new considerations for future research that emerge when an intersectional lens is incorporated to view work-life flexibility policies including how basic assumptions about the use and impacts of work-life flexibility policies might be modified to account for variance in how flexibility may operate and link to outcomes. For example, we assume that work-life boundaries may be more permeable and operate in more varied ways for employees with many highly salient and stigmatized work-life intersectional identities (e.g., women of color with lower status; single working mothers) compared to employees with fewer impactful intersectional characteristics.

PART I: COMPARING TRADITIONAL AND INTERSECTIONAL LENSES ON WORK-LIFE FLEXIBILITY POLICIES

Overview of Traditional Approach

Work-life flexibility policies have historically been viewed in the work-life literature through what we refer to as a *traditional* work–nonwork theoretical lens: as organizational resources that when accessed and used are rationally assumed to either reduce conflict (e.g., Greenhaus & Beutell, 1985) and buffer strain between or to facilitate and enrich (cf. Greenhaus & Powell, 2006) relationships between work and nonwork roles. For example, ten Brummelhuis and Bakker (2012) argue in their integrative model that individual resources link across work and home roles such that demands in one domain such as home deplete resources for the other, resulting in work-home role conflict (see also Greenhaus & Beutell, 1985). At the same time, resources accumulated in one domain such as work can help with managing the demands of the other domain such as home (see also Greenhaus & Powell, 2006).

Through this lens, work-life flexibility is presumed to provide control to workers to manage work role boundaries (Capitano et al., 2019) and demands, enabling employees to alter the timing or location of the work role (Kossek & Lautsch, 2022) or the freedom to manage time for tasks completed with a results orientation instead of just hours worked (Kelly et al., 2010). A traditional view of work-life flexibility policies (Kossek & Lautsch, 2018) integrates boundary theory (Ashforth et al., 2000), implementation approaches (Kossek et al., 2022), and theory on HR systems strength pertaining to cultural support for work-life policies (Bowen & Ostroff, 2004; Perry-Smith & Blum, 2000). Work-life flexibility policies are conceptualized as vehicles that enable individuals to exert control over the work role boundary along five dimensions: (1) temporal, when the role is conducted; (2) spatial, where the role is conducted; (3) size, which reflects the scope of the role; (4) continuity, which affects the ability to disengage from the role for discrete periods (e.g., days and weeks); and (5) permeability, referring to the extent to which the work role boundary is separated from (thick with few cross-role interruptions) or integrated with (thin with frequent role crossings) other roles (Kossek et al., 2022). Boundary control is not a personal trait but rather the ability to control one's border crossings between work and nonwork roles along these multi-dimensional features of the role boundary (Allen et al., 2013; Kossek et al., 2022; Kossek, Lautsch, & Eaton, 2006).

Whether work-life flexibility policies confer control, and whether that control ultimately enhances performance in work and nonwork domains, is conditioned by implementation that is enacted by multiple stakeholders and across levels. Implementation occurs as policy features are adapted through use to align with the demands of a particular context (Herrera-Sanchez et al., 2017). While limited aspects of implementation have been examined in the traditional literature on work-life flexibility policies, particularly the role of supervisors as gatekeepers (Crain & Stevens, 2018; Hammer et al., 2009; Kossek et al., 2011; Straub, 2012), other implementation elements are comparatively under-examined including the efforts of individuals to shape flexibility use and outcomes, the demands and resources of the home context, coworker support, and the alignment of flexibility policies with the broader HR system within the firm (Kossek et al., 2022). Regarding this latter point, while organizational cultural support is often referenced in general as important for implementation in many work-life flexibility policies, we believe that the concept and operationalization of HR systems strength may provide an avenue for researchers to assess cultural support in relation to human resource practices.

Specifically, Bowen and Ostroff (2004) note that HR systems are characterized by (1) substantive intent or the purpose the policies are designed to achieve (e.g., performance) and (2) process: the set of practices, such as flexibility policies, that are implemented to reflect employer goals and values. HR systems are stronger when content and process are integrated such that ambiguity about policy intent and use is reduced and compliance with policy is increased; individual differences are less likely to shape attitudes and behavior as a result (Bowen & Ostroff, 2004). Historically, work-life flexibility policies have been implemented in weak system contexts; their usability has often been ambiguous as they have been offered with the limited employer and cultural support (Eaton, 2003). Consequently, career-oriented employees have under-utilized work-life flexibility policies (Kossek & Lautsch, 2018), and users – often women – have faced stigma, backlash, and negative attributions for using flexibility for family demands (Leslie et al, 2012; Perrigino et al., 2018). Effective work-life flexibility policy implementation requires alignment with employer goals and values in a strong HR system, which enhances coordination with other related HR practices (e.g., compensation and career development).

Overview of Intersectional Approach

The traditional work-life literature has given limited attention to diversity beyond gender and child- and older adult-care demands, often overlooking intersectional relationships between these identities as well as recent research on intersectionality (Crenshaw, 1989, 1991). Work-life intersectionality considers how the work-life interface differs for individuals with multiple stigmatized social identities in the context of organizational and social systems that may perpetuate inequity. Intersectionality theory originated in the work of Crenshaw (1989, 1991) who, focusing on the experience of Black women, uncovered the limitations of a "single-axis framework" in which race, gender, or class might be examined separately:

> Because the intersectional experience is greater than the sum of racism and sexism, any analysis that does not take intersectionality into account cannot sufficiently address the particular manner in which Black women are subordinated. (1989, p. 140)

Intersectional arguments echo many aspects of feminist critiques of essentialism (or the idea that social categories like race or gender have a core and unchanging essence so that the group can be represented by any member of it). Such arguments have similarly noted that the experiences of Black women become invisible in analysis that examines only white women as placeholders for all women (Carbado & Harris, 2019), which has historically (due to limited sample size) been the case in research grounding traditional views of work-life flexibility.

Intersectionality has expanded the consideration of not only race, gender, and class but also sexuality, religion, immigration status, and ability and has been influential in many literatures – including its introduction to work-life research with the work of Özbilgin et al. (2011). Central to any intersectional analyses are issues of identity (including interlocking multiple identities and identity stigma) along with power and resources. Such a view is also consistent with seminal research on work and family, suggesting that just as work-life experiences do not occur in separate spheres (Bailyn, 1993; Kanter, 1983), so too should work-life research challenge the assumptions that employees' nonwork identities are separate from each other and that they occur independently from how individuals carry out their work role and shape their access to, experiences with, and benefits from using work-life flexibility.

Identity

From an intersectional perspective, individuals derive a self-identity from a multiplicity of social identities attached to social categories (e.g., age and gender) and the meanings associated with them (Corlett & Mavin, 2014). Identities combine to shape lived experience in a manner that is interactional rather than additive. Merely considering the effects of, for example, race and gender as in a quantitative study with indicator variables for both categories, is not intersectionality (Ryan & Briggs, 2019). Instead, social categories can be seen as mutually constituting. Further, the identity categories examined within an intersectional perspective (e.g., gender, race, sexuality, and ability) are linked to stigma in that they are "devalued or derogated by persons within a particular culture at a particular point in time" (Paetzold et al., 2008, p. 186). In the context of health research, for example, Jackson-Best and Edwards (2018) argue that intersectional approaches should consider the joint effects of stigma emanating from not only multiple health conditions (e.g., disability and HIV/AIDS) but also other identity sources such as race and sexuality.

Power and Resources

The embedding of identities within a social context has particularly been overlooked in the work-life literature, which has instead maintained an "overwhelming focus on the analysis of individual-level variables… trivializing much wider power issues" (Özbilgin et al., 2011, p. 183). The social categories of intersectionality such as race, gender, and sexuality have meaning that is shaped by a particular historical and cultural context that imbues them (or not) with power and resources. Thus, an intersectional lens is inherently multilevel and focused upon systems that maintain or disrupt inequity.

Drawing on previous reviews (Else-Quest & Hyde, 2016; Özbilgin et al., 2011; Ryan & Briggs, 2019), we define *work-life intersectionality* as the ways in which: (1) several categories of social identities and values (e.g., race, gender, class, religion, sexuality, ability, and nationality) may combine to create joint effects on work-life relationships in ways that (2) may affect inequality in access to and/or benefits from societal resources for managing the work–nonwork interface, and the distribution of nonwork responsibilities; and (3) which can often result in social context dynamics creating stigmatization and disadvantaging employees' opportunities for well-being on and off the job. Such joint intersections are shaped by organizational and societal structures that may perpetuate inequality. Thus, three conditions are assumed to be integrated to capture one's extent of work-life intersectionality: (1) the possessing of several interdependent nonwork social identities, (2) that when combined are stigmatized (i.e., seen as undesirable by others), and (3) are also related to having lower access to and/or benefits from work-life support resources occurring in a particular cultural context. It is important here to note that some individuals such as a white man or a white woman can hold both privileged and stigmatized intersectional identities beyond their gender and race such as sexual orientation or disability status and may benefit from intersectional invisibility such that some of these other stigmatized identities may not be visible until raised through seeking out work-life flexibility policies due to considerations for their other identities, for example, adopting a baby with a partner or seeking flexible arrangements due to a chronic illness or having to take custody of children, etc. This is consistent with the work of Atewologun et al. (2016) who studied intersectional identity work and found that intersecting identities of gender, ethnicity, and rank can be experienced by individuals as simultaneously providing advantages (e.g., senior rank) and disadvantages (e.g., female gender and minority ethnicity).

While consensus has not yet emerged in empirical research on the operationalization of intersectionality in general, "it is generally considered a compounded variable, with more marginalized identities representing greater intersectional risk" (Standley & Foster-Fishman, 2021, p. 205). Studies show that individuals who identify with more than one stigmatized group report receiving more unfair treatment compared to individuals who identify with one or no stigmatized categorizations (Remedios & Snyder, 2018). We similarly suggest that higher work-life intersectionality considerations exist for an individual where they have more intersecting identities that confer greater stigma as well as lesser resources and power. Higher work-life intersectionality would entail considering more stigmatized identities simultaneously in a context that systematically disempowers members of certain groups, whereas lower work-life intersectionality would indicate consideration of fewer identities in a given context.

Comparing and Contrasting Traditional and Intersectional Approaches

Summarizing the two approaches above, Table 1 identifies six central distinctions between the traditional and intersectional approaches to examining work-life flexibility policies: theoretical lenses, level of analysis, analytical approach, common terminology, traditionally studied samples, and attention to context.

Regarding *theoretical lenses*, the traditional approach developed its own theories – including now-seminal perspectives on work-family conflict (Greenhaus & Beutell, 1985), work-family enrichment (Greenhaus & Powell, 2006), spillover theory (Edwards & Rothbard, 2000), and boundary management theory (Ashforth et al., 2000) – in response to emergent issues associated with the impact of increased globalization, changing workforce demographics, and technology developments that first began to impact family life in the late 1970s and early 1980s (Katzell & Austin, 1992). In contrast, recent developments of intersectionality theory (e.g., Hall et al., 2019) were preceded by the integration of a variety of identity-based theories including social identity (Tajfel & Turner, 1979) and optimal distinctiveness (Brewer, 1991). Although shifting currently toward the use of "work-life," "work-family" has been the *common terminology* of the traditional approach, with this focus reflected in the *traditionally studied samples* of nuclear families consisting of married individuals with children. In contrast, the intersectionality approach commonly refers to "work–nonwork" or "work-life" issues to capture broader experiences beyond the work/family domains and encompass marginalized groups of individuals – although there are some critiques that these groups remain understudied in management-focused empirical research (Hall et al., 2019).

The traditional approach primarily focuses on the individual *level of analysis*, with *analytical approaches* centered around discrete variables (e.g., comparing work-family conflict experiences between men and women; Byron, 2005). Interestingly, however, intersectional analyses are primarily person-centered, meaning that clusters of various attributes and identities jointly operate to shape outcomes (Kossek et al., 2012; Hall et al., 2019). Thus, the intersectionality approach is multilevel in scope primarily from a sociological standpoint with person-centered approaches recognizing that these clusters of attributes and identities within individuals are shaped by various layers of *context* (e.g., history and gendered norms; Crenshaw, 1989). Although the traditional approach also considers context, it does so primarily in terms of recognizing the top-down influences of supervisor support and the work-family and work-life cultures within organizations, whereas the intersectional perspective calls for a bottom-up approach that centers on the most marginalized (Crenshaw, 1989; Hooks, 1984).

Finally, there are *opportunities* for both approaches to benefit from more theoretical development and empirical research addressing their key foundations. We develop additional theory and unpack these opportunities in Part II (traditional approach) and Part III (intersectional approach) of our manuscript. In Part II, we present a general model showing how access and use of flexibility policies relate to boundary control and work and home performance for all individuals. While we maintain that our model will hold in general, as we developed the model, we noticed an important gap that diversity theorizing is not strongly integrated into work-family theories. In Part III, we consider how taking an intersectional approach to reviewing the model opens rich horizons for future research.

PART II: WORK-LIFE FLEXIBILITY MODEL: ENRICHING THE TRADITIONAL BOUNDARY CONTROL AND IMPLEMENTATION PERSPECTIVE

In this section, we discuss the propositions in Fig. 1 and our theoretical model that integrates boundary control and multilevel policy implementation lenses to examine how work-life flexibility alters performance in work and nonwork domains.

Drawing on the work of Kossek et al. (2022), we argue through six propositions (see boxes in Fig. 1) that the use of work-life flexibility policies provides individuals with the ability to control five dimensions (temporal, spatial, size, continuity, permeability) of the work role boundary. This construct is referred to in the figure as "Boundary Control." We suggest that this relationship is conditioned by the extent to which and how the organization implements work-life flexibility policies. Control over the work role boundary in turn affects performance outcomes for both work and nonwork roles. We use the term "nonwork" to reflect the multi-faceted commitments individuals have to their families, friends, communities, and personal interests. Work performance is defined as the behaviors individuals use to carry out job role responsibilities to meet employer goals (Motowidlo & Kell, 2012). Nonwork performance is defined as the behaviors one uses to carry out nonwork role responsibilities to meet nonwork goals. These include the family role (e.g., parent, spouse, and partner), and other nonwork roles that are meaningful to one's personal identity (e.g., student and citizen) (e.g., Wilson & Baumann, 2015).

As we elaborate below, we expect positive effects of flexibility on performance in nonwork roles, due to increased availability for nonwork tasks, but more

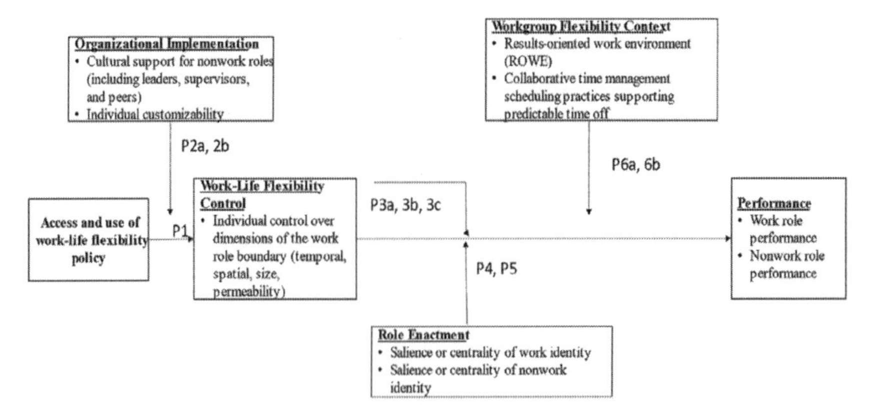

Fig. 1. Work-Life Flexibility Policies: From a Traditional View toward Work-Life Intersectionality Considerations.

equivocal effects on work performance. The work performance of individuals who can reshape the work boundary may benefit if they are motivated by their work arrangement to work more efficiently, for example, at times of peak efficiency (Shepard et al., 1996) or to extend their work efforts as reciprocation for the opportunity to work flexibly. At the same time, their reduced availability to their colleagues can also impair work performance.

Finally, we suggest that the impact of using flexibility on performance in work and nonwork realms is moderated by how individuals enact flexibility to align with their work and nonwork identities and their group context. Additionally, theory has under-addressed work contextual factors that may shape the ability to benefit from workplace flexibility (Van Dyne et al., 2007). Yet there are key differences that condition the impacts of flexibility not only in terms of variation in the ways that individual's work and nonwork identities (Stryker & Serpe, 1982) shape how one synthesizes the management of role engagement across multiple roles (Kossek & Lautsch, 2012) but also in how teams structure work tasks and processes to support each other. For example, making highly frequent personal interruptions to modify the work boundary to be available for nonwork matters may lessen the benefits of work-life flexibility for work performance for individuals who do not have a highly salient work identity. At the group level, teams that operate with a mechanistic focus on process and "face-time" rather than results, and without a collaborative approach to work scheduling also will reduce the benefits of flexibility (Perlow, 2012). Our model incorporates work and nonwork identity salience as well as workgroup norms and processes to illustrate how phenomena at multiple levels influence flexibility's effects on work and nonwork performance.

Our first set of propositions focuses on links between policy use, work boundary control, and variation in organizational implementation of policies.

Use of Work-Life Flexibility Policies and Control Over the Work Role Boundary

Where flexibility policies are used, it is clear from the literature that the *intent* is to provide discretion to *control* varied features (temporal, spatial, size, continuity, permeability) of the work boundary (Kossek et al., 2022). For example, one review defined flextime as "the ability to exercise some choice over when work is carried out" (de Menezes & Kelliher, 2011, p. 456) or when to arrive or leave work, affording control over temporal aspects of the work role boundary. Similarly, a policy such as hoteling, which provides a teleworker the option to book space at a main or satellite work site as needed, is intended to provide control over the spatial limits of the work role boundary. Policies that allow individuals to job share, a variant of part-time work in which two employees share hours and duties, offer each the possibility to control the size of the work role boundary. Bring your own device to work (BYOD) policies (Bamboo HR, 2022) facilitate employee control over the permeability of the work role boundary, as they may enable the individual choice to use personal devices to access work enterprise systems and to manage access to personal texts or emails during the day.

Consistent with the intent of work-life flexibility policies to provide some control over the work role limits, which we briefly examined above, studies show positive linkages of use to control perceptions. For instance, as Gajendran & Harrison (2007, p.1535) note in their meta-analysis: "telecommuting … is associated with increased perceptions of autonomy." Thus, we propose that employees who use work-life flexibility policies are more likely to have the ability to control the work role boundary compared to similar employees who do not use policies.

> *P1*. Employees who use work-life flexibility policies experience greater control over the temporal and spatial characteristics, size, continuity, and permeability of the work role boundary than those who do not use work-life flexibility policies.

Certainly, using certain work-life flexibility policies can enable control over the work role's spatial boundary, for example, by providing one the authority to determine whether to work at home or in the office on a given day. However, it does not guarantee that one is necessarily protected from attempts from management or others in the organization to reduce the control that one has acquired from policy use. Thus, it is critical to conceptually distinguish policy use from the extent of boundary control because, as we contend, flexibility policies – despite their intentions – do not inevitably increase control. Below we examine how the strength of the relationship between policy use and control over the work role boundary depends on an organization's policy implementation approach.

Organizational Implementation Approach

We define the *organizational implementation approach* as the cultural and structural ways that an organization implements flexibility policies to provide employees the discretion to control the work role boundary. It is assessed via two characteristics that we found were prevalent in the employer implementation literature: cultural support for flexibility policy use and customizability. We contend that these attributes can enhance or weaken linkages between the use of a flexibility policy and boundary control.

Cultural Support for Flexibility Policy Use

Research has well documented that firms can vary in the extent to which they support the use of flexibility policies (Williams et al., 2013). Managers are critical actors in the implementation process as they serve as gatekeepers to flexibility use affecting cultural support (Kossek et al., 2015). Managers also make attributions regarding whether their staff use flexibility for performance or personal reasons, and these judgments influence employees' performance evaluations and career success (Leslie et al., 2012). A lack of cultural support for nonwork roles and, in particular, flexibility not only restricts the use of a work-life flexibility policy but also limits the extent of boundary control afforded by policy use due to the increased likelihood of boundary violations from colleagues (Trefalt, 2013). The potential for increased boundary control from a flexibility policy would be lessened, for example, if team norms persist in expecting policy users' attendance at on-site meetings during a part-timer's day off or on one's established telework day.

Customizability

Research shows that HR policies (such as flexibility) are most effective when they are implemented in ways that meet the needs of multiple constituencies and when they are adaptable and evolve to meet changing employee needs (Tsui & Milkovich, 1987). Control is likely to be enhanced, the more flexibility policies are "flexible" in how they are implemented so they can be customized to meet employees' needs (Kossek & Lautsch, 2012). For example, a customizable flextime policy might allow working parents to adjust start times in the summer when children are not in school, enhancing their temporal control. Similarly, a customizable reduced load work arrangement might enable an employee attending university to adjust whether they work three or four days per week, allowing them to pursue further education and accommodate their shifting class schedule. The more that implementation of a policy can be adapted to meet a worker's personal needs, the greater control the individual will experience from the use of the policy.

> *P2*. The use of work-life flexibility policies enhances control over the work role boundary to a greater degree when policies are: (a) more culturally supported by the organization and its members (e.g., supervisors, leaders, peers) and are (b) individually customizable to meet personal needs.

Individual Implementation of Work-Life Flexibility

Just as job crafters vary in how they shape and perform their jobs (Wrzesniewski & Dutton, 2001), so too we argue that individuals vary in how they implement "work-life flexibility" (Kossek & Lautsch, 2012). Individuals vary in how they carry out work-life flexibility in ways that allow them to support the multiple roles they fill; how they do so is influenced by their personal identities and their perceptions of their nonwork and work social environments (Weick, 1979). Ashforth et al. (2000) noted that the more that roles are highly important to one's identity, the more likely that individuals will want to manage boundaries to engage in that role within and across domains. Below we examine the main effects of work-life flexibility on nonwork performance through increased nonwork availability mechanisms; and compare control over boundary size to other forms, followed by the moderating effects of nonwork identity salience.

Effects of Control Over the Work Role Boundary on Performance in the Nonwork Domain

Physical and Psychological Availability

We suggest that work-life flexibility affects individuals' performance in nonwork roles by shaping their availability to engage in nonwork activities. We define availability in terms of both physical availability (presence) and psychological availability (readiness to engage). *Physical availability*, the ability to be physically present in a role, facilitates "being there." *Psychological availability* is the "sense of having the physical, emotional, or psychological resources to personally engage at a particular moment" (Kahn, 1990, p. 714). It has been shown to foster the energy (Russo et al., 2015), creativity (Binyamin & Carmeli, 2010), and engagement (Kahn, 1990; May et al., 2004) necessary to perform well at work and home.

Increases in *physical availability* may be achieved through increased control over any of the five dimensions of the work role boundary. For example, an individual who manages care for a chronically ill child may exert work-life flexibility to control the size of the work boundary by reducing work hours or adjusting continuity by taking a medical leave. Or they may shift the spatial boundary by frequently teleworking or use flextime to shift temporal boundaries to restructure meetings and schedule medical appointments. Or they may constantly multi-task, shifting between work emails and tasks and nonwork activities (e.g., contacting the pharmacy, getting homework, checking in on the child), increasing permeability. These examples illustrate how having greater work-life flexibility to control different dimensions of the work role boundary is likely to increase physical and psychological availability to perform the nonwork role. Not being physically present can reduce one's ability to participate fully in nonwork activities, to perform well in them, and to be psychologically engaged. Studies of the impact of a military lifestyle, for instance, have shown that the recurring periodic separations that military families experience are negatively related to well-being and marital satisfaction (Burrell et al., 2006). Consistent with the theory on boundaries (Ashforth et al., 2000) and availability (Kahn, 1990), we propose that individuals who have higher control to alter the work role boundaries across the five dimensions will be likely to be more physically available and have higher performance in nonwork roles. Such physical availability may also feed into and can support psychological availability, as individuals can be more able to be psychological available when physically present. As role salience identity theory (Stryker & Serpe, 1982) suggests, the more time people physically allocate to a role, the greater their psychological attachment.

> *P3a.* Control over the work role boundary increases employees' physical and psychological availability for nonwork roles, which enhances their performance in the nonwork domain.

Moderating Effects of Type of Work Role Boundary Control on the Relationship Strength Between Availability and Nonwork Performance

Compared to other dimensions, we theorize that the relationship between work role boundary control and *psychological availability* may be most facilitated by having higher control over the size of the work role boundary. If individuals reduce the size (e.g., working a reduced load role such as 32 rather than a typical 40 hours a week), they will experience a lower level of work-related demands (Duxbury & Halinski, 2014), thereby increasing psychological resources like energy and attention for the nonwork role. This view is in accord with work-family role conflict theory, which maintains that individuals have limited resources to fulfill their roles, and that resources devoted to meeting demands in one domain make it difficult to satisfy demands in another domain (Greenhaus & Beutell, 1985).

Nonwork role performance can also be expected to be enhanced when individuals can access multiple mechanisms linking control and performance, rather than merely one. Control over the size of the work role boundary may increase *both* physical and psychological availability for nonwork roles, enhancing resources to detach from work, preventing job creep and fostering better nonwork engagement (Rothbard et al., 2005). Control over the size of the work role boundary may have a stronger effect on nonwork performance than other forms of boundary control.

For example, individuals whose telework provides increased control over spatial boundaries but are required to engage in work conference calls while a child does homework can experience enhanced physical availability but not necessarily enhanced psychological availability. Similarly, having increased control over the temporal boundary via flextime may allow an individual to reorder their day to physically attend an early doctor's appointment, but may not reduce burdens or add resources to enhance such psychological availability. Unlike size control, with spatial and temporal control, total work and nonwork performance demands are not reduced but merely reshuffled in time and space. Similarly, policies enabling individuals to create a more permeable work boundary to constantly text and email family while working may increase physical availability to respond to nonwork needs, but any potential gains in psychological availability may be offset by added strains from multi-tasking.

> *P3b*. Control over the size of the work role boundary enhances performance in the nonwork domain to a greater degree than does control over the other dimensions of control over the work role boundary (temporal and spatial characteristics, continuity, and permeability).

Control Bundling and Chilling Effects

Consistent with the idea of "complementary capabilities" from social capital theory, which maintains that actors, and individuals in their networks, may have abilities or resources that become more powerful when deployed in combination (Adler & Kwon, 2002), we argue that different forms of work-life flexibility to control the work boundary can have bundling as well as chilling effects. Economists studying bundles of human resource management (HRM) practices suggest that the marginal effect of altering a single HRM practice will be much less than the results achieved when sets of complementary practices are implemented together as a coherent system of practices (Ichniowski et al., 1997). This logic has been suggested for work-life programs more generally (Perry-Smith & Blum, 2000).

Drawing on this literature, we suggest that the benefits of work-life flexibility on nonwork role performance are deepened when multiple types of flexibility are present or "bundled together." For instance, individuals whose employers provide a flextime program that allows employees to vary the start of work between 8 a.m. and 10 a.m. with corresponding changes in departure from work gain some ability to adjust the temporal dimension of the work role boundary. But they might not have the full availability required to assist with complex family needs such as an aging parent with repeated appointments for medical treatments that require a long commute and hours in hospitals. In such cases, temporal control over the work boundary would have greater positive effects on nonwork performance if combined with the ability to work from other locations (spatial) offering more accessibility for older adult-caregiving, or with a reduction in workload and hours (size) to enhance availability for the health care tasks.

Such reasoning is consistent with recent flexibility literature reviews urging researchers to follow the lead of HRM scholars to consider synergies across bundles of flexibility practices (de Menezes & Kelliher, 2011). Some work-life empirical work has begun to explore interrelationships across work-family and work-life programs and practices and supports the usefulness of this approach. Greenhaus et al. (2012), for example, found that the relationship between family-supportive supervision and balance was stronger for employees in family-supportive organizational environments than unsupportive environments. Accordingly, we propose that different types of work-life flexibility complement each other so that their effects on availability for and performance in nonwork tasks will be heightened when used in combination.

The converse is also true. We propose that a "chilling effect" exists whereby having lower work-life flexibility related to one dimension of the work boundary weakens the benefits of other types of flexibility control. For example, an individual who telecommutes (and has control over the spatial characteristics of the work role boundary) may experience limited gains in their availability to attend parent–teacher meetings at a child's school if their workload is very high (boundary size) or if they are required to work set hours even when working at home (temporal boundary). Being unable to control the size and permeability and scheduling of the work role will weaken the benefit of working at home in such situations. Supporting this argument is Hunton's research (2005) showing that telecommuting from locations that limit control over work intrusions into the nonwork domain (e.g., teleworking from home rather than a satellite office) will reduce one's ability to carry out one's job and attend to personal issues.

P3c. Each form of boundary control enhances performance in the nonwork domain to a greater degree when the other forms of boundary control are high than when they are low.

Individual Work-Life Flexibility Enactment and Nonwork Performance

In this section, we turn to moderators that condition the effect of control over the work role boundary on nonwork performance. We argue that whether work-life flexibility leads to higher *nonwork* performance depends on the strength of one's nonwork identity salience.

Salience of Nonwork Identity

We suggest that the effects proposed in *3a* will be magnified as the person is able to focus on a nonwork role that is highly meaningful. Having work-life flexibility does not always mean that one will necessarily make oneself more available to perform nonwork activities; it depends on the person and the situation. Individuals differ in the values and priorities they hold regarding work and nonwork roles (Carlson & Kacmar, 2000). Roles that are highly salient to an individual are a means of self-definition and personal satisfaction (Amatea et al., 1986). Work and nonwork role identities reflect the degree to which one attaches social value and meaning to work and nonwork roles, and individuals vary in their identities, such as they may be work-centric, or more generally nonwork centric such as family centric (Kossek & Lautsch, 2012). Individuals enact work-life flexibility in varied ways based on these varying identity configurations (Capitano et al., 2017; Kossek & Lautsch, 2012). Consistent with Ashforth et al.'s (2000) argument that individuals are more likely to want to enact role identities that are highly meaningful, we suggest that individuals are more likely to apply their ability to control the work role boundary to increase their availability for nonwork activities if they highly identify with nonwork roles.

Previous studies are consistent with this idea that increased salience of one's nonwork identity will shape motivation to use boundary control to attain greater availability and performance in the nonwork domain. Studies show, for example, that both men and women are likely to be equally interested in using flextime and telework, but individuals with higher involvement and identification in caregiving such as women are more likely to use work-life flexibility to support nonwork identities such as caregiving (Brescoll et al., 2013) as it is seen as a way to not only enable control over the work role but also facilitate one's ability to allocate availability toward family performance (Hammer et al., 2005). Individuals who highly identify with nonwork roles are also likely to increase their work boundary permeability to stay available to family while at work (Ashforth et al., 2000), or use control over work scheduling (the temporal boundary) to support nonwork involvement. We argue that such individuals are likely to have higher nonwork performance because they will be more available to nonwork demands.

A key mechanism by which individuals with high nonwork identity salience achieve availability for their nonwork role demands is through controlling work-to-nonwork interruptions (Kossek et al., 2012). Interruptions have been defined as incidents that temporarily suspend progress on tasks (Baethge & Rigotti, 2013). They have also been defined as "breaks," "distractions," "intrusions," and as an unexpected encounter that limits the flow and continuity of work or nonwork task completion (Jett & George, 2003). Interruptions are linked to a reduced ability to immerse oneself in a task (Chen & Karahanna, 2014), to reduced creativity (Amabile, 1998), and to reduced task quality (Gupta et al., 2013). Frequent role transitions lead to process losses in being able to complete a task due in part to switching costs or inefficiencies in moving back and forth to transition between two roles (Alzahabi et al., 2017; Kossek & Lautsch, 2012), and to less focus on the role at hand (Ashforth et al., 2000; Neale & Griffin, 2006). Minimizing interruption behaviors avoids inefficiencies and process losses and maximizes one's sustained availability in a highly salient nonwork domain.

> *P4*. Each form of boundary control enhances performance in the nonwork domain to a greater degree for employees whose nonwork identity salience is high than for employees whose nonwork identity salience is low.

Effect of Work-Life Flexibility on Performance in the Work Domain

Having work-life flexibility may have both upsides and downsides for work performance. We assume that the positive effects of flexibility on work performance are driven by two mechanisms: (1) *reciprocity* – individuals appreciate work-life flexibility and respond with increased work effort; (2) *efficiency* – with the ability to adapt the temporal, spatial, size, continuity, or permeability dimensions of the work role boundary, individuals are more able to work when, where, and how they will be most productive. At the same time, we suggest that there may be disadvantages associated with work-life flexibility that reflect a third mechanism that shapes the relationships between flexibility and work performance; and (3) reduced *availability* to others in the workplace and potential relationship damage that may accrue as a result. The effect of work-life flexibility on work performance, then, is dependent on whether the gains that flexibility leads to in terms of efficiency and reciprocity are outweighed by the disadvantages associated with not being available for colleagues (Van Dyne et al., 2007). Given these competing gains and losses, we do not predict a main effect for the relationship between flexibility and work performance, but focus on moderators that shift the relationship toward being beneficial or detrimental.

We suggest below that both individuals and work groups may shape how flexibility is implemented and the extent to which relevant mechanisms – reciprocity, efficiency, or availability – affect work performance. Individuals who have higher boundary control, which we define as the extent to which one has control over the work role may alter its effects on work performance through their efforts to shape interruptions to manage their work and nonwork availability in a manner that best reflects the salience of their work identity. Workgroup contexts such as supportive team results-oriented work environments and scheduling practices also influence the relationship between using flexibility and work performance.

Salience of Work Identity

It is plausible that having greater control over the work role boundary might improve the efficiency and effort that individuals achieve in their work performance. Greater work-life temporal flexibility may allow individuals to select work hours that correspond to their own peak hours of productivity (Shepard et al., 1996). In addition, greater location flexibility might, for example, allow a teleworking programmer who finds inspiration in the middle of the night to work more efficiently at that time. Teleworkers, who have control over spatial work role boundaries may benefit from avoiding long-hours spent commuting and may increase their productivity and output by devoting some portion of those time savings to additional work (Beauregard & Henry, 2009); this argument is consistent with empirical findings of positive associations between hours of work and flexibility (e.g., Golden, 2001). Yet we argue that efficiency gains may not be realized if individuals do not have a highly salient work identity or if they allow nonwork to constantly interrupt work focus. A work arrangement like telecommuting, for example, may place the worker in greater proximity to family members enabling more interruptions during work time. If this happens frequently, some of the beneficial outcomes of work-life flexibility for work performance will not be realized. Although not all interruptions detract from individual effectiveness, and instead sometimes provide a needed break (Jett & George, 2003), high levels of interruptions can be assumed to reduce efficiency in the work role. Individuals for whom the work role is highly salient will be likely to enact their work-life flexibility in a manner that allows them to limit nonwork interruptions of the work role (e.g., a teleworker who decides to regularly keep the door to the home office shut while working). While some individuals may allow a diminishing of efficiency to be available for nonwork issues in a timely manner, others may prefer to limit nonwork interruptions, maintaining work focus and efficient performance. Here the gains in efficiency and work performance from having work-life flexibility are likely to be maintained.

> *P5*. Control over the work role boundary enhances performance in the work domain for employees whose work identity salience is high and weakens performance in the work domain for employees whose work identity salience is low.

Workgroup Flexibility Context

Workgroups shape how flexibility is enacted and the extent to which each of these mechanisms – reciprocity, efficiency, and availability – affects work performance (Van Dyne et al., 2007). Employees are nested in workgroups that influence how members construe the opportunities and constraints of how work is to be conducted and the effects of flexibility on work performance. Not all workgroups support work-life flexibility or develop positive norms around its use (Blair-Loy & Wharton, 2002). Work-life flexibility is often offered as an individual "accommodation" without considering how its enactment relates to group norms (Van Dyne et al., 2007). Below we consider two key elements of the group context that we identified in the literature as influencing relationships between work-life flexibility and work performance.

Results-oriented Work Environment

The effects of individual control over work role boundaries on work performance may be conditioned by whether the team has a results-oriented work environment (ROWE). Teams with such environments are characterized by a cultural shift away from a traditional bureaucratized process-oriented work context to focus on work action and goal achievement. Members are socialized to avoid focusing on "face-time," physical presence, and the number of hours worked as means to facilitate productivity (Kelly et al., 2010). Individuals are empowered to "do whatever they want, whenever they want, as long as the work gets done" (Ressler & Thompson, 2008). Kelly et al. (2010) describe a ROWE as empowering group members to alter when and where they work without having to get permission from a manager so long as they coordinate with coworkers. Staff can reconsider meetings, questioning whether they are necessary, who should attend, and who could provide input asynchronously online.

With this type of environment, individuals with higher control over work boundaries are more likely to experience higher work performance because they can better restructure work boundaries (i.e., alter schedules, permeability, location, continuity, or size) to allow them to manage work–nonwork demands more synergistically. Further, those who work from home or work nontraditional hours face less stigma or negative attributions (Ressler & Thompson, 2008), thereby further strengthening the relationship between work-life flexibility and work performance since energy will not be used justifying how work-life flexibility is being enacted.

Such a group culture increases norms of reciprocity and efficiency. It also may motivate availability for critical work tasks, as teams learn to prioritize high-value tasks that are the most critical. Since efficiencies are focused on completing high-value tasks rather than low-value tasks (e.g., avoiding long meetings that are unproductive, psychologically depleting, and decrease physical availability for completing work tasks), groups adhering more highly to results-oriented cultural norms that focus on key tasks will have enhanced psychological resources and energy to perform work. This team context is consistent with a long line of research on implementing flexibility policies such as telework, which commonly recommends that managers shift from a face-time to a results-oriented supervisory approach to foster efficiency and reciprocity instead of undermining teleworker performance (Lautsch et al., 2009). In sum, the positive effects of work-life flexibility on work performance will be stronger in a group with a higher results-oriented work environment culture.

Collaborative Time Management Scheduling Practices and Predictable Time Off
Evidence is growing that work groups that organize work scheduling collaboratively better support predictable time off (PTO) and team back up when individuals need to adjust work boundaries, and promote stronger linkages between work-life flexibility and work performance. Perlow (2012) conducted a PTO experiment, where members in a consulting firm that had historically had a long-hours culture were given planned time off each week using collaborative time management to reduce overwork. Team members engaged in structured dialogue for 30 minutes at weekly meetings to ensure that work was getting done efficiently (Perlow, 2012). The structured dialogue forced the team to examine group processes and to reconsider how the team was working. These discussions enabled workers to voice their flexibility needs and to be more able to reap the full benefits of work-life flexibility and greater boundary control because they would not be interrupted or expected to work while using flexibility. This also increased workers' ability to plan for nonwork needs (e.g., dinner and exercising), which would foster positive psychological spillover for renewed work engagement. Members in such cultures are less likely to be burned out when working, as they have had time to recover from previous work (Sonnentag & Fritz, 2015). In contrast, Sexton et al. (2017) found that when physicians chose to work a three-day compressed work week, but were overscheduled in high face-time cultures with no collaborative scheduling for team backup, individual work performance suffered and burnout increased. Thus, team contexts with collaborative scheduling require group members to think about work tasks in the collective. Members cross-train each other and agree to be back-ups to support member substitutability for work tasks. Such cultures foster norms of reciprocity and efficiency, enhancing work performance as clients' task demands are less likely to build up during absences. Such practices support coworkers backing each other up and foster group problem-solving on

work tasks and increased awareness of members' work-life needs, freeing up people to be able to enact flexibility in ways that support work performance without worrying about stigma, increasing efficiency (Van Dyne et al., 2007).

> *P6a.* Control over the work role boundary enhances performance in the work domain to a greater degree for work groups that have a strong results-oriented work environment than for work groups that have a weak results-oriented work environment.

> *P6b.* Control over the work role boundary enhances performance in the work domain to a greater degree for work groups that have collaborative time management scheduling practices supporting predictable time off than for work groups that do not have collaborative scheduling practices supporting predictable time off.

PART III: ENRICHING THE MODEL WITH CONSIDERATIONS FOR FUTURE RESEARCH FROM A WORK-LIFE INTERSECTIONALITY LENS

As noted in Part I of the paper and summarized in Table 1, attention to intersectionality in a work-life context illuminates how traditionally assumed work-family relationships may need to be revisited to address the dynamics of employees' diverse flexibility implementation experiences and outcomes. For example, work-life intersectionality may alter one's needs and preferences for work-life flexibility as well as access to work-life flexibility resources and benefits from use. An intersectional lens also suggests a need to consider how individuals' experiences with flexibility policies occur in an embedded context that is shaped by existing societal structures and power dynamics relevant to the work–nonwork interface. To illustrate these arguments, below we re-examine our model in Fig. 2 by adding in six intersectional considerations which provide new research directions to broaden work-life flexibility research to better fit with an increasingly diverse workforce and society. Recall that in Section 1, we defined *work-life intersectionality* as having multiple intersecting identities (e.g., gender, caregiving, and race), that are stigmatized and linked to having less access to and/or benefits from resources to support managing the work-life interface in a social context. It pertains to the ways in which multiple categories of social identities (e.g., race, gender, class, religion, sexuality, ability, and nationality) are influenced by a historical and social context that shapes power relation, which we assume create interactive effects on work-life flexibility.

Work-Life Flexibility Initiation: Invoking Policy Use and Access to Work-Life Flexibility

Intersectional Consideration #1

Compared to other employee groups, access to work-life flexibility is often more limited for employees with higher work-life intersectionality, as their "choices" are

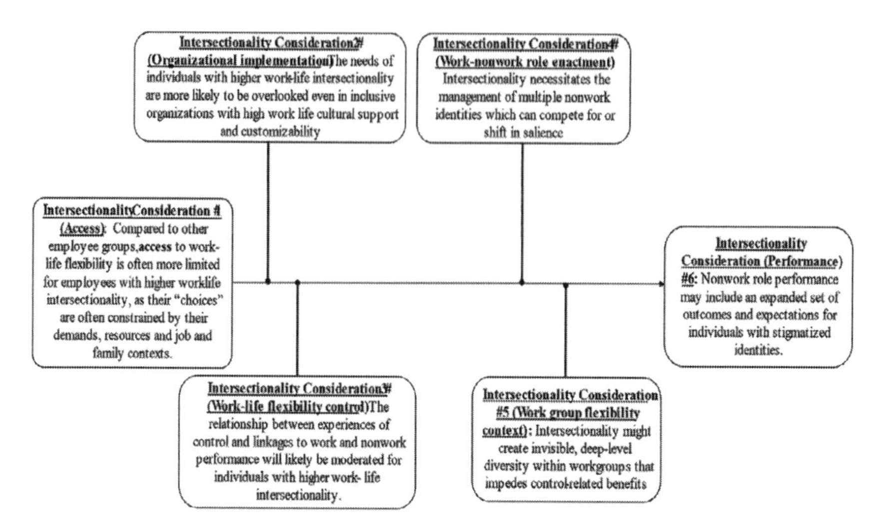

Fig. 2. Work-Life Flexibility Policies: Moving toward Work-Life Intersectionality Considerations.

often constrained by their demands, resources and job and family contexts. While the traditional work–nonwork theoretical lens underlying our model is more focused on policy use and its outcomes, when we moved to consider a work-life intersectionality lens we noticed that members of some social groups (e.g., according to age, race, or gender) lack equal access to flexibility, often coinciding with their membership in specific occupations, and this disparity is largely overlooked in research. As Alderfer (1983) maintains, job groups systematically overlap with demographic groups creating under and over representation, or what is often called occupational segregation. This segregation is often linked in organizations to hierarchy and power structures that limit or enhance access to work-life flexibility. For example, women and minorities with children are often overly represented in lower-level jobs in service work (e.g., housekeeping, food service, and nursing) or in manufacturing such as food manufacturing (Kossek & Lee, 2020), where they have less access to request flexible scheduling compared to men. Research has also shown that lower-wage workers and those without high-school education are less likely to have access to some types of work-life flexibility policies such as flextime (Miller, 1992), and that concentration in such less-desirable jobs is persistent for these relatively disadvantaged workers (Blau et al., 2013).

Further, the effects of occupational segregation often intensify for those with multiple stigmatized identities; for example, analysis of gender- and race-based occupational segregation shows that while Latino men are the most segregated within the US economy, Latina women are the most concentrated in low-wage work (Alonso-Villar et al., 2012) where access to work-life flexibility is limited. Thus, occupational segregation related to social structures that push people into various jobs may affect access to varying types of flexibility that may be systematically linked to work-life intersectionality and warrants further study.

Granted some prior research has addressed variation in individual preferences for work-life flexibility. For example, research has shown that differences exist across an array of dimensions in terms of who desires to work flexibly. Reviews of survey evidence show, for example, that preferences for flexibility in general and for specific types of work-life flexibility policies vary by gender, life-stage, parenting-stage, occupation, and country (Thornthwaite, 2004). Yet most of this literature overlooks how preferences and needs occur not in a vacuum, but in a social context and power structure where some workers are more likely to be advantaged in their access to flexibility by virtue of their jobs. For example, workers in entry-level retail jobs may express no desire for reduced load or part-time work but this may be because their work hours are already notably low and unstable, creating strains, particularly for parents unable to arrange or afford childcare (Henly & Lambert, 2014). Thus, the literature often overlooks how choices may be more limited for some job groups, frequently making this discussion decontextualized.

We should note that preferences also reflect differences in the policy environment of the country (e.g., the existence of public childcare, and the right to request a flexible schedule) (cf. Kossek & Kelliher, 2022) as well as organizational features (e.g., managerial support for work-life) and individual/home experiences and demands (e.g., partner work hours) (Thornthwaite, 2004). Moreover, preferences are distinct from intent to use policies, as workers may prefer to work part-time or to take a parental leave, for example, but not feel free to do so due to fears of backlash from use such as lower pay and job loss (Kossek & Lautsch, 2018; Perrigino et al., 2018) or a simple lack of availability based on traditional employment policies that exclude some job groups. Thus, any discussion of access, preferences, and work-life intersectionality also opens the need to examine more deeply a disconnect between the different types of flexibility that are being offered by organizations and the preferences of all types of workers. For example, in one study of unionized employees working mothers who were in social work and service jobs desired part-time work, but the union which had more male members did not support part-time work as an option for these working mothers to access (Kossek et al., 2014).

Another gap in the mainstream management flexibility literature relates to i-deals, or idiosyncratic flexibility deals (e.g., Hornung et al., 2009), defined as negotiated, individualized customized flexible work schedules. Such research tends to focus on privileged highly paid workers with market power who are also likely to have extra family resources (e.g., a stay-at-home spouse) and financial resources for caregiving (Kossek & Kelliher, 2022). These studies also assume considerable worker latitude to have a choice over flexibility and again show a decontextualized and individualistic approach to work-life flexibility preferences and access (e.g., Hornung et al., 2009).

Organizational Implementation

Intersectionality Consideration #2

The needs of individuals with higher work-life intersectionality- are more likely to be overlooked even in inclusive organizations with high work-life cultural support and customizability of flexibility policies. As noted in *P2* in Fig. 1 in the traditional model, we argue that the use of work-life flexibility policies will be more likely to increase boundary control when implemented in an organizational context with cultural support for flexibility and nonwork roles, and with policies that are customizable to meet individual needs. While these aspects of organizational implementation benefit all workers, they may not be sufficient to be fully inclusive of individuals with higher work-life intersectionality.

For example, despite the widespread increase in support for flexible work during the pandemic, research in Canada and the UK. has shown workers with disabilities felt less supported by organizations during the pandemic than their colleagues with no disability (Gignac et al., 2021; Peters et al., 2022). Similarly, a national study of women in STEM found that male professors experienced far fewer boundary disruptions and loss of boundary control than their women in STEM counterparts as they were far less likely to have to manage child and older adult care, or had far less responsibility for domestic labor (cooking, cleaning), with the widespread move to remote work (Kossek et al., 2021). This situation revealed that women professors' joint gender and mother identities were more likely to be stigmatized as it made visible the fact that they were less than "ideal workers" for being focused on caregiving identity during the day. For example, many female faculty perceived they were not socially, supported by their work colleagues if they had to have their children being on camera while in a conference call, which made visible their multitasking work and care, engaging in nonwork interruptions and less physical and psychological availability for work. In contrast, male faculty often had far greater access to have a spouse with primary or sole responsibility for managing child care, which helped to keep their gender and parent joint status largely invisible and less likely stigmatized while teleworking. Thus, work-life flexibility experiences are assumed to be related to the extent of one's work-life intersectionality, defined as when an individual has not just the mere combination of two or more identities, but these identities are stigmatized and linked to less access to and benefits from resources to support managing the work-life interface.

An intersectional lens raises the issue that organizations can sometimes have high support for flexibility but individuals with higher work-life intersectionality may still not experience the environment as inclusive. Shore et al. (2011) define inclusion as the degree to which an individual perceives they are a valued member of their workplace through treatment that simultaneously supports their belongingness and uniqueness. Regarding work-life flexibility, some companies have implemented policies in ways that even if providing high levels of cultural support may not be very inclusive of marginalized groups particularly pertaining to those with members having higher work-life intersectionality (e.g., single-parent women of color or low-income immigrant mothers who are often stigmatized and have less access to and benefits from resources for managing the work-life interface). For example, mothers who do not have access to paid family leave in the U.S. may be unable to afford to take leave unless they are in a traditional two-parent family.

Besides often overlooking intersectional family structures that may shape the usability of work-life flexibility policies, some companies also exclude access based on gender, hierarchy and job level, flexibility type and comprehensiveness across job groups and regions, local leader preferences, norms, institutional, and societal contexts. We give an example of each of these forms of exclusion that can occur even in firms that overall look strong on general work-life flexibility support. For example, some organizations take a gendered approach to caregiving policy use and culturally limit access and use to certain workers such as only allowing mothers with young children or daughters with a sick parent to work part-time, without offering similar options to fathers or sons. Hierarchical work-life exclusion as noted also affects the usability of policies that may formally be on the books at the organizational level but not available at the job group level within the firm. For example, a company may only allow managers to telework but not clerical workers, even though both types of workers could do some of their tasks at home and the policy is listed as available at the firm level on national surveys. Thus, organizations that recognize and adapt to work-life intersectionality have higher usability and inclusiveness of flexibility policies across many demographic, functional, and hierarchical job groups (Ryan & Kossek, 2008).

We have noted that the many types of flexibility from part-time work to permeability and the ability to disconnect are important for supporting a diversity of work-life needs. Thus, an organizational approach to work-life flexibility implementation that would support intersectionality also tends to be comprehensive. For example, a firm would not only invest in telework but also all forms of flexibility we discussed from control over work size, to time off, and scheduling. Such a firm that strongly supports work-life intersectionality would be characterized by having a full range of flexible options available to many different types of jobs, workers, and geographies and suited to many work-life flexibility needs, that is, every job or person would be able to use some meaningful form of work-life flexibility. Although factory workers may not have jobs conducive to telework, they may request flextime or part-time work or have the right to bring a personal cell phone on the floor. Or while employees without children cannot take paid maternity or paternity leave, they might be able to take paid dependent care leave to care for their parents or a disabled sibling.

Implementing policies in ways that support work-life intersectionality is likely to enhance the positive effects of policy use on control because cultural acceptance of flexibility is likely to be higher in firms where many people can work flexibly throughout the firm. Since working flexibly is seen as socially normative, use of flexibility will not be seen as socially deviant, or limited to sometimes marginalized groups such as working mothers, or stigmatized "nonideal workers" who do not engage in overworking as a way to advance in career (Williams et al., 2013). Firms that more highly support work-life intersectionality are more likely to have learned how to implement flexibility more effectively. For example, such firms might have a higher investment in cross-training or staff an extra worker for improved backup, enabling users to experience and exercise greater control.

Control and Work and Nonwork Performance

Intersectionality Consideration #3

The relationship between experiences of control and linkages to work and nonwork performance will differ for individuals with higher work- life intersectionality. There are several reasons why higher work-life intersectionality might alter the relationships described in *P3 and P5* suggested above in Fig. 1 between work-life flexibility policy use, control, and positive outcomes. Individuals who have multiple stigmatized identities, when enacting in combination may also be associated with more demands, and less access to resources and less power to navigate social contexts, which may mean that individuals who use work-life flexibility policies may experience lower control and benefits from use for several reasons. Having multiple stigmatized identities can exacerbate unfair treatment from others (Remedios & Snyder, 2018), which may result in attenuating benefits from work-life flexibility policy use. For example, in a work-life flexibility policy context, supervisors' attributions (Leslie et al., 2012) and face-time expectations (Barsness et al., 2005) could lead to differential treatment across policy users. Consider a single man who utilizes a work from home flexibility arrangement for caregiving reasons as opposed to overworking late at night. Based on precarious manhood theory, the decision might be regarded unfavorably because it is viewed as "weak" and a violation of masculine gender norms (Rudman & Mescher, 2013), particularly if the policy is viewed as more intended for women (Kirby & Krone, 2002). Yet based on singlism – which identifies a stigma associated with the status of being single or unmarried (DePaulo & Morris, 2005) – the decision might be regarded unfavorably if there is a sentiment that the policy is intended for individuals with family responsibilities (Aryee et al., 2013). Although these interpretations more accurately reflect *mis*attributions based on a limited understanding of the underlying intentions and breadth of work-life flexibility policies, individuals with multiple stigmatized identities might be more likely to experience backlash-related effects involving reduced career outcomes, such as lower pay, different attributions for use (Leslie et al., 2012) and more negative performance appraisals compared to individuals with only one or no stigmatized identity (Perrigino et al., 2018).

Further, individuals with high work-life intersectionality are likely to have an underlying lack of personal resources or additional demands that undermine the link between work-life flexibility policy use, control, and positive outcomes. Beyond concerns that work-life balance rhetoric neglects vulnerable workers – including low-wage women of color (Kolhatkar, 2021) – various aspects of intersectionality involving the unique cultural, community, and religious considerations create additional demands and resource drain not considered or addressed in work-life flexibility policies (Kamenou, 2008). It is plausible that the connection between policy use and positive outcomes will only hold for traditionally studied samples (Casper et al., 2007) and disempower those with multiple stigmatized identities (Ravenswood & Harris, 2016) – unless inclusivity is embedded within work-life flexibility policy implementation for different employees – some higher and some lower on work-life intersectionality.

In addition, the expectations and actions of supervisors on how flexibility is to be used and differentially supported may have adverse impact on individuals with higher work-life intersectionality characteristics. For example, it has been documented that people who participate in remote meetings in which cameras and microphones are expected to be on such that children and others in the background can be seen and heard experience increased "zoom fatigue"

(Shockley et al., 2021). In some of these front-facing meetings, it is possible that to appear more diverse, the burden of being visible – if not physically present – falls more on women and people of color, who may have more concealing to do, resulting in trade-offs and process loss to the work tasks (Kossek et al., 2021). Further, individuals with higher work-life intersectionality may receive less protection if they use policies. Low-status employees are also less likely to have access to those in power who can advocate for their use of flexible policies (Briscoe & Kellogg, 2011).

Moreover, differences in access to family resources may moderate the benefits of using different flexibility forms for some employees who are members of multiple stigmatized social groups. Consider a single Latina mother who works as an administrative assistant living in a small house with spotty internet. She may not have the space to work in a quiet home office, and her smaller home may make it difficult for her to derive the full benefits of using a remote work option. Further, women of color who telework are more likely to be the head of their household and may be less likely to have a spouse who is staying at home to watch the children while working. As a result, despite the use of a flexibility policy, they may engage in more multi-tasking and be less productive due to lower boundary control at their work location. They also are more likely to have nonwork responsibilities not only for their children but other adult members of their families and with extended members of their community as well (Pew Research Center, 2022). Therefore, even though they are teleworking they may need to juggle these additional family demands while working from home, unlike some with lower demands. Many of these work-life intersectionality-related differences that attenuate the likely control and performance benefits from flexibility can be attributed to culture such as the disproportionate reality of people of color living in multi-generational households (Pew Research Center, 2022), which may complicate the attractiveness of using of some flexibility policies to enable control over work location (e.g., telework and flexplace). For example, women of color may be more reluctant to work from home if there is less space in the home to work separately from others, even though this living arrangement may have other benefits, such as childcare savings if there are grandparents in the home who can watch their grandchildren.

However, on the positive side, more study is also needed to consider the possible increased usefulness of flexibility policies for those with higher intersectional work-life needs. For example, the recently expanded access to flexibility policies can be a double-edged sword for women (Villamor et al., 2022) particularly regarding remote work as the decreased emphasis on physical presence with remote work has allowed increased efficiency for workers of color and other stigmatized employees who may no longer feel the need to conceal their nonwork roles or other salient identities to appear as part of their team (Kossek et al., 2021). This process loss from constant code-switching may be reduced in an environment where workers do not feel as though they are constantly under the threat of being judged and working to fend off such stereotypes (Block et al., 2011). Future research should consider the ways in which work-life intersectionality may attenuate and strengthen the positive relationship between work-life flexibility policy use, control, and positive outcomes.

Individual Implementation

Intersectionality Consideration #4

Work-life intersectionality necessitates the management of multiple nonwork identities which can compete for or shift in salience and extent of stigmatization. While the traditional work–nonwork model of work-life flexibility does contemplate how the implementation of flexibility may be impacted by the salience of nonwork identities, it has not extended to consideration of multiple intersectional identities. One area ripe for future development concerns the agency of individuals and the potential strengths of intersectional identities. Identities are in flux, and aspects of one's identities may be more salient or influential depending on both the identity work of the individual and the context (Corlett & Mavin, 2014). Intersectional identities, while generally stigmatized, may be less so in certain contexts, as in the work of Czarniawska and Sevon (2008) showing that foreign women professors are not doubly disadvantaged but instead enjoy greater success. Further, recent scholarship within Indigenous traditions has noted the need to avoid a deficit model in which holding an Indigenous identity is associated exclusively with limitations and stigma, overlooking the rich cultural resources also associated (Bryant et al., 2021).

As an example, since women of color are neither perceived as the prototypical woman nor the prototypical male member of their subordinated race, they may escape some of the parenting stigma that white women face due to intersectional invisibility (Purdie-Vaughns & Eibach, 2008). Just as some Black women can be agentic and not suffer the double-bind backlash for not following proscriptive stereotypes for women to be caring (Rosette & Livingston, 2012; Rudman et al., 2001), it is possible that Black women are able to bring their whole selves to their roles without incurring similar backlash. However, it could be the case that enacting flexible work-life policies is what renders those with multiple marginalized identities who would otherwise be invisible, visible (Lyons et al., 2018). For example, while white men have intersecting privileged identities of gender and race, some may have less visible stigmatized identities such as being gay or disabled that may become more salient if work-life flexibility is sought on account of their sexual orientation or disability status, such as requesting part-time or remote work after adopting a baby or to manage an illness. And across national cultures, such a request may be less stigmatized in some nations (e.g., the UK) where the right to request flexibility is supported through national legislation as an employment right (Kossek & Kelliher, 2022).

The MOSAIC model (Hall et al., 2019) provides a framework that allows for the consideration of how multiple marginalized nonwork identities can shift in salience. While Black women, for instance, deal with a variety of positive and negative stereotypes, seeking flexible work-life policies may invoke other stereotypes that may highlight their nonwork identity, such as being a single parent (Kennely, 1999), which can be accompanied by new stereotypes to fend off (Block et al., 2011). As reflected in the MOSAIC model, varied caregiving needs of one's layered identities may result in anticipated needs for flexibility such as needing to work a reduced load or remotely via flextime and flexplace, whereas sudden needs for flexibility that may make one's multiple identities more salient may be more difficult to navigate. In the case of Black women, contending against stereotypes (Merriweather & Block, 2016) related to their intersecting identities of being both a woman and expected to be more family-focused in addition to being Black with the proscriptive expectations to work more (Hall et al., 2019) can affect one's willingness to utilize flexibility policies. Additionally, employees who have multiple, marginalized identities may fear being further stigmatized due to having higher intersecting salient nonwork identities and incurring backlash, which can affect team processes as they may try to use flexibility (e.g., flexible scheduling and remote work) in ways that help them keep these identities less visible. All these factors contribute to the work-life inequality that affects those with intersecting identities differently than what has been traditionally discussed in the literature.

Further, having the potential of more nonwork identities to manage, which increases the capacity through which shifting can occur, can affect the implementation processes of efficiency, reciprocity, and availability. As stated previously regarding efficiency, code-switching can lead to process loss that can be attenuated if flexibility is enacted in such a way to minimize the trading off between multiple nonwork identities and one's work identity. Kossek et al. (2022) have found that under-represented individuals appreciate when their departments offer diversity, equity, and inclusion training because this training aligns with their values, leading workers to reciprocate with positive attitudes such as higher satisfaction and commitment. Similar reciprocity dynamics could exist for those with multiple nonwork identities who are able to shift the salience of such identities and who could benefit more from work-life flexibility policies. Regarding availability, individuals with multiple stigmatized identities may have more nonwork constraints and expanded views of their desire to invest in their nonwork role which affects their work visibility and availability. While shifting the competing salience of one's multiple nonwork identities could lead to decreased availability for the work role, it could also lead to increased availability for multiple nonwork roles and thereby improved nonwork performance.

Workgroup Implementation

Intersectionality Consideration #5

The work-life intersectionality of members might create invisible, deep-level diversity within workgroups that impedes control-related benefits.

As discussed above, the traditional model on work-life flexibility acknowledges that not all workgroups and teams are supportive of flexibility and identifies two key practices that enhance flexibility outcomes: ROWE and collaborative time management. These practices change the workgroup culture in ways that enhance norms of reciprocity, efficiency, and availability to team members as well as the importance of completing high-value tasks. Whether and how these dynamics might differ for individuals with multiple stigmatized identities is yet unknown.

There has, however, been an extensive related literature examining the effects of diversity in teams, which has actively debated whether heterogeneity within teams is beneficial or harmful, at least in terms of group performance (Horwitz & Horwitz, 2007). Within this literature, it is common to distinguish two types of diversity on teams: (1) visible or "surface-level" diversity, typically linked to bio-demographic characteristics such as race, age, or gender and (2) task-related or cognitive diversity related to experience and skills to perform the work (Harrison et al., 1998; Pelled, 1996). Reviews have concluded that only the latter task-related diversity enhances performance, with no effect for bio-demographic diversity (Horwitz & Horwitz, 2007).

An acknowledged limitation of these conclusions is that they are grounded in only few studies of bio-demographic diversity (Horwitz & Horwitz, 2007). Further, the distinction between visible-sociodemographic and task-related diversity overlooks the experience of many with stigmatized but invisible differences such as members of the LGBTQ+ community. Bowen and Blackmon (2003) have shown that individuals with "invisible" sources of diversity including sexual orientation may exist within "spirals of silence" (p. 1393) in which they avoid disclosing their personal circumstances due to the risk that colleagues will not support them, leading them to also avoid exercising voice in the workplace in general. The hesitation to disrupt the dominant discourse of the workplace on the part of these individuals is driven by perceptions of lower power and greater risk and thus is likely an experience shared by those with multiple stigmatized identities (some of which may be visible, as well). The results-focused work environment and collaborative time management practices envisioned as enhancing work-life flexibility implementation are premised on open communication within the workgroup. Instead, an intersectional lens shows that not all individuals may be empowered to equal participation in those collaborative processes. On the one hand, this may lead individuals with stigmatized identities to avoid disclosing nonwork needs, increasing their availability to colleagues and work performance at the expense of nonwork outcomes. On the other hand, without the ability to express their true needs, these same individuals may not utilize the control offered by their work-life flexibility policy to work at their most efficient times and places.

Work-Life Intersectionality and Nonwork Performance

Intersectionality Consideration #6

Nonwork role performance may include an expanded set of outcomes and expectations for individuals with stigmatized work-life identities. Here we focus on nonwork performance, highlighting how the nature of nonwork performance may require revisiting an intersectional approach. Consideration of nonwork outcomes is equally relevant for both the traditional and intersectional approaches given that both inherently recognize employees' role responsibilities and lives outside of the workplace. We believe that consideration of intersectionality from an identity standpoint opens up more nonwork identities and variation in nonwork resources and demands and – because we are thinking about identities more broadly – we may need to think about more experiences, impacts, and types of outcomes. For example, the pathways within our model should yield a positive impact on family engagement – which refers to attention paid to family members and absorption in family activities (Rothbard, 2001) – for both traditionally studied samples and those with stigmatized identities. Relatedly, boundary control afforded through work-life flexibility policies should benefit a variety of nonwork outcomes associated with participation in community, school, and leisure activities regardless of whether intersectionality is a prevalent theme or consideration (Keeney et al., 2013). Yet while these expanded nonwork outcomes are receiving increased attention (e.g., work-school conflict; Park & Sprung, 2015), integrating intersectionality considerations sheds light on the depth to and nuance with which they can be addressed. We provide three examples below.

First, boundary control afforded through work-life flexibility policies can facilitate *othermothering*, defined as "acceptance of responsibility for a child not one's own, in an arrangement that may or may not be formal" (Edwards, 2000, p. 88). Stemming from communal lifestyles in West Africa and exacerbated through the familial instabilities caused by enslavement in the United States and beyond (where Black women would take on caregiving responsibilities for children whose parents had been sold to other slaveowners; James, 1993), the fulfillment of duties associated with the modern day practice of taking on the role of a "community mother" to care for others' children is a unique nonwork performance outcome that may be particularly specific to Black women and can be facilitated through work-life flexibility policy use.

Second, boundary control afforded through work-life flexibility policies can facilitate *community activism*. Intersectional activism efforts aimed at promoting social justice preceded academic research on the topic (Moradi & Grzanka, 2017). Nonetheless, many grassroots efforts – including the #SayHerName social movement – remain prevalent today (Brown et al., 2017; Heaney, 2021). Although research on allyship recognizes the participation of "advantaged" individuals, individuals with intersectional stigmatized identities may be more likely to play a larger, central, or more active role in such efforts (Dahling, et al., 2016; Radke et al., 2020). Work-life flexibility policies that afford spatial and temporal control can enhance the degree to which individuals engage in community activism by allowing for greater participation in activities including voting, petition signing, civil disobedience, protesting, and attending meetings (Swank & Fahs, 2013).

Third, boundary control afforded through work-life flexibility policies can facilitate *educational attainment while working*. On the one hand, those with intersectional identities in pursuit of higher education may demonstrate more of a "hustle" compared to traditionally studied samples in work-life research, including their use of part-time work (perhaps facilitated by size control) in blue collar occupations to pay their way through school compared to white collar workers afforded more temporal and spatial control whose organizations sponsor their MBA degree (Reed & Brown, 2013). On the other hand, individuals' previous experiences of stigmatization associated with their intersectional identities might diminish self-efficacy when pursuing higher education while working or might serve to deter this pursuit altogether (Corsi et al., 2021; Mirza, 2018; Mkhize & Pillay, 2018). Regardless of which perspective is more applicable to a specific individual with an intersectional identity, the use of work-life flexibility policies should reduce work-school conflict while the organizational support embedded in the ability to use the policy can further enhance their self-efficacy.

DISCUSSION

We drew on Kossek et al.'s (2022) boundary control and implementation framework on work-life flexibility policies which established that different types of control and implementation domains are important for shaping the relationships between policies and outcomes. In this paper, we extended those ideas to (1) specify the mechanisms (availability, reciprocity, efficiency) and moderators (e.g., organizational, group, and individual) to work and nonwork performance; and (2) explore individual employee intersectionality considerations related to flexibility access, use and consequences. In the first part we examined mechanisms and moderators shaping the relationship between boundary control, use, and performance using a traditional variable-centered approach. Then we reviewed the model in the intersectionality section of this paper to extend this work by drawing attention to which types of people are more likely to access, differentially use, and likely benefit from different types of control. That is, whether individuals get to use flexibility policies, how they experience them, and the outcomes they achieve may depend in part on who they are in terms of the extent of their overlapping work-life identities.

Contributions to the Work-Life Literature

First, our model advances understanding because it *makes transparent the mechanisms by which work-life flexibility policy use affects work and nonwork performance*. Boundary control enhances performance at home through its effects on availability for nonwork demands and at work through its impacts on efficiency, reciprocity, and availability for the work role. This perspective opens new research avenues distinguishing the use of specific policies and the amount of control over different dimensions of the work role boundary. We contribute to the development of theory by suggesting that scholars identify the consequences of boundary control via availability, efficiency, and reciprocity on performance in multiple domains. We also added to the literature by considering how reciprocity, efficiency, and availability can operate differently depending on organizational, team, and individual moderators that are related to the synthesis of multiple work-life identities and roles through intersectionality.

Second and most importantly, given that the diversity and work-life literatures are under-integrated, we noted that an intersectional view can extend current flexibility research by advancing perspectives to question whether and the extent to which work-life flexibility enhances boundary control and for whom. An intersectional lens suggests a need to consider how individuals' experiences with work-life flexibility policies occur reflected in a broader cultural and historical context. We hope this paper encourages future work to not only use variable-centered approaches to understand work-life flexibility but also with the integration of identity and intersectionality we propose to move toward more person-centered approaches. This paper suggests scholars need to increasingly pay attention to which types of people are using and likely benefiting from different types of control afforded by various work-life flexibility policies. This leads us to suggest the need for future research to incorporate intersectional views that look at clustered relationships between multiple forms of work-life diversity to augment the traditional work-life literature and provide a re-conceptualization of work-life flexibility policies as practices enhancing work role boundary control to support work-life inclusion. Although work-life flexibility policies offer opportunities to increase employee control over the work role boundary to enhance nonwork and work performance, we surmised that this assumption may need to be empirically examined with more diverse samples that include many intersectional analyses. The theoretical underdevelopment of the work-life flexibility literature regarding intersectionality remains problematic since intersectionality may be an indicator of reduced access to flexibility policies and attenuated benefits of control for performance for some employee groups, particularly those with many identities that may lead to their marginalization in society such as gender, class, religion, and race among many others.

Future work-life flexibility policy research needs to integrate variable and person-centered approaches. We call for research to incorporate the concept of work-life intersectionality into future theorizing. Adding an intersectional lens may advance work-life flexibility research theoretically by considering how multiple forms of identity such as race, gender, sexuality, and nonwork identities and demands intersect to enhance or attenuate assumed work-life relationships related to conflict and enrichment due to differential resource access, power dynamics, and differential work-life demands and needs and benefits of use. For example, an intersectional lens may help explain why the pandemic and ways that employers managed flexibility access and use for different jobs differentially affected many employees with multiple stigmatized identities such as women of color in frontline jobs such as nurses and teachers.

Future research should also consider how work-life intersectionality impacts the shifting of salience between work and nonwork identities and empirically explore the MOSAIC framework (Hall et al., 2019) as applied to work-life flexibility. This model of stereotype activation through intersectional and associated categories could demonstrate how individuals among the spectrum of work-life intersectionality may have varied work and nonwork outcomes. Considering how intersectional categories can be activated and made visible through the enactment of flexibility policies would illuminate how such structures are embedded into organizational life. It is possible that different nonwork identities are made salient in different combinations based on the use of various flexible work-life policies. Future research could explore which work and nonwork identities may significantly intersect with which combination of policies that could result in differing work and nonwork outcomes. For instance, an Asian-American woman may benefit from intersectional invisibility (Purdie-Vaughns & Eibach, 2008) for neither being the prototypical woman on account of her race and ethnicity nor the prototypical Asian-American on account of her gender. However, if she were to utilize a flexibility policy, such as remote work, that would enable her to better care for an aging parent, this may highlight her ethnicity and the widely held societal belief of the Asian community and respect for older persons. While this is not a negative stereotype per se, it could have practical implications for flexibility policy use that should be considered from a Human Resources perspective.

In practice, organizations can think proactively about how the availability of work-life flexibility policies have differing implications for those with varied work-life intersectionality. Just as it is essential that organizations consider how flexible work-life policies cluster to create optimum work–nonwork management (Kossek et al., 2022), so too is it necessary that Human Resources professionals consider the various cluster of demographics within their organizations and how the latter impact the former and vice versa. Third, we advance theorizing by suggesting that scholars should assume that work-life flexibility typically has mixed consequences for performance in multiple domains that may not be aligned unless one holistically understands supportive organizational, group, and individual (including intersectionality related) implementation conditions. Previous reviews suggest that flexibility often has varied results for employees and employers (Allen et al., 2013; de Menezes & Kelliher, 2011; Kossek & Lautsch, 2018). Yet work-life research typically focuses either on performance in one domain but not the other or alternatively assumes a "dual agenda" (Bailyn, 2011) of beneficial effects of work-life flexibility for both employees and employers without investigating moderators that may condition these effects. Our model comprehensively specifies the conditions under which flexibility promotes performance and demonstrates how it can have differential consequences for work and nonwork outcomes. Work-life flexibility and control over the work role boundary is likely to enhance nonwork performance, but it may negatively affect work performance at the same time, if implemented poorly by the organization in ways that do not foster customization, inclusion, or cultural support. Or flexibility may be enacted by individuals with too many interruptions of the work role; or conversely employees may not use their flexibility to become more available for nonwork roles, but instead overwork. And groups may enable or constrain employees who have work-life flexibility from performing well at work if they adopt a heavy face-time-oriented culture and do not support collaborative scheduling or PTO or respect many forms of work-life diversity.

For the dual agenda of joint work and nonwork gains through work-life flexibility initiatives to be realized would require attention to implementation across levels as well as to intersectional considerations. The starting point would be equalized access to an expansive and customizable set of flexibility practices, implemented with cultural support within organizations to limit backlash and enhance inclusivity. Although the work-life literature understands the importance of cultural support and informal customizability (e.g., i-deals), greater consideration of formalized customizability within the HR system – as well as the strength of the HR system itself – is required. As workgroups transition to work-life flexibility, they must enact supportive practices such as a ROWE and collaborative time management, in a manner that is respectful and adaptive to power dynamics that may inhibit some group members from full participation in the open discussions these practices require. Future research and practice should consider, for example, the distinct approaches that might best work to include individuals with both visible and invisible sources of stigma in flexible work coordination. Individuals and nonwork partners similarly have roles in work-life flexibility implementation as both the salience of work and nonwork identities, and unique demands and resources of the nonwork setting shape multi-domain outcomes.

Finally, adding an intersectional lens suggests a need to broaden examination of nonwork performance in management research. People experience diversity in their home circumstances, and in the communities in which they live outside of work, which can create unique priorities in terms of nonwork outcomes. The management literature has sorely under-emphasized the importance of well-being and performance in the nonwork domain despite its criticality for most employees who increasingly vary in nonwork resources and demands. Thus, human resource studies should include not just work measures of performance and effectiveness but measures of nonwork performance and effectiveness as a basic practice.

Adding an intersectional lens also suggests that research needs to follow individuals and organizations as they adapt to changing nonwork (as one ages and undergoes work-life changes) and work environments (e.g., a pandemic); *work-life flexibility should be understood as an evolving process occurring over time*. For example, (1) organizations can change how they implement policies to be more work-life inclusive to support work-life intersectionality. For example, they might conduct studies to ensure access to and use of policies is effective for employees across many work-life backgrounds; or (2) work groups can change work cultures, and team scheduling and time off practices to be more respectful of many overlapping intersectional work-life identities; This would entail giving all employees some say in how work-life flexibility is implemented to provide equal access and benefits. And importantly (3) individuals can shift the salience that they attach to particular identities over the life course, and how they intersect which can alter how they enact work-life flexibility in a particular societal institutional context. For example, a single employee who generally liked to work in the office may seek to now move to remote work when they get married and have a new child, and their spouse has an immigrant family that lives overseas resulting in increased older adult care and family commitments during different hours of the day. Collectively, these areas provide a rich integration of critical conditions that matter for understanding linkages between work-life flexibility and performance at work and home.

In sum, future research must be conducted to identify the aggregate employer conditions (organization, team, individual) under which work-life flexibility can enhance performance in both domains, consistent with a dual agenda perspective. Experiments in the lab and the field should be done to understand the multilevel conditions that identify what it would it take for flexibility to promote performance in both domains concurrently. Such studies would also need to attend to implementation in the home and societal domains which are often under-examined in human resource and management studies. Lastly, policy-capturing studies should be conducted that involve partnering with innovative employers who are implementing such practices, perhaps ahead of research science to capture innovative and creative solutions occurring in workplaces. Similarly, intervention studies to identify the barriers to transferring best practices in implementing flexibility and in fostering widespread dissemination of HRM best practices are sorely needed for future study.

CONCLUSIONS

The effective implementation of work-life flexibility policies in ways that benefit performance for an increasingly diverse workforce in a transformed workplace that is increasingly crossing diverse boundaries at work and home is not well-understood. To advance understanding, we developed theory conceptualizing work-life flexibility policy use as sources of work role boundary control and identify multilevel moderators of the conditions under which using policies enhances control over the work role and performance on and off the job. Many employers have moved away from providing job security and lengthy careers in an increasingly turbulent economic world often undergoing massive disruptions in work organization. Societal safety nets for family support are also devolving in many countries. Work-life flexibility balances these pressures serving as a social vehicle arbitrating employees' needs to have greater control over their personal and family lives, and employers' interests in controlling how, when, and where work roles are enacted in a 24/7 world. Our integrative theory fosters new insights to broaden research to examine the dynamics of accessing and using flexibility policies and their linkages to employees' control over the work boundary and their work-life intersectionality in order to better close the work-life flexibility implementation gap.

ACKNOWLEDGMENT

We thank Tina Garwood and the Mitchell E. Daniels Junior School of Business Purdue University for administrative support.

REFERENCES

Acker, J. (2006). Inequality regimes: Gender, class and race in organizations. *Gender & Society*, *20*, 441–464.

Adler, P., & Kwon, S., (2002). Social capital prospects for a new concept. *The Academy of Management Review*, *27*, 17–40.

Alderfer, C. (1983). An intergroup perspective on group dynamics. In J. Lorsch (Ed.), *Handbook of organizational behavior* (pp. 190–222). Prentice Hall.

Allen, T., Johnson, R., Kiburz, K. M., & Shockley, K. (2013). Work–family conflict and flexible work arrangements: Deconstructing flexibility. *Personnel Psychology*, 66, 345–376.

Alonso-Villar, O., Del Rio, C., & Gradin, C. (2012). The extent of occupational segregation in the United States. *Industrial Relations (Berkeley)*, *51*(2), 179–212.

Alzahabi, R., Becker, M., & Hambrick, D. (2017). Investigating the relationship between media multitasking and processes involved in task-switching. *Journal of Experimental Psychology: Human Perception and Performance*, *43*, 1872–1894.

Amabile, T. M. (1998). How to kill creativity. *Harvard Business Review*, Sept./Oct., 77–87.

Amatea, E., Cross, E., Clark, J., & Bobby, C. (1986). Assessing the work and family role expectations of career-oriented men and women: The life role salience scales. *Journal of Marriage and the Family*, *48*, 831–838.

Aryee, S., Chu, C. W. L., Kim, T.-Y., & Ryu, S. (2013). Family-supportive work environment and employee work behaviors: An investigation of mediating mechanisms. *Journal of Management*, *39*(3), 792–813.

Ashforth, B. E., Kreiner, G. E., & Fugate, M. (2000). All in a day's work: Boundaries and micro role transitions. *Academy of Management Review*, *25*, 472–491.

Atewologun, D., Sealy, R., & Vinnicombe, S. (2016). Revealing intersectional dynamics in organizations: Introducing 'intersectional identity work'. *Gender, Work and Organization*, *23*, 223–247.

Baethge, A., & Rigotti, T. (2013). Interruptions to workflow: Their relationship with irritation and satisfaction with performance, and the mediating roles of time pressure and mental demands. *Work & Stress*, *27*, 43–63.

Bailyn, L. (1993) *Breaking the mold.* Basic Books.

Bailyn, L. (2011). Redesigning work for gender equity and work-personal life integration. *Community, Work & Family*, *14*, 97–112.

Bailyn, L., Fletcher, J., & Kolb, D. (1997). Unexpected connections: Considering employees' personal lives can revitalize your business. *Sloan Management Review*, Summer, 11–19.

Bamboo HR. (2022). https://www.bamboohr.com/hr-glossary/bring-your-own-device-byod/

Barsness, Z. I., Diekmann, K. A., & Seidel, M.-D. L. (2005). Motivation and opportunity: The role of remote work, demographic dissimilarity, and social network centrality in impression management. *Academy of Management Journal*, *48*(3), 401–419.

Beauregard, T. A., Adamson, M., Kunter, A., Miles, L., & Roper, I. (2020). Diversity in the work–life interface: Introduction to the special issue. Equality, Diversity and Inclusion: *An International Journal*, *39*(5), 465–478.

Beauregard, T. A., & Henry, C. L. (2009). Making the link between work–life balance practices and organizational performance. *Human Resource Management Review*, 19, 9–22.

Bergman, L., & Magnusson, D. (1997). A person-oriented approach in research on developmental psychopathology. *Development and Psychopathology*, *9*(2), 291–319.

Binyamin, G., & Carmeli, A. (2010). Does structuring of human resource management processes enhance employee creativity? The mediating role of psychological availability. *Human Resource Management*, *49*, 999–1024.

Blair-Loy, M., & Wharton, A. (2002). Employees' use of work-family policies and the workplace social context. *Social Forces*, *80*, 813–845.

Blau, F. D., Brummund, P., & Yung-Hsu Liu, A. (2013). Trends in occupational segregation by gender 1970-2009. *Demography*, *50*(2), 471–492. https://doi.org/10.1007/s13524-012-0151-7

Block, C. J., Koch, S. M., Liberman, B. E., Merriweather, T. J., & Roberson, L. (2011). Contending with stereotype threat at work: A model of long-term responses. *The Counseling Psychologist*, *39*(4), 570–600.

Bowen, D. E., & Ostroff, C. (2004). Understanding HRM–firm performance linkages: The role of the "strength" of the HRM system. *Academy of Management Review*, *29*(2), 203–221.

Bowen, F., & Blackmon, K. (2003). Spirals of silence: The dynamic effects of diversity on organizational voice. *Journal of Management Studies*, *40*(6), 1393–1417.

Brescoll, V., Glass, J., & Sedlovskaya, A. (2013). Ask and ye shall receive? The dynamics of employer-provided flexible work options and the need for public policy. *Journal of Social Issues*, *69*, 367–388.

Brewer, M. B. (1991). The social self: On being the same and different at the same time. *Personality and Social Psychology Bulletin*, *17*(5), 475–482. https://doi.org/10.1177/0146167291175001

Briscoe, F., & Kellogg, K. C. (2011). The initial assignment effect: Local employer practices and positive career outcomes for work-family program users. *American Sociological Review*, *76*(2), 291–319.

Brown, M., Ray, R., Summers, E., & Fraistat, N. (2017). #SayHerName: A case study of intersectional social media activism. *Ethnic and Racial Studies*, *40*(11), 1831–1846.

Bryant, J., Bolt, R., Botfield, J. R., Martin, K., Doyle, M., Murphy, D., Graham, S., Newman, C. E., Bell, S., Treloar, C., Browne, A. J., & Aggleton, P. (2021). Beyond deficit: 'Strengths-based approaches' in Indigenous health research. *Sociology of Health & Illness*, *43*(6), 1405–1421.

Bundale, B. (2022). *Remote work debate intensifies as companies mandate return to office after-labour day*. https://www.ctvnews.ca/business/remote-work-debate-intensifies-as-companies-mandate-return-to-office-after-labour-day-1.6053351

Burrell, L. Adams, G., Durand, D., & Castro, C. 2006. The impact of military lifestyle demands on well-being, Army, and family outcomes. *Armed Forces & Society*, *33*, 43–58.

Byron, K. (2005). A meta-analytic review of work–family conflict and its antecedents. *Journal of Vocational Behavior*, *67*(2), 169–198.

Capitano, J., DiRenzo, M., Aten, K., & Greenhaus, J. (2017). Role identity salience and boundary permeability preferences: An examination of enactment and protection effects. *Journal of Vocational Behavior*, *102*, 99–111.

Capitano, J., McAlpine, K. L., & Greenhaus, J. H. (2019). Organizational influences on work–home boundary permeability: A multidimensional perspective. In M. R. Buckley, A. R. Wheeler, J. E. Baur, & J. R. B. Halbesleben, J. R. B (Eds.), *Research in personnel and human resources management (research in personnel and human resources management)* (Vol. 37, pp. 133–172). Emerald Publishing Limited.

Carbado, D. W., & Harris, C. I. (2019). Intersectionality at 30: Mapping the margins of anti-essentialism, intersectionality, and dominance theory. *Harvard Law Review*, *132*(8), 2193–2239.

Carlson, D., & Kacmar, K. (2000). Work-family conflict in the organization: Do life role values make a difference? *Journal of Management*, *26*, 1031–1054.

Casper, W. J., Eby, L. T., Bordeaux, C., Lockwood, A., & Lambert, D. (2007a). A review of research methods in IO/OB work-family research. *Journal of Applied Psychology*, *92*(1), 28–43.

Casper, W. J., Weltman, D., & Kwesiga, E. (2007b). Beyond family-friendly: The construct and measurement of singles-friendly work culture. *Journal of Vocational Behavior*, *70*(3), 478–501.

Chen, A., & Karahanna, E. (2014). Boundaryless technology: Understanding the effects of technology-mediated interruptions across the boundaries between work and personal life. *AIS Transactions on Human-Computer Interaction*, *6*, 16–36.

Corlett, S., & Mavin, S. (2014). Intersectionality, identity and identity work. *Gender in Management*, *29*(5), 258–276. https://doi.org/10.1108/GM-12-2013-0138

Corsi, M., Zacchia, G., & Zuazu, I. (2021). Intersectional gaps in self-efficacy among post-graduate students in international renewable-energy programs: The role of maternal employment. *Social Sciences*, *10*(7), 242.

Crain, T. L., & Stevens, S. C. (2018). Family-supportive supervisor behaviors: A review and recommendations for research and practice. *Journal of Organizational Behavior*, *39*, 869–888.

Crenshaw, K. (1989). Demarginalizing the intersection of race and sex: A black feminist critique of anti-discrimination doctrine, feminist theory and anti-racist politics. *University of Chicago Legal Forum*, *1989*, 139–167.

Crenshaw, K. (1991). Mapping the margins: Intersectionality, identity politics, and violence against women of color. *Stanford Law Review*, *43*(6), 1241.

Czarniawska, B., & Sevon, G. (2008). The thin edge of the wedge: Foreign women professors as double strangers in academia. *Gender, Work and Organization*, *15*(3), 235–287.

Dahling, J. J., Wiley, S., Fishman, Z. A., & Loihle, A. (2016). A stake in the fight: When do heterosexual employees resist organizational policies that deny marriage equality to LGB peers? *Organizational Behavior and Human Decision Processes*, *132*, 1–15.

De Menezes, L., & Kelliher, C. (2011). Flexible working and performance: A systematic review of the evidence for a business case. *International Journal of Management Reviews*, *13*, 452–474.

DePaulo, B. M., & Morris, W. L. (2005). Singles in society and in science. *Psychological Inquiry*, *16*(2–3), 57–83.

Duxbury, L., & Halinski, M. (2014). When more is less: An examination of the relationship between hours in telework and role overload. *Work*, *48*, 91–103.

Eaton, S. C. (2003). If you can use them: Flexibility policies, organizational commitment, and perceived performance. *Industrial Relations*, *42*(2), 145–167. https://doi.org/10.1111/1468-232X.00285

Eddleston, K. A., & Mulki, J. 2017. Toward understanding remote workers' management of work–family boundaries: The complexity of workplace embeddedness. *Group & Organization Management*, *42*, 346–387.

Edwards, A. E. (2000). Community mothering: The relationship between mothering and the community work of Black women. *Journal of the Motherhood Initiative for Research and Community Involvement*, *2*(2), 87–100.

Edwards, J. R., & Rothbard, N. P. (2000). Mechanisms linking work and family: Clarifying the relationship between work and family constructs. *Academy of Management Review*, *25*(1), 178–199.

Else-Quest, N. M., & Hyde, J. S. (2016). Intersectionality in quantitative psychological research: I. Theoretical and epistemological issues. *Psychology of Women Quarterly*, *40*(2), 155–170. https://doi.org/10.1177/0361684316629797

Fleming, S. (2020). July 8. Working flexibly is now the new normal for employees. Poll. https://www.weforum.org/agenda/2020/07/working-flexibly-new-normal-poll/

Gajendran, R. S., & Harrison, D. A. (2007). The good, the bad, and the unknown about telecommuting: Meta-analysis of psychological mediators and individual consequences. *Journal of Applied Psychology*, *92*, 1524–1541.

Gignac, M. A. M., Shahidi, F. V., Jetha, A., Kristman, V., Bowring, J., Cameron, J. I., Tonima, S., & Ibrahim, S. (2021). Impacts of the COVID-19 pandemic on health, financial worries, and perceived organizational support among people living with disabilities in Canada. *Disability Health Journal*, *14*(4), 101161. https://doi.org/10.1016/j.dhjo.2021.101161

Golden, L. (2001). Flexible work schedules: What are we trading off to get them? *Monthly Labor Review*, *124*, 50–67.

Greenhaus, J. H., & Beutell, N. J. (1985). Sources of conflict between work and family roles. *Academy of Management Review*, *10*, 76–88.

Greenhaus, J. H., & Powell, G. N. (2006). When work and family are allies: A theory of work-family enrichment. *The Academy of Management Review*, *31*(1), 72–92.

Greenhaus, J., Ziegert, J., & Allen, T. (2012). When family-supportive supervision matters: Relations between multiple sources of support and work-family balance. *Journal of Vocational Behavior*, *80*, 266–275.

Gupta, A., Li, H., & Sharda, R. (2013). Should I send this message? Understanding the impact of interruptions, social hierarchy and perceived task complexity on user performance and perceived workload. *Decision Support Systems*, *55*, 135–145.

Hall, E. V., Hall, A. V., Galinsky, A. D., & Phillips, K. W. (2019). MOSAIC: A model of stereotyping through associated and intersectional categories. *Academy of Management Review*, *44*(3), 643–672. https://doi.org/10.5465/amr.2017.0109

Hammer, L. B., Kossek, E. E., Yragui, N. L., Bodner, T. E., & Hanson, G. C. (2009). Development and validation of a multidimensional measure of family supportive supervisor behaviors (FSSB). *Journal of Management*, *35*(4), 837–856. https://doi.org/10.1177/0149206308328

Hammer, L. L., Neal, M., Newsom, J. T., Brockwood, K. J., & Colton, C. L. (2005). A longitudinal study of the effects of dual-earner couples' utilization of family-friendly workplace supports on work and family outcomes. *Journal of Applied Psychology*, *90*, 799–810.

Harrison, D. A., Price, K. H., & Bell, M. P. (1998). Beyond relational demography: Time and the effects of surface and deep-level diversity on work group cohesion. *Academy of Management Journal*, *41*, 96–107.

Heaney, M. T. (2021). Intersectionality at the grassroots. *Politics, Groups, and Identities*, *9*(3), 608–628. https://doi.org/10.1080/21565503.2019.1629318

Henly, J. R., & Lambert, S. (2014). Unpredictable work timing in retail jobs: Implications for employee work-life outcomes. *Industrial and Labor Relations Review*, *67*(3), 986–1016.

Herrera-Sánchez, I. M., León-Pérez, J. M., & León-Rubio, J. M. (2017). Steps to ensure a successful implementation of occupational health and safety interventions at an organizational level. *Frontiers in Psychology*, *8*, 2135.

hooks, b. (1984). *Feminist theory: From margin to center*. South End Press.

Hornung, S., Rousseau, D. M., & Glaser, J. (2009). Why supervisors make idiosyncratic deals: antecedents and outcomes of i-deals from a managerial perspective. *Journal of Managerial Psychology*, *24*(8), 738–764. https://doi.org/10.1108/02683940910996770

Horwitz, S. K., & Horwitz, I. B. (2007). The effects of team diversity on team outcomes: A meta-analytic review of team demography. *Journal of Management*, *33*(6), 987–1015.

Hunton, J. E. (2005). Behavioral self-regulation of telework locations: Interrupting interruptions! *Journal of Information Systems*, *19*, 111–140.

Ichniowski, C., Shaw, K., & Prennushi, G. (1997). The effects of human resources management practices on productivity: A study of steel finishing lines. *American Economic Review*, *87*, 291–313.

Jackson-Best, F., & Edwards, N. (2018). Stigma and intersectionality: A systematic review of systematic reviews across HIV/AIDS, mental illness, and physical disability. *BMC Public Health*, *18*, 919.

James, S. M. (1993). Mothering: A possible Black feminist link to social transformation. In S. M. James & A. A. Busia (Eds.), *Theorizing Black feminisms: The visionary pragmatism of Black women* (pp. 32–44). Routledge.

Jett, Q., & George, J. (2003). Work interrupted: A closer look at the role of interruptions in organizational life. *The Academy of Management Review*, *28*(3), 494–507.

Kahn, W. A. (1990). Psychological conditions of personal engagement and disengagement at work. *Academy of Management Journal*, *33*, 692–724.

Kamenou, N. (2008). Reconsidering work–life balance debates: Challenging limited understandings of the 'life' component in the context of ethnic minority women's experiences. *British Journal of Management*, *19*, S99–S109. https://doi.org/10.1111/j.1467-8551.2008.00575.x

Kanter, R. (1983). *Men and women of the corporation*. Basic Books.

Katzell, R. A., & Austin, J. T. (1992). From then to now: The development of industrial-organizational psychology in the United States. *Journal of Applied Psychology*, *77*(6), 803–835. https://doi.org/10.1037/0021-9010.77.6.803

Keeney, J., Boyd, E. M., Sinha, R., Westring, A. F., & Ryan, A. M. (2013). From "work–family" to "work–life": Broadening our conceptualization and measurement. *Journal of Vocational Behavior*, *82*(3), 221–237. https://doi.org/10.1016/j.jvb.2013.01.005

Kelly, E., Ammons, S., Chermack, K., & Moen, P. (2010). Confronting the ideal worker norm in a White-collar organization. *Gender and Society*, *24*(3), 281–303.

Kelly, J. (2022). *JP Morgan requires employees to return to their offices by July striking-a blow to the remote work trend?* https://www.forbes.com/sites/jackkelly/2021/04/28/jp-morgan-requires-employees-to-return-to-their-offices-by-july-striking-a-blow-to-the-remote-work-trend/?sh=4b2ec5394cdc

Kennedy, A. (2022). Finding a new normal: Embracing flexibility for a better era of working. *Forbes*. https://www.forbes.com/sites/forbescommunicationscouncil/2022/03/02/finding-a-new-normal-embracing-flexibility-for-a-better-era-of-working/?sh=7adc9091171c

Kirby, E., & Krone, K. (2002). The policy exists but you can't really use it: Communication and the structuration of work-family policies. *Journal of Applied Communication Research*, *30*(1), 50–77. https://doi.org/10.1080/00909880216577

Kolhatkar, S. (2021). *What about work-life balance for low-wage women of color?* https://www.yesmagazine.org/social-justice/2021/10/04/work-life-balance-low-wage-women-of-color

Kossek, E. E., Dumas, T. L., Piszczek, M. M., & Allen, T. D. (2021). Pushing the boundaries: A qualitative study of how stem women adapted to disrupted work–nonwork boundaries during the COVID-19 pandemic. *Journal of Applied Psychology*, *106*, 1615–1629.

Kossek, E. E., Gettings, P., Misra, K., & Berg, P. (2014). Balanced and imbalanced workplace flexibility: Cultures of flexibility practice across organizations. Paper presented at National Academy of Management meetings, Philadelphia, PA.

Kossek, E. E., & Kelliher, C. (2022). Making flexibility more i-deal: Advancing work-life equality collectively. *Group and Organization Management*. https://doi.org/10.1177/10596011221098823

Kossek, E. E., & Lautsch, B. (2012). Work-family boundary management styles in organizations: A cross-level model. *Organizational Psychology Review*, *2*, 152–171.

Kossek, E. E., & Lautsch, B. (2018). Work-life flexibility for whom? Occupational status and work-life inequality in upper, middle, and lower level jobs. *The Academy of Management Annals*, *12*(1), 5–6.

Kossek, E. E., Lautsch, B., & Eaton, S. (2006). Telecommuting, control, and boundary management: Correlates of policy use, job control, and work-family effectiveness. *Journal of Vocational Behavior*, *68*, 347–367.

Kossek, E. E., & Lee, K.-H. (2020). The Coronavirus & work–life inequality: Three evidence-based initiatives to update U.S. work–life employment policies. *Behavioral Science & Policy*. https://behavioralpolicy.org/journal_issue/covid-19/

Kossek, E. E., & Michel, J. (2011). Flexible work scheduling. In S. Zedeck (Ed.). *Handbook of industrial-organizational psychology* (Vol. 1, pp. 535–572). APA.

Kossek, E. E., Perrigino, M., & Lautsch, B. L. (2022). Work-life flexibility policies from a boundary control and implementation perspective: A review and research framework. *Journal of Management*. https://doi.org/10.1177/01492063221140354

Kossek, E. E., Perrigino, M., Russo, M., & Morandin, G. (2023). Missed connections between the leadership and work-life fields: Work-life supportive leadership as the key to the dual agenda. *Academy of Management Annals*, *17*(1), 181–217.

Kossek, E. E., Pichler, S., Bodner, T., & Hammer, L. B. (2011). Workplace social support and work–family conflict: A meta-analysis clarifying the influence of general and work–family-specific supervisor and organizational support. *Personnel Psychology*, *64*(2), 289–313.

Kossek, E. E., Ruderman, M., Braddy, P., & Hannum, K. (2012). Work-nonwork boundary management profiles: A person-centered approach. *Journal of Vocational Behavior*, *81*, 112–128.

Kossek, E. E., & Thompson, R. (2016). Workplace flexibility: Integrating employer and employee perspectives to close the research-practice implementation gap. In L. Eby & T. Allen (Eds.), *Oxford handbook of work and family* (pp. 255–270). Oxford.

Kossek, E. E., Thompson, R., & Lautsch, L. (2015). Balanced flexibility: Avoiding the traps. *California Management Review*, *57*, 3–25.

Lautsch, B. A., Kossek, E. E., & Eaton, S. C. (2009). Supervisory approaches and paradoxes in managing telecommuting implementation. *Human Relations*, *62*, 795–827.

Leonard, B. (2013). Is flex blurring the boundaries between work and home? *HR News*. Society for Human Resource Management. https://www.shrm.org/hr-today/news/hr-news/pages/flex-work-overtime.aspx

Leslie, L., Manchester, C., Park, T., & Mehung, S. (2012). Flexible work practices: A source of career premiums or penalties? *Academy of Management Journal*, *56*, 1407–1428.

Lobel, S. A., & St. Clair, L. (1992). Effects of family responsibilities, gender, and career identity salience on performance outcomes. *Academy of Management Journal*, *35*(5), 1057–1069.

Lyons, B. J., Martinez, L. R., Ruggs, E. N., Hebl, M. R., Ryan, A. M., O'Brien, K. R., & Roebuck, A. (2018). To say or not to say: Different strategies of acknowledging a visible disability. *Journal of Management*, *44*(5), 1980–2007.

May, D. R., Gilson, R. L., & Harter, L. M. (2004). The psychological conditions of meaningfulness, safety, and availability and the engagement of the human spirit at work. *Journal of Occupational and Organizational Psychology*, *77*, 11–37.

Merriweather, T. J., & Block, C. B. (2016). For colored girls who have considered management: The effect of intersectional stereotypes on perceptions of managers. Paper presented in the "Multiple Minority Identities in the Workplace" Symposium at the Academy of Management Annual Meeting, Anaheim, CA.

Miller, B. (1992). *The distribution of family oriented benefits*. EBRI Issue Brief No. 130. Employee Benefits Research Institute.

Mirza, H. S. (2018). Black bodies 'out of place' in academic spaces: Gender, race, faith and culture in post-race times. In J. Arday & H. S. Mirza (Eds.), *Dismantling race in higher education* (pp. 175–193). Cham: Palgrave Macmillan. https://doi-org.ezproxy.lib.purdue.edu/10.1007/978-3-319-60261-5_10

Mkhize, Z., & Pillay, A. (2018). Exploring Black female post-graduate science students' experiences and understandings of their intersectional identities. *Alternation Journal*, *25*(2), 249–272.

Moradi, B., & Grzanka, P. R. (2017). Using intersectionality responsibly: Toward critical epistemology, structural analysis, and social justice activism. *Journal of Counseling Psychology*, *64*(5), 500–513.

Motowidlo, S., & Kell, H. (2012). Job performance. In *Industrial and Organizational Psychology II* (Vol. 12). https://doi.org/10.1002/9781118133880.hop212005

Neale, M., & Griffin, M. A. (2006). A model of self-held work roles and role transitions. *Human Performance*, *19*(1), 23–41.

Özbilgin, M. F., Beauregard, T. A., Tatli, A., & Bell, M. P. (2011). Work-life, diversity and intersectionality: A critical review and research agenda. *International Journal of Management Reviews*, *13*(2), 177–198.

Paetzold, R. I., Dipboye, R. L., & Elsbach, K. D. (2008). A new look at stigmatization in and of organizations. *The Academy of Management Review*, *33*(1), 186–193.

Park, Y., & Sprung, J. M. (2015). Weekly work–school conflict, sleep quality, and fatigue: Recovery self-efficacy as a cross-level moderator. *Journal of Organizational Behavior*, *36*(1), 112–127.

Pelled, L. H. (1996). Demographic diversity, conflict, and work group outcomes: An intervening process theory. *Organizational Science*, *7*, 615–631.

Perlow, L. (2012). *Sleeping with your smart phone*. Harvard Business Publishing.

Perrigino, M., Dunford, B., & Wilson, K. (2018). Work-family backlash: The dark side of work-life balance policies. *The Academy of Management Annals*, *12*, 600–630.

Perry-Smith, J. E., & Blum, T. C. (2000). Work-family human resource bundles and perceived organizational performance. *Academy of Management Journal*, *43*, 1107–1117.

Peters, S. E., Dennerlein, J. T., Wagner, G. R., & Sorensen, G. (2022). Work and worker health in the post-pandemic world: A public health perspective. *The Lancet Public Health*, *7*(2), e188–e194.

Pew Research Center. (2022, March). *"Financial issues top the list of reasons U.S adults live in multigenerational homes" demographics of multigenerational households*. Pew Research Center. https://www.pewresearch.org/social-trends/2022/03/24/the-demographics-of-multigenerational-households/

Purdie-Vaughns, V., & Eibach, R. P. (2008). Intersectional invisibility: The distinctive advantages and disadvantages of multiple subordinate-group identities. *Sex Roles: A Journal of Research*, *59*(5–6), 377–391.

Radke, H. R., Kutlaca, M., Siem, B., Wright, S. C., & Becker, J. C. (2020). Beyond allyship: Motivations for advantaged group members to engage in action for disadvantaged groups. *Personality and Social Psychology Review*, *24*(4), 291–315.

Ramarajan, L. (2014). Past, present and future research on multiple identities: Toward an intrapersonal network approach. *Academy of Management Annals*, *8*(1), 589–659.

Ravenswood, K., & Harris, C. (2016). Doing gender, paying low: Gender, class and work–life balance in aged care. *Gender, Work & Organization*, *23*, 614–628.

Rawls, J. (1971). *A Theory of Justice: Original Edition*. Harvard University Press. JSTOR, https://doi.org/10.2307/j.ctvjf9z6v

Reed, N., & Brown, A. (2013). In every way I'm hustlin': The post-graduate school intersectional experiences of activist-oriented adjunct and independent scholars. *Workplace: A Journal for Academic Labor*, *22*, 71–81.

Remedios, J. D., & Snyder, S. H. (2018). Intersectional oppression: Multiple stigmatized identities and perceptions of invisibility, discrimination, and stereotyping. *Journal of Social Issues*, *74*(2), 265–281.

Ressler, C., & Thompson, J. (2008). *Why work sucks and how to fix it*. Penguin Group.

Rosette, A. S., & Livingston, R. W. (2012). Failure is not an option for Black women: Effects of organizational performance on leaders with singly versus dual-subordinate identities. *Journal of Experimental Social Psychology*, *48*(5), 1162–1167.

Rothbard, N. P. (2001). Enriching or depleting? The dynamics of engagement in work and family roles. *Administrative Science Quarterly*, *46*(4), 655–684.

Rothbard, N. P., Phillips, K., & Dumas, T. (2005). Managing multiple roles: Work-family policies and individuals' desires for segmentation. *Organization Science*, *16*, 243–258.

Rudman, L. A., & Glick, P. (2001). Prescriptive gender stereotypes and backlash toward agentic women. *Journal of Social Issues*, *57*(4), 743–762. https://doi.org/10.1111/0022-4537.00239

Rudman, L. A., & Mescher, K. (2013). Penalizing men who request a family leave: Is flexibility stigma a femininity stigma? *Journal of Social Issues*, *69*(2), 322–340.

Ruiz Castro, M., & Holvino, E. (2016). Applying intersectionality in organizations: Inequality markers, cultural scripts and advancement practices in a professional service firm. *Gender, Work & Organization*, *23*(3), 328–347.

Russo, M., Shteigman, A., & Carmeli, A. (2015). Workplace and family support and work-life balance: Implications for individual psychological availability and energy at work. *The Journal of Positive Psychology*, *11*(2), 173–188.

Ryan, A., & Kossek, E. (2008). Work-life policy implementation: Breaking down or creating barriers to inclusiveness. *Human Resource Management*, *47*, 295–310.

Ryan, A. M., & Briggs, C. Q. (2019). Improving work-life policy and practice with an intersectionality lens. *Equality, Diversity and Inclusion: An International Journal*, *39*(5), 533–547. https://doi.org/10.1108/EDI-01-2019-0049

Sexton, J., Schwartz, S., Chadwick, W., Rehder, K., Bare, J., Bokovoy, J., Doram, K., Sotile, W., Adair, K., & Profit, J. (2017). The associations between work–life balance behaviours, teamwork climate and safety climate: Cross-sectional survey introducing the work–life climate scale, psychometric properties, benchmarking data and future directions. *BMJ Quality & Safety*, *8*, 632–640.

Shepard, E., Clifton, T., & Kruse, D. (1996). Flexible work hours and productivity: Some evidence from the pharmaceutical industry. *Industrial Relations*, *35*, 123–139.

Shockley, K. M., Gabriel, A. S., Robertson, D., Rosen, C. C., Chawla, N., Ganster, M. L., & Ezerins, M. E. (2021). The fatiguing effects of camera use in virtual meetings: A within-person field experiment. *Journal of Applied Psychology*, *106*(8), 1137–1155. https://doi.org/10.1037/apl0000948

Shore, L., Randel, A., Chung, B., Dean, M., Holcombe Ehrhart, K., & Singh, G. (2011). Inclusion and diversity in work groups: A review and model for future research. *Journal of Management*, *37*, 1262–1289. https://doi.org/10.1177/0149206310385943

Sonnentag, S., & Fritz, C. (2015). Recovery from job stress: The stressor detachment model as an integrative framework. *Journal of Organizational Behavior*, *36*, S72–S103.

Standley, C. J., & Foster-Fishman, P. (2021). Intersectionality, social support, and youth suicidality: A socioecological approach to prevention. *Suicide & Life-Threatening Behavior*, *51*(2), 203–211.

Straub, C. (2012). Antecedents and organizational consequences of family supportive supervisor behavior: A multilevel conceptual framework for research. *Human Resource Management Review*, *22*, 15–26.

Stryker, S., & Serpe, R. (1982). Identity salience and psychological centrality: Equivalent, overlapping, or complementary concepts? *Social Psychology Quarterly*, *57*, 16–35.

Swank, E., & Fahs, B. (2013). An intersectional analysis of gender and race for sexual minorities who engage in gay and lesbian rights activism. *Sex Roles*, *68*(11), 660–674. https://doi.org/10.1007/s11199-012-0168-9

Swank, E., & Fahs, B. (2013). An intersectional analysis of gender and race for sexual minorities who engage in gay and lesbian rights activism. *Sex Roles: A Journal of Research*, *68*(11–12), 660–674. https://doi.org/10.1007/s11199-012-0168-9

Tajfel, H., & Turner, J. C. (1979). An integrative theory of inter-group conflict. In W. G. Austin & S. Worchel (Eds.), *The social psychology of inter-group relations* (pp. 33–47). Brooks/Cole.

ten Brummelhuis, L. L., & Bakker, A. B. (2012). A resource perspective on the work–home interface: The work–home resources model. *American Psychologist*, *67*(7), 545–556. https://doi.org/10.1037/a0027974

Thomas, L. T., & Ganster, D. C. (1995). Impact of family-supportive work variables on work-family conflict and strain: A control perspective. *Journal of Applied Psychology*, *80*(1), 6–15. https://doi.org/10.1037/0021-9010.80.1.6

Thornthwaite, L. (2004). Working time and work-family balance: A review of employees' preferences. *Asia Pacific Journal of Human Resources*, *42*(2), 166–184. https://doi.org/10.1177/1038411104045360

Trefalt, S. (2013). Between you and me: Setting work-nonwork boundaries in the context of workplace relationships. *Academy of Management Journal*, *6*, 1802–1829.

Tsui, A., & Milkovich, G. (1987). Personnel department activities: constituency perspectives and preferences. *Personnel Psychology*, *40*, 519–537.

Van Dyne, L., Kossek, E., & Lobel, S. (2007). Less need to be there: Cross level effects of work practices that support work-life flexibility and enhance group processes and group-level OCB, *Human Relations*, *60*, 1123–1153.

Wrzesniewski, A., & Dutton, J. E. (2001). Crafting a job: Revisioning employees as active crafters of their work. *Academy of Management Review*, *26*, 179–201.

Weick, K. (1979). *The social psychology of organizing*. Addison Wesley.

Williams, J., Blair-Loy, M., & Berdahl, J. (2013). Cultural schemas, social class, and the flexibility stigma. *Journal of Social Issues, Special Issue: The Flexibility Stigma*, *69*, 209–234.

Wilson, K., & Baumann, H. (2015). Capturing a more complete view of employees' lives outside of work: The introduction and development of new interrole conflict constructs. *Personnel Psychology*, *68*, 235–282.

INDEX

Printed and bound by CPI Group (UK) Ltd, Croydon, CR0 4YY

28/09/2023

08122185-0001